Mac OS X, v10.3 Panther

Kate Binder

Contents

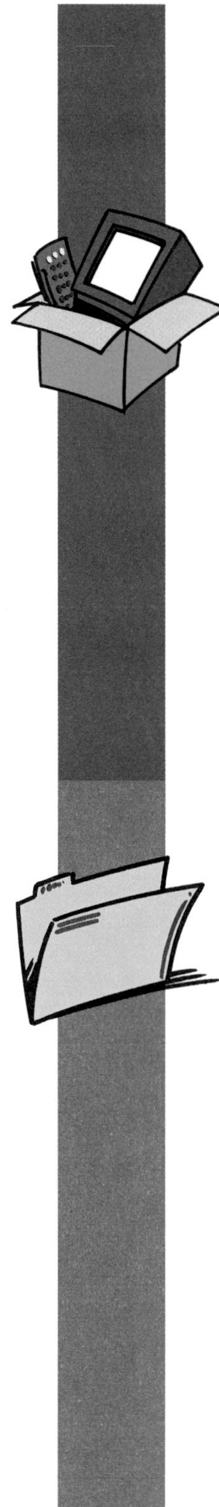

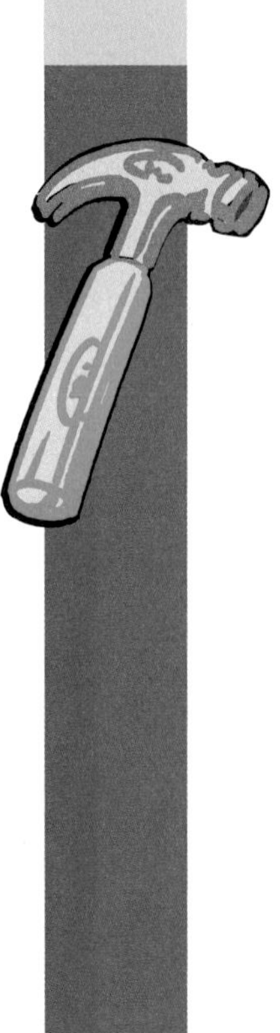

NOTES

12 Creating a Home Network 220

13 Maintaining Your System 230

Glossary 248

Index 256

Associate Publisher
Greg Wiegand

Acquisitions Editor
Laura Norman

Development Editor
Laura Norman

Managing Editor
Charlotte Clapp

Project Editor
Dan Knott

Production Editor
Megan Wade

Indexer
Ken Johnson

Technical Editor
Brian Hubbard

Publishing Coordinator
Sharry Lee Gregory

Designer
Anne Jones

Easy Mac OS X, v10.3 Panther

International Standard Book Number: 0-7897-3074-x

Library of Congress Catalog Card Number: 2003114780

Printed in the United States of America

First Printing: January 2004

07 06 05 04 4 3 2

Trademarks

All terms mentioned in this book that are known to be trademarks or service marks have been appropriately capitalized. Que Publishing cannot attest to the accuracy of this information. Use of a term in this book should not be regarded as affecting the validity of any trademark or service mark.

Warning and Disclaimer

Every effort has been made to make this book as complete and as accurate as possible, but no warranty or fitness is implied. The information provided is on an "as is" basis. The author and the publisher shall have neither liability nor responsibility to any person or entity with respect to any loss or damages arising from the information contained in this book.

Bulk Sales

Que Publishing offers excellent discounts on this book when ordered in quantity for bulk purchases or special sales. For more information, please contact

U.S. Corporate and Government Sales
1-800-382-3419
corpsales@pearsontechgroup.com

For sales outside of the U.S., please contact

International Sales
1-317-428-3341
international@pearsontechgroup.com

We Want to Hear from You!

As an associate publisher for Que Publishing, I welcome your comments. You can email or write me directly to let me know what you did or didn't like about this book—as well as what we can do to make our books better.

When you write, please be sure to include this book's title and author as well as your name, email address, and phone number. I will carefully review your comments and share them with the author and editors who worked on the book.

Email: `feedback@quepublishing.com`

Mail: Greg Wiegand
Associate Publisher
Que Publishing
800 East 96th Street
Indianapolis, IN 46240 USA

For more information about this book or another Que Publishing title, visit our Web site at `www.quepublishing.com`. Type the ISBN (excluding hyphens) or the title of a book in the Search field to find the page you're looking for.

About the Author

Kate Binder is a longtime Mac lover and graphics expert who works from her home in New Hampshire. She has written articles on graphics, publishing, and photography for magazines including *Publish, PEI,* and *Desktop Publishers Journal.* Kate is also the author of several books, including *The Complete Idiot's Guide to Mac OS X* and *Easy Adobe Photoshop 6*, and coauthor of books including *Microsoft Office: Mac v.X Inside Out, SVG for Designers,* and *Get Creative: The Digital Photo Idea Book.* To those interested in a successful career as a computer book writer, Kate recommends acquiring several retired racing greyhounds (find out more at www.adopt-a-greyhound.org)—she finds her five greyhounds extraordinarily inspirational.

Dedication

This one's for Junior—now revealed to the world as Patrick John Fluckinger, born August 28, 2003. Long may you wave, kiddo.

Acknowledgments

As usual, I owe an enormous debt of gratitude to editor Laura Norman, who knew just how to coax work out of me while simultaneously offering a true friend's support to "the pregnant lady"—and then to a very new mom. Thanks, also, to the rest of the jolly crew at Que, some of whom have been putting up with me for quite a while now, and to my husband Don, who continues to make me lunch every day no matter how cranky I get. And finally, I owe Joe O'Malley at the Nashua, New Hampshire, CompUSA store big-time for letting me shoot screenshots on the sales floor. Thanks, Joe!

Introduction to *Easy Mac OS X, v10.3 Panther*

Mac OS X is like no operating system, Macintosh or otherwise, that came before it. It's incredibly stable and powerful, and it looks sleek and new and very unfamiliar to long-time Mac users. But underneath, it has the same old friendly nature that Mac lovers have always enjoyed.

With *Easy Mac OS X, v10.3 Panther*, you'll learn how to take advantage of powerful and useful Mac OS X features such as the built-in instant messaging program iChat, automatic file and printer sharing with Windows PCs, and the ability to find just about anything you could want online with Sherlock. Along the way, you'll get used to being able to run a dozen programs at one time on a stable system that doesn't crash. This book's step-by-step approach tells you just what you need to know to accomplish the task at hand, quickly and efficiently. All the skills you need to get the most out of Mac OS X, both online and on the desktop, are covered here.

If you want, you can work through the tasks in *Easy Mac OS X, v10.3 Panther* in order, building your skills steadily. Or, if you prefer, use this book as a reference to look up just what you need to know *right now*. Either way, *Easy Mac OS X, v10.3 Panther* lets you see it done and then do it yourself.

1 Each step is fully illustrated to show you how it looks onscreen.

It's as Easy as 1-2-3

Each part of this book is made up of a series of short, instructional lessons, designed to help you understand basic information that you need to get the most out of your computer hardware and software.

2 Each task includes a series of quick, easy steps designed to guide you through the procedure.

3 Items that you select or click in menus, dialog boxes, tabs, and windows are shown in **bold**.

44

PART 3

Looking Up Synonyms

Start

Click

Click

Click

Click

1. After you select the word for which you want to see synonyms, open the **Tools** menu and choose **Thesaurus**.
2. The Thesaurus dialog box opens. If two or more choices are in the **Meanings** list, click the one that most closely matches the meaning you want.
3. In the **Replace with Synonym** list, click the word you want to use.
4. Click the **Replace** button to close the thesaurus and replace your original word with the synonym.

End

INTRODUCTION

Another feature of FrontPage is the built-in thesaurus that can suggest some *synonyms*, alternative words with the same meaning, for text that you've typed.

TIP

Canceling the Thesaurus
If you don't like any of the suggested synonyms better than your original word, click **Cancel** in the Thesaurus dialog box to close it.

HINT

Finding More Choices
To display a new list of synonyms based on one of the suggestions in the Replace with Synonym list, click the suggestion and then click the **Look Up** button.

Introductions explain what you will learn in each task, and **Tips and Hints** give you a heads-up for any extra information you may need while working through the task.

drop

How to Drag:
Point to the starting place or object. Hold down the mouse button (right or left per instructions), move the mouse to the new location, then release the button.

See next page:
If you see this symbol, it means the task you're working on continues on the next page.

End

End Task:
Task is complete.

Selection:
Highlights the area onscreen discussed in the step or task.

Click:
Click the left mouse button once.

Right-click:
Click the right mouse button once.

Click & Type:
Click once where indicated and begin typing to enter your text or data.

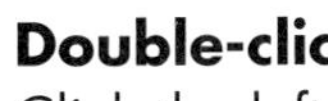

Double-click:
Click the left mouse button twice in rapid succession.

Pointer Arrow:
Highlights an item on the screen you need to point to or focus on in the step or task.

PART 1

Getting Started

Mac OS X was introduced, after much anticipation and even more hype, in the spring of 2001. Surprisingly, it has lived up to its hype. With Mac OS X, users have an operating system that is many times more powerful than older systems, completely modern, capable of handling the latest innovations in hardware, and as easy to use as any Mac system that has gone before.

The starting point for any exploration of Mac OS X is the desktop: what you see when your Mac has finished starting up. The desktop is operated by a program called the Finder, and it's a central location where you'll gain access to your disks and their contents, move files around, and keep track of what your computer's up to—sort of like a hotel or office building lobby. This section covers the basics of working with the Finder, as well as other functions that work the same no matter what program you're using.

Mac OS X's Desktop

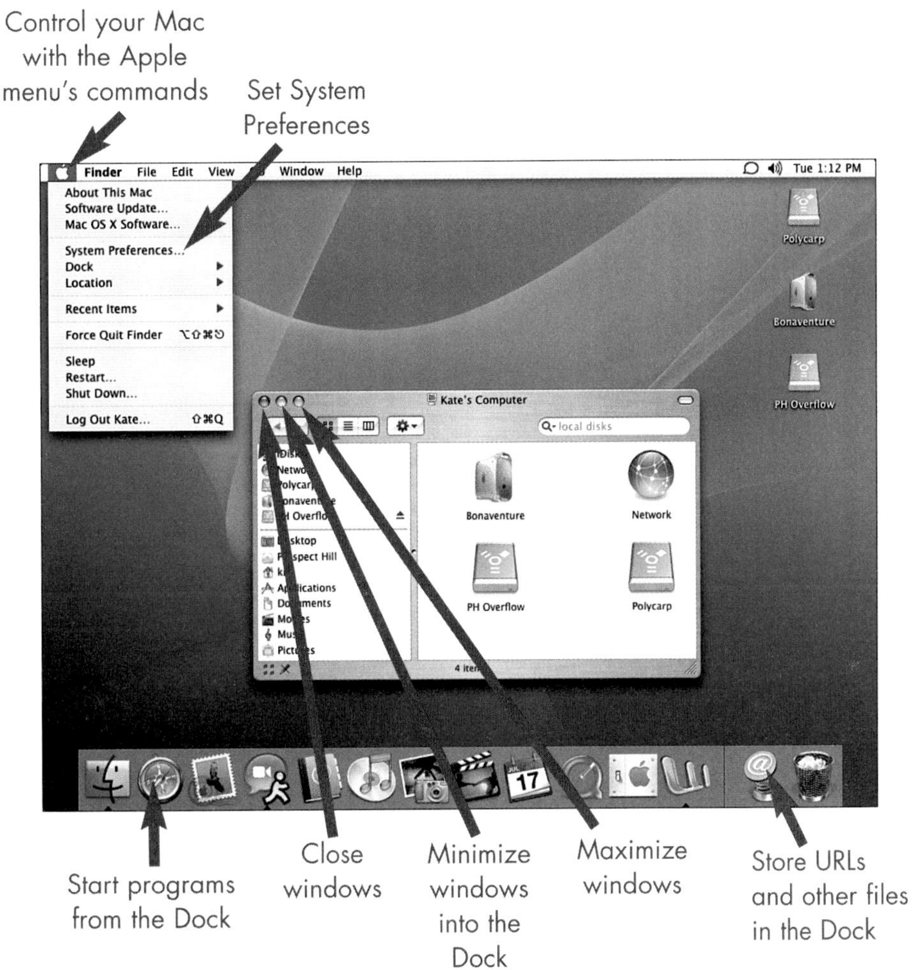

Touring the Desktop

Click & Drag

Double-click

Click

Click

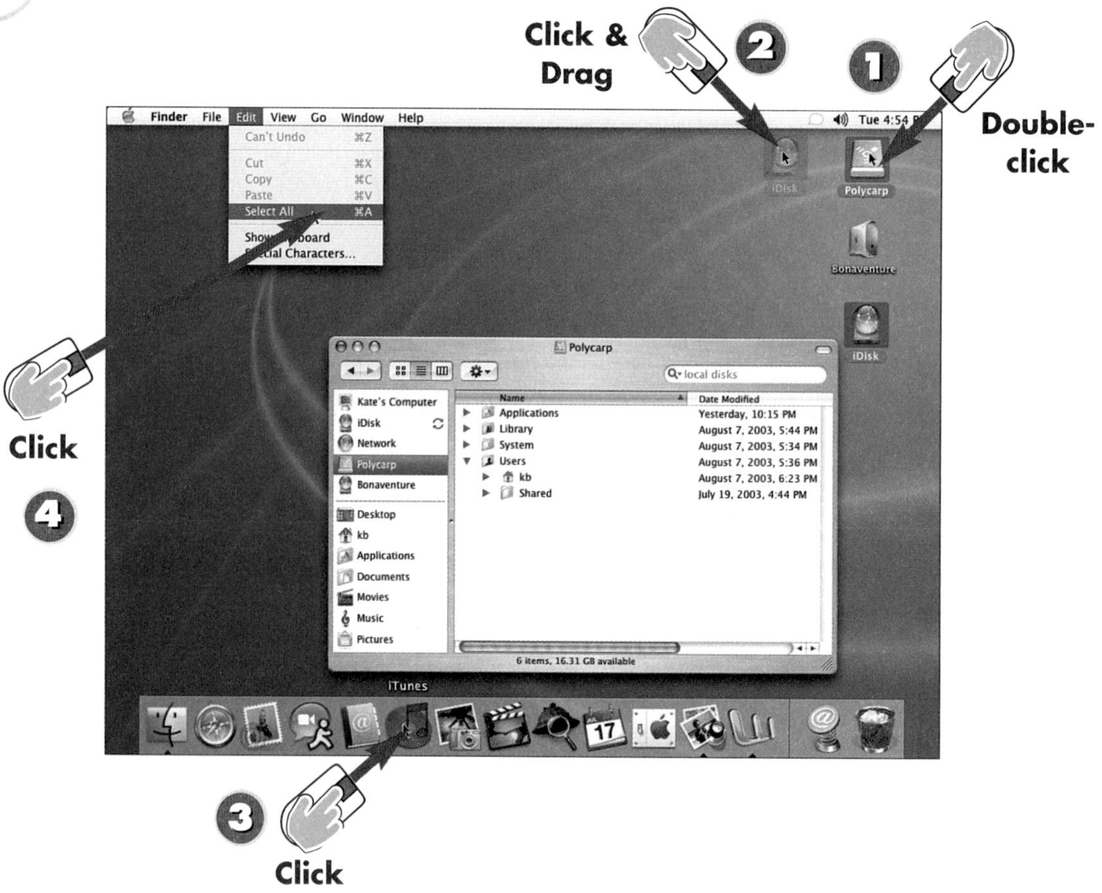

1. Double-click to view a window showing the contents of a drive or folder.

2. Click and drag to move icons on the desktop.

3. Click objects in the Dock to activate them.

4. Click a menu name, drag the mouse down, and release the mouse button on a command to execute that command.

INTRODUCTION

If you've used a Mac before, Mac OS X's desktop won't look completely new to you—just a bit unfamiliar. On the other hand, if you're new to computers, concepts like *windows*, *icons*, and *menus* might need a little explanation. Either way, this tour of the Mac OS X desktop should set you on your way.

HINT

It's Okay to Explore

If you're not sure what something on the desktop does, try clicking or double-clicking it. Mac OS X will let you know before it does anything destructive to your system, so it's safe to explore and experiment.

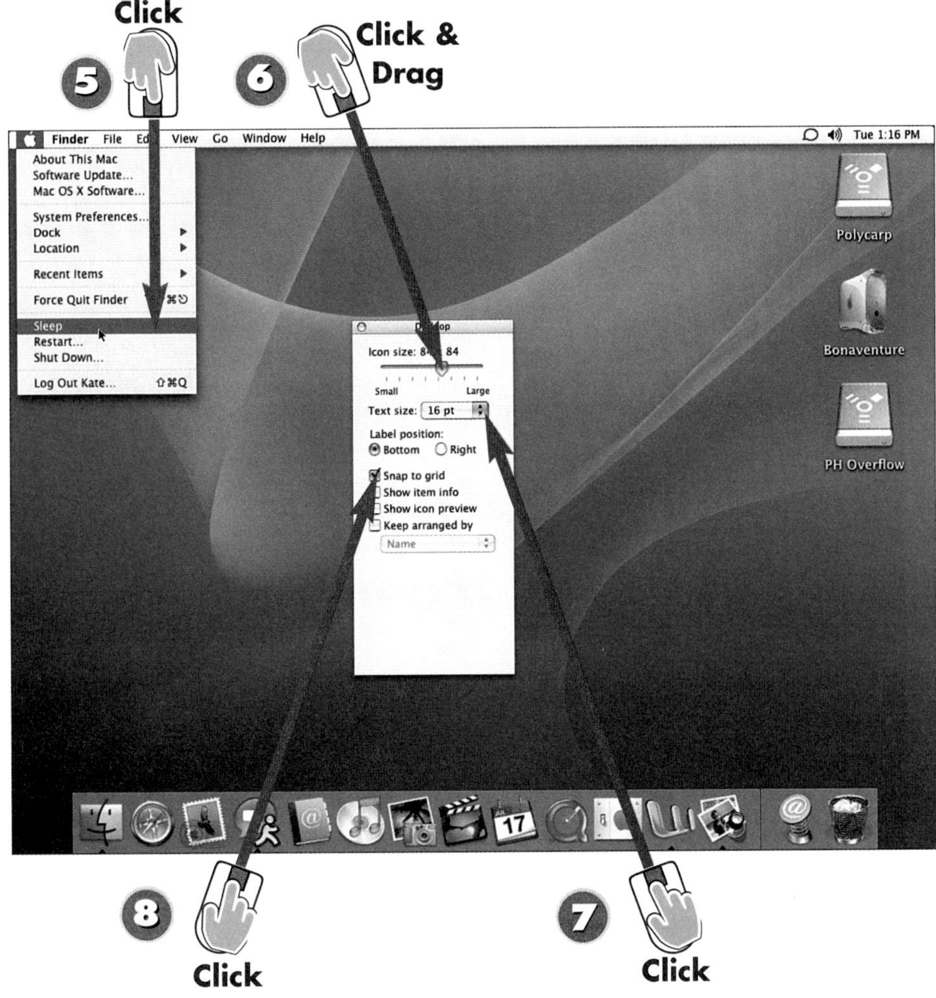

5. Use the **Apple** menu to access systemwide functions.

6. Choose **View**, **Show View Options** to open the View Options dialog box. Drag the **Icon size** slider to change the size of desktop icons.

7. Change the **Text Size** and **Label Position** to modify the appearance of icon labels.

8. Check any of the other options to display more information about files, folders, and drives on the desktop.

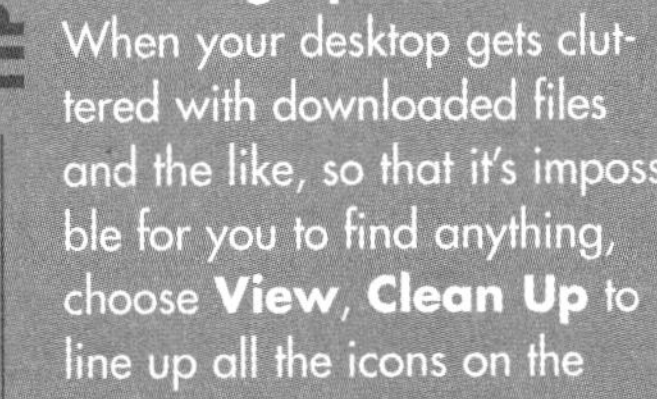

TIP

Cleaning Up the Place
When your desktop gets cluttered with downloaded files and the like, so that it's impossible for you to find anything, choose **View**, **Clean Up** to line up all the icons on the desktop in neat rows, so you can see what you've got.

HINT

Making the Desktop Your Own
Turn to the task called "Changing Your Desktop Picture" in Part 5, "Customizing the Mac," to learn how to change the desktop picture so you'll truly feel at home when you sit down in front of your Mac.

Using the Dock

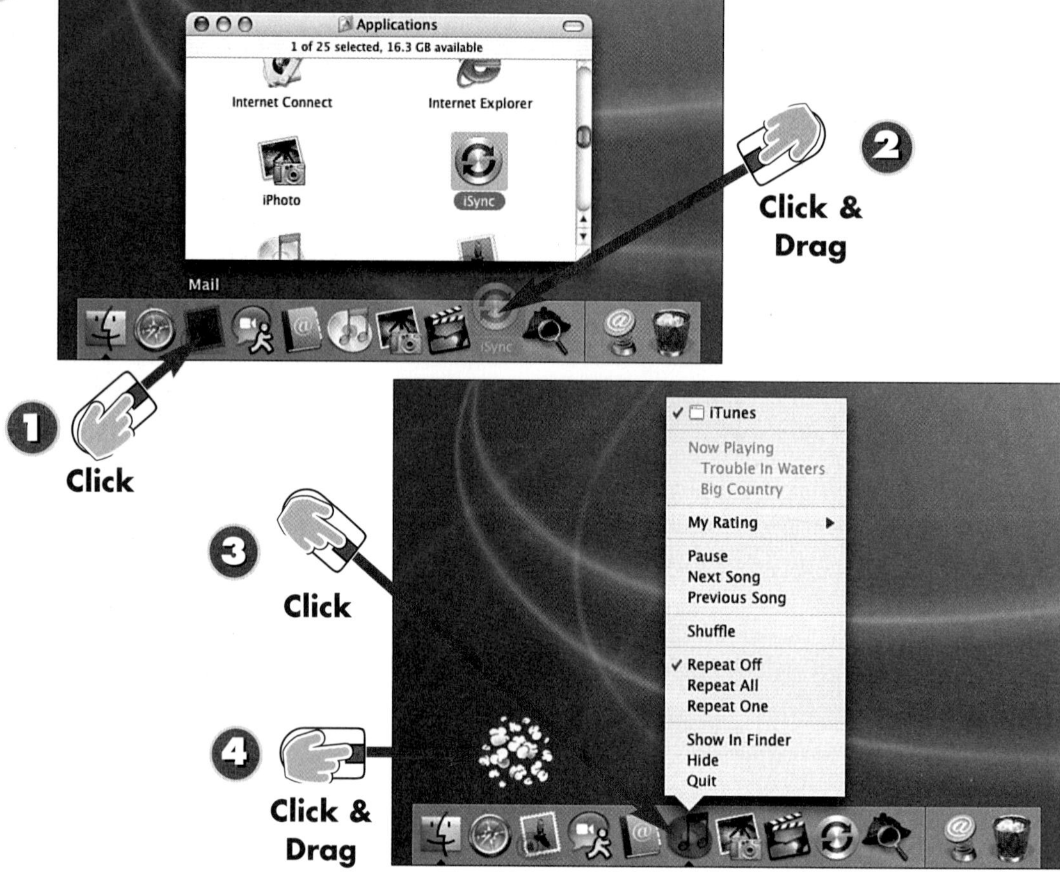

1. Click a program icon in the Dock to switch to that program (if it's running) or to start it up (if it's not running).
2. Drag programs into the Dock's left side and documents or folders into the Dock's right side to store them for easy access.
3. Click and hold an icon in the Dock to see a menu of actions you can perform on that object.
4. Drag icons of files, folders, and inactive programs off the edge to remove them from the Dock in a puff of virtual smoke.

INTRODUCTION

The *Dock* serves more than one function. First, it's where you can see which programs are running and switch among them. The Dock contains an icon for each active program at any given time. Second, it's a good place to store things you use often, whether they're programs, folders, or documents. And finally, it's where you'll find the Trash (you'll learn how to use the Trash in Part 2, "Working with Disks, Folders, and Files"). The Dock has a vertical line dividing its two sides. Program icons are stored on the left side, whether the programs are running or not, and folders and documents you add to the Dock yourself are stored on the right side. You'll find that you aren't able to drag a program onto the right side of the Dock or a document onto the left side.

HINT

Disappearing Act

When you drag programs or documents off the Dock, they disappear in a puff of smoke. But don't worry about the original files—they're still on your hard drive right where you left them. Dock icons are just pointers to the files, not the files themselves.

Moving and Resizing Windows

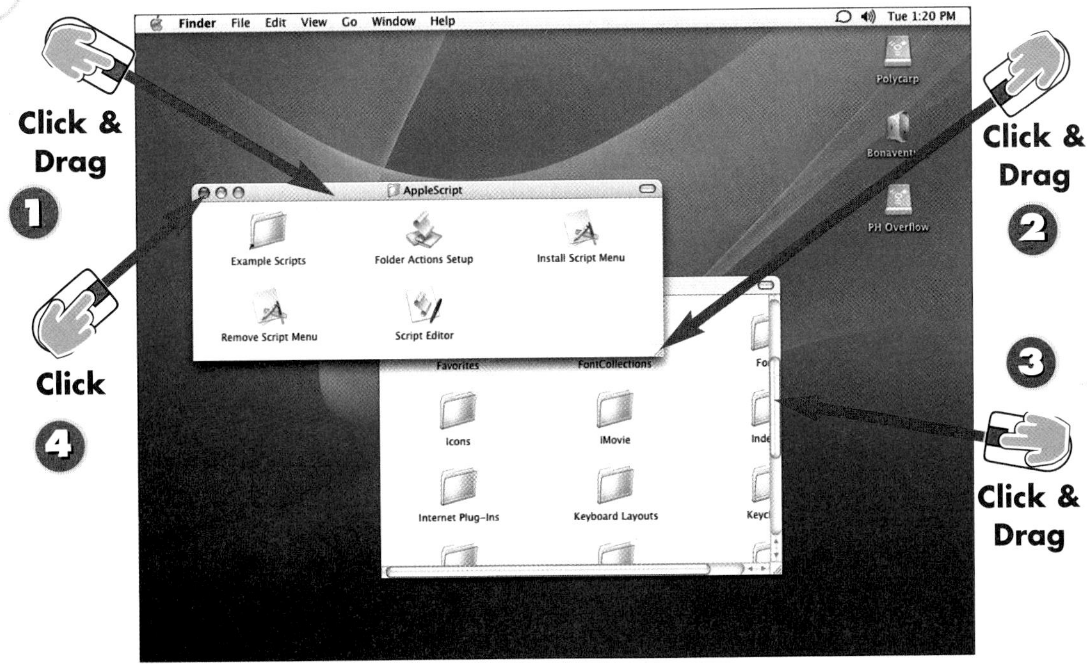

1. To move a window so you can see what's underneath it, click its title bar and drag the window to a new position.
2. Click and drag the lower-right corner of a window to change the window's size.
3. View the hidden contents of a window by clicking and dragging the scrollbars.
4. To close a window, click the red button at the left end of the window's title bar.

INTRODUCTION

Mac OS X is full of windows: document windows, folder windows, more windows than you can count. The Finder shows you the contents of each folder or disk in a window, and programs put each document in a window. Knowing how to get windows to go where you want them to is an important skill for any Mac user.

HINT

More to Windows Than Meets the Eye

Keep reading for more about wrangling windows. The next task shows you how to minimize and maximize your windows—the results might not be quite what you're expecting.

Minimizing and Maximizing Windows

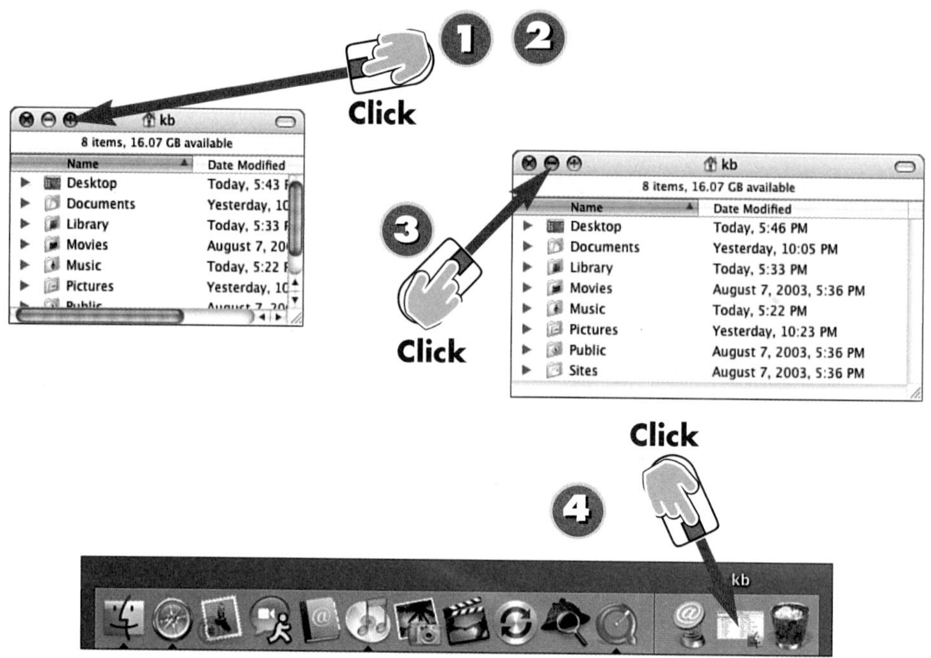

1. Click the green button at the left end of a window's title bar to size the window so that it shows its entire contents.
2. Click the green button again to return the window to its previous size.
3. Click the yellow button at the left end of a window's title bar to shrink the window downward into the right side of the Dock.
4. Click the window's icon in the Dock to put it back onto the desktop.

INTRODUCTION

Although windows are a great way to look inside folders, they never seem to open at just the right size for what you're trying to see. Getting the most from your windows requires learning to maximize their size and minimize them out of sight.

HINT

Window Identification
Each minimized window in the Dock has a small icon attached to its lower-right corner that identifies the program to which the window belongs. Folder and disk windows belong to the Finder, so they have a Finder logo.

HINT

The Wonders of Windows
The Dock continuously updates the appearance of minimized document windows. For example, if you minimize a QuickTime movie window while the movie's running, you can continue to monitor the movie's progress while its window is in the Dock.

Managing Multiple Windows

Start

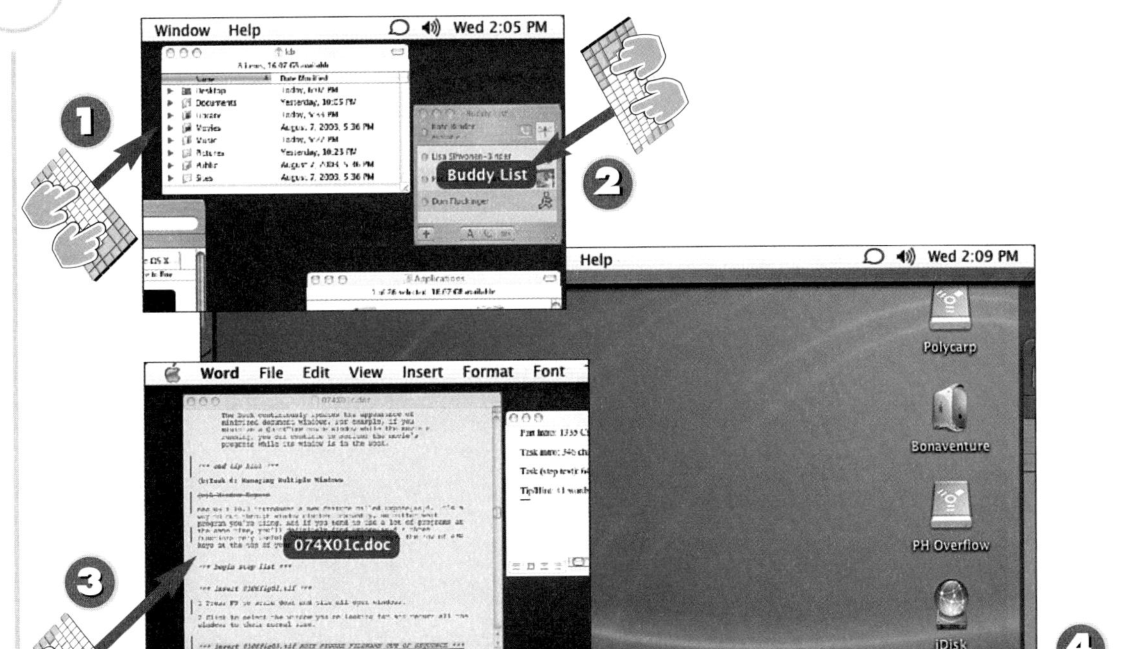

1. Press **F9** to scale down and tile all open windows.

2. Click to select the window you're looking for and return all the windows to their normal size.

3. Press **F10** to tile all the windows in the current program and shade other windows.

4. Press **F11** to hide all windows so you can see the desktop.

INTRODUCTION

Mac OS X 10.3 introduces a new feature called Exposé. It's a way to cut through window clutter instantly, no matter what program you're using. And if you tend to use a lot of programs at the same time, you'll definitely find Exposé's three functions very useful. They use the function keys, the row of *F* keys at the top of your keyboard.

TIP

For Those Who Prefer the Mouse

If you prefer to use the mouse, choose **Apple menu**, choose **System Preferences**, and click **Exposé** to assign the Exposé functions to three of the corners of the screen. Then perform any of these magical actions by simply positioning your mouse in the appropriate screen corner.

Using Contextual Menus

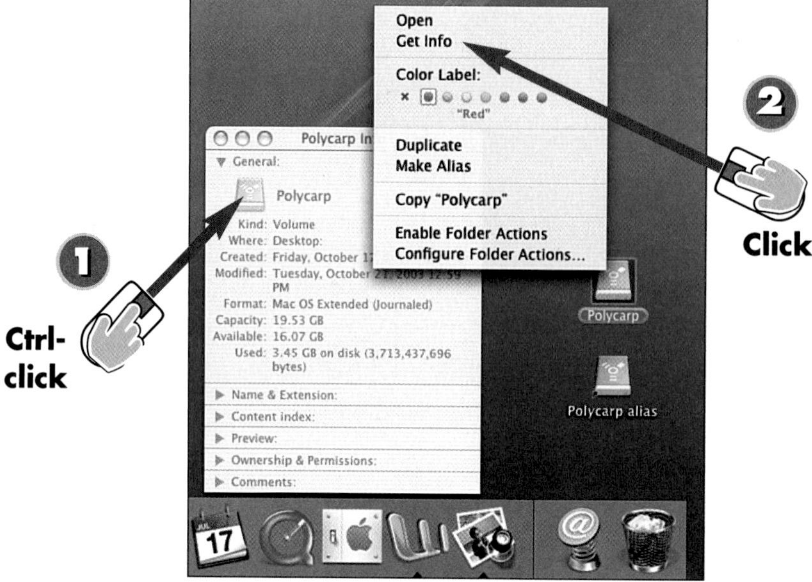

1. Press **Ctrl** and click any object on the desktop.

2. Click the contextual menu command you want to perform.

INTRODUCTION

The more you use your Mac, the more you'll appreciate time-saving techniques. Contextual menus pop up right where you're working, instead of requiring you to mouse up to the menu bar or take your hands off the mouse to use keyboard commands. Their contents vary depending on what you're doing at the time.

TIP

Remember the Context

Contextual menus contain different options depending on what you click to see them. Try Ctrl-clicking the desktop itself, and don't forget to try Ctrl-clicking objects in document windows, such as pictures or misspelled words.

HINT

Making Contextual Menus Even Easier

If you have a multibutton mouse, you can program one of the buttons to perform a Ctrl-click. The most popular option in this case is to use the right mouse button, so you can right-click to see contextual menus.

Taking a Screenshot

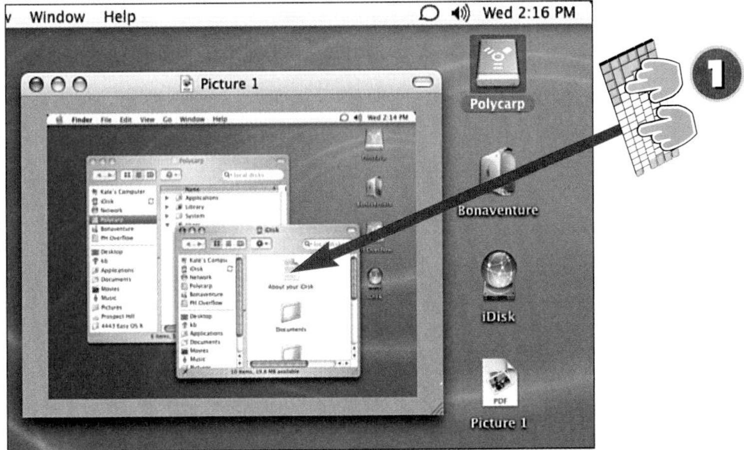

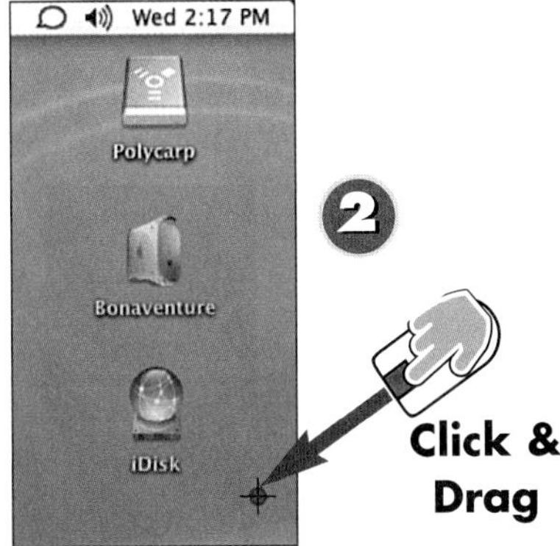

1. To shoot the whole screen, press **Cmd-Shift-3**. The picture is saved in a file called **Picture 1** on your desktop.
2. To shoot part of the screen, press **Cmd-Shift-4**. Click and drag the mouse to select the area you want to shoot.

INTRODUCTION

There will come a time when you'll want to take a shot of your Mac's screen for one reason or another. Maybe you need to show a technical support person exactly what's going wrong with your Web browser, or perhaps you just want to preserve a picture of an amazing high score list in your favorite game.

TIP

Oops!
If you change your mind about taking a screen shot after pressing Cmd-Shift-4, click the mouse anywhere to cancel the operation.

HINT

Open, Sesame
Mac OS X saves screenshots in PDF format. If you double-click one, it opens in Preview or Adobe Reader, depending on how your system is set to deal with PDFs. You can open them in any graphics program, such as Adobe Photoshop.

Getting Help

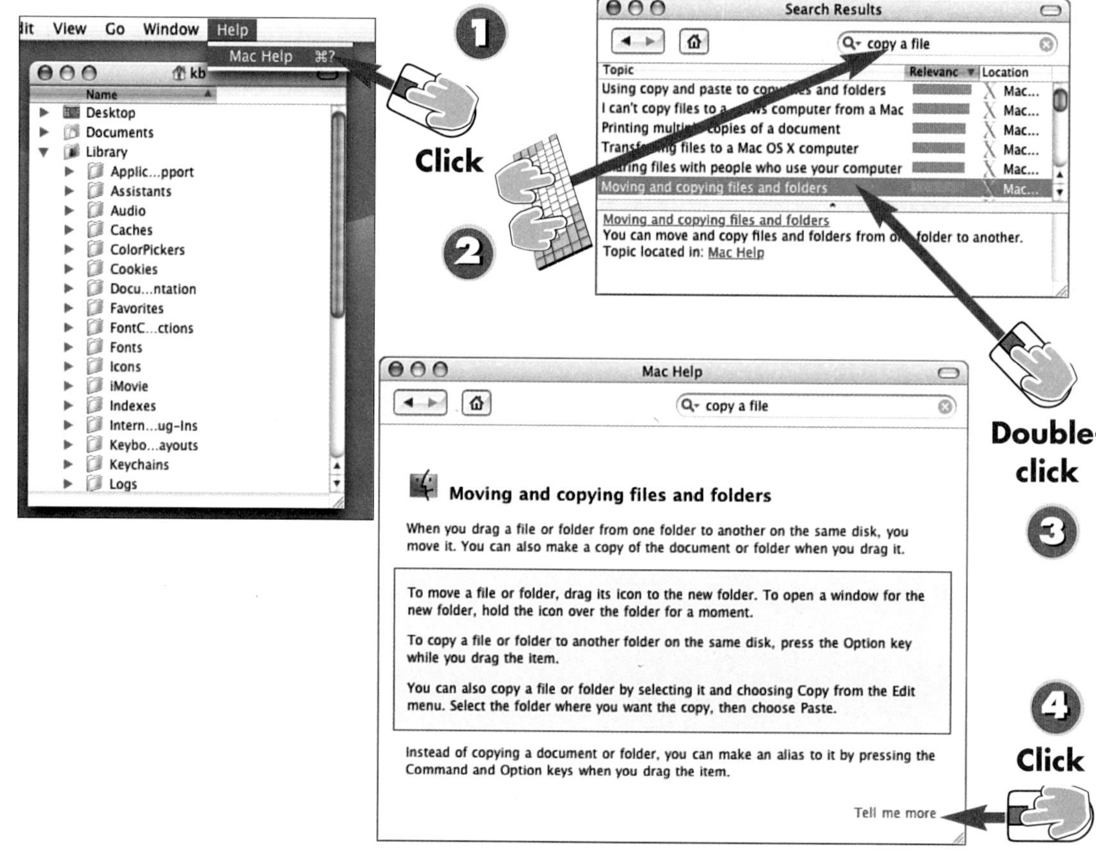

1. Choose the command you want from the **Help** menu. In the Finder, choose **Help**, **Mac Help**.
2. Type a phrase or question in the text entry field and press **Enter**.
3. Double-click a line in the search results to see that Help section.
4. The Mac Help window opens showing the information. Click **Tell me more** to get additional information.

INTRODUCTION

In Mac OS X, the Help Viewer offers access to help for all your programs no matter where you are when you invoke the Help Viewer, so you don't have to start up or switch to those programs.

HINT

More and More Help
Some programs have several commands in the Help menu. Usually, the first command or two opens the Help Viewer, or that program's equivalent. The other commands take you places like the software developer's Web site, where you can find helpful information.

Restarting or Shutting Down the Mac

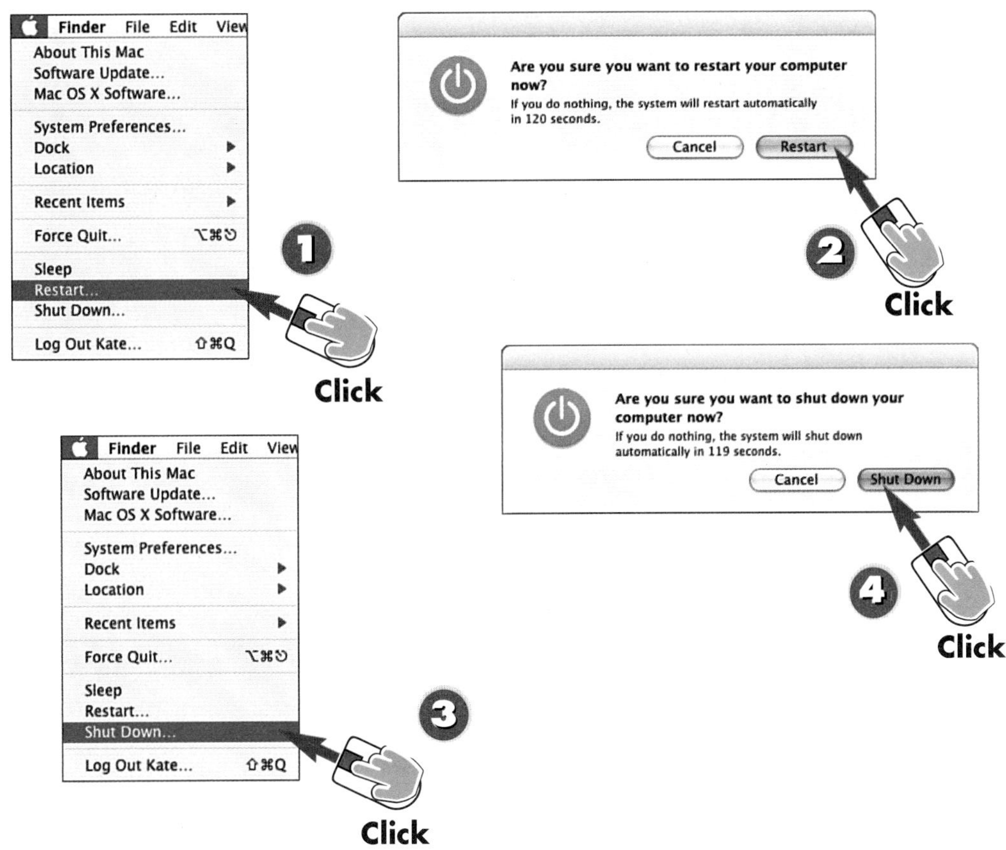

1. To restart the Mac, choose the **Apple** menu and click **Restart**.
2. In the dialog box, click **Restart**. Click **Cancel** to exit the dialog box without restarting.
3. To shut down the Mac, choose **Apple menu**, **Shut Down**.
4. In the dialog box, click **Shut Down**. Click **Cancel** to exit the dialog box without shutting down.

INTRODUCTION

As commands that affect the entire system, Restart and Shut Down are located in the Apple menu, so you can access them from any program rather than having to switch to the Finder, as in previous versions of the Mac OS. You'll use Restart most often after installing new software, and you'll use Shut Down when you want to turn your computer all the way off.

TIP

No Fresh Start Needed
You don't have to restart the Mac if you only want to switch users. Choose **Apple menu**, **Log Out** instead; this command quits all running programs and presents you with the login screen, but it doesn't require the computer to completely reboot.

Setting Basic System Preferences

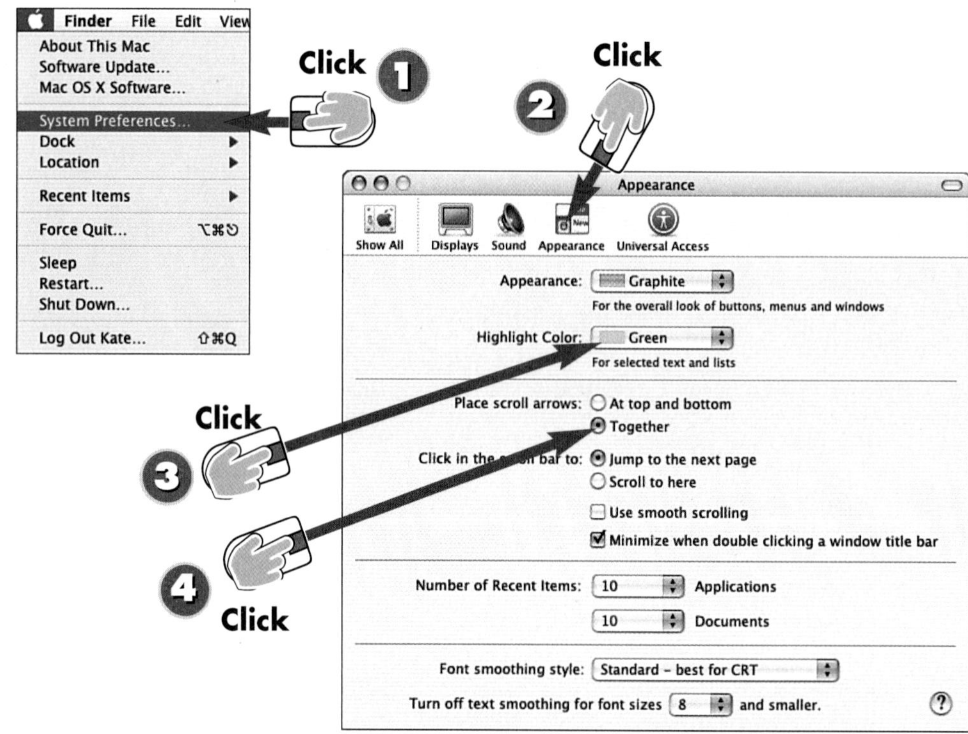

1. Choose **Apple menu**, **System Preferences**.
2. Click **Appearance** to display the Appearance preferences.
3. Choose colors from the **Appearance** pop-up menu (for scrollbars, buttons, and menus) and the **Highlight Color** pop-up menu (for selected text and objects in list view).
4. Click a radio button to put scrollbar arrows together or at the top and bottom of each window.

INTRODUCTION

You can't customize everything about your Mac, but you can get darn close (for more customization techniques, turn to Part 5). Here's a look at the most basic preferences you'll want to set on a new Mac.

HINT

Blue Versus Graphite

Your Appearance color preference starts out set to Blue. If you switch it to Graphite, all your dialog box buttons, menu highlights, and window components turn graphite gray. The only problem you might encounter with that setting is that the Close, Minimize, and Maximize buttons—normally red, yellow, and green, respectively—also turn gray. You can still tell them apart by placing the cursor over them; an X appears in the Close button, a minus sign in the Minimize button, and a plus sign in the Maximize button.

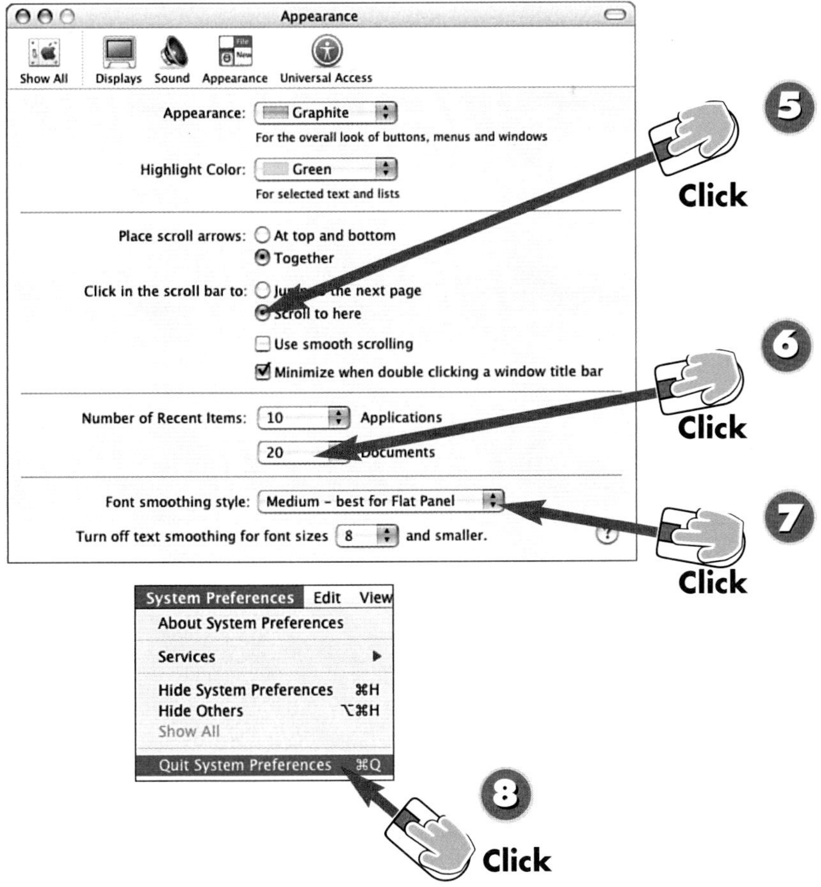

5 Click a radio button to choose how far clicking in the scrollbar scrolls the window.

6 Choose the number of recently used applications and documents that will appear in the Apple menu.

7 Choose a font smoothing style and size from the pop-up menus.

8 Choose **System Preferences**, **Quit System Preferences** to apply your changes.

TIP

Scroll, Scroll, Scroll Your Window

Choosing a scrollbar setting might be a little confusing unless you've used different operating systems in the past. Here's the scoop: Jump to the next page moves the view up or down one screenful when you click in the scrollbar. With long documents, you might prefer Scroll to here, which moves the view to the location within the document that approximates the location of your click. In other words, click halfway down the scrollbar to see the document's midpoint. These settings apply within both application windows and folder windows in the Finder.

HINT

Font Smoothing

If font smoothing is off, be aware that some dialog boxes can look odd. You'll still be able to use those dialog boxes, but button labels and the like might be positioned a bit oddly and you might see a dialog box warning you of this fact on occasion.

Using Universal Access

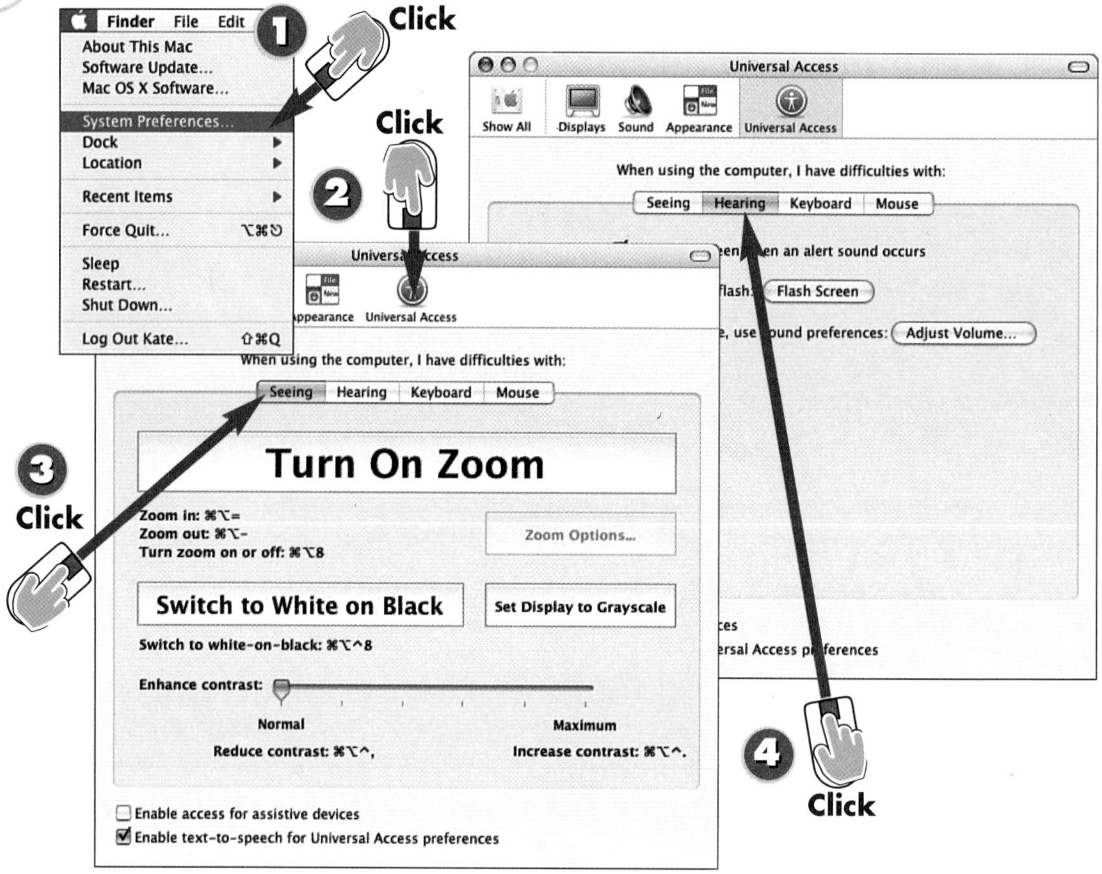

1. Choose the **Apple** menu, and then choose **System Preferences**.

2. Click **Universal Access**.

3. Click the **Seeing** tab and click the buttons to turn on the Zoom feature or switch to white text on a black background.

4. Click the **Hearing** tab and click the check box to flash the screen when an alert sound is played.

INTRODUCTION

Universal Access provides alternative ways of viewing the Mac's screen, hearing the sounds it makes, using the keyboard, and using the mouse. For example, if you can't hear alert sounds, you can set the screen to flash instead, calling your attention to what's happening just as clearly as an alert sound would.

TIP

Shortcuts to Access
No matter which Universal Access settings you want to use, you should click **Allow Universal Access Shortcuts**. This option activates the keyboard shortcuts shown on each tab of the Universal Access preferences pane.

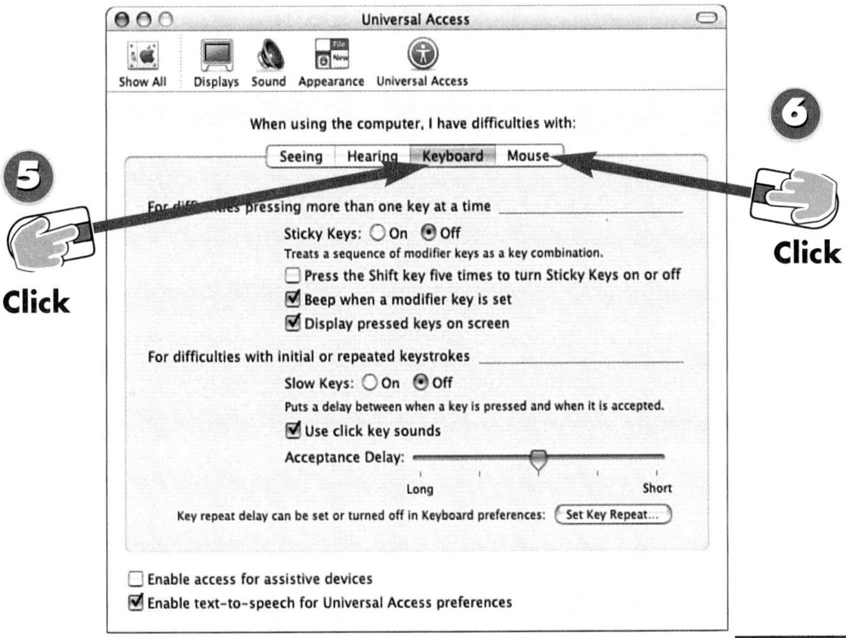

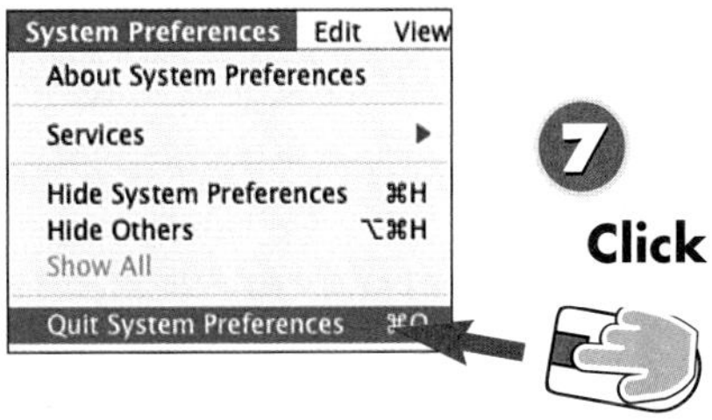

5 Click the **Keyboard** tab and choose from the various keyboard options.

6 Click the **Mouse** tab and choose from the various mouse options.

7 Choose **System Preferences**, **Quit System Preferences** to apply your changes.

HINT

Special Assistance

The Enable access for assistive devices setting at the bottom of the Universal Access preferences pane enables you to use special equipment to control your Mac, such as head tracking devices with which you can move the cursor by moving your head.

HINT

Yakkety Yak

The Enable text-to-speech for Universal Access preferences check box turns on your Mac's speech in this single area so that if you hold the cursor over a button or tab, you'll hear the text label for that object read out loud.

PART 2

Working with Disks, Folders, and Files

The tasks in this part might not be glamorous or exciting, but they're the foundation of everything you do on your Mac. It's all about files, folders, and the disks that hold them. Every time you create a new document or receive an email attachment, that information is stored in a file on your hard drive, and the file is in turn stored within a folder. Mac OS X provides many ways for you to view and modify folder contents and file attributes, so you're in control of your Mac.

The tasks in this part teach you how to create new folders and view their contents in different ways, how to move and copy files, how to organize your hard drive and keep it uncluttered, and how to use Apple's .Mac online service to perform regular backups of your important files and synchronize your vital information across multiple computers.

You might notice that windows on your Mac OS X desktop have two distinct guises—a "plain" dress that looks like any document window and a "fancy" version that includes a rack of buttons down the side. These are, respectively, multiwindow mode and single-window mode. Don't be deceived, though—you can have windows of both types open at the same time. This important new aspect of Mac OS X is covered in the first task in this part.

Exploring the OS X File System

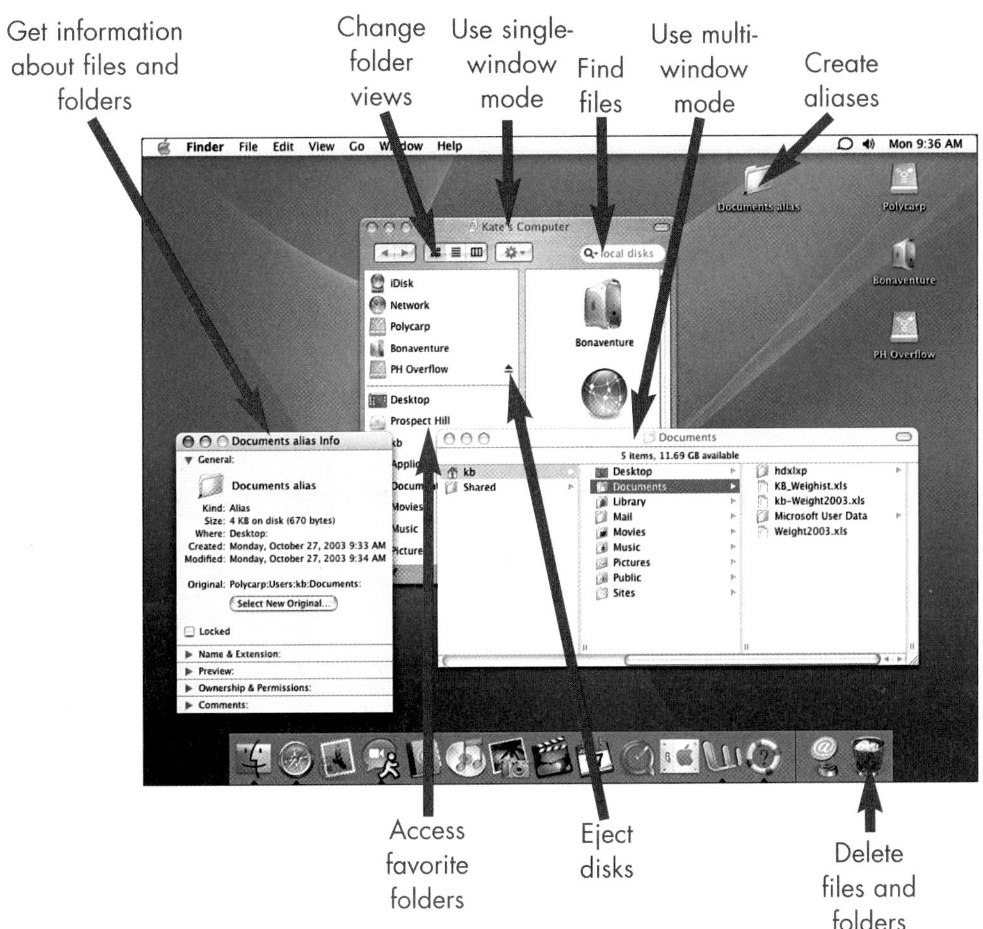

Using Single-Window Mode

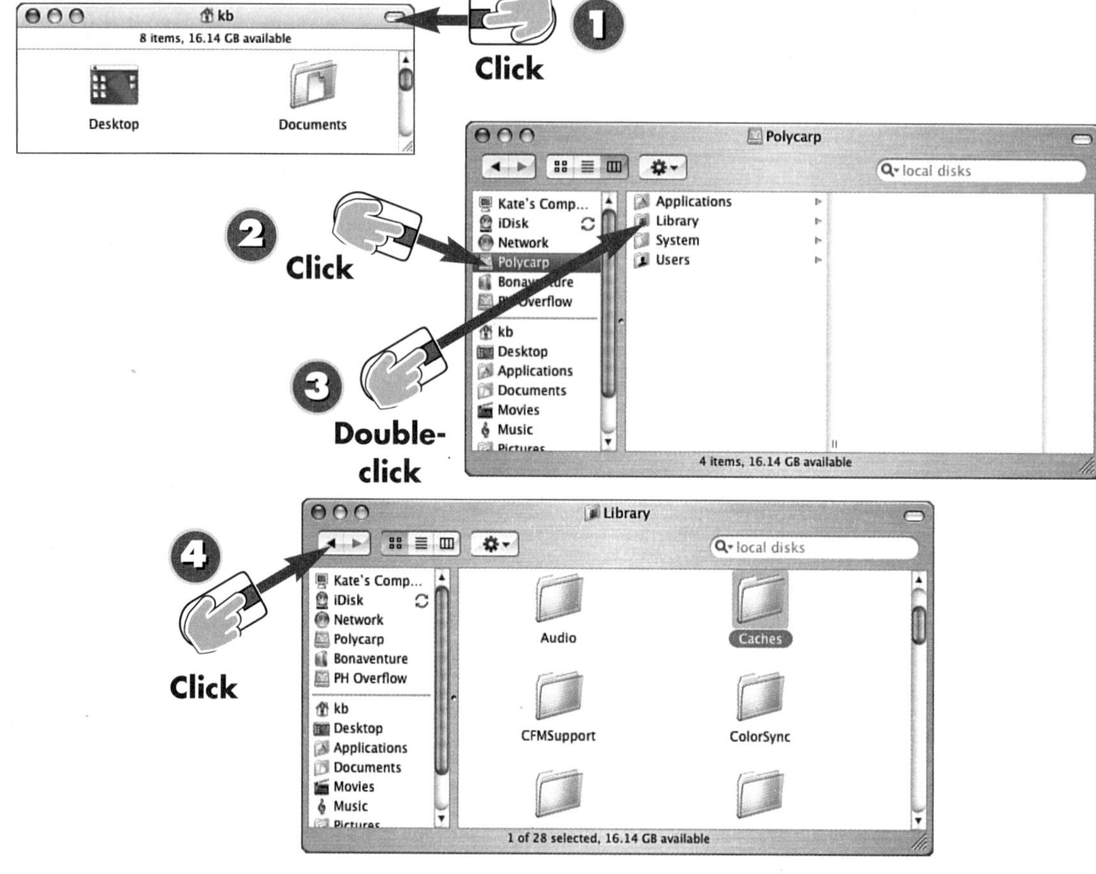

1. If you're using multiwindow mode, click the transparent button in the upper-right corner of the window to switch to single-window mode.
2. Click a folder or disk in the Places sidebar to see its contents.
3. Double-click folders in the main window to see their contents.
4. Click the left and right arrows to go back and forward in the series of windows you've viewed (similar to the Back and Forward buttons in a Web browser window).

INTRODUCTION

Traditionally, the Mac has spawned a new window for each folder or disk you open. Mac OS X introduced single-window mode, in which the contents of each folder or disk appear in the same window, like each successive page in a Web browser displays in the same window. It takes a little getting used to, but it's a better way of working.

HINT

Single Versus Multi

Single-window mode is at its most useful when you need to see the contents of only one window. If you're copying or moving files from one folder to another, you'll probably find good old-fashioned multiwindow mode a better bet.

HINT

More Fun

Don't forget that you can switch window views in single-window mode by clicking the Icon, List, and Column view buttons at the top of the window. A special button next to these three summons up a contextual menu for any selected file in the window.

Customizing the Toolbar

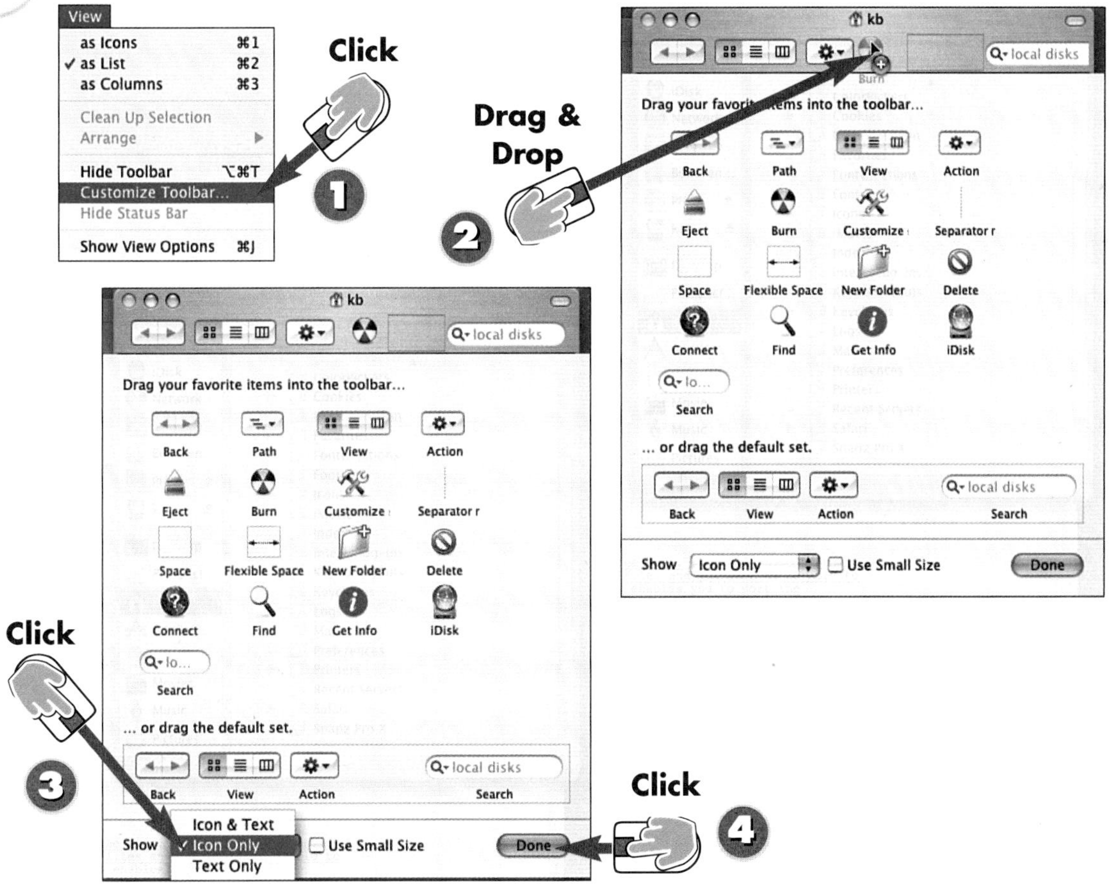

1. Choose **View**, **Customize Toolbar**.

2. Drag buttons onto the toolbar to add them.

3. Choose an option from the **Show** pop-up menu.

4. Click **Done**.

INTRODUCTION

The row of buttons across the top of a window when you're in single-window mode is called the *toolbar*. These buttons offer you quick access to the most common functions in the Finder, such as changing window views and creating new folders. You can choose which buttons you want to display.

TIP

Back Where You Started

When you're customizing your toolbar, you can restore the default set of buttons by dragging the whole set from the bottom of the Customize dialog box up to the toolbar.

TIP

Cutting Back

To remove buttons from the toolbar, choose **View**, **Customize Toolbar** and drag the buttons you don't want off the toolbar.

Using Different Folder Views

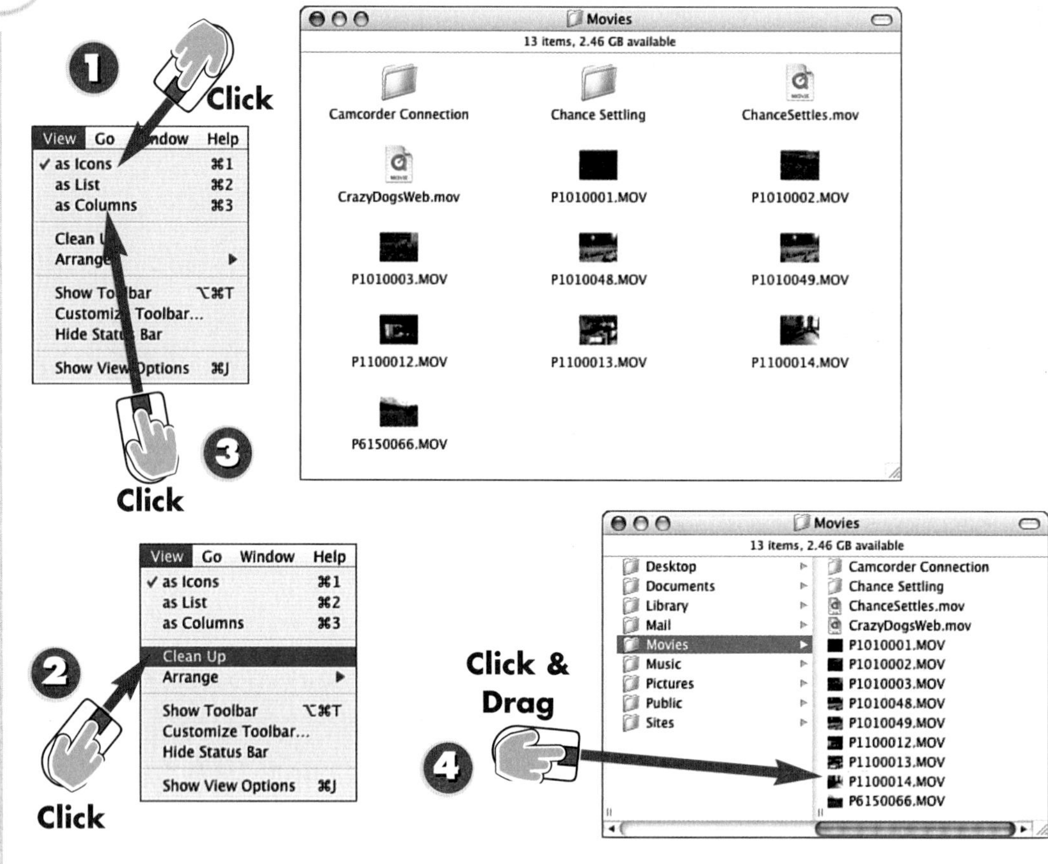

1. To switch to Icon view, choose **View**, **as Icons**.

2. If the icons are stacked on top of each other, choose **View**, **Clean Up** to space them out so you can see them all.

3. To switch to Column view, choose **View**, **as Columns**.

4. Drag the bar between two columns to adjust the columns' width.

INTRODUCTION

You can view Finder windows in three ways. Icon view is convenient when a folder contains just a few files and you want to be able to tell them apart quickly. List view enables you to sort the contents of a window, and Column view provides a quick way of burrowing down into a series of nested folders.

TIP

Wide Angle View

To adjust column widths in column view, drag the small double line at the bottom of the column divider. It's only visible if the column contains a list of files and folders; you can't adjust empty columns.

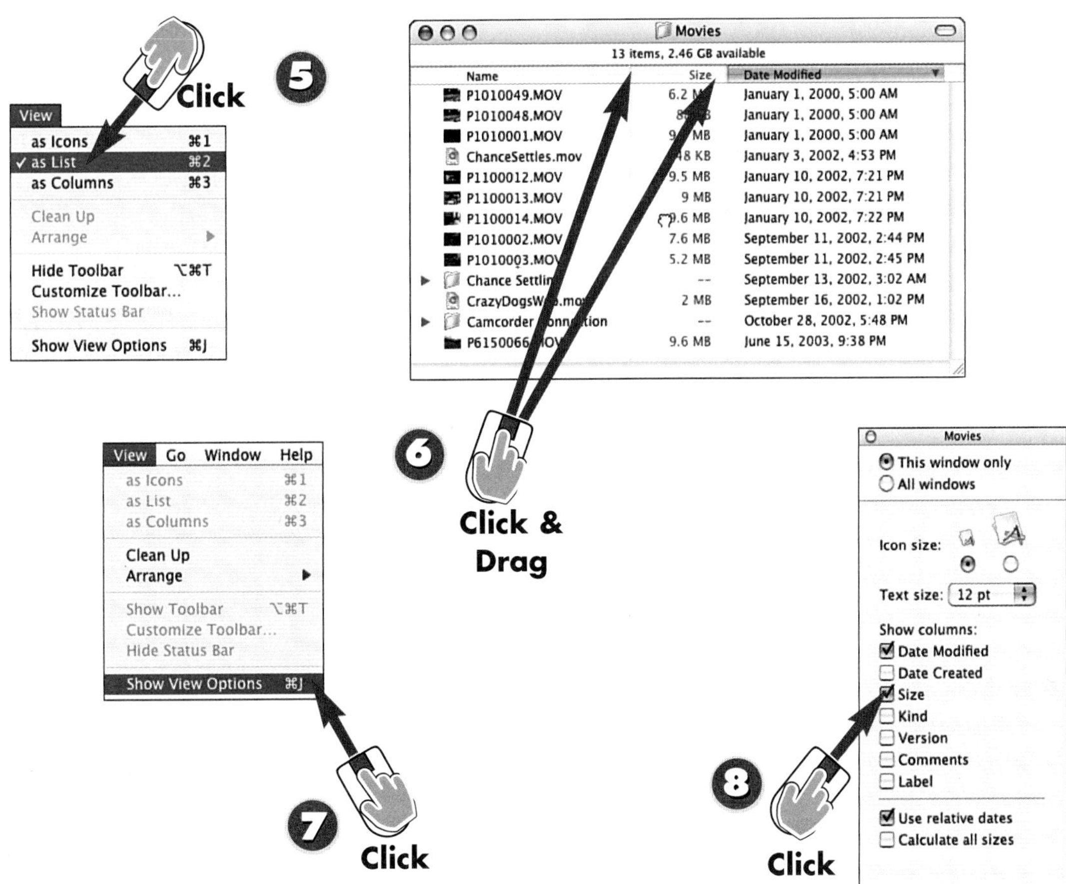

5 To switch to List view, choose **View**, **as List**.

6 Drag the right edge of a list column header to change that column's width, or drag a column header to a different position to change the order of the columns.

7 Choose **View**, **Show View Options** to select which list columns are visible.

8 Check boxes to choose which columns are visible in the active window.

TIP

Getting There via Buttons

In single-window mode, you can click the buttons in the upper-left corner of the window to switch window views without going all the way up to the View menu. Turn to the task "Using Single-Window Mode," earlier in this part, to learn more about using single-window mode.

TIP

Switch Hitting

Lists can be sorted in ascending or descending order. Click the active column header to switch from ascending to descending order or vice versa.

Using the Go Menu

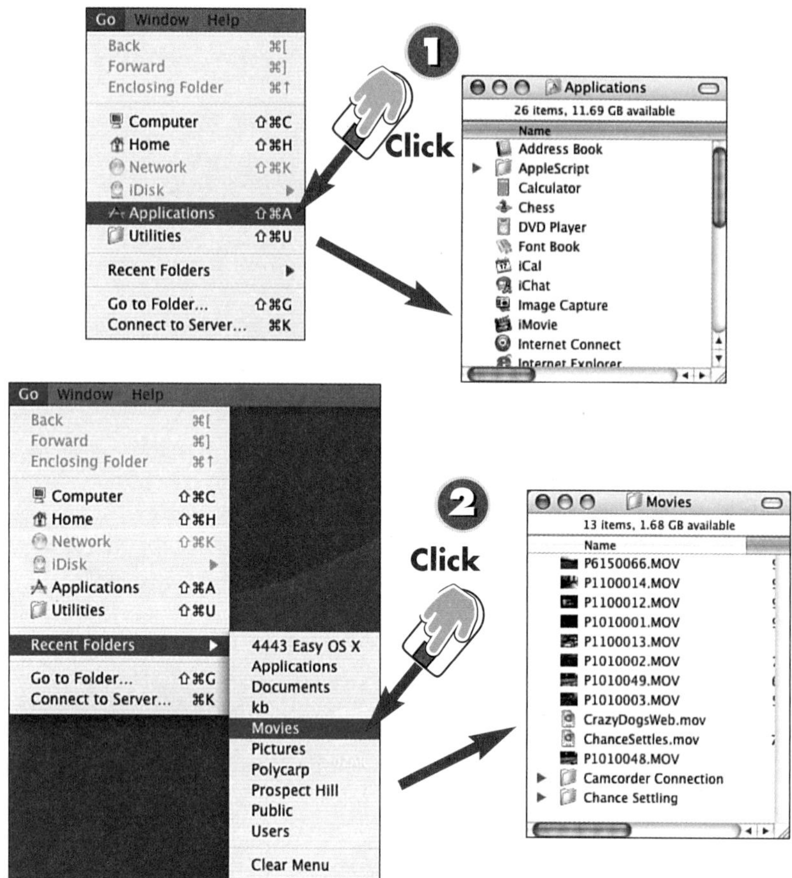

1. To go to one of Mac OS X's special folders, choose **Go** and choose **Computer**, **Home**, **Applications**, or **Utilities**.

2. To go to one of the folders you've opened recently, choose **Go**, **Recent Folders** and choose a folder.

INTRODUCTION

To make getting around your system easier, the Go menu contains commands that instantly take you to specific locations, including any of the special folders Mac OS X creates for your programs and documents. The Go menu also keeps track of the last several folders you've opened so you can return to any of them with a single click.

TIP

Using the Keyboard

You can also go to the special folders with keyboard commands. Press **Cmd-Shift-C** to see the Computer window; press **Cmd-Shift-H** to open your home folder; press **Cmd-Shift-A** to open the Applications folder; and press **Cmd-Shift-U** to open the Utilities folder.

Using Folder Pathnames

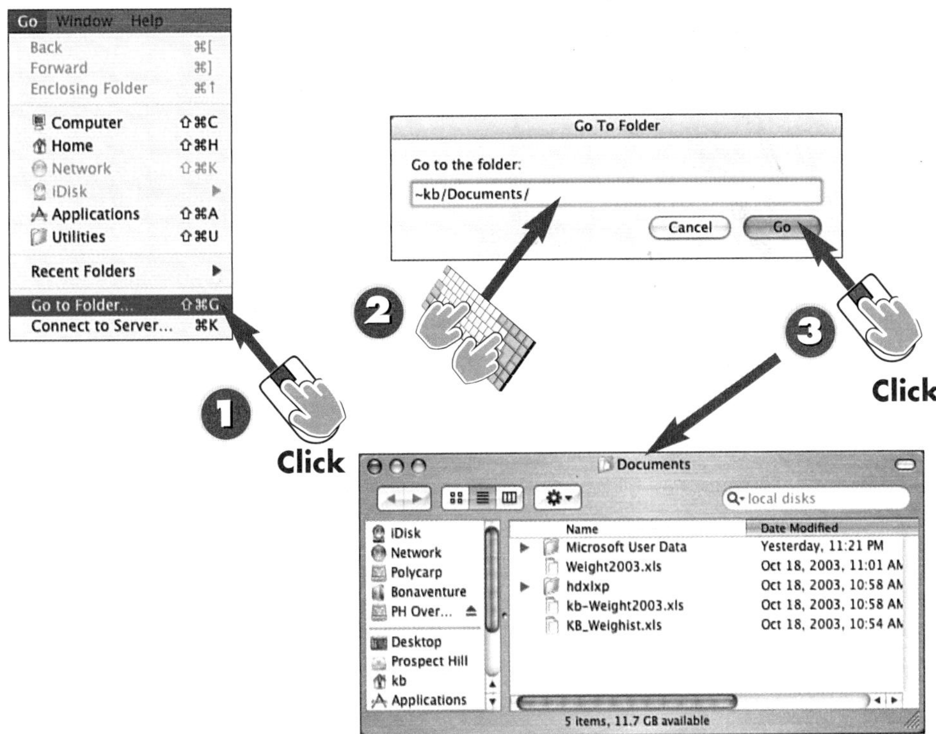

1. In the Finder, choose **Go**, **Go to Folder**.
2. Type the pathname of the folder you want to go to.
3. Click **Go** to open the folder.

INTRODUCTION

With Mac OS X, you can navigate your hard drive with the mouse or the keyboard. To use the keyboard, you type *pathnames* that list the nested folders your destination resides in, such as **~/Documents/** to go to the Documents folder in your home folder.

TIP

Pathname Protocols
When you're entering pathnames, type **~** to indicate your home folder. Separate each pair of folder names with a **/**.

HINT

Follow the Path
To get an idea how pathnames work, press **Cmd** and click the title bar of a folder window in the Finder. You'll see a list of the nested folders all the way back out to your hard drive.

Selecting Files

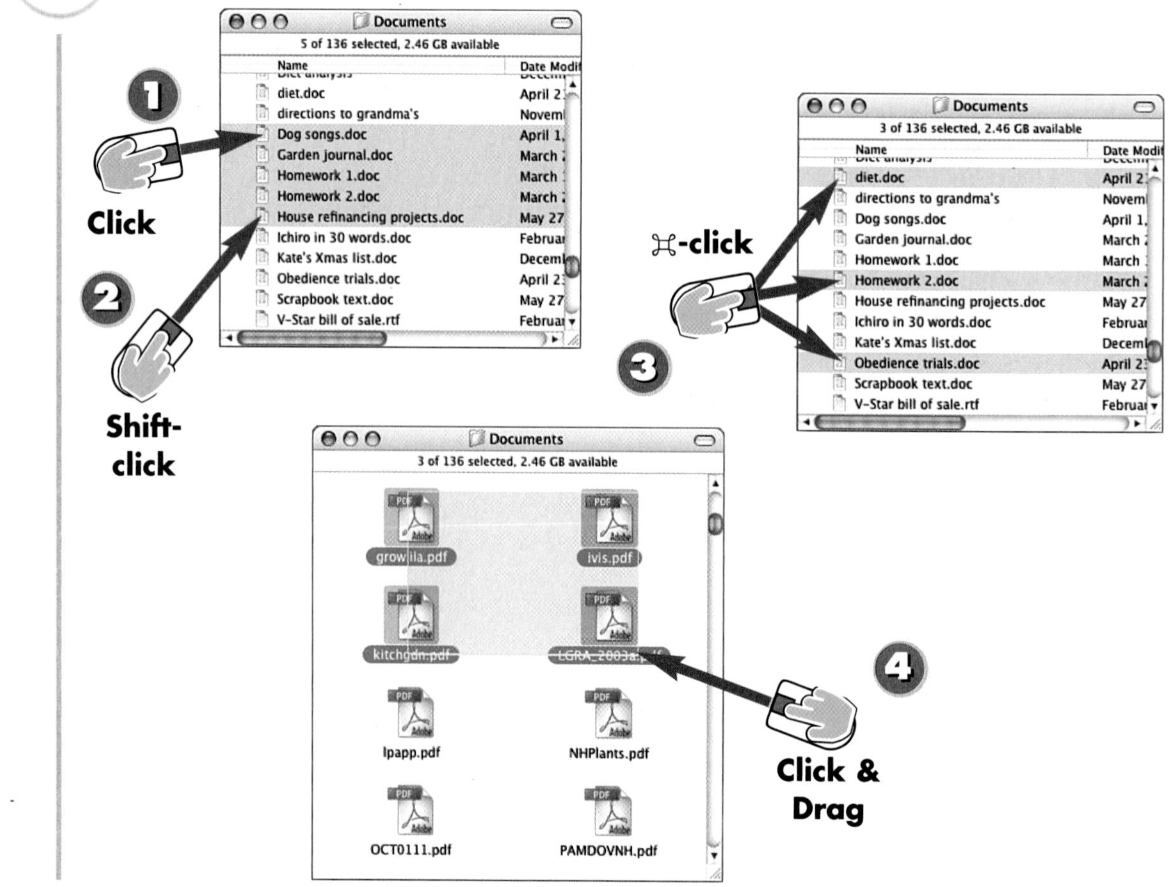

1. In any folder view, click a file or folder to select it.
2. Shift-click another file or folder to select it along with all the items between it and the first object you selected.
3. Cmd-click to select noncontiguous items.
4. In icon view, click and drag to select a group of icons.

INTRODUCTION

It might seem obvious, but before you can do anything with a file, folder, or disk in the Finder, you must select it so that the Finder knows which object(s) you want it to operate on. A couple of selection methods enable you to select more than one item at a time while leaving out those you don't want to use at the moment.

TIP

Selecting Everything at Once

To select all the items in a folder (or on the desktop), click the folder's title bar to make sure it is the active folder; then either press **Cmd-A** or choose **Edit**, **Select All**.

Moving and Copying Files and Folders

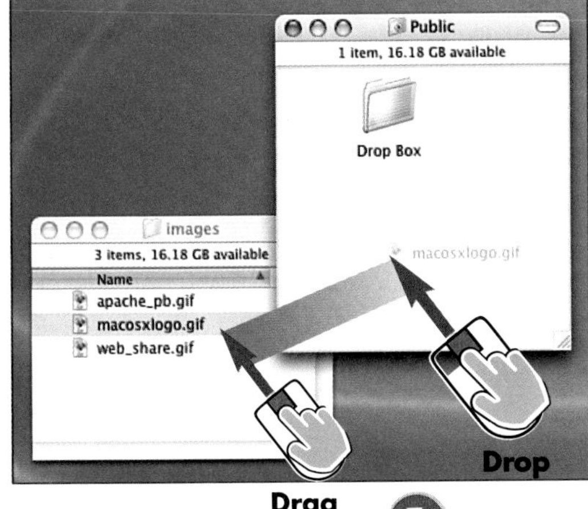

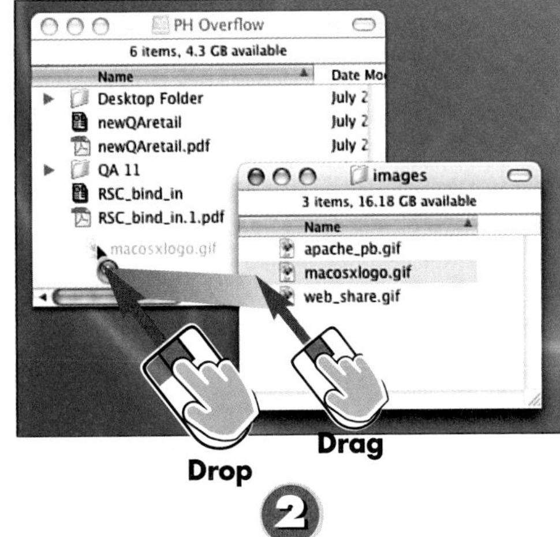

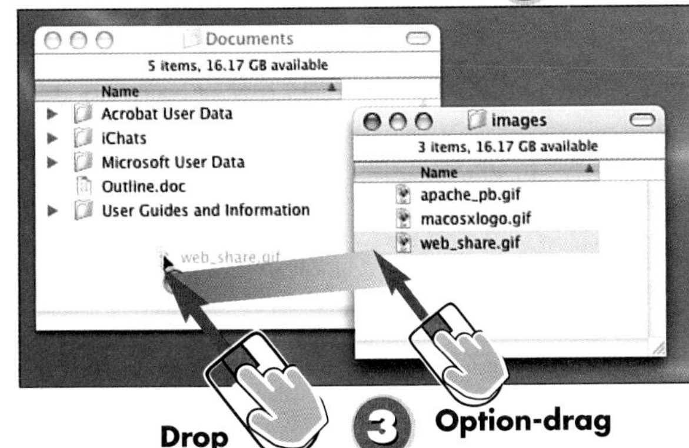

1. To *move* an item to another folder on the same disk, drag and drop it into the folder's window.
2. To *copy* an item to a location on a different disk, drag and drop it into the folder's window.
3. To copy an item to a different location on the same disk, press **Option** while you drag and drop it into the folder's window.

INTRODUCTION

Keeping your computer tidy is mostly a matter of putting things where they belong. That means moving and copying files and folders to different locations. These operations can be tricky in Mac OS X because it requires you to be authorized to open folders to which you're copying items.

TIP

Another Way to Copy
To make a copy of an item in the same place, press **Option** and drag the icon a little away from its current location or choose **File**, **Duplicate**.

TIP

Using Copy and Paste to Copy Files
Ctrl-click the file you want to copy and choose **Copy** from the menu. **Ctrl-click** in an open area of the folder's window where you want to copy the item and choose **Paste Item**.

Making a New Folder

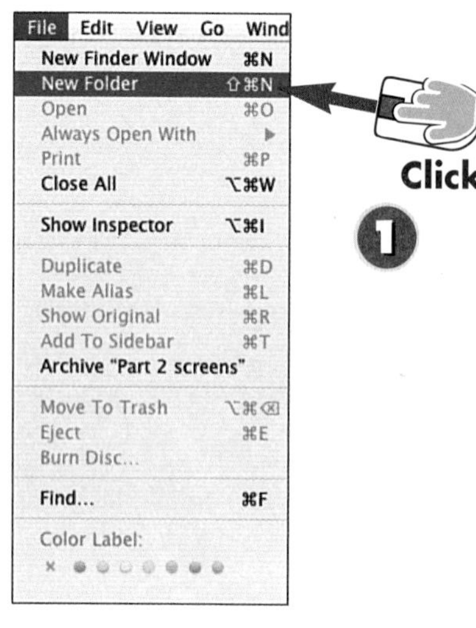

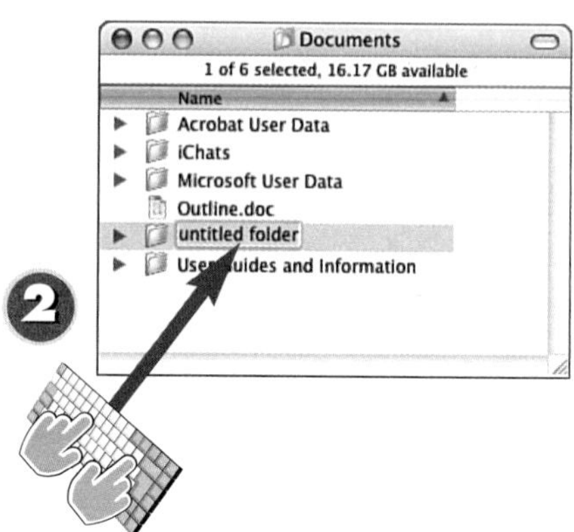

1. To create a new folder, choose **File**, **New Folder** (or press **Cmd-Shift-N**).

2. Type a name for the untitled folder; to change the name, see the next task.

INTRODUCTION

This is one task that often trips up long-time Mac users, who are used to pressing Cmd-N to create a new folder. That keyboard shortcut brings up a new Finder window now, instead of creating a new folder. You'll get used to the change, and you'll find that being able to create new Finder windows this way is pretty useful, too.

TIP

You Don't Have to Start from Scratch
If you need several folders with the same name and, perhaps, a different number tacked onto the end of each, create the first one and create copies of it as described earlier in the task "Moving and Copying Files and Folders." Then replace **"copy"** in the folder name with the numbers or text you want.

Renaming Folders and Files

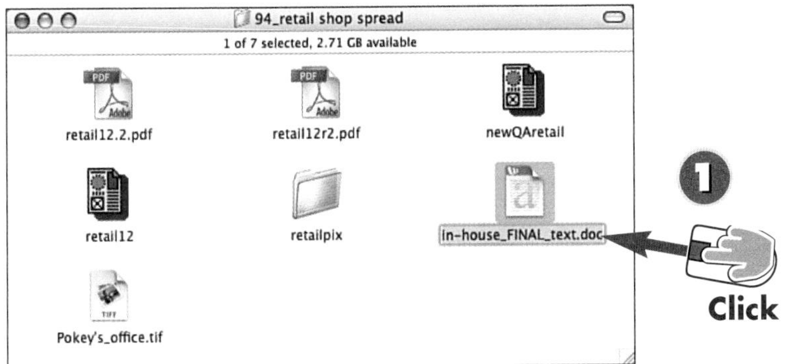

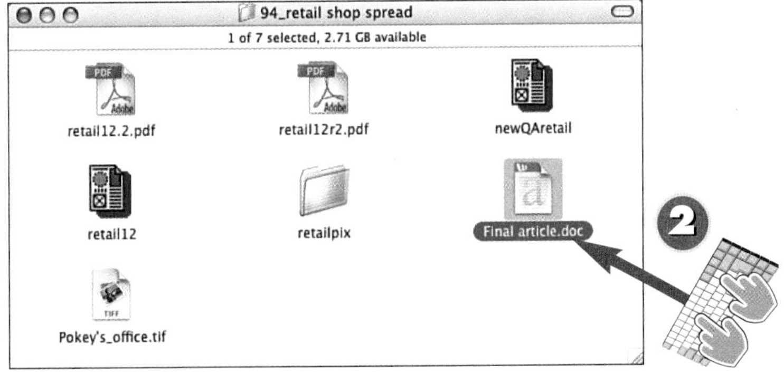

1. Click to select the item whose name you want to change and keep the mouse cursor positioned over the name.
2. When the item's name becomes highlighted, type to replace the old name with the new one. Press **Enter** when you're done.

INTRODUCTION

Some people like to include dates and similar information in filenames so anyone can tell what's inside; others don't care if anyone else can make sense of their filenames. Whichever camp you fall into, you'll need to know how to change the names of files and folders.

HINT

Adding Extensions

Don't you hate documents with blank, white icons? You can't open them by double-clicking because your Mac doesn't know which program to use. If you know which kind of document it is, add the correct filename extension so it will open.

HINT

Extended Filenames

Filenames have two components: the name and the extension, such as **.pdf** or **.doc**. Mac OS X uses extensions to determine which program can open which files, so don't change an extension unless you know what you're doing.

Making an Alias

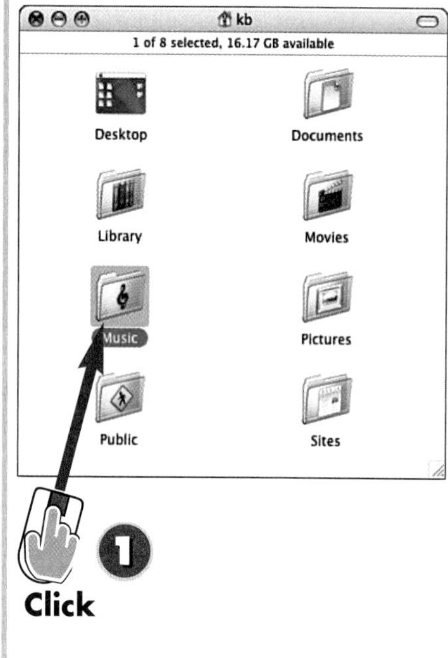

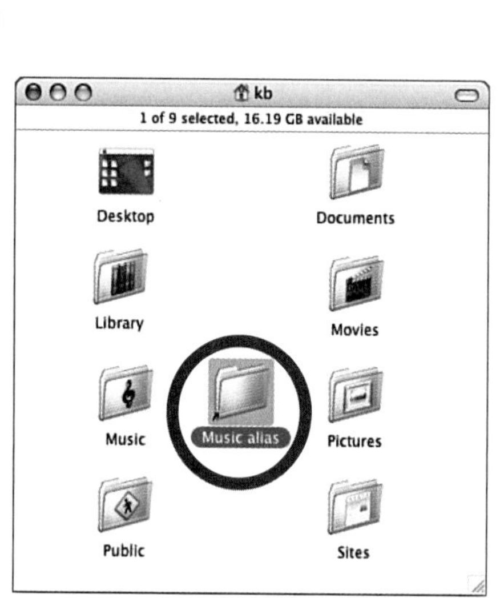

1. Click the original file or folder to select it.
2. Choose **File**, **Make Alias**.
3. Move the alias wherever you want it; you can recognize it by the small arrow in the icon's lower-left corner.

INTRODUCTION

An *alias* is a file that provides access to another file, folder, or program. To make locating and opening an item you've stored several folder levels deep in your home folder or anywhere else on your Mac easier, you can put an alias of that file on your desktop. Deleting an alias does not delete the item it points to.

TIP

Avoid Dock Obesity

One way to put a lot of files in your Dock is to put aliases in a folder, put the folder in your home folder, and drag it into the Dock. When you click and hold the folder's icon in the Dock, you see a list of files from which you can choose.

HINT

One, Two, Many Aliases

You can make as many aliases of an item as you want, and you can store them anywhere that makes sense to you, even on another disk. If your Mac can't find the alias's original when you double-click the alias, it will politely let you know.

Viewing File Information

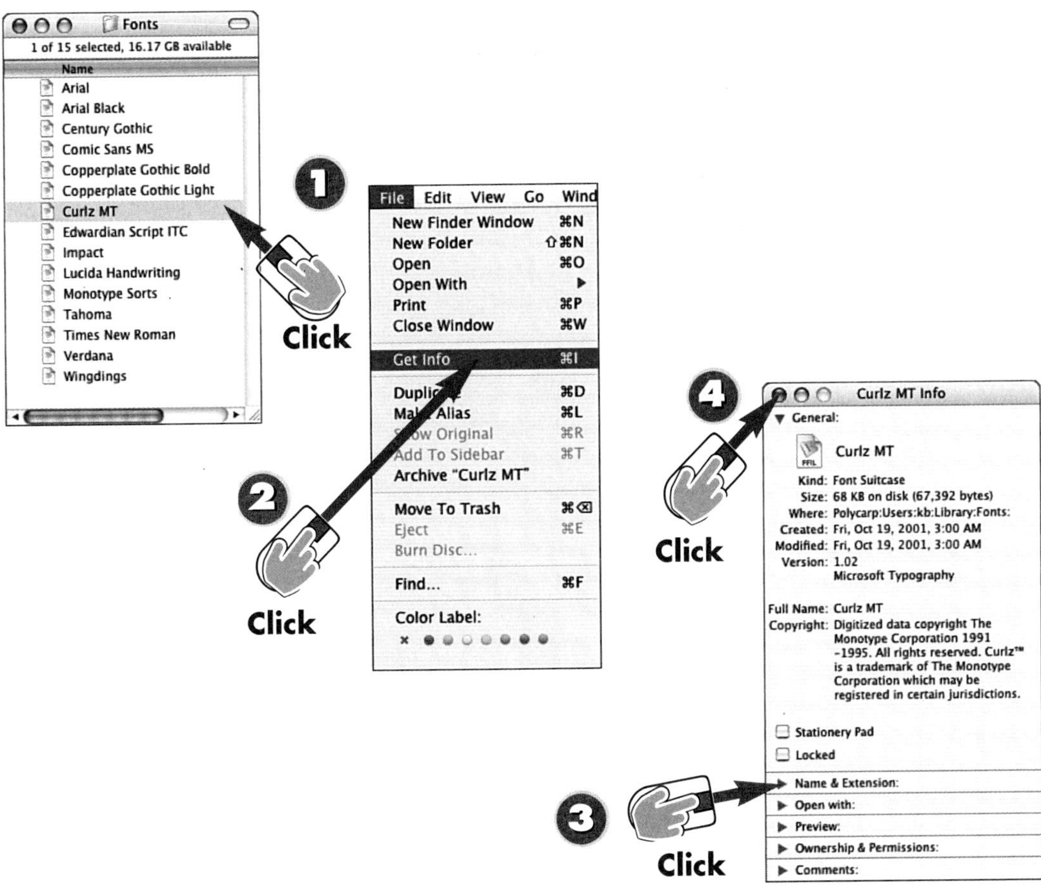

1. Click a file to select it.
2. Choose **File**, **Get Info**.
3. The Info window opens to the General pane; to see the contents of another pane, click the gray triangle next to its name.
4. Click the red **Close** button to close the Info window when you're done.

INTRODUCTION

Each file or folder on your computer has a lot of information associated with it—not just the data it contains, such as recipes or pictures or programming code, but data about the file, such as when it was created, the last time it was modified, and which program made it.

TIP

Avoiding a Trip to the Menu Bar

You can also press Cmd-I or use a contextual menu to get information about an item.

HINT

Getting Info

Some file information can be changed in the Info window, if you're the owner of a file. You can change the name and extension, the program that opens a document, and the file's ownership (if you're an *admin user*), and you can add comments.

Opening a File

Start

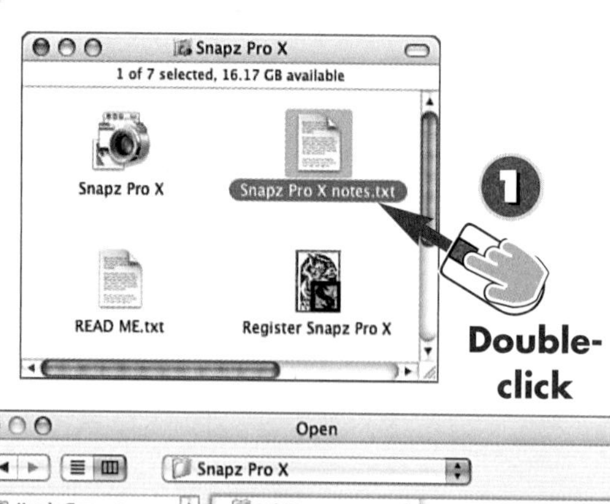

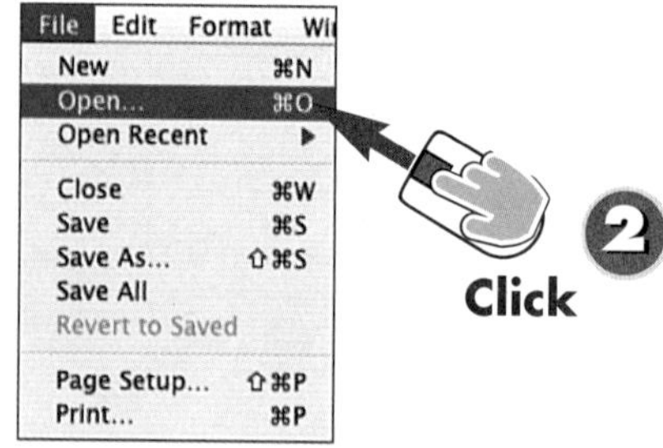

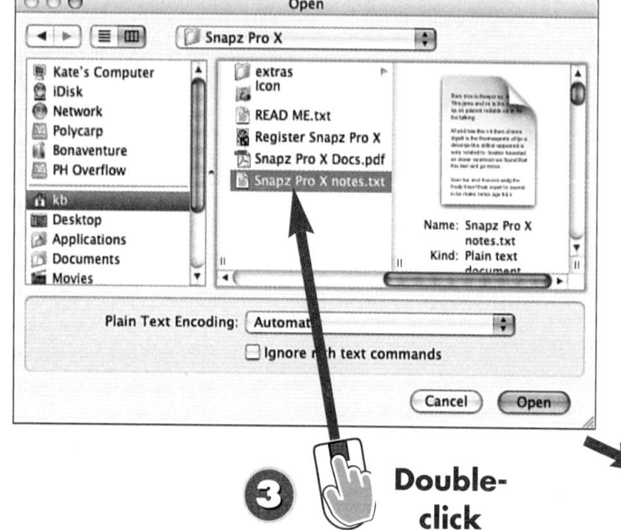

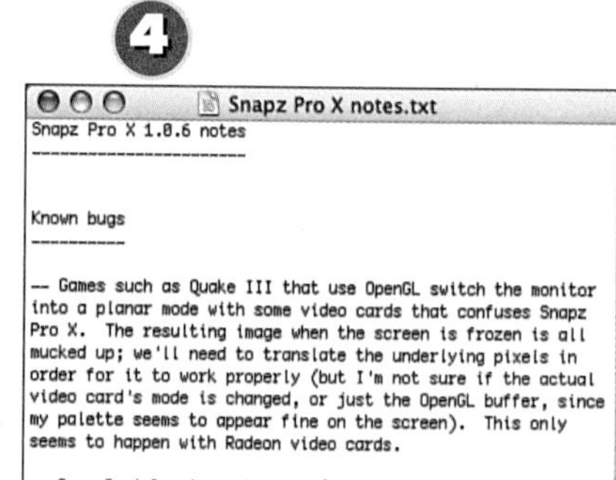

1. In the Finder, double-click the file's icon. The file opens in the program that created it.

2. To open a file from within a running program, choose **File**, **Open**.

3. Navigate to the file in the pick list and double-click it or click **Open**.

4. The file opens in the program window.

End

INTRODUCTION

When you're looking at a file's icon in the Finder, you can open that file in the correct program without having to first start up the program. Conversely, if you're already using that program, you can open more files without having to return to the Finder to locate them.

TIP

Programs

Some programs are picky about which types of files they'll open, so your file might be unavailable in an Open dialog box. If a pop-up menu below the pick list has an option such as Show All Files, choose this option to make your file available.

HINT

It's a Drag

A third method of opening a file is to drag it on top of a program icon, either in the Finder or in the Dock. The program starts up, if it wasn't already running, and opens the file if it can.

Choosing a Program to Open a File

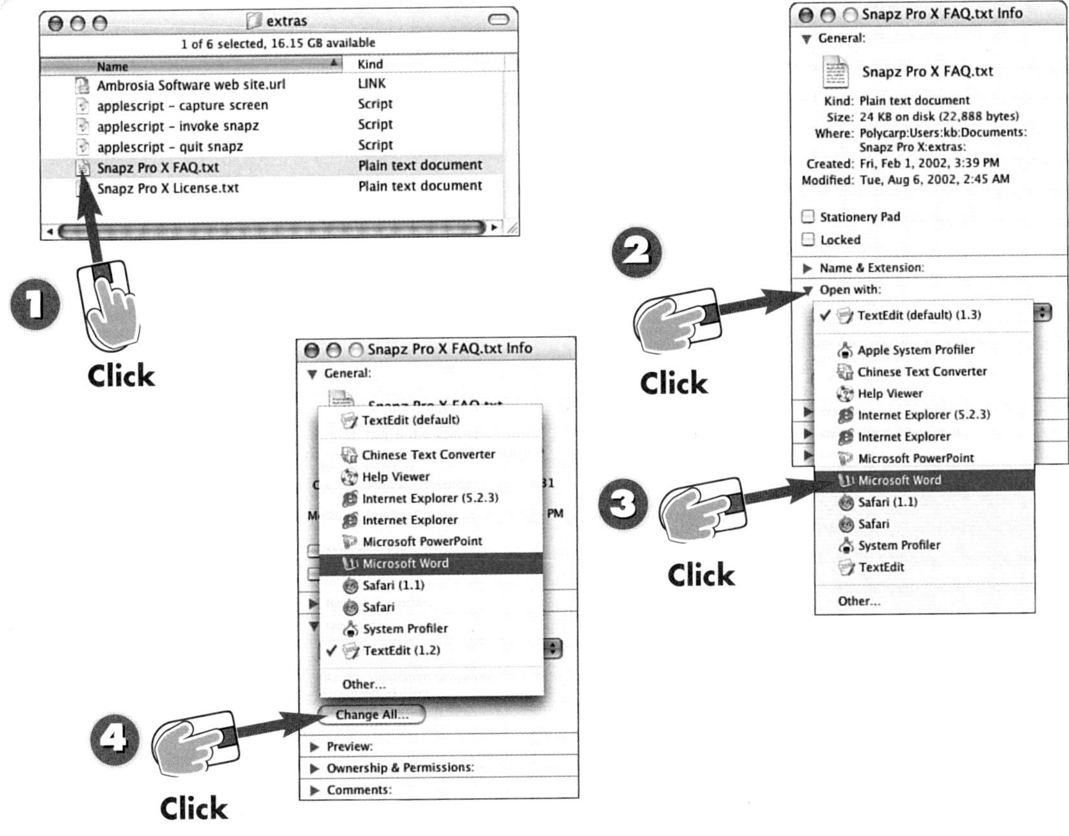

1. Click to select the file and press **Cmd-I** to see its Info window.
2. Click the gray triangle next to **Open with** in the Info window.
3. Choose an application from the pop-up menu, or choose **Other** to navigate to the program you want if it's not listed.
4. Click **Change All** if you want to make the same change for all documents with the same extension.

INTRODUCTION

Sometimes you disagree with your Mac about which program it should use to open a file you double-click. For example, perhaps you want to open PDF files in Adobe Reader instead of Preview, or RTF word processor files in Microsoft Word instead of TextEdit. You have the power to make the change—here's how.

TIP

There's More than One Way

The directions here enable you to open a file in the right program by double-clicking its Finder icon. But if you're in a hurry, you can just start the program, choose **File**, **Open** as described earlier in the task "Opening a File."

Deleting a File

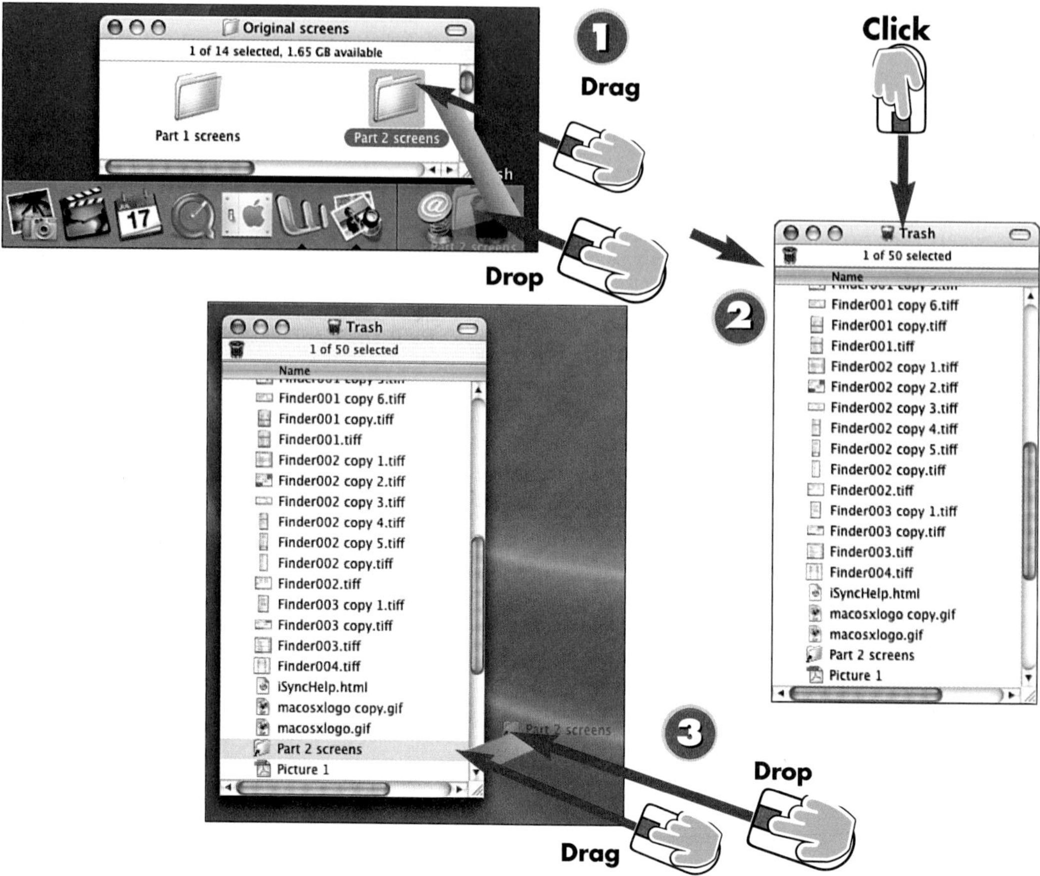

1. Drag the file to the **Trash** icon on the Dock and drop it when the Trash icon is highlighted.
2. Click the **Trash** to open a window showing its contents.
3. Drag items that you don't want to delete out of the Trash window and drop them in a new location.

INTRODUCTION

Mac OS X stores files you don't want any more in a trash can. You can rummage through the Trash to retrieve files you didn't mean to discard, just as you can in the real world. But—again, just like the real world—the Trash doesn't empty itself; you have to remember to empty it to truly delete the discarded files.

HINT

An Open and Shut Case

You can't open files in the Trash, but you can open folders located there. If you need to open a file you've found in the Trash, drag it onto the desktop first.

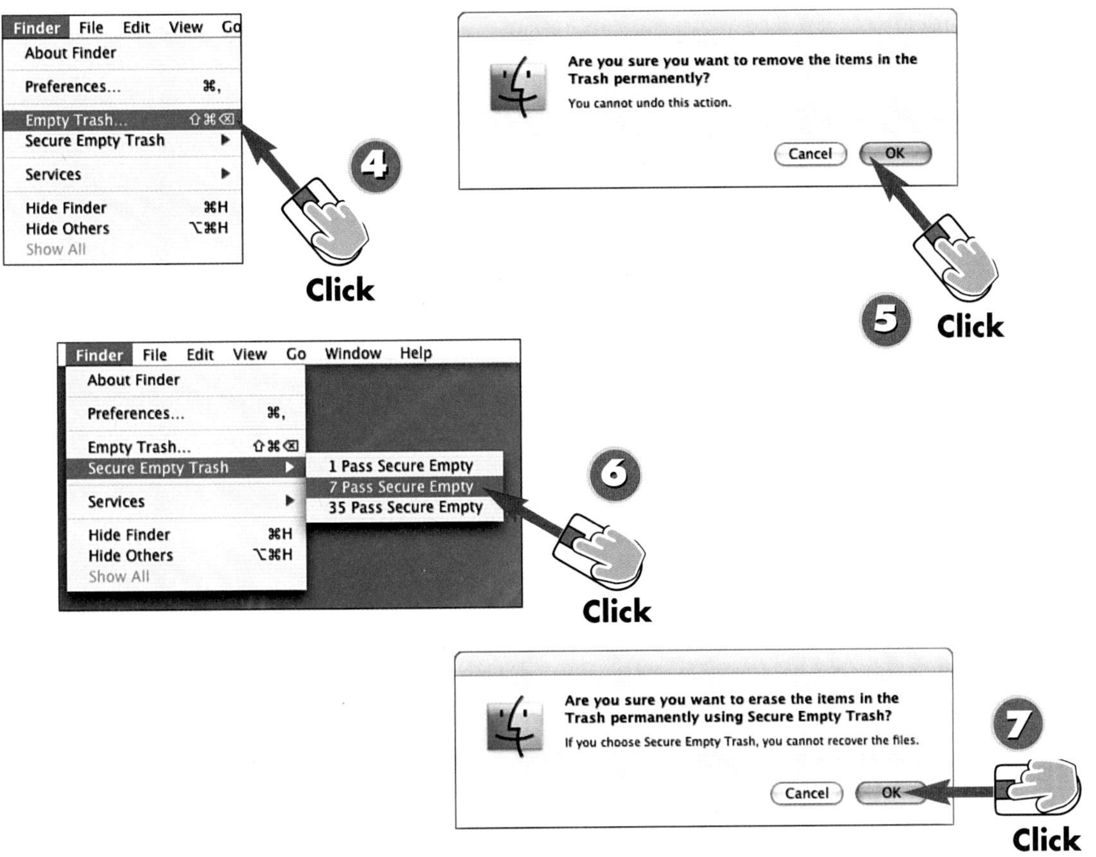

4 To delete all the objects in the Trash, choose **Finder**, **Empty Trash**.

5 Click **OK** on the confirmation dialog box or **Cancel** to keep the items in the Trash.

6 To delete the objects in the Trash so they can't be recovered by special software, choose **Finder**, **Secure Empty Trash** and pick one of the three options.

7 Click **OK** to confirm the deletion.

HINT

Deleting Files Securely

Secure Empty Trash solves an old Mac problem: Emptying the Trash doesn't really delete files; it just lets the Mac forget where it put them. Secure Empty Trash writes gibberish data over the files so they can never be found, even by "computer detectives."

Finding Files

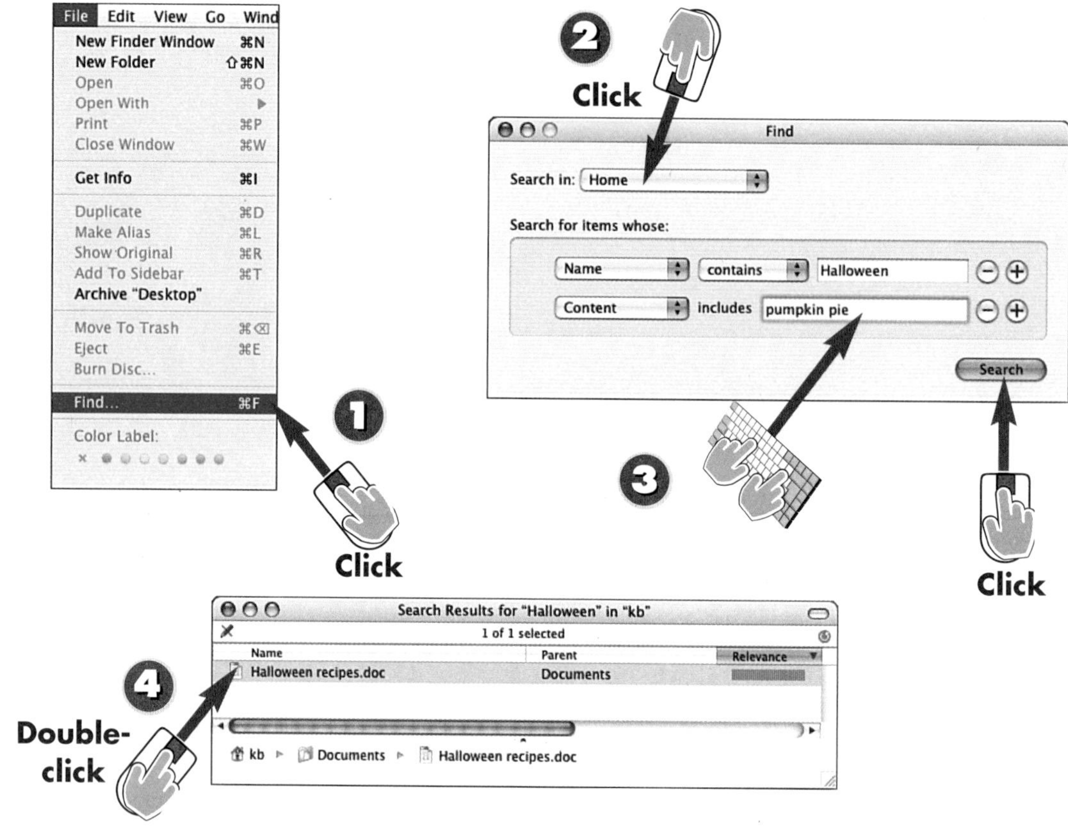

1. In the Finder, press **Cmd-F** or choose **File**, **Find**.
2. Choose a location to search from the **Search in** pop-up menu at the top of the Find dialog box.
3. Fill in the criteria on which you want to search and click **Search**.
4. In the Search Results window, double-click to open a file, or drag it out of the window to the desktop or to another folder.

INTRODUCTION

No matter how organized you are, you'll lose a file from time to time. The more you use your Mac, the more it will happen to you as your collection of documents and folders grows. Fortunately, Mac OS X comes with a handy way to look for files you've lost based on their names, contents, dates modified, or other criteria.

TIP

Quick and Dirty
In single-window mode, a Find text field appears on the toolbar at the top of the window. If you're in a hurry, you don't have to bring up the Find dialog box—just type the search terms right in the window.

HINT

Zeroing In
Don't overlook the pop-up menus next to each criterion; they enable you to refine your searches. You can look for files whose names end with that word or files that were modified after a certain date, rather than simply on that date.

Accessing Your Favorite Files and Places

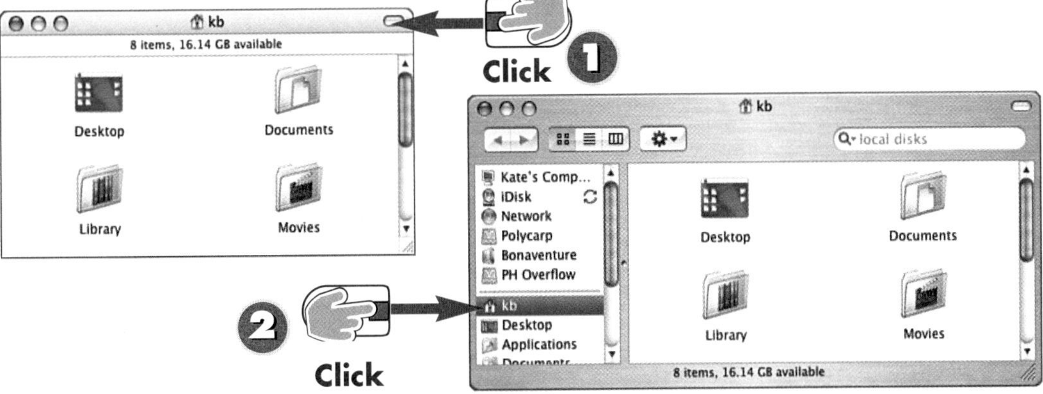

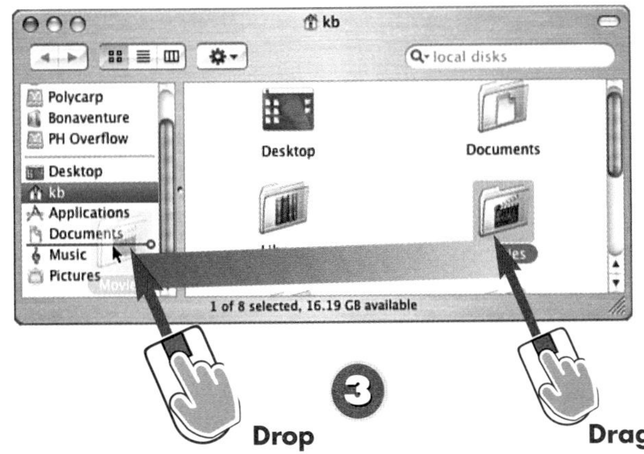

1. If you don't see the Places sidebar, click the clear button at the upper-right corner of the window to enter single-window mode.
2. Click a disk or folder to view its contents in the window.
3. Drag folders into the lower section of the Places sidebar to customize it.

INTRODUCTION

Mac OS X 10.3 offers a new way to store and access your favorites. They're visible in a column called the Places sidebar at the left side of every window when you're using single-window mode. The top section of the Places list contains disks attached to your Mac, and the lower section contains anything you want.

HINT

Quick Copy, Quick Move
You can move or copy files to disks or folders in the Places sidebar by dragging them from the main section of the window over a disk or folder icon in the sidebar.

HINT

Customizing the Custom List
To change the order of items in the bottom half of the Places sidebar, just drag and drop them into the order you prefer. Drag folders out of the lower section of the Places sidebar to remove them from the list.

Burning a Data CD

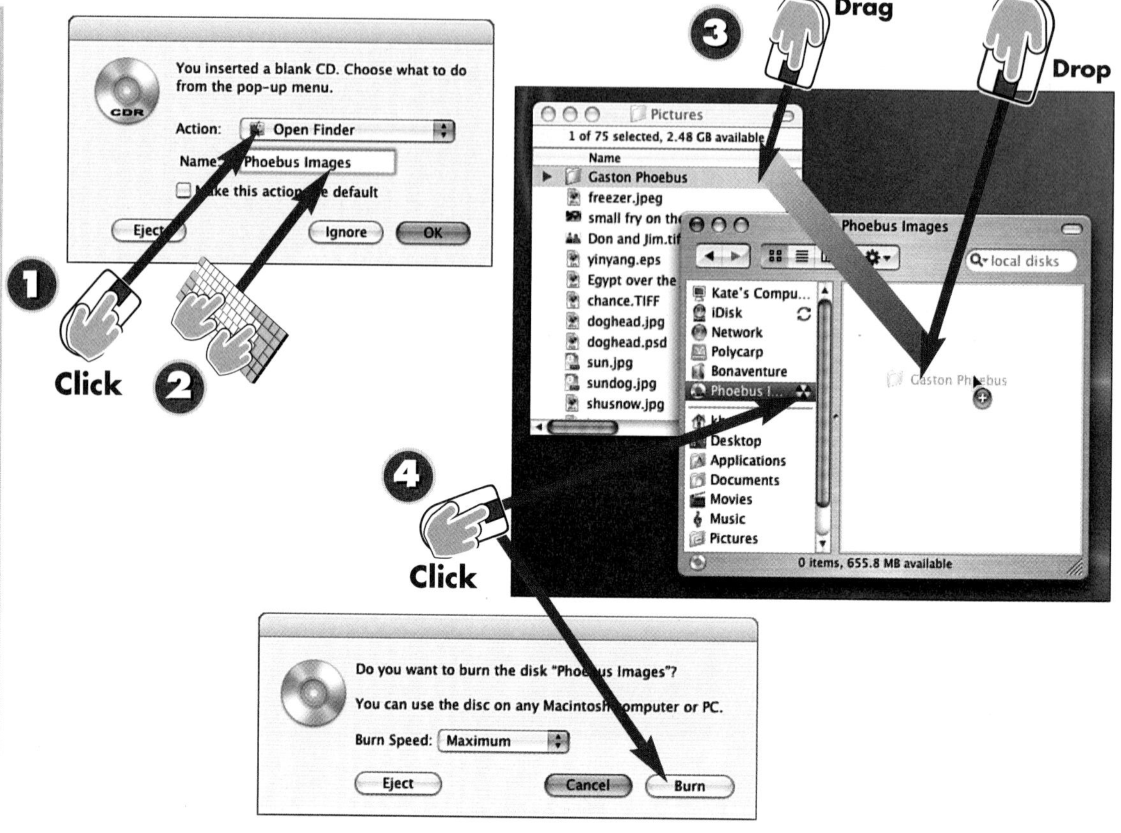

1. Insert a blank CD-R or CD-RW disc in the CD-R or CD-RW drive. A dialog box asks what you want to do with the disc; choose **Open Finder** from the pop-up menu.
2. Type a name for the disc.
3. Drag files and folders into the CD's window.
4. Click the **Burn** icon next to the CD's name in the Places sidebar. Or choose **File**, **Burn Disc** and then click **Burn** in the dialog box.

INTRODUCTION

These days the CD is usually the cheapest, easiest medium to use for transporting large amounts of data from one computer to another. Many Macs have built-in CD-R or CD-RW drives that can burn CDs quickly, and the Finder can help accomplish the task.

TIP

The Different Flavors of CDs

CD-R? CD-RW? They all look just like music CDs, so what's the difference? CD-Rs are writable only once, and CD-RWs can be erased and rerecorded. CD-Rs, naturally, are cheaper, so stick to CD-RWs for home use and CD-Rs for discs you give to other people.

Organizing Files and Folders with Labels

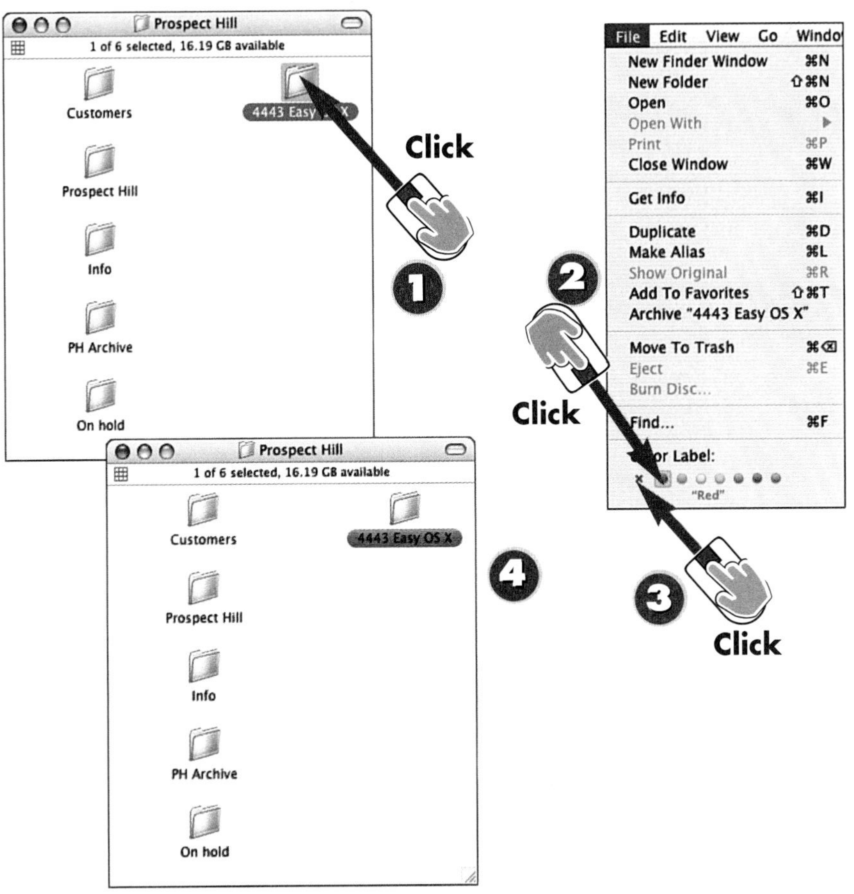

1. In the Finder, select a file or folder to label.
2. Open the **File** menu, scroll to the bottom, and choose a label color.
3. To remove a label, choose the **X** at the left end of the color list.
4. The name of the item appears in the chosen color.

INTRODUCTION

You can think of labels as actually being color coding. With a label, you can assign a color to a file or folder so that it jumps out at you when you're digging through a folder for it, or you can search for files by label color. Labels also enable you to create custom sort orders for folder contents in List view.

TIP

Sorting by Labels
Choose **View**, **Show View Options** and click the **Labels** check box to add a Labels column to the window. Then return to the window and click the **Labels** column header to sort by the value in that column.

HINT

Labeling the Fast Way
Adding a label color is one of the things you can do to a file or folder via a contextual menu. Turn to "Using Contextual Menus" in Part 1, "Getting Started," to learn more.

Archiving a File or Folder

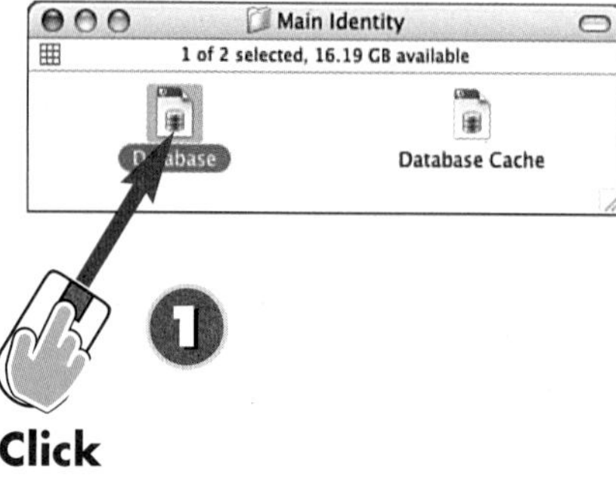

Click

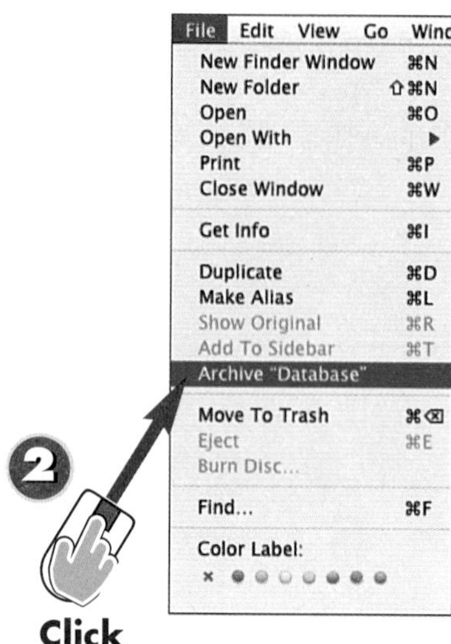

Click

Double-click

1. In the Finder, select a file or folder to archive.
2. Choose **File**, **Archive**.
3. To de-archive a file, double-click the archive.

INTRODUCTION

Archiving a folder and its contents is a way to package it as a single, compressed file so that it takes up as little disk space as possible and so that its contents can't be lost or modified. You can archive folders and files before attaching them to email messages, and you can archive files and folders to free up disk space.

HINT

Watch Out for Archive Clutter

When you de-archive a file, the archive is left intact, so you end up with two copies of the file: the archive and the decompressed version. Watch out for these extra files so that you don't lose track of which is the version you're working on.

Ejecting a Disk

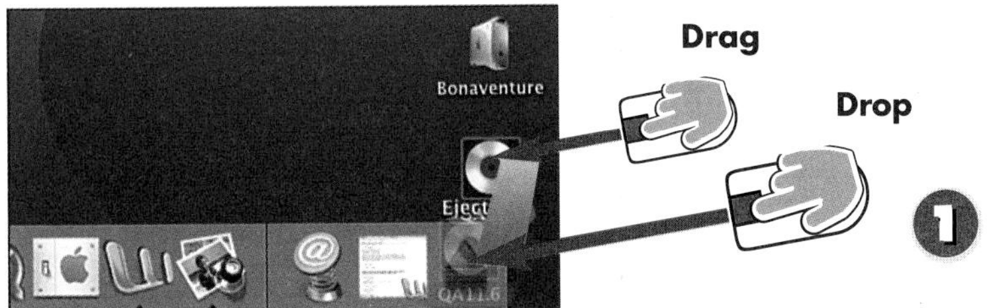

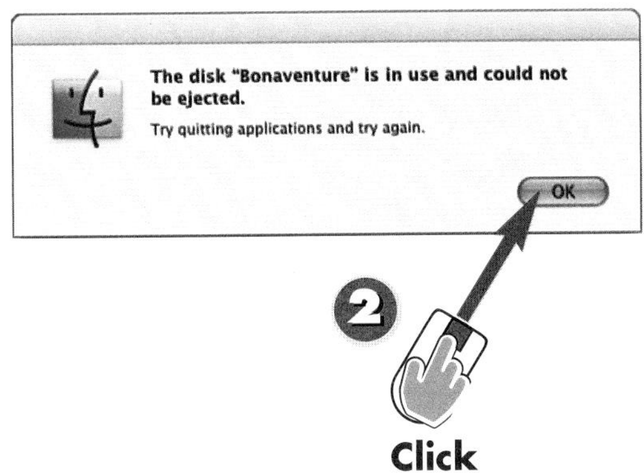

1. Drag the disk icon to the Dock and drop it on the Eject button to eject the disk.

2. If files are open on the disk, the Mac lets you know. Click **OK**, close the open files, and try again.

INTRODUCTION

For most of the Mac's history, users have dragged disks to the Trash to eject them. With Mac OS X, that analogy is no more. Now an Eject symbol takes the place of the Trash when you're dragging a disk. And there's more than one way to eject a disk, so you can pick the most convenient method.

TIP

Alternative Ejection Methods

Don't want to drag a disk to the Dock? Select the disk on the desktop and choose **File**, **Eject**. Or choose **Eject** from its contextual menu. In single-window mode, select the disk in the Places sidebar and click the Eject button next to the disk's icon or choose **Eject** from the Action menu in the window's title bar.

Undoing a Finder Action

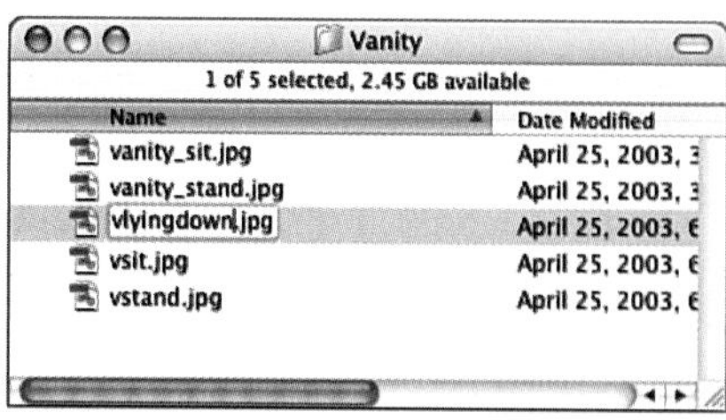

1. If you mistakenly rename, copy, delete, or move a file or folder, choose **Edit**, **Undo** to restore the item to its original state.

2. To redo the change after undoing it, choose **Edit**, **Redo**.

INTRODUCTION

We all make mistakes. Fortunately, you can almost always recover from a mistake on the Mac. A big part of that safety net is the Undo command, which enables you to change your mind after modifying the name or location of a file or folder.

HINT

Fools Rush Ahead

You can't undo some actions, such as duplicating a file or folder or applying a label. In that case, however, you can just drag the unwanted item to the Trash or remove the label via the File menu. Watch out for actions that are harder to reverse, such as actually emptying the Trash, burning a disc, or even rearranging file and folder icons.

Tidying Up Your Folders

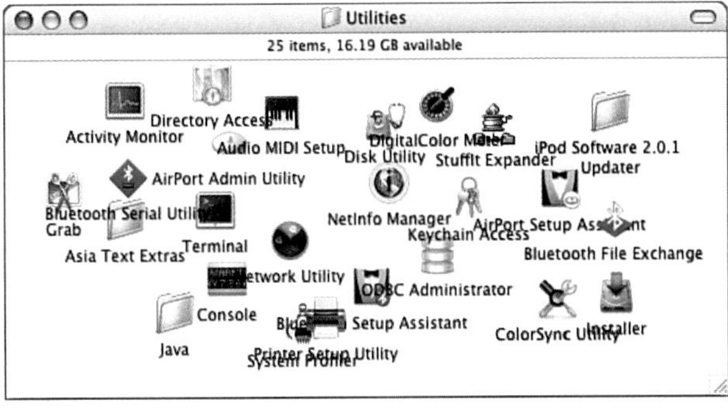

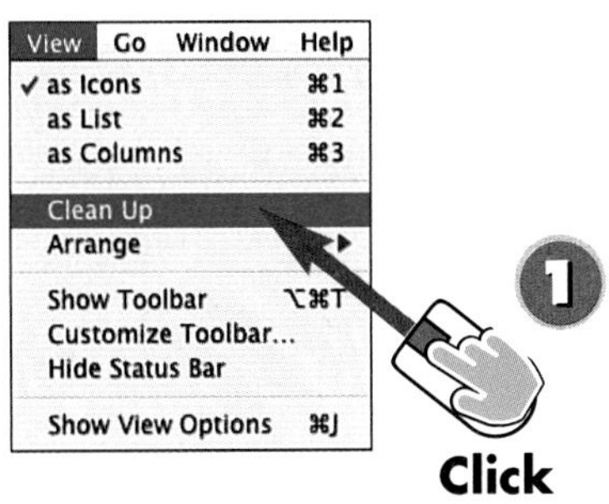

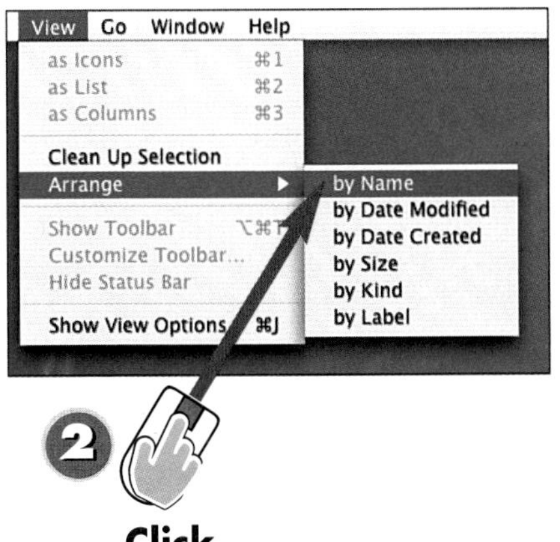

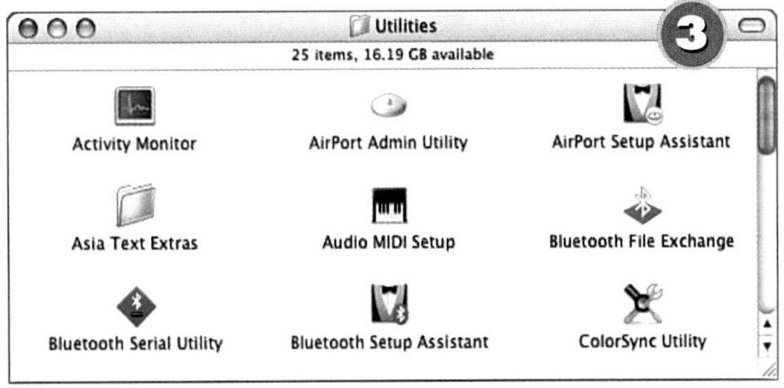

1. With a window open, choose **View**, **Clean Up** to line up the window's icons neatly.
2. Choose **View**, **Arrange** and an option from the submenu to re-sort the icons in your preferred order.
3. The icons are then arranged in the desired order.

INTRODUCTION

Icon view is a great way to look at folder windows. Mac OS X icons are beautifully detailed and scale to large sizes if you prefer. But they can end up stacked on top of each other or separated from each other by wide gulfs of white space. Fortunately, getting Icon view folders in shape so you can see what's what is an easy task.

TIP

Constant Organization
To keep the folder organized all the time, choose **View**, **View Options** and click the **Keep arranged by** check box; then choose an option from the pop-up menu. To keep icons lined up on a grid, click the **Snap to Grid** check box.

TIP

Bigger Is Better
If you want to enjoy your icons more, try viewing them at a larger size. Choose **View**, **View Options** and drag the slider at the top of the View Options palette to scale icons up to as large as 128 pixels square—almost 2" across!

Mounting Your iDisk

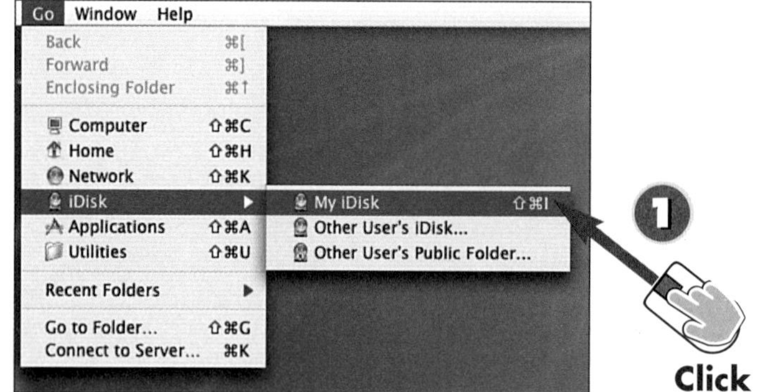

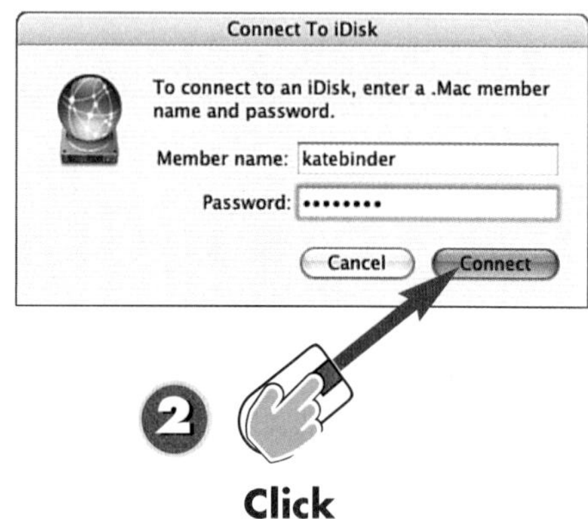

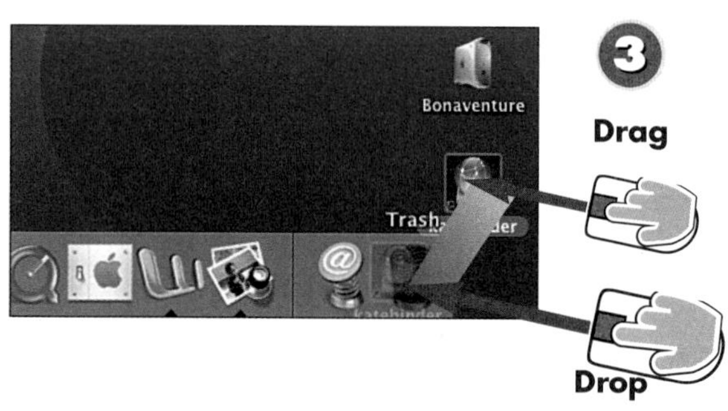

1. In the Finder, either choose **Go**, **iDisk**, **My iDisk** or press **Cmd-Shift-I**.
2. If you haven't entered your .Mac username and password in System Preferences, type that information into the dialog box that appears and click **Connect**.
3. To dismount the iDisk so that it no longer appears on the desktop, drag it to the Eject button in the Dock.

INTRODUCTION

Apple's special online services for Mac users, referred to collectively as .Mac (dot-Mac), include the use of an *iDisk*—an online storage area. You can mount your iDisk right on your desktop, where it appears along with your hard drive and any removable disks you insert (Zip disks, DVDs, or CDs).

TIP

Keeping Your iDisk at Home

For easy access to your iDisk, go to the **.Mac** pane in **System Preferences**. Click **iDisk** and click the **Create a local copy of your iDisk** check box. The iDisk copy appears on your desktop all the time; changes you make to it are automatically made to the real iDisk.

Storing Files on Your iDisk

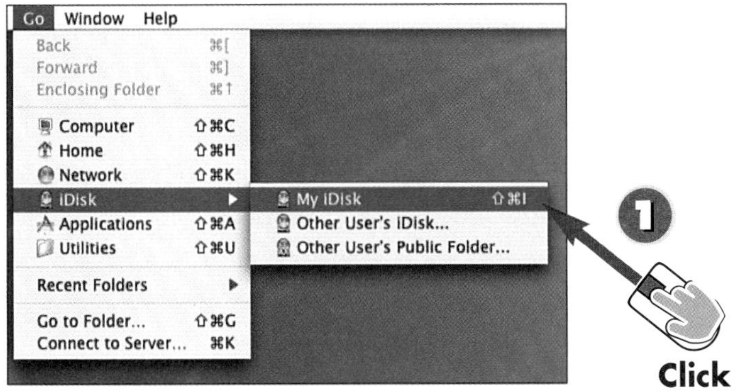

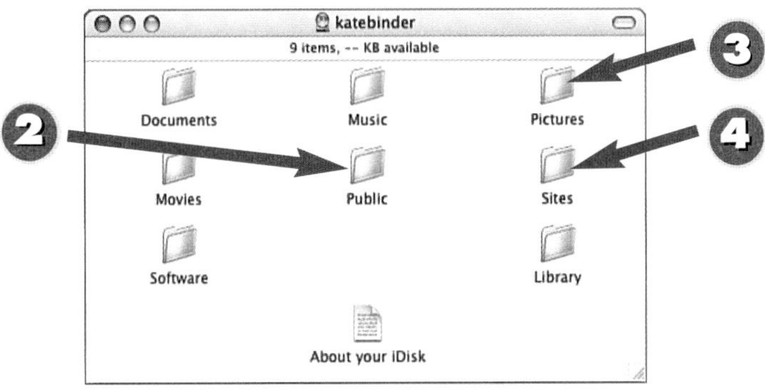

1. In the Finder, mount your iDisk by choosing **Go**, **iDisk**, **My iDisk** or pressing **Cmd-Shift-I**.
2. Drag files into the iDisk Public folder if you want other people to be able to download them.
3. Drag files into the Pictures folder if you want to be able to use them to create e-cards or put them on your .Mac Web pages.
4. Drag files into the Sites folder if you want to use them to build your Web site.

INTRODUCTION

What can you put on your iDisk? Actually, what *can't* you put on your iDisk? You can store the files to make up your own Web site, stash pictures and iMovies to share with friends and family members, and even back up important files. The nicest thing about an iDisk is that you can reach it from anywhere you can get online.

HINT

Folders Everywhere
Documents provides private storage for anything you want to keep there. The Movies folder is where you can stash QuickTime movies you want to use in a Web site. And Music is intended for storing music files and iTunes playlists.

HINT

And More Folders
The contents of two iDisk folders aren't subtracted from your quota of disk space. They're Library, which contains maintenance files for the iDisk itself, and Software, where you can download the latest free programs and demos.

PART 3

Installing and Using Applications

The programs make using your Mac worthwhile, whether it's the applications that come with Mac OS X (such as Preview, TextEdit, and Safari) or the ones you buy and install yourself (such as Microsoft Word, Adobe Photoshop, or your favorite games). Most of the software you'll use every day runs natively in Mac OS X, but you can still use older programs (that require Mac OS 9) by running them in Classic.

Classic is like a computer within your computer; with this system feature, you can start up a Mac OS 9 "bubble" in which Mac OS 9 programs can run. When you're using a Classic program, you'll see the gray Mac OS 9 menu bar and the rainbow-colored Apple menu icon instead of the white Mac OS X menu bar and blue Apple menu icon.

In this part you'll learn how to use a couple of the system's built-in programs, how to install new programs, how to switch among multiple programs running at the same time, and more techniques to make your Mac day run smoothly. You'll also learn how to start up and run Classic so you can use those older applications.

Mac OS X's Programs

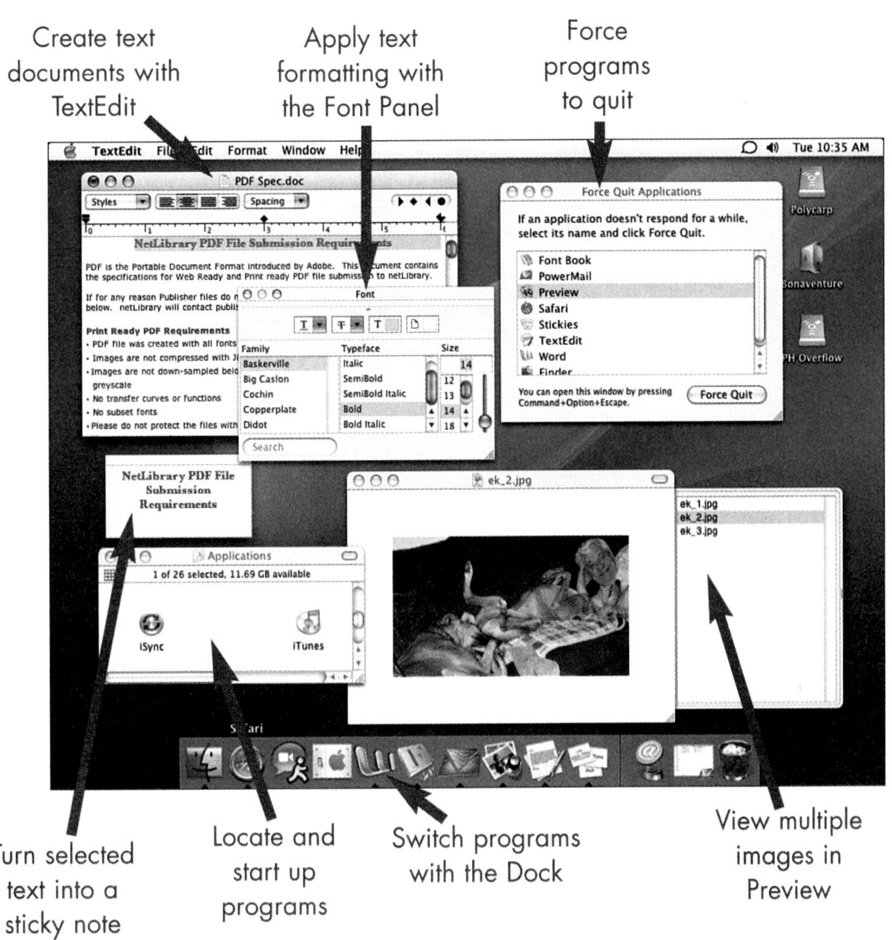

Installing Programs

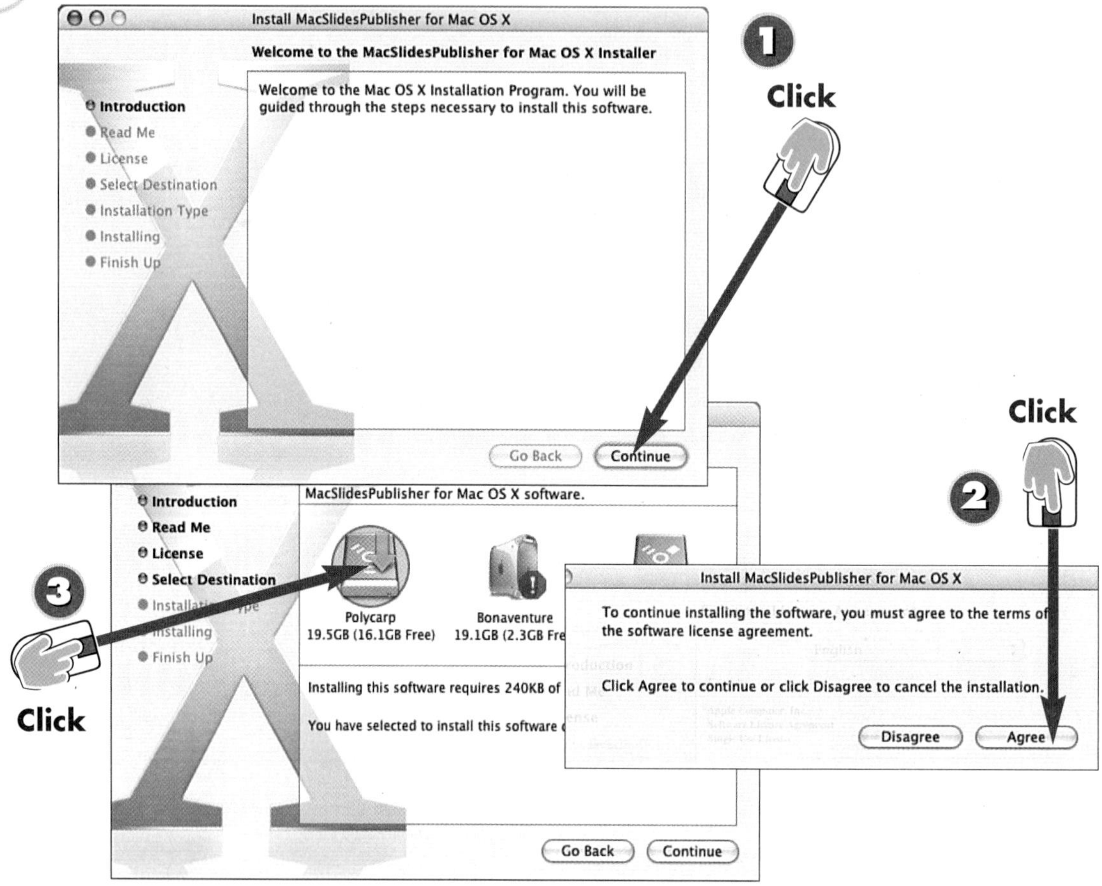

1. After you read each screen of the installer, click the **Continue** button at the bottom of the window to move to the next screen.
2. Read the program information and the license agreement; then click **Agree** to agree to the license terms (or Disagree if you don't want to install the program after all).
3. If you have more than one hard drive, choose the drive where you want to install the software.

INTRODUCTION

Some Mac programs are small enough that you can drag them off their disks right into the Applications folder, but others require an installer program to make sure all their pieces get to the right places. When you run Apple's Installer, you have to enter an admin password to authorize the installation.

HINT

Applications in the Applications Folder
You can install programs anywhere you want, but it's best to put them in the Applications folder on your startup drive. That way all users of your Mac can run the programs.

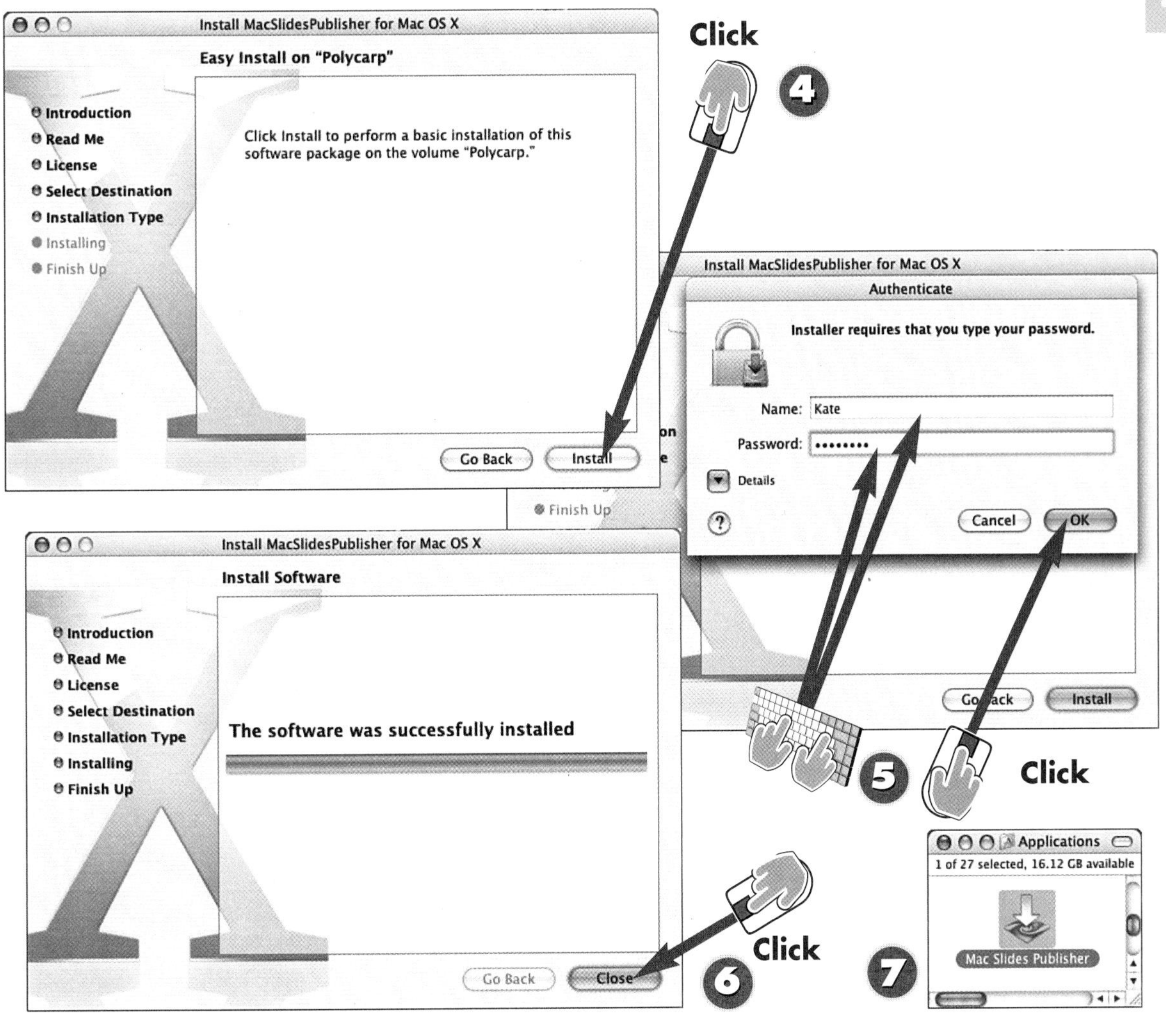

4 Click **Install** to begin the installation process.

5 Enter an admin username and password to authorize the installation and click **OK**.

6 When the installation is complete, click **Close** to quit Installer.

7 The application's icon now appears in the Applications folder (or whatever folder you chose).

HINT

Installation Options
Many installer scripts ask you to choose whether to install optional software such as sample files, fonts, or bonus features. The Easy Install or Full Install option usually installs everything that's available.

HINT

Easy Uninstalling
Some installer programs have an Uninstall option in case you decide you no longer want the software installed on your Mac. Using an installer to uninstall programs ensures that all the extra pieces scattered through your system are uninstalled.

Finding and Starting Up Programs

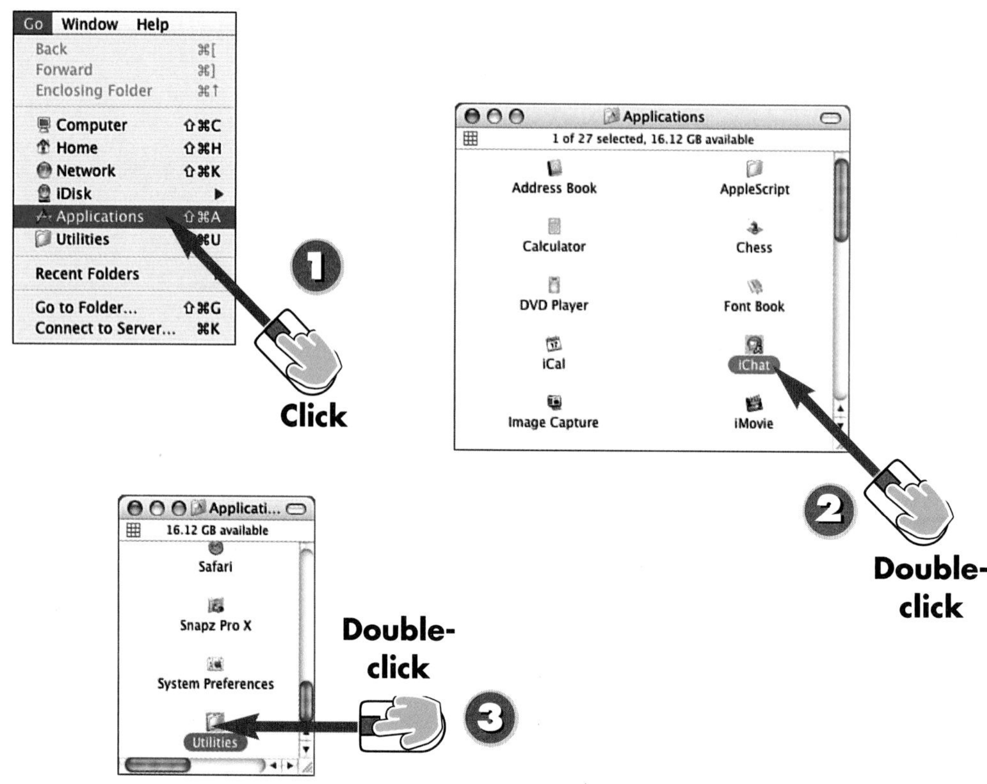

1. In the Finder, either press **Cmd-Shift-A** or choose **Go**, **Applications** to open the Applications folder.

2. Locate the program you want to use and double-click its icon to start it up.

3. If you can't find a program, look in the Utilities folder within the Applications folder.

INTRODUCTION

Mac OS X is a very structured operating system, with a place for everything and everything in its place. Applications are no exception to this rule; all your programs live in one place where you and other users of your Mac can find them easily.

TIP

Regaining Control of Your Programs
You can start a program by double-clicking a document icon, but sometimes the document doesn't open in the program you want. Turn to the task titled "Choosing a Program to Open a File" in Part 2, "Working with Disks, Folders, and Files," to learn how to specify the program to which a document belongs.

Saving Files

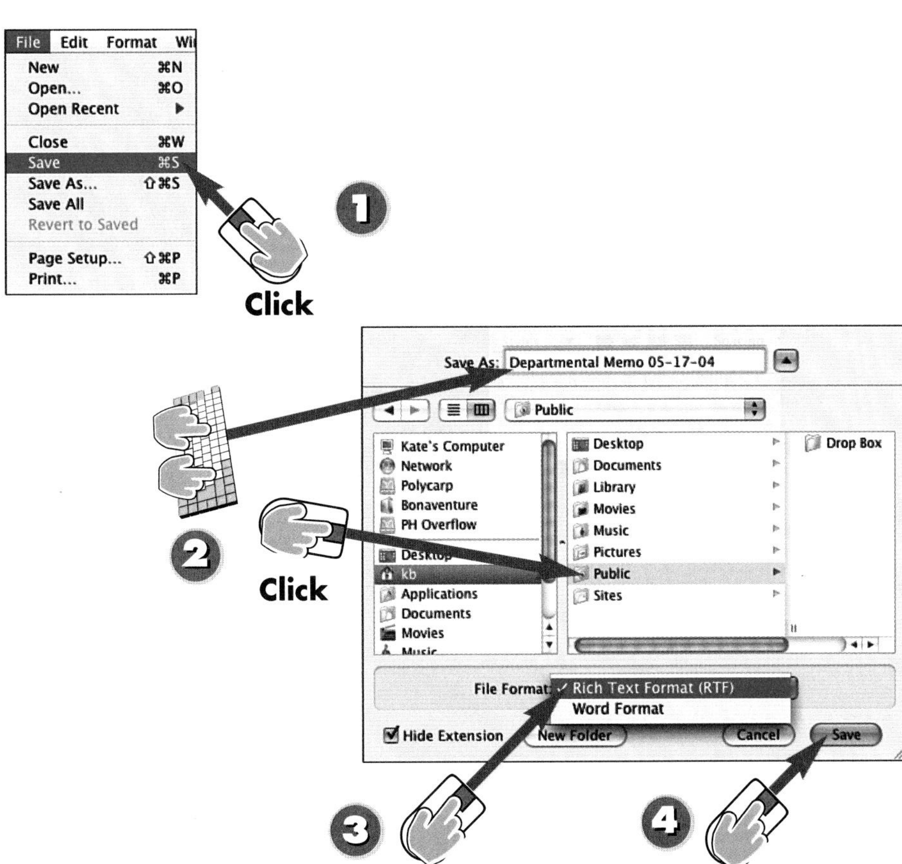

1. In the application in which you want to save a file, either choose **File**, **Save** or press **Cmd-S**.Give the file a name and choose a location in the pick list.
2. Give the file a name and choose a location in the pick list.
3. Choose file options such as format and compression (the available options vary depending on the program).
4. Click **Save**.

INTRODUCTION

Every program is different, of course, but some operations work almost the same no matter which program you're using. One of those is saving a file. Each program saves files in different formats, depending on which type of data that program works with, but the general process is the same no matter what. Here's how it goes.

TIP

Pay Attention!
Save dialog boxes usually open to the last place you saved a file in that program, which is unlikely to be the same place you want now. To save to the desktop, press **Cmd-D**—you'll have to put the file away later, but you'll be able to find it for the moment.

HINT

Save Early, Save Often
Don't wait until you're done working on a file to save it—start early and keep hitting the Save command as you continue to work. That way the file will be stored on your hard drive in case of a drive crash or power outage.

Writing with TextEdit

Start

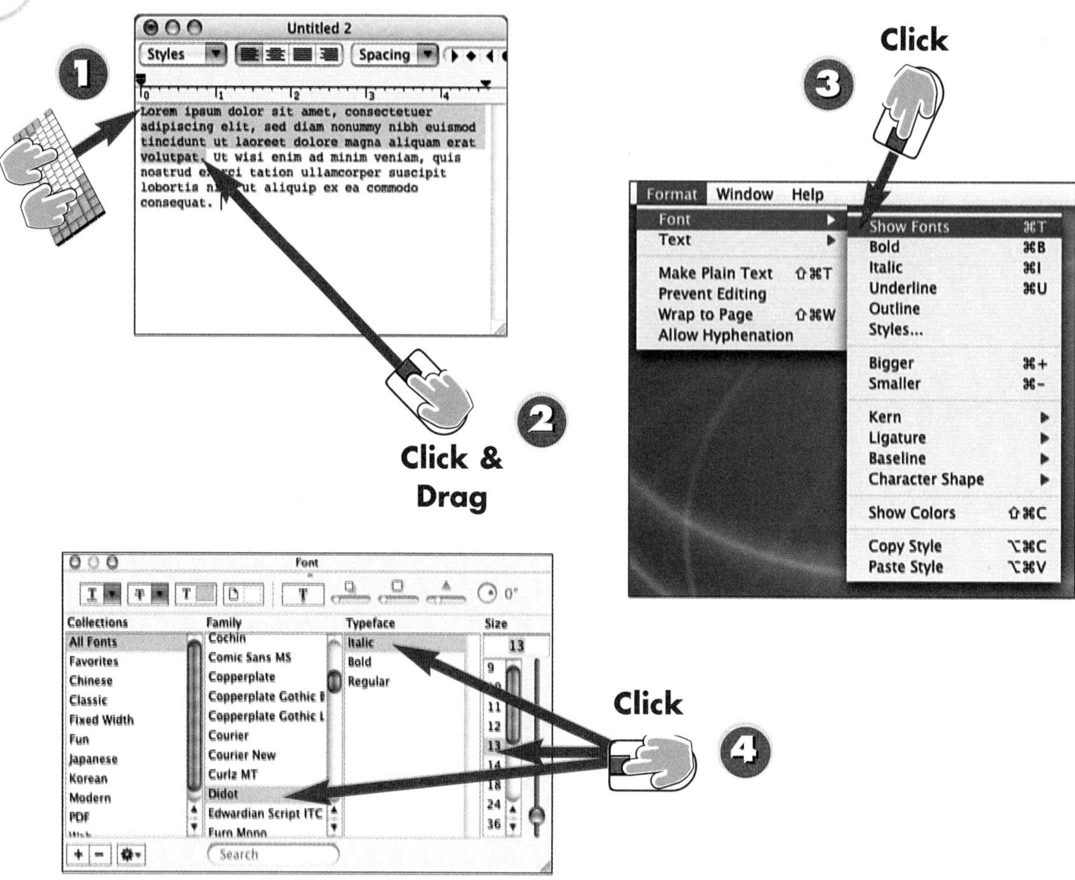

1. Start **TextEdit** (located in the Applications folder) and begin typing in the new document window.
2. To copy text to another location, click and drag to select the text and press **Cmd-C**; place the cursor where you want the text to appear and press **Cmd-V** to paste it.
3. To change the font, select the text and choose **Format**, **Font**, **Show Fonts**.
4. Choose a new font, typeface, and size in the Font panel. The change is applied immediately.

INTRODUCTION

Successor to TeachText and SimpleText, Mac OS X's TextEdit program can do a lot more than either of its ancestors. It's really a very compact, fast word processor with a lot of formatting options and tools as well as the capability to read and write Microsoft Word documents.

TIP

Learning How to Spell
TextEdit gives questionable words a red underline; **Ctrl-click** each and choose an option from the contextual menu. The Learn Spelling command adds the word to a systemwide dictionary, so all your built-in applications will know it in the future.

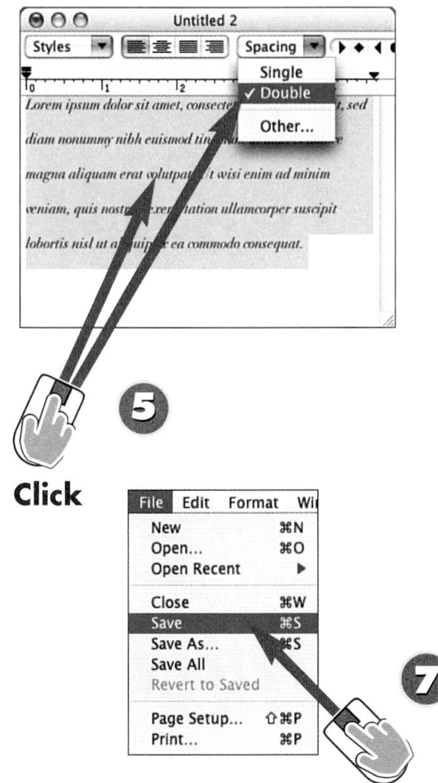

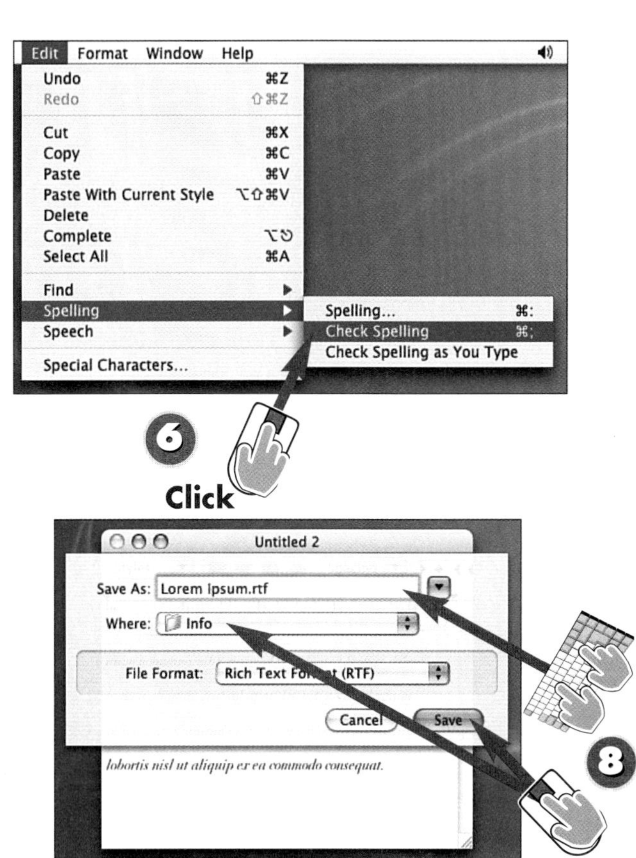

5 To change the text alignment or spacing, click and drag to select the text and choose an option from the controls at the top of the document window.

6 To run a spell check, choose **Edit**, **Spelling**, **Check Spelling**.

7 Choose **File**, **Save** to save the file.

8 Give the file a name and choose a location to save it in; then click **Save**.

HINT

Getting What You Pay For

TextEdit's capability to open and save files in Microsoft Word format could keep you from having to invest in Word. TextEdit doesn't support Word's entire feature set, however, so some advanced features such as tables and hyperlinks can be lost when you edit a Word file in TextEdit.

HINT

Word Compatibility

When you're saving your document in step 8, you can choose RTF (Rich Text Format) or Word format. Either way, your document can be opened in Microsoft Word and retains all its formatting.

Using the Font Panel

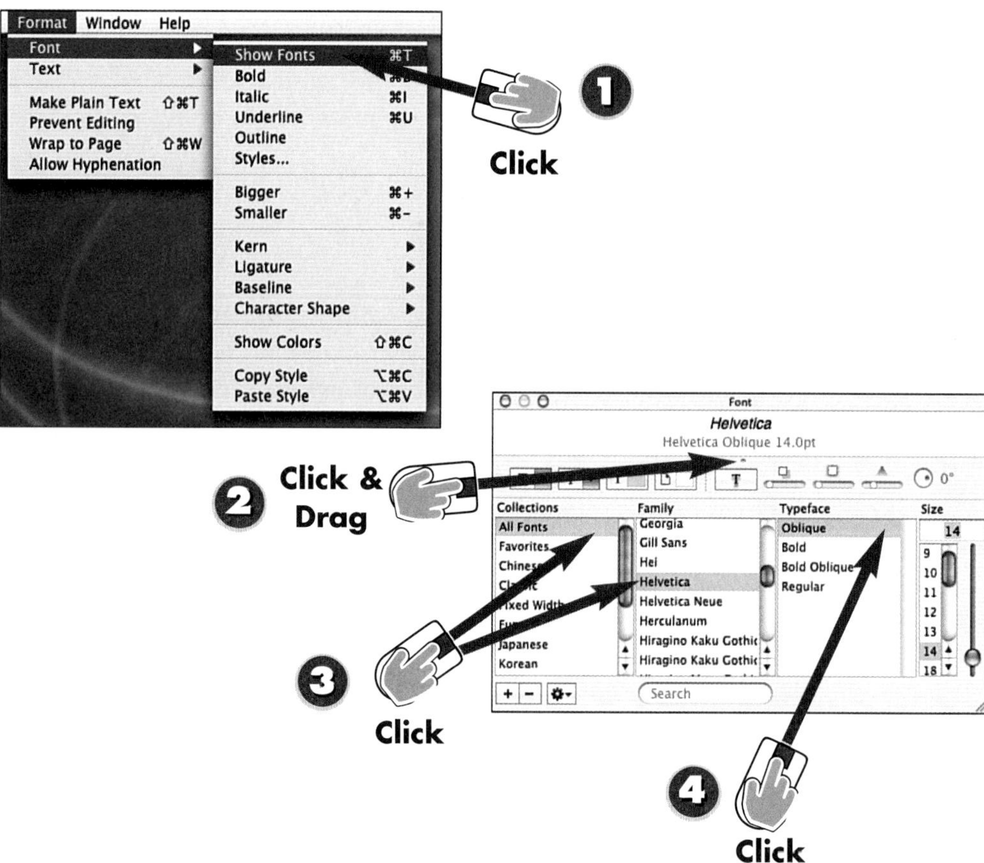

1. In TextEdit, choose **Format**, **Font**, **Show Fonts** to display the Font panel.
2. Click the dot below the window's title bar and drag downward to reveal the preview area.
3. Click **All Fonts** in the Collections column and choose a font family from the Family column.
4. Choose a style from the Typeface column.

INTRODUCTION

Mac OS X handles fonts very well. A lot of thought went into designing ways to make excellent typography more accessible to the average Mac user. The Font panel, which is the same in all the built-in applications, is part of that effort—it contains a wide variety of settings, from basic to advanced, for modifying the way text is formatted.

TIP

Favorite Type Styles

If you create a combination of type settings you plan to use again, click the **Action** menu at the bottom of the Font panel and choose **Add to Favorites**. Then you can apply this style to other text selections by choosing **Font**, **Style** from the menu bar.

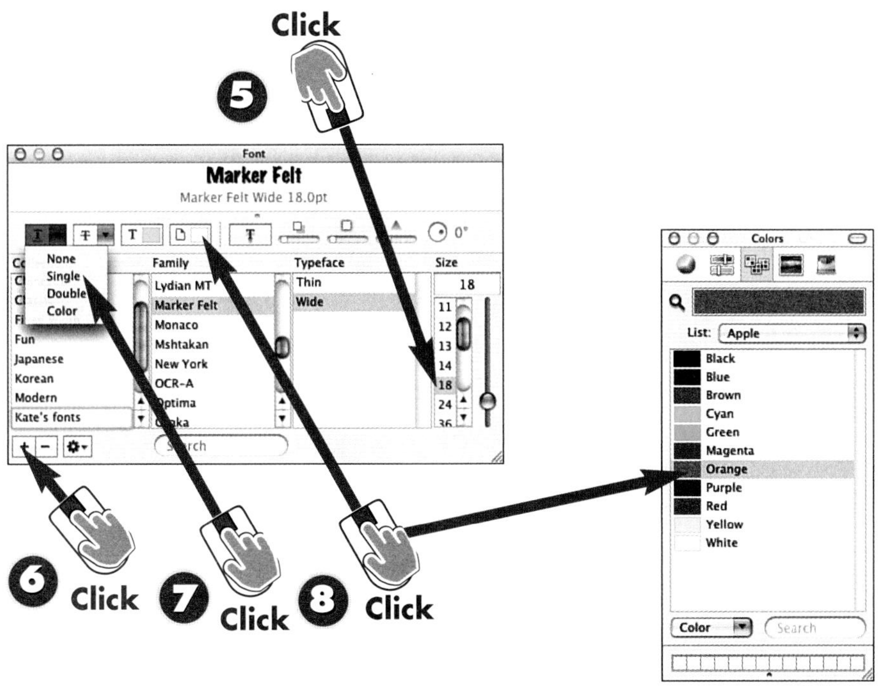

5 Choose a size from the Size column, or enter a value above the column.

6 Click the **Add** button to create a new font collection.

7 Click the **Strikethrough** or **Underline** button and choose an option to add strikethrough or underline style to the selected text.

8 Click the **Text Color** and **Paper Color** buttons to open the Colors panel; then choose a color for the text or the background.

HINT

Beyond the Font Basics
If you're interested in working more specifically with type, check out the Font Book program (located in the Utilities folder within Applications). This utility helps you install and manage fonts.

HINT

Collectible Fonts
Collections of your corporate fonts or the fonts for a particular project enable you to access those fonts without digging through a long list of fonts. To add a font to a collection, just drag its name from the Family column on top of the collection name.

Sending Text to TextEdit

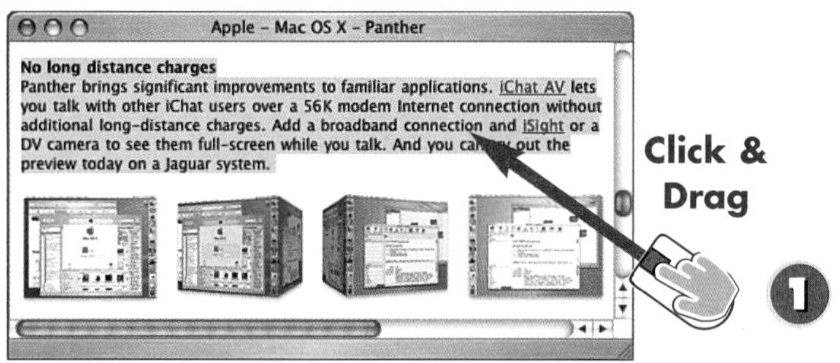

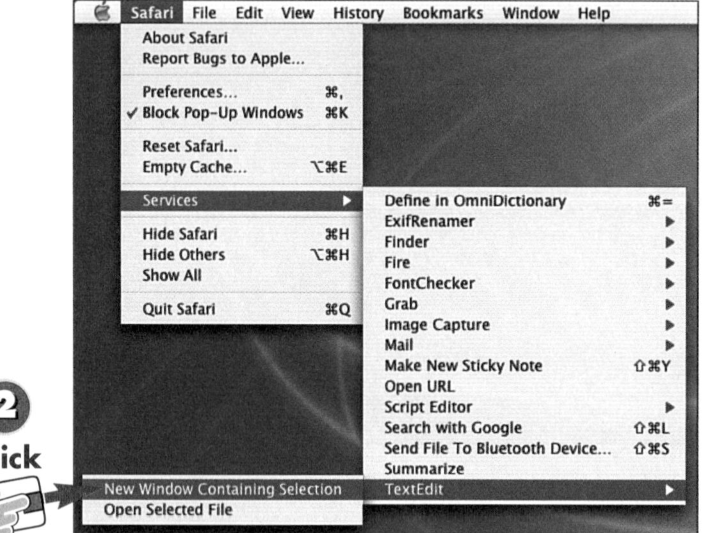

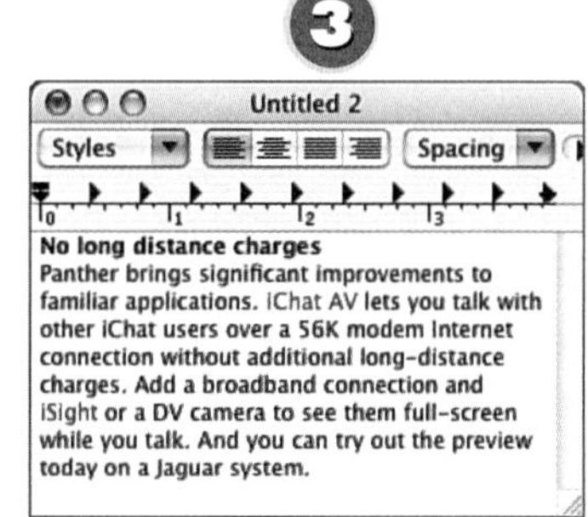

1. Select the range of text you want to move into TextEdit.
2. From the Application menu, choose **Services**, **TextEdit**, **New Window Containing Selection**.
3. The text appears in an untitled TextEdit window. Save the file as directed earlier in the task "Writing with TextEdit."

INTRODUCTION

In each program's Application menu (the menu named after the program), you'll find a Services command with submenus named after other programs. You can use this service to move text from Mail, Safari, or another program into a brand-new document in TextEdit.

HINT

Why Services Rule

Why use this service when you could just copy and paste the text? Because it's less intrusive; you stay in the program you're using, and the text is sent to TextEdit in the background to await your attention.

Turning Text into a New Sticky Note

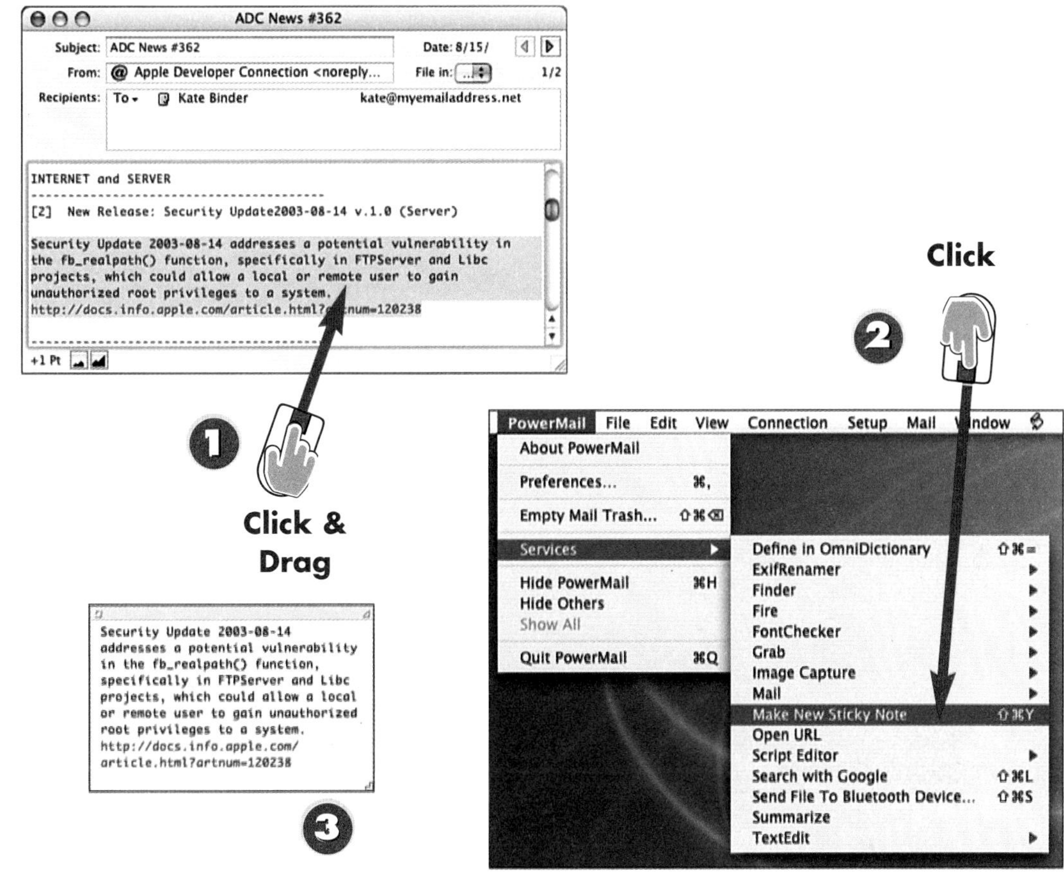

1. Click and drag to select the range of text you want to make into a sticky note.
2. From the Application menu, choose **Services**, **Make New Sticky Note**.
3. The selected text appears in a sticky note on your desktop.

INTRODUCTION

This is one of the most convenient services in Mac OS X. It works the same way as the text to TextEdit service described in the previous task, only it starts up Stickies and creates a new note to hold the text. If you're like most Mac users, you'll use this task a dozen times a day.

HINT

Making Stickies Less Obtrusive

If you use Stickies a lot but the millions of floating stickies drive you crazy, try keeping it hidden by choosing **Stickies**, **Hide Stickies**. You can switch quickly to Stickies using the Dock, so they're always there when you need them, just not in your way.

Viewing Images with Preview

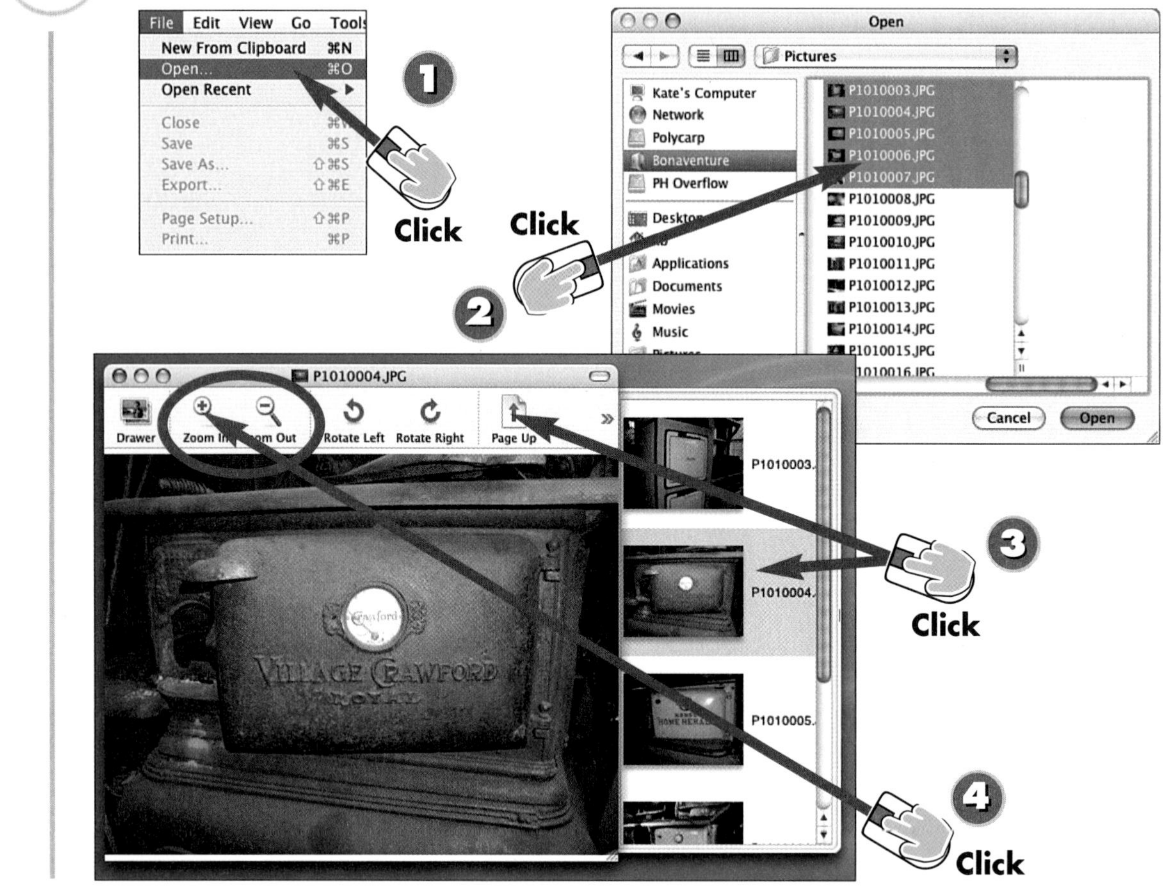

1. Start up Preview (located in the Applications folder) and choose **File**, **Open**.
2. Choose the images you want to open in the pick list and click **Open**.
3. Click a thumbnail or click the **Page Up** and **Page Down** buttons to switch images (press **Cmd-B** if you don't see the toolbar).
4. Click the **Zoom In** and **Zoom Out** buttons to view the image at a different magnification.

INTRODUCTION

Preview is a handy program designed for two purposes: looking at pictures and opening PDF files. It works well for both of those jobs. You can't edit either graphic images or PDFs with Preview, but that's not what it's for. Preview's drawer feature makes it particularly useful for reviewing several images at once, all in a single window.

TIP

Converting Formats
To save an image in a different format from within Preview, choose **File**, **Export**. In the Export dialog box, give the file a new name and select a location and a format; then click **Save**.

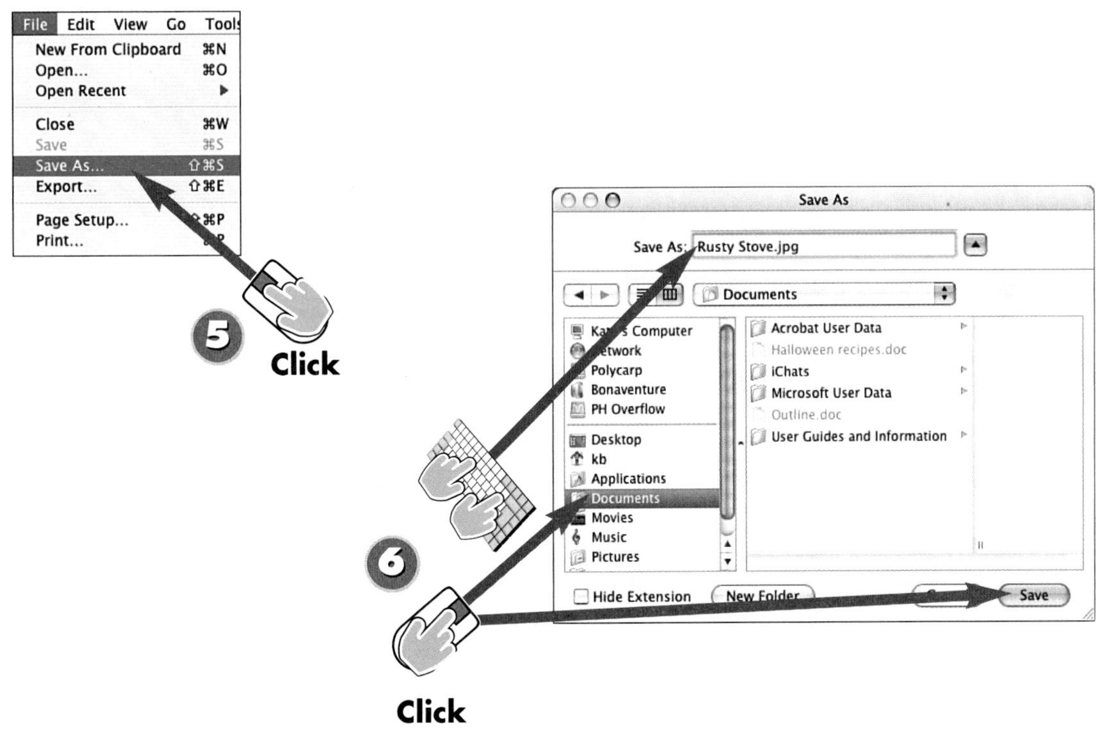

5 Choose **File**, **Save As** to save the file with a different name.

6 In the Save As dialog box, give the file a new name and choose a location; then click **Save**.

TIP

Getting Your Thumbnails in Order
Preview's drawer shows you largish thumbnails accompanied by the images' filenames. But you can change the size of the thumbnail images or get rid of them and just view the filenames. Choose **Preview**, **Preferences** and click **General** to make the change.

HINT

PDFs in Preview
Mac OS X is set to automatically open PDF files in Preview. When you're viewing a PDF file, the arrows at the left end of the window's toolbar enable you to move from page to page.

Switching Programs with the Dock

1 Click

2 Option-click

3 Click

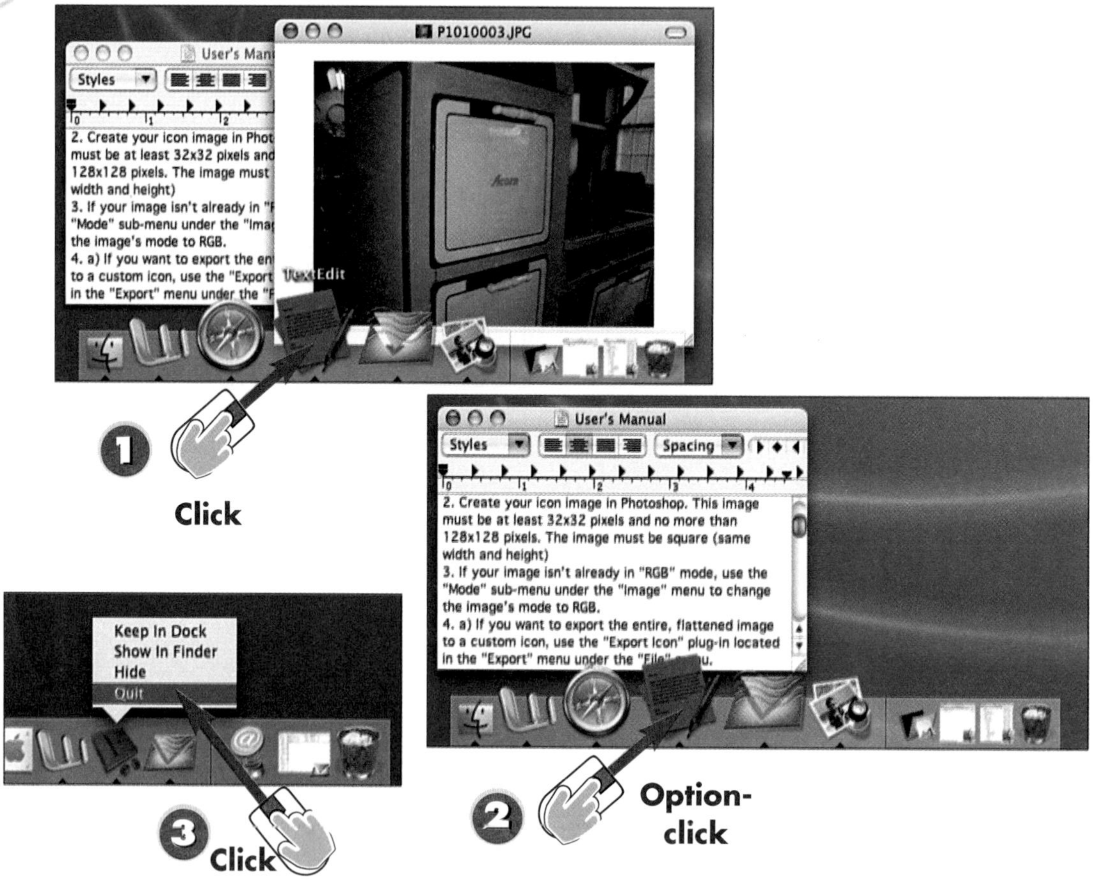

1. Move your mouse to the bottom of the screen and click a program icon on the Dock.
2. To hide windows belonging to the current program when you switch to the new program, press **Option** as you click.
3. To quit a program you're not using, click and hold its Dock icon (or Ctrl-click) and choose **Quit** from the contextual menu.

End

INTRODUCTION

The Dock acts as central storage for running programs and frequently used programs, but it has other functions, too. One of those is as an application switcher—a method of bringing different programs to the foreground so you can use them in turn. The Dock's location at the bottom of the screen makes it the most convenient way to switch applications.

TIP

Don't Touch That Mouse!
If you prefer to use the keyboard to switch programs, press **Cmd-Tab** to see a list of the currently running programs in the center of the screen. Press Cmd-Tab as many times as needed to cycle through the list to the program you want.

Hiding Programs

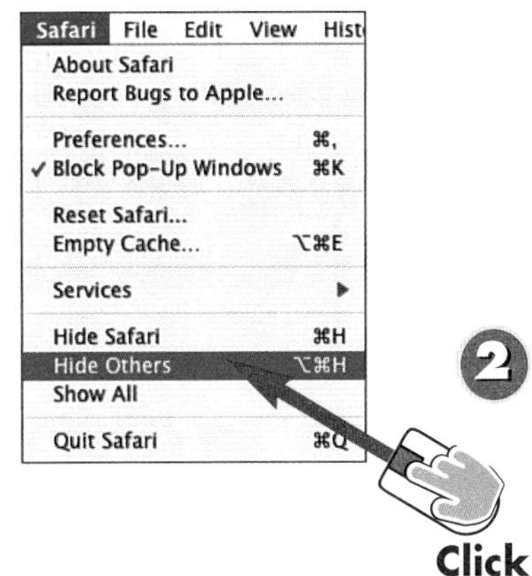

1. In the Application menu, choose **Hide** (or press **Cmd-H**) to hide the program you're currently using.
2. In the Application menu, choose **Hide Others** (or press **Cmd-Option-H**) to hide all other programs that are currently running.
3. To get one window out of the way instead of hiding the program, double-click its title bar or click the yellow **Minimize** button to send it to the Dock.

INTRODUCTION

Mac OS X enables you to run many programs at the same time because it hands over memory to each program as it's needed. But if you do like to run multiple programs, your screen can get pretty cluttered. Hiding program windows and palettes is a lifesaver for people who never quit programs until they shut down their Macs.

TIP

Another Way to Hide
Another way to hide programs is to **Option-click** the desktop or a window from another program to simultaneously switch to the Finder or the other program, respectively, and hide the previous program.

HINT

A Window Exposé
Yet another way to maneuver among running programs and open windows is to use a feature introduced with Panther: Exposé. Turn to "Managing Multiple Windows" in Part 1, "Getting Started."

Forcing Programs to Quit

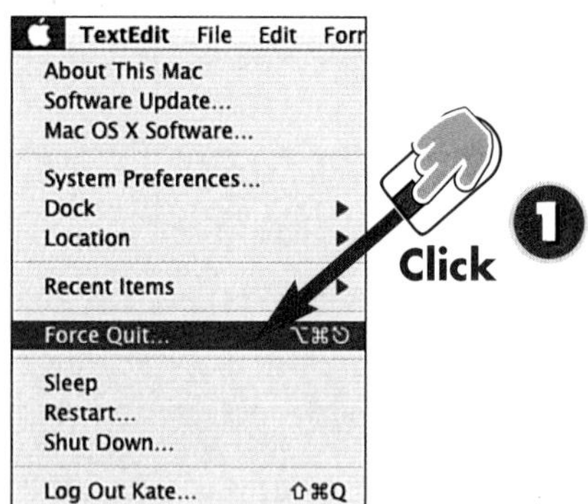

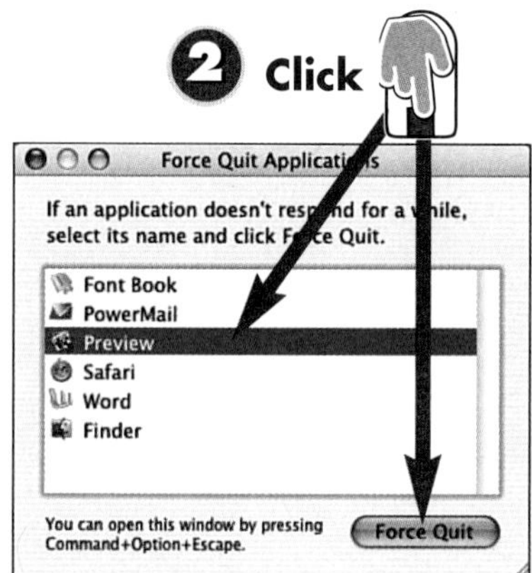

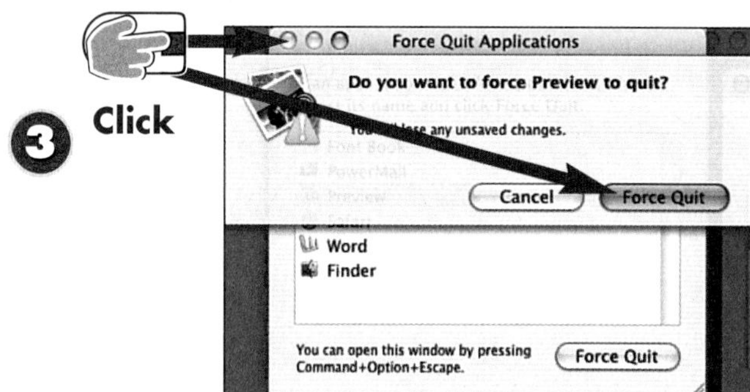

1. Choose **Apple menu**, **Force Quit** or press **Cmd-Option-Esc**.
2. In the Force Quit Applications dialog box, choose the program you want to quit and click **Force Quit**.
3. Click **Force Quit** again and click the **Close** button to dismiss the dialog box.

INTRODUCTION

Macs are great, but that doesn't mean they're perfect. From time to time, a program might act up, refusing to do what you want or perhaps refusing to do anything at all. When this happens and the regular Quit command doesn't work, you can force that program to quit.

HINT

Red Alert
If a program's name appears in red in the Force Quit Applications dialog box, that program is being particularly uncooperative. This indicates that the program is not only ignoring your wishes, but also not responding to the system.

HINT

Quitting Safely
In earlier Mac systems, force quitting a program disrupted the entire system, so it was a good idea to restart your Mac, but that's no longer the case. Force quitting is now entirely safe, guaranteed not to crash your Mac.

Starting and Stopping Classic

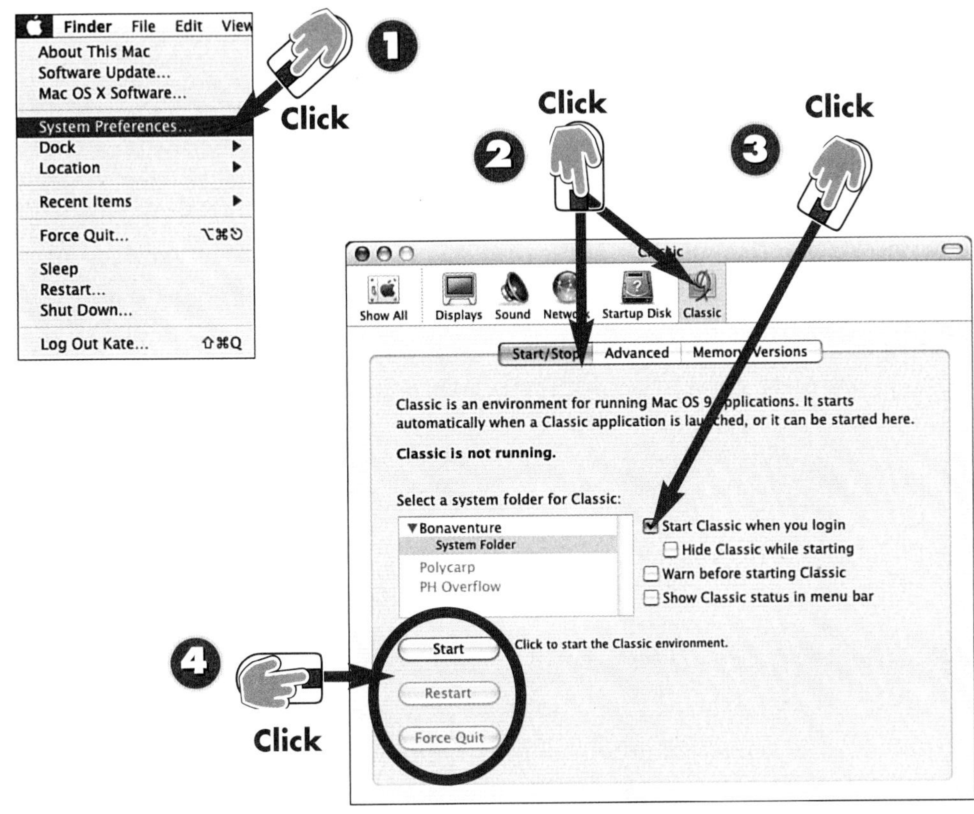

1. Choose **Apple menu**, **System Preferences**.
2. Click **Classic** to open the Classic pane, click **Start/Stop**, and then click the **Start** button to run Classic.
3. If you expect to run Classic programs most of the time, click **Start Classic when you login**.
4. Click **Stop** to shut down Classic, **Restart** to start Classic up again, or **Force Quit** if it has crashed.

INTRODUCTION

Classic is a special environment inside your system where you can run Mac OS 9. If you want to use software that doesn't run in Mac OS X, Classic is the way to do that. Normally, double-clicking a Classic application or document starts up Classic, but you can start it up independently if you need more control over it.

HINT

Classic for Experts
The Advanced pane in Classic preferences enables you to perform system maintenance on Classic as you would on a free-standing Mac OS 9 system. You can control how it starts up or rebuild its desktop as well as putting it to sleep when it's not being used.

PART 4

Setting System Preferences

Preferences make the world go round—or, at least, they make your Mac more *your* Mac. You can control so many aspects of your everyday computing experience that it's worth a trip to the System Preferences window every once in a while just to remind yourself what's there. Be sure to explore all the tabs of each preference pane, too, to make sure you know what all your options are.

The System Preferences command in the Apple menu opens a command center for preferences. It contains buttons for each preference pane, organized into categories. The top row of buttons, the *shelf*, holds your favorite preferences—just drag buttons into the shelf to customize it.

In this part you'll learn how to set preferences for everything from how your mouse or trackpad works to what size objects are displayed on your monitor. A couple of tasks—"Setting Trackpad Preferences" and "Monitoring Battery Use"—deal with preferences for laptop users only; if your Mac isn't an iBook or a PowerBook, you won't even see these settings, so don't worry about them.

The System Preferences Window

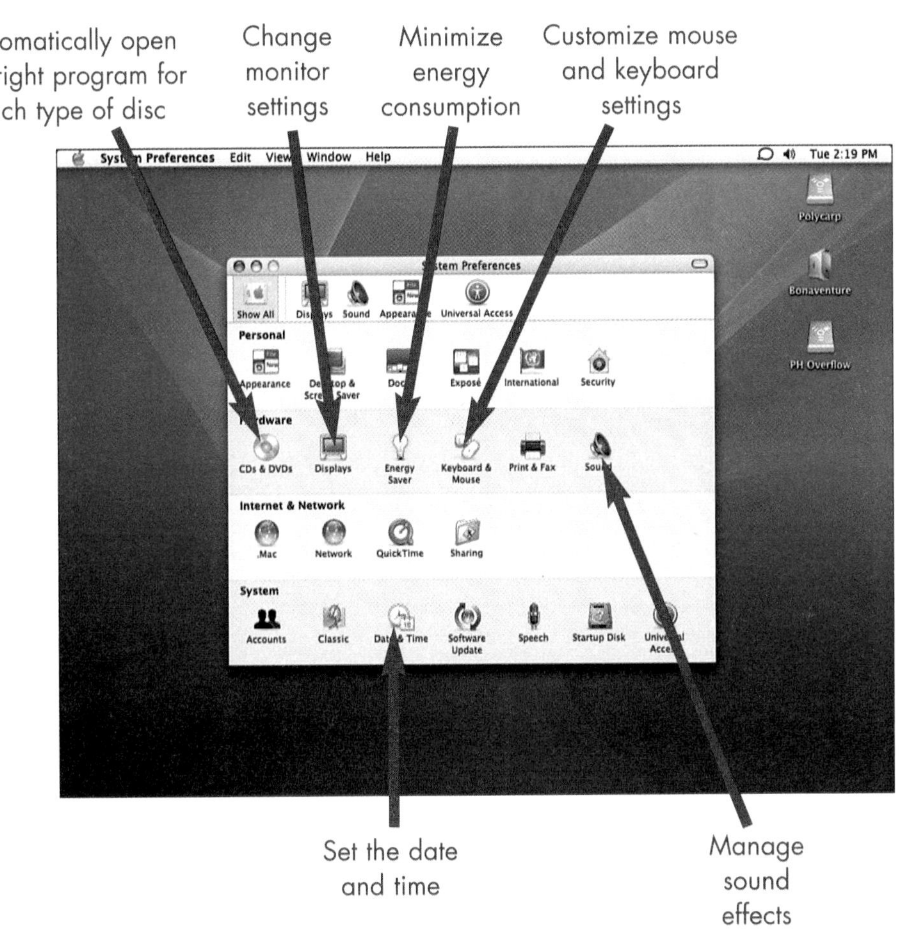

Setting System Preferences

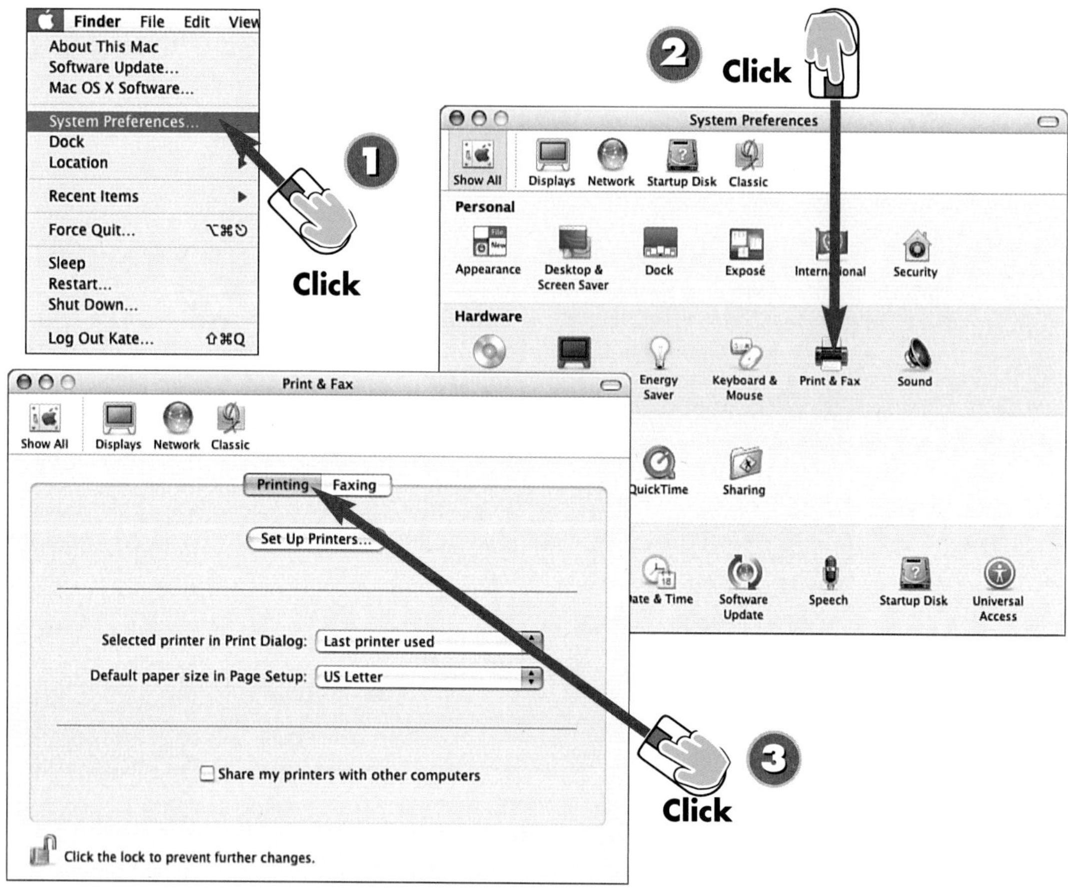

1. Choose **Apple menu**, **System Preferences** to display the System Preferences window.
2. Click **Show All** to see all the icons; then click the icon for the preferences you want to change.
3. Click buttons across the top of the preference pane to access various settings.

INTRODUCTION

In a flashback to the days of the Mac's System 6, Mac OS X stores all its preferences in a central window called System Preferences. It's accessible via the Apple menu, so you can reach it from any program. Third-party preference panes, such as those for aftermarket mouse devices or trackballs or for software system enhancements, can also be found in System Preferences.

TIP

Easy Access
If you find yourself going back to a particular preference pane all the time (such as Startup Disk), drag its icon to the shelf at the top of the System Preferences window so you can access that pane more easily.

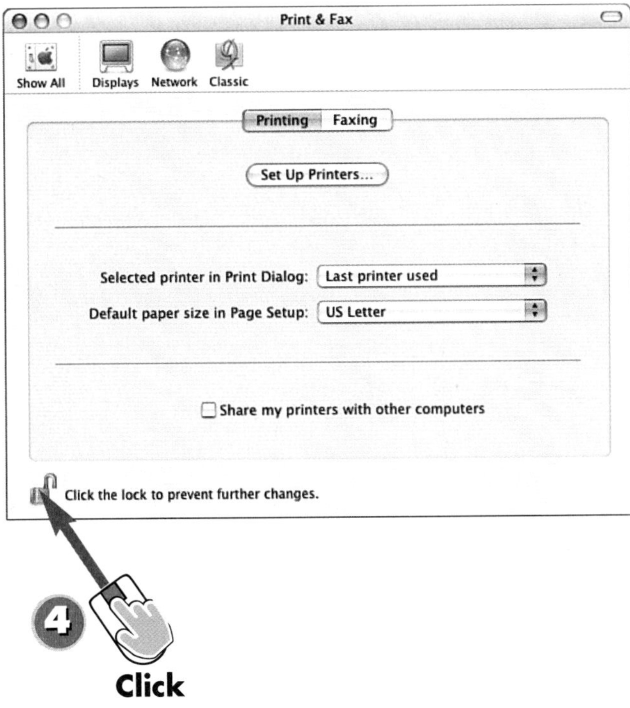

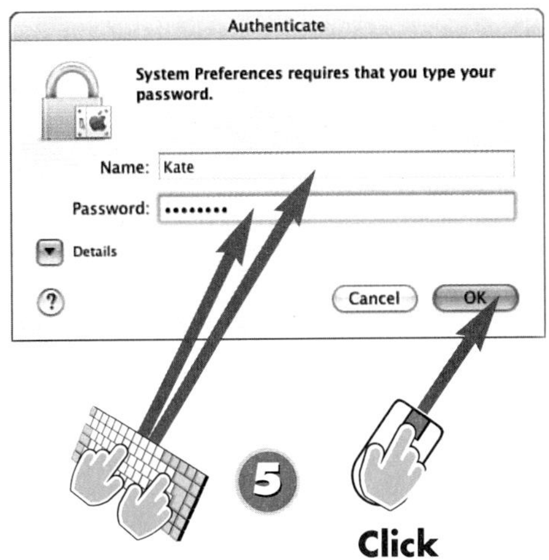

4. Lock the preferences by clicking the **padlock** icon.

5. If the preferences are locked (indicated by a closed padlock icon in the lower-left corner of the window), enter an admin name and password when prompted.

HINT

Down by the Dock

If you haven't changed what's in your Dock since you got your Mac or installed Mac OS X, you'll find System Preferences there. You don't have to leave it there, but if you make many trips to the System Preferences, the Dock can be quicker.

TIP

Now You Know Your ABCs

If the System Preference categories don't make sense to you, so that you're always hunting for the icon you want, choose **View**, **Organize Alphabetically**. This command reorders the icons in good old alphabetical order, instead of dividing them by category.

Changing Your Alert Sound

1 Click

2 Click

3 Click

4 Click & Drag

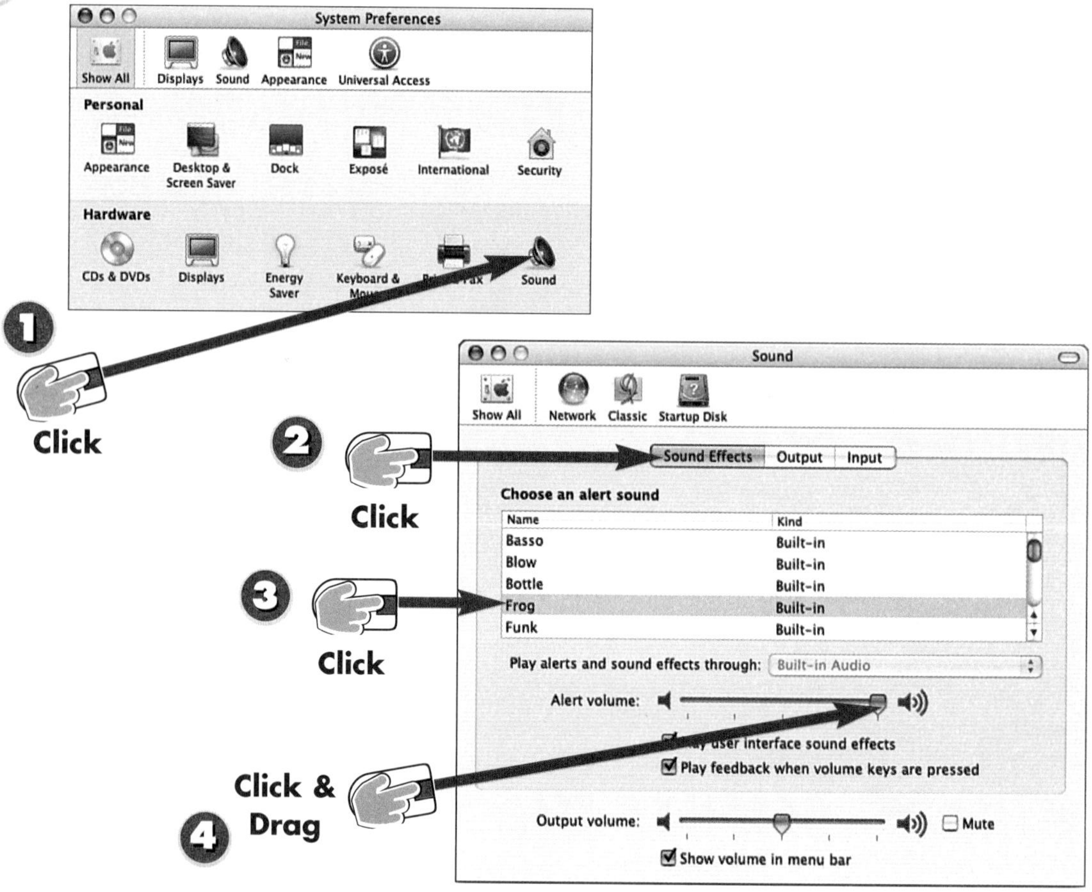

1. Click the **Sound** icon in the System Preferences window to display the sound preferences.

2. Click the **Sound Effects** tab to see your choices.

3. Click a sound in the pick list to hear it.

4. Drag the **Alert volume** slider to set the volume level for alert sounds.

INTRODUCTION

The alert sound is that annoying beep you hear when you do something your Mac doesn't like or when you tell it to do something it can't do. The nice part about this is that you can change the sound that's played, as well as adjusting its volume independently of the system's overall volume level.

HINT

Blowing Your Own Horn

If you don't like any of the alert sound choices, you can add your own. They must be in AIFF format, and you need to store them in the Sounds folder within the Library folder within the System folder on your main hard drive.

Changing Display Settings

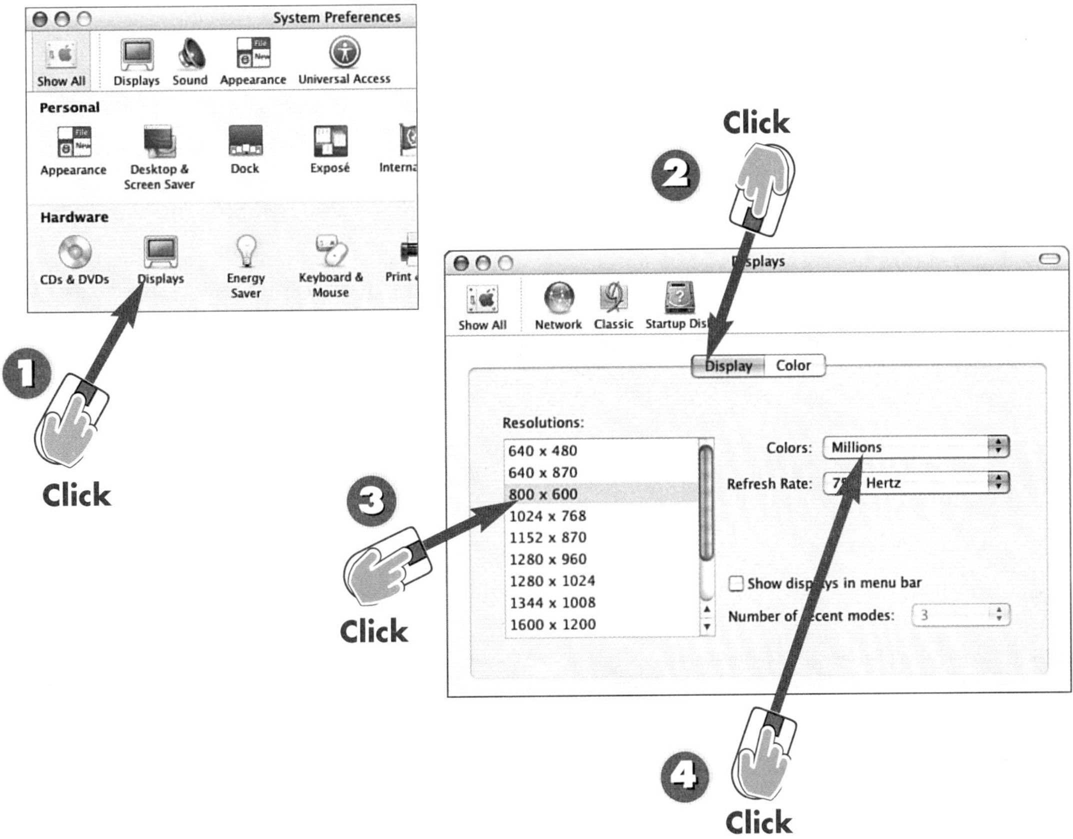

1. Click the **Displays** icon in the System Preferences window to display monitor preferences.

2. Click the **Display** tab to see your choices.

3. Click a setting in the **Resolutions** pick list to determine the scale of the images on your monitor.

4. Choose an option from the **Colors** pop-up menu to change the number of colors displayed on your monitor.

INTRODUCTION

Your monitor's display resolution is the number of pixels it displays horizontally and vertically. You can change the resolution of most monitors. With a lower resolution, everything on the screen is bigger and you can't see as many windows at one time, and with a higher resolution everything is smaller, but you can fit more.

TIP

Don't Keep Your Resolutions

If you expect to change your settings often, click **Show displays in menu bar** in the Displays preference pane to add a menu that you can use to switch resolutions.

HINT

The More, the Merrier

Expert users generally choose the highest resolution that still allows them to read text onscreen. It makes onscreen objects seem small at first, but you adjust to that quickly. You can fit more windows onscreen at higher resolutions.

Changing the Mouse Speed

Start

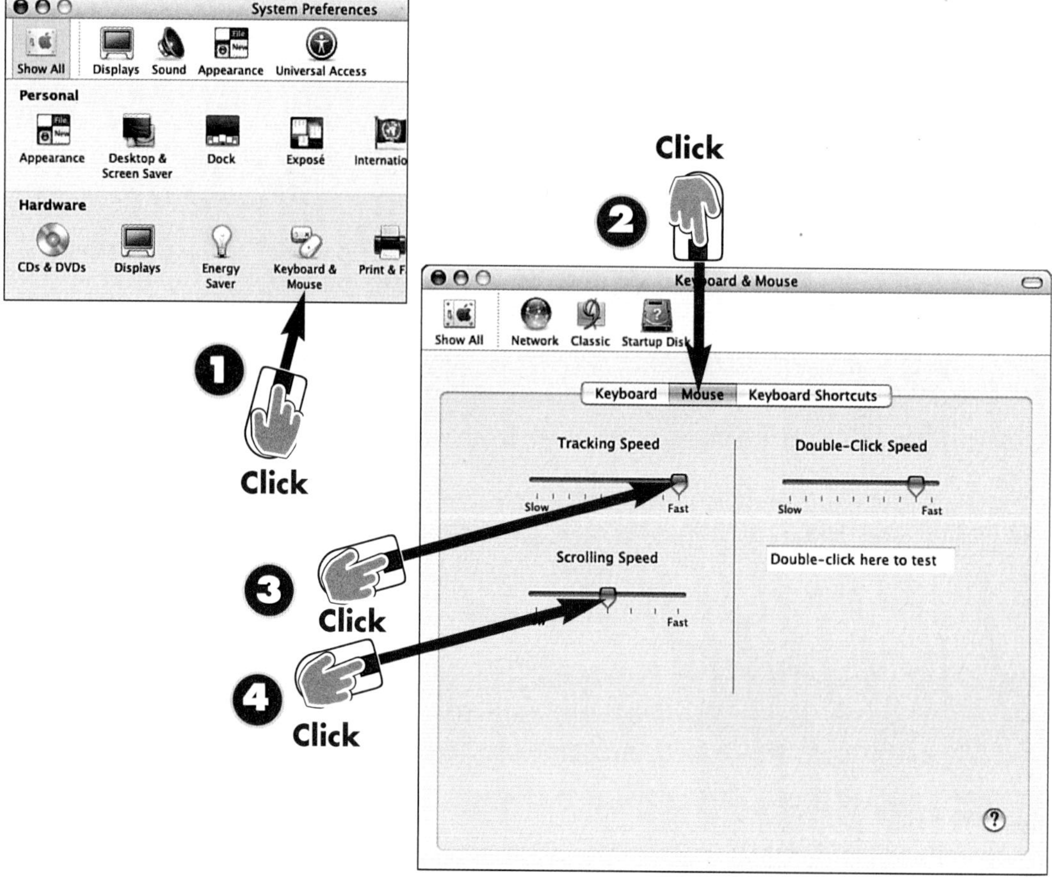

1. Click the **Keyboard & Mouse** icon to display mouse preferences.
2. Click the **Mouse** tab to see the mouse settings.
3. Drag the **Tracking Speed** slider to change how quickly the mouse moves across the screen.
4. Drag the **Scrolling Speed** slider to change how fast windows scroll when you use a mouse with a scroll wheel.

INTRODUCTION

When you're in a hurry, there are few things more annoying than a slow mouse, or one that's so fast you can't keep track of it. Whether your mouse moves too slowly or too quickly for your taste, you can adjust its setting until it's just where you like it. You can also change the speed at which you must click for two clicks to register as an official double-click.

HINT

Scrolling, Scrolling, Scrolling

If you haven't tried a mouse with a scroll wheel yet, you should make a point of checking one out. This handy little control makes scrolling through long documents or long Web pages a breeze.

Changing Keyboard Settings

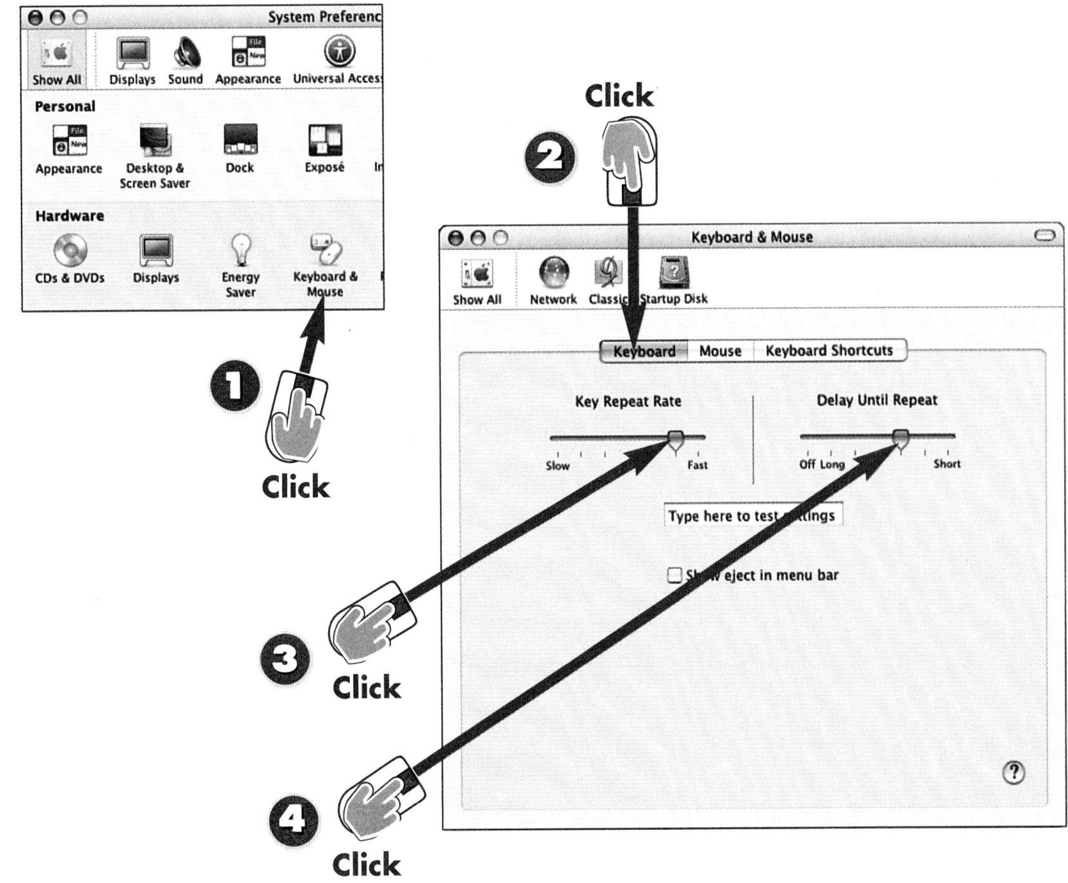

1. Click the **Keyboard & Mouse** icon in the System Preferences window to display keyboard preferences.
2. Click the **Keyboard** tab to see the keyboard settings.
3. Drag the **Key Repeat Rate** slider to control how quickly keys repeat when you hold them down.
4. Drag the **Delay Until Repeat** slider to control how long the Mac waits before starting to repeat keys when you hold them down.

INTRODUCTION

Most aspects of the way a keyboard works are determined by the hardware—in other words, the keyboard itself. However, there are a couple of keyboard settings you can adjust, having to do with how quickly your Mac repeats keys when you hold down a key.

TIP

Another Cool Extra Menu

Like many preference panes, the keyboard settings include a useful menu that you can opt to display, or not, as you wish. In this case, the option puts an Eject menu in the menu bar, which enables you to eject disks in removable drives such as CD or DVD drives.

Setting Energy Saver Options

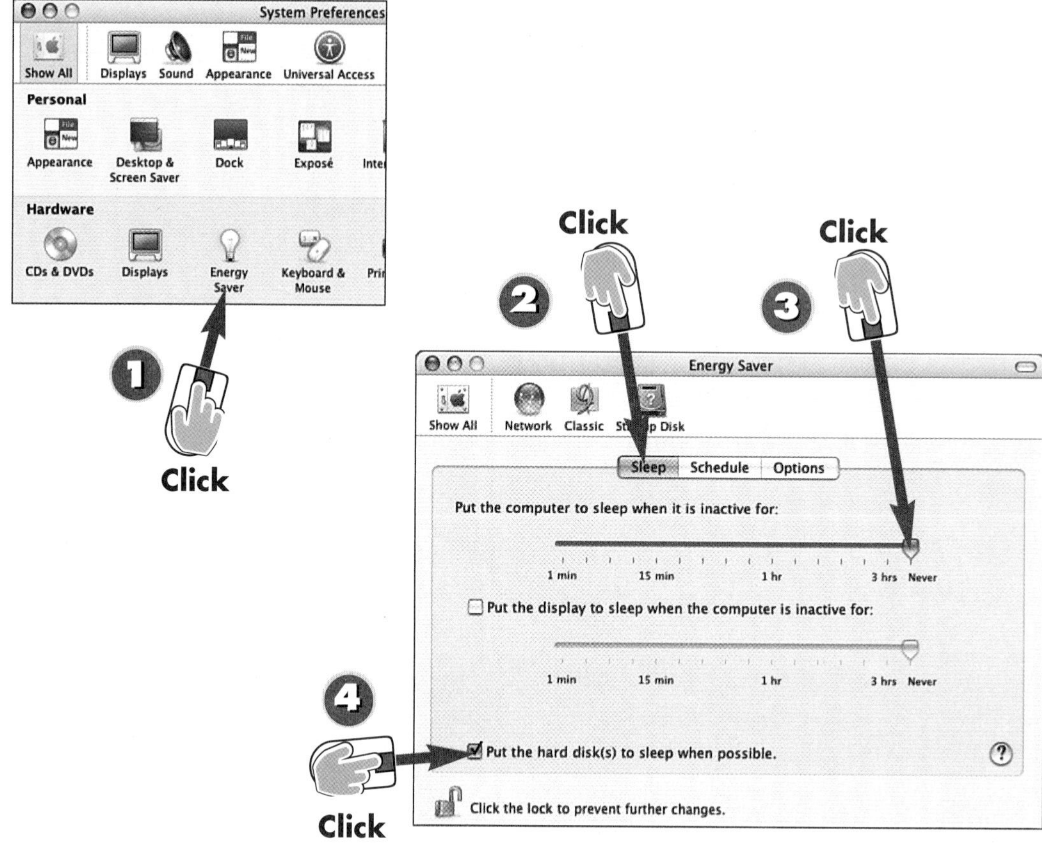

1. Click the **Energy Saver** icon in the System Preferences window to display energy preferences.
2. Click the **Sleep** tab to display sleeping options.
3. Drag the top slider to choose when your Mac will sleep and the bottom slider to set a separate time for when your monitor will sleep.
4. Click the check box if you want the hard drive to sleep.

INTRODUCTION

You might not think your quiet little computer, sitting over there in the corner not even moving, could eat up that much electricity—but think again. That's why the Energy Saver settings are important; they enable you to reduce your Mac's power consumption during times when you're not using it. Be sure to take as much advantage of Energy Saver as possible.

HINT

Hurry Hurry

If you're always in a hurry when you come back to your computer, don't set the hard drive to sleep. The monitor wakes up from sleep instantly, but it takes a few moments for the hard drive to spin back up to speed when it wakes up.

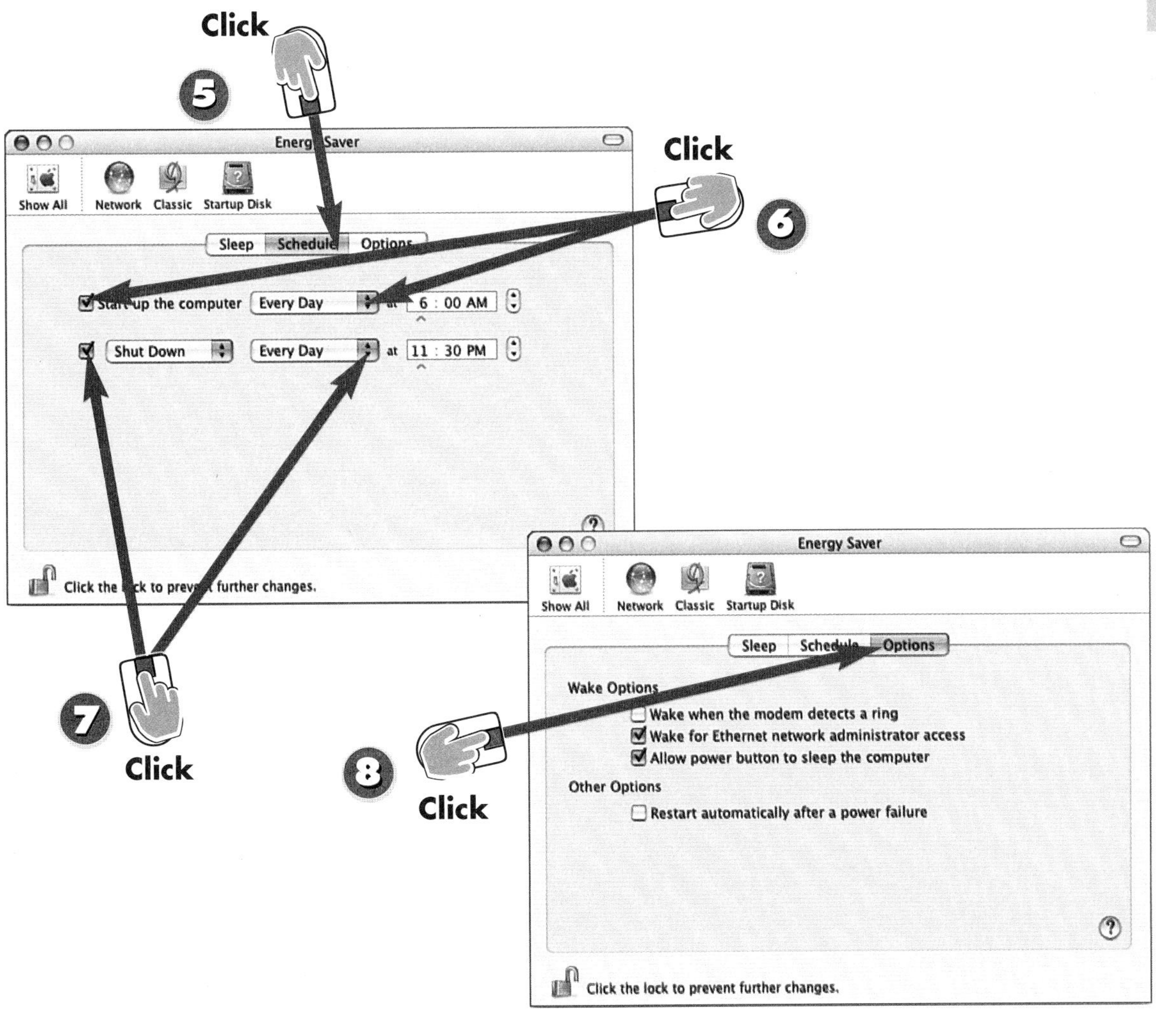

Click

Click

Click

Click

5. Click the **Schedule** tab to display scheduled startup and shutdown options.

6. Check the box and choose a day and time to start up the Mac automatically.

7. Check the box and choose a day and time to shut down the Mac automatically.

8. Click the **Options** tab if you want to change the circumstances under which the Mac will sleep and wake up.

TIP

Are You Getting Sleepy?
For computers, sleep is a state between powered up and powered down. A sleeping computer consumes much less power, but it's not completely turned off. Of course, it wakes up much more quickly than it boots up from a powered-down state.

HINT

Sleepy Time
In step 7, you can also set your Mac to sleep at a particular time instead of shutting down. This is a good choice if you keep programs running all the time that you don't want to have to start up again every day.

Setting Options for Inserted Discs

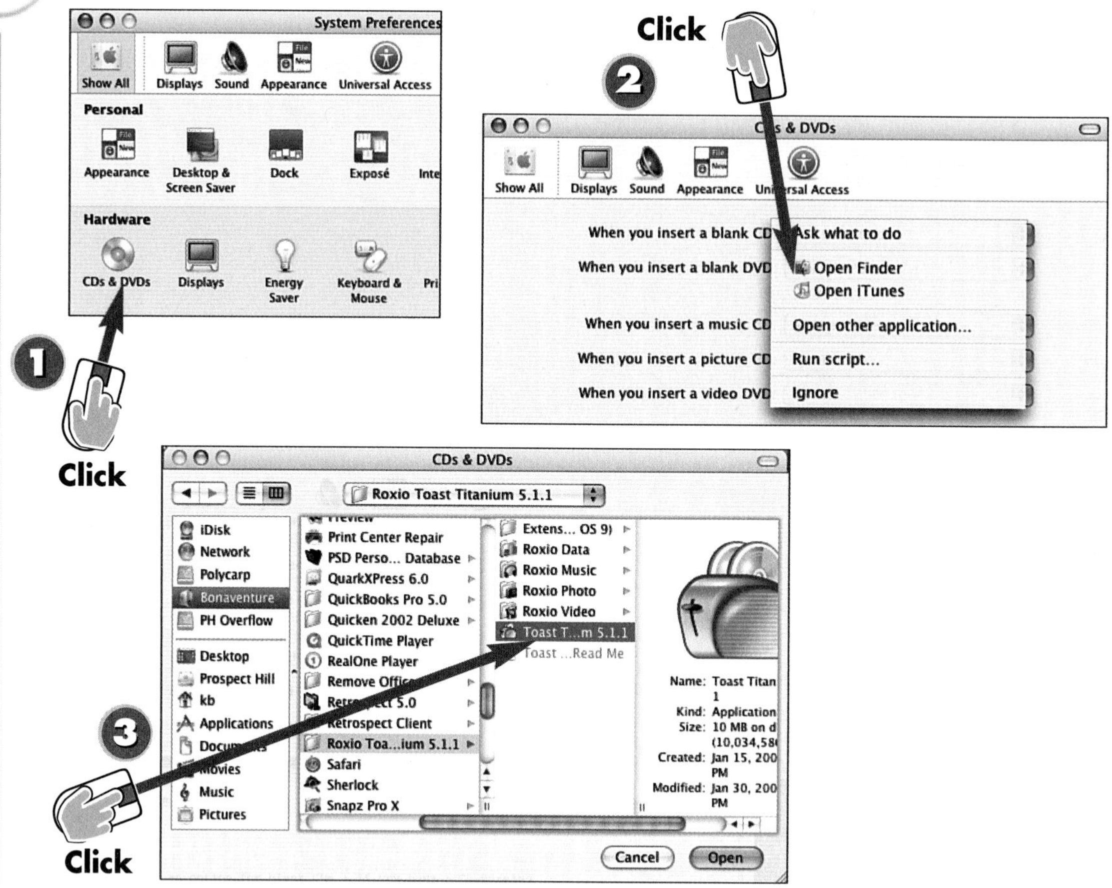

1. Click the **CDs & DVDs** icon in the System Preferences window to display removable disc preferences.
2. Choose an option for blank CDs.
3. If you have a CD-burning program such as Toast, choose **Open other application** and navigate to the program in the Applications folder.

INTRODUCTION

Wouldn't it be nice if your Mac knew just what to do when you inserted a CD or DVD into its drive? The CDs & DVDs preferences enable you to have your Mac start up a specified program when you insert a blank disc that you're going to write yourself or when you insert a prewritten data, music, or movie disc.

HINT

Ignore Me, Please

Sometimes, the Ignore option is the best choice. If you set the Mac to ignore discs you insert, you'll be able to decide what to do with each disc at the time, without having to quit a program that started up when you didn't want it to. You might do this if you use multiple methods to burn CDs—for example, using Toast or the Finder, depending on the circumstances.

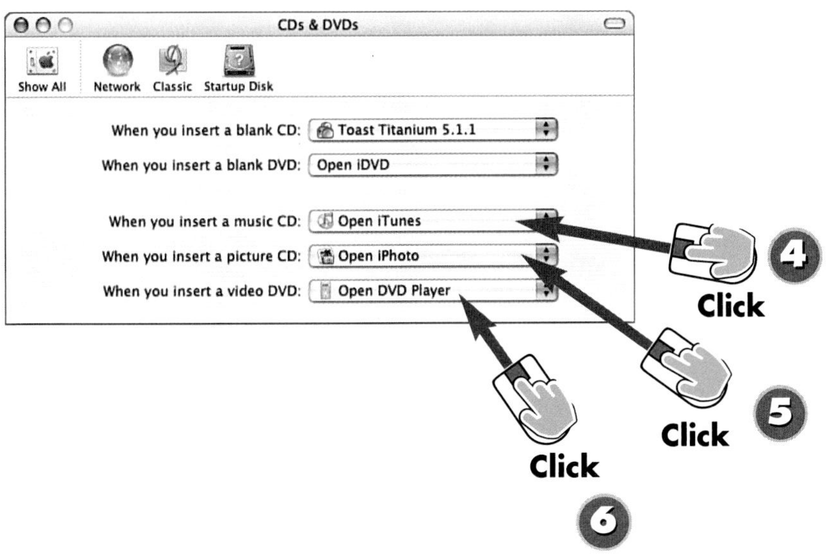

4 Choose an option for blank DVDs; if you use iDVD or another DVD program, choose **Open other application**.

5 Choose an option for music CDs; Open iTunes is the best choice unless you prefer a different program for playing music.

6 Choose an option for picture CDs; Open iPhoto is the best choice unless you prefer a different program for viewing photos.

7 Choose an option for video CDs; Open DVD Player is the best choice unless you prefer a different program for viewing movies.

TIP

It Never Hurts to Ask
If you're not sure what you want to happen when you insert a particular type of disc, just choose **Ask what to do**.

HINT

Burn, Baby, Burn
You can burn CDs and DVDs using the Finder's Burn Disc command. But if you want a choice of formats to ensure you can send the right type of disc to various customers, you'll need a program such as Toast (**www.roxio.com**).

Setting the Time and Date

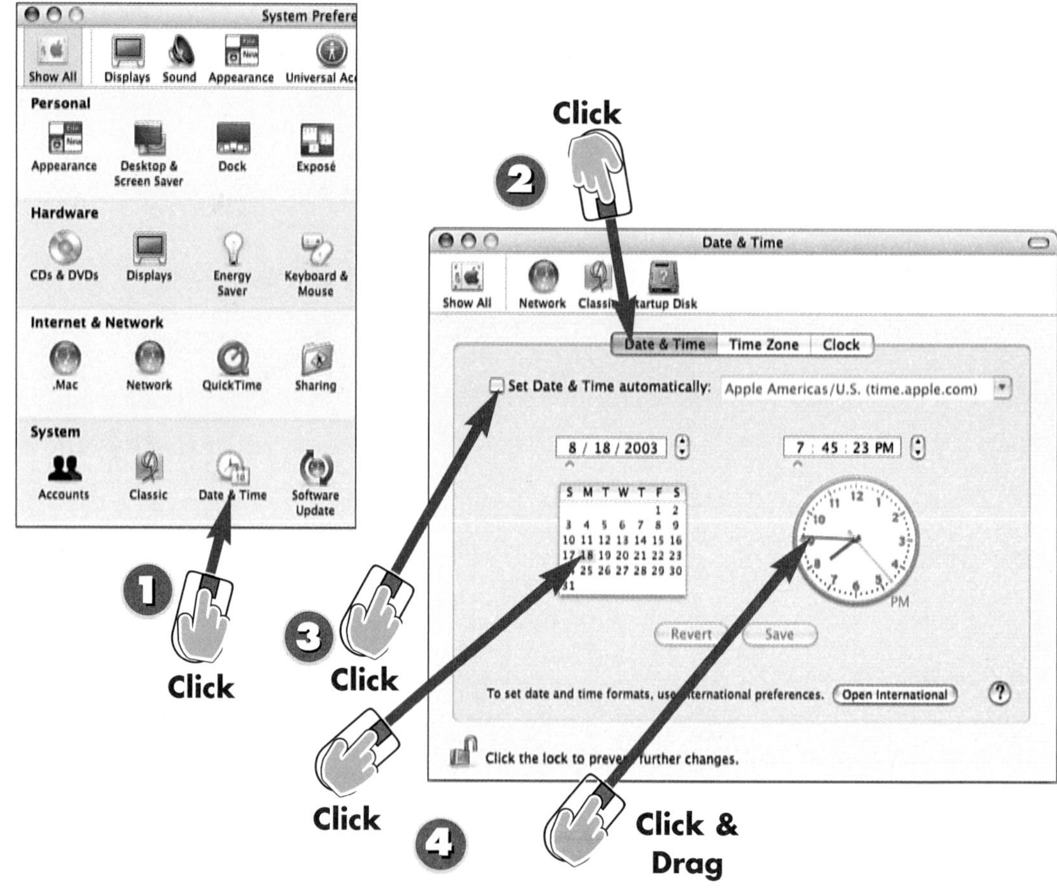

1. Click the **Date & Time** icon in the System Preferences window to display time and date preferences.

2. Click the **Date & Time** tab to see your choices.

3. If the Set Date & Time automatically box is checked, click to remove the check mark.

4. Click a day on the calendar to set the date, or type in the date; drag the hands on the clock to set the time, or type in the time.

INTRODUCTION

If you opt to set the date and time yourself, you can do it by clicking a calendar or dragging clock hands—no messy typing needed! If you have a constant or frequent online connection, you can choose instead to have your Mac's clock set automatically over the Internet.

HINT

Do You Have the Correct Time?

If you use a timeserver to set your Mac's clock automatically over the Internet, be sure you've chosen the correct time zone in the Time Zone tab of the Date & Time preferences.

HINT

A Clockwork Preference

The third tab in the Date & Time preferences pane is the Clock tab, where you'll find settings for the menu bar clock. You can even choose an analog clock with hands instead of the regular digital display.

Adjusting the System Volume

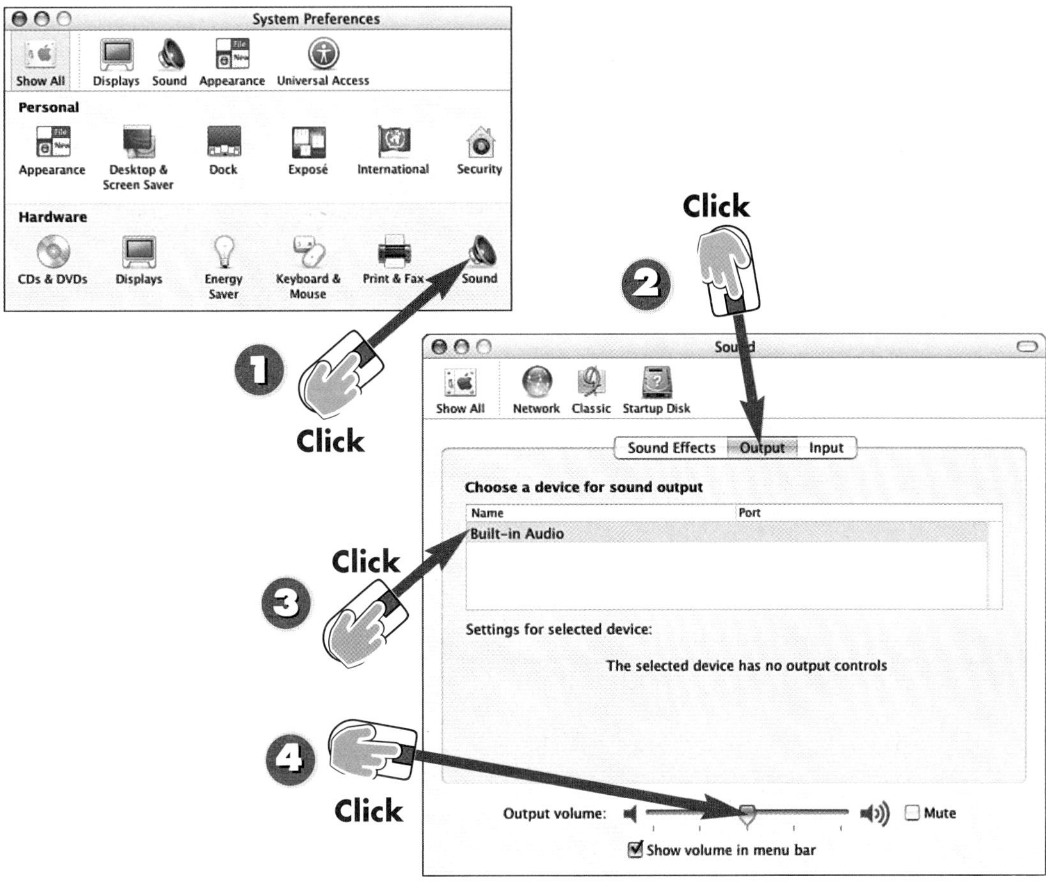

1. Click the **Sound** icon in the System Preferences window to display sound preferences.

2. Click the **Output** tab to see your choices.

3. If you have more than one output method (internal speaker and external speakers), choose the device you want to use from the pick list.

4. Drag the **Output volume** slider to change the volume for all sounds produced by your Mac.

INTRODUCTION

A small thing such as the volume of the sounds your Mac plays can have such an impact on your experience while using the computer. You can always increase the volume when you're working in the next room or you want to turn up the radio and sing along, or lower it when you don't want to wake the baby.

TIP

Muting for Discretion's Sake

Click the **Mute** check box next to the Output volume slider if you want to turn the volume all the way down. When the sound is muted, you'll see a screen flash instead of hearing an alert sound.

TIP

Getting Louder (or Softer) Faster

Click the **Show volume in menu bar** check box to put an extra menu in your menu bar that's simply a volume slider. To use it, click its icon, release the mouse button, and click and drag the slider.

Setting Trackpad Preferences

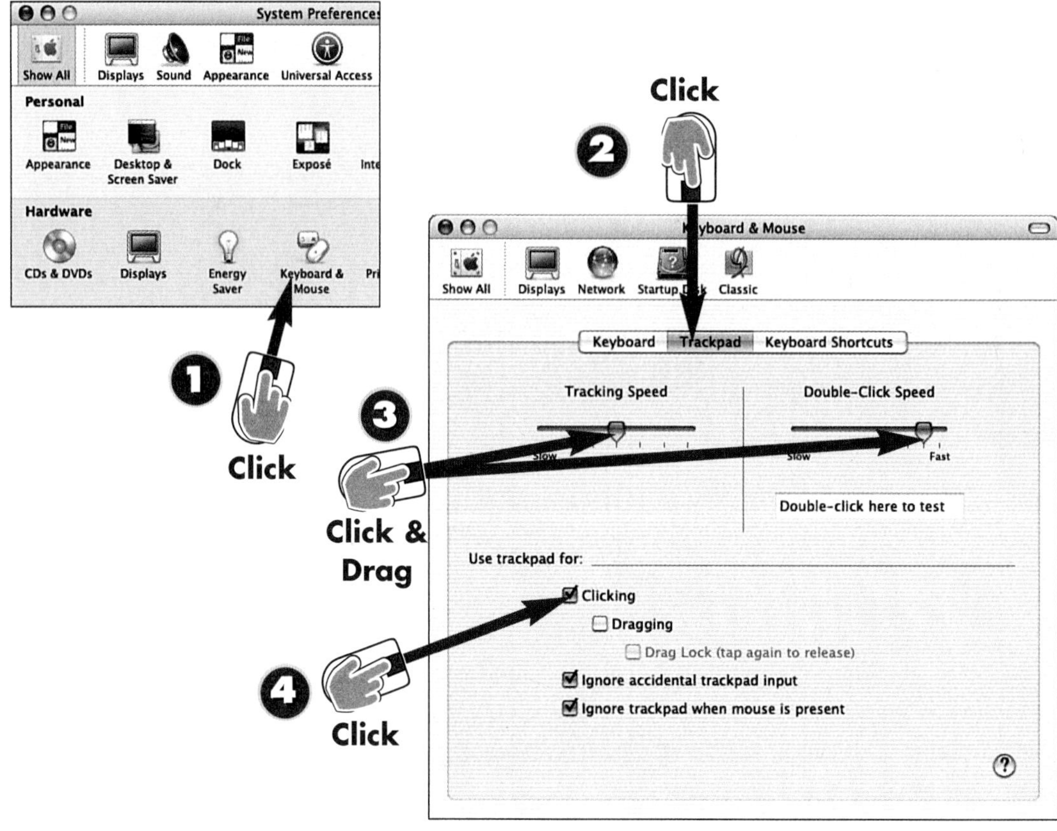

1. Click the **Keyboard & Mouse** icon in the System Preferences window to display mouse preferences.
2. Click the **Trackpad** tab to see the trackpad settings.
3. Drag the **Tracking Speed** slider to set how fast the trackpad cursor moves, and drag the **Double-Click Speed** slider to set how fast you have to double-click.
4. In the **Use trackpad for** section, click the check boxes to change your click and drag settings.

INTRODUCTION

Trackpads—those snazzy rubber pads laptops use instead of trackballs these days—are funny creatures. Because they don't feel the same as a mouse, you might want to use different speed and double-clicking settings for a trackpad than you would for a mouse. Feel free to experiment until you're comfortable with the settings you have.

HINT

Trackpad Settings

Don't overlook the last two check boxes: Ignore accidental trackpad input reduces the sensitivity of the trackpad so you don't click or drag accidentally, and Ignore trackpad when mouse is present turns off the trackpad when you plug in a mouse.

HINT

A Trackpad but no Laptop

If you love trackpads but don't use a PowerBook, you can still satisfy your craving. Try a standalone trackpad such as the Cirque Easy Cat—the USB version plugs right into your Mac—and your fingertips will be cruising along in no time.

Monitoring Battery Use

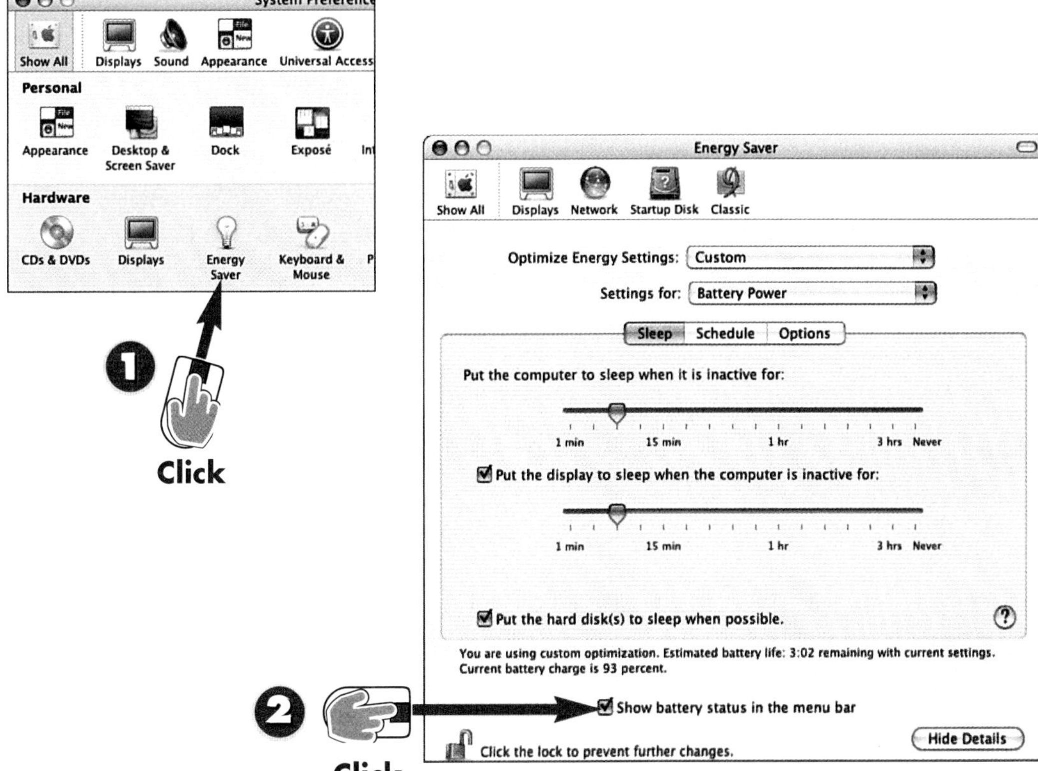

1. Click the **Energy Saver** icon in the System Preferences window to display power preferences.
2. Click the **Show battery status in the menu bar** check box to display your battery's charge status in the menu bar.

INTRODUCTION

If you're a laptop user, you know how important it is to keep track of the charge in your PowerBook's battery. Running out of power at a crucial moment could be a disaster—you'll definitely want to turn on this extra menu to make sure the worst never happens to you.

HINT

Saving More Power
Be sure to take a look at the other Energy Saver functions—you can save a lot of power by setting your preferences the right way. See the task "Setting Energy Saver Options" earlier in this part to learn more about Energy Saver settings.

PART 5

Customizing Your Mac

It's your Mac—why not have some fun with it? There are myriad ways to make your Mac your own, from changing its desktop picture, its icons, and even your own login icon to changing the way the Finder works and responds to you. You can even change the Finder's language to any of a couple dozen alternatives, including Asian languages, or you can set up your Mac to talk to you—and listen for your responses.

Your custom settings are associated with your login name, so they're automatically put into action each time you log in. When other users log in, their own settings are activated. That means a single Mac can offer each user a custom experience. Your custom settings can include useful preferences such as network locations and more fun preferences such as your desktop wallpaper.

In this part you'll learn how to customize the Finder, the Dock, the desktop, your screen saver, and your security preferences. You'll also learn about using Speakable Items to give voice commands to your Mac and how to make your Mac talk to you. If you move your computer around or switch networks a lot, you'll benefit from the "Creating Custom Network Locations" task, which shows how to create custom location settings that change all your network preferences with a single click.

Taking Advantage of Custom Settings

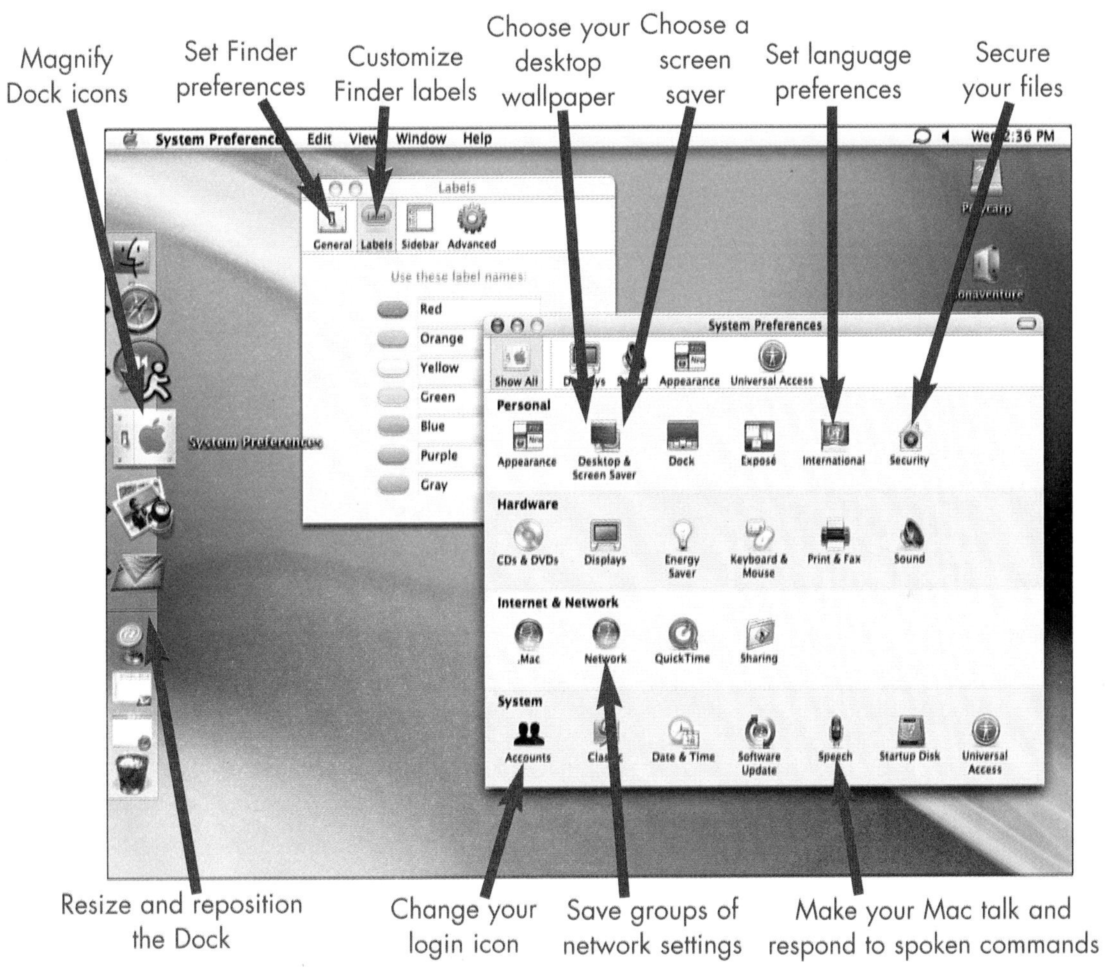

Moving the Dock Around

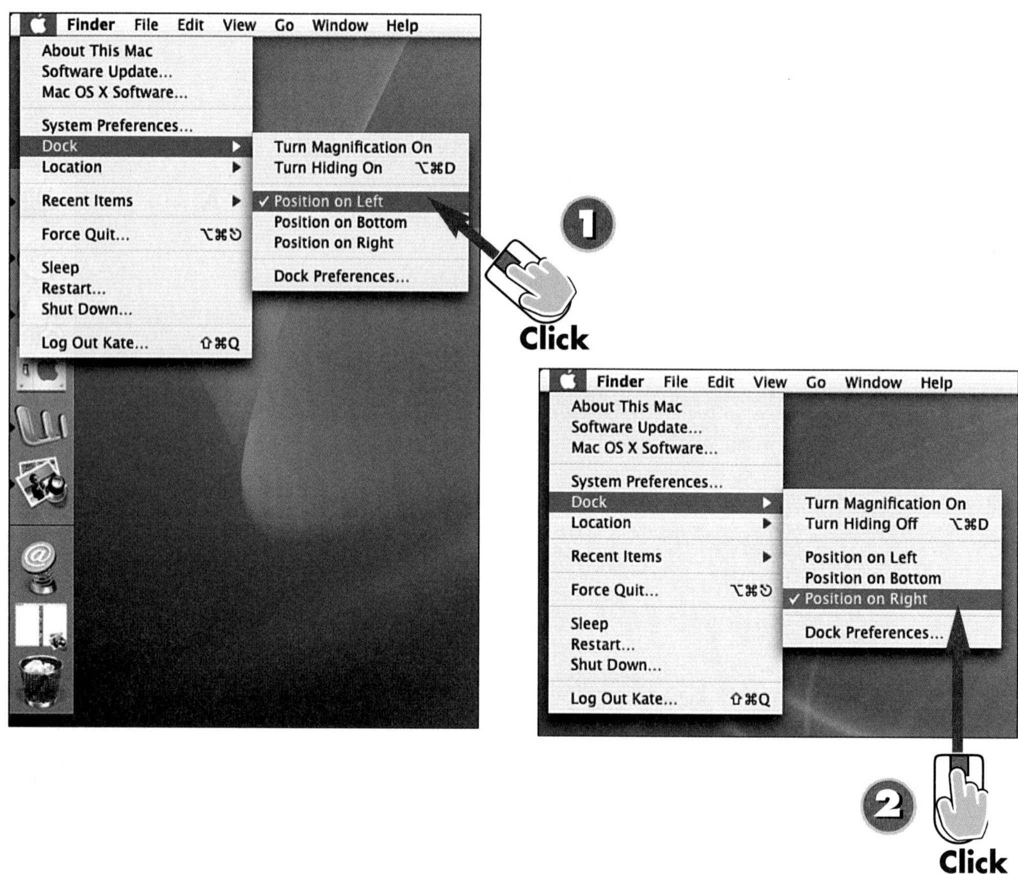

1. Choose **Apple menu**, **Dock**, **Position on Left** to move the Dock to the left edge of the screen.
2. Choose **Apple menu**, **Dock**, **Position on Right** to move the Dock to the right edge of the screen.

INTRODUCTION

Although the Dock normally lives at the bottom of your screen, it doesn't have to stay there. If you prefer, you can put it on the left or right side of the screen instead. No matter which edge of the screen it's on, the Dock works the same way and you can set its preferences to suit your tastes.

TIP

Hide and Go Dock
To hide the Dock, choose the **Apple** menu, **Dock**, **Turn Hiding On**; the Dock sinks off the edge of the screen whenever you're not using it. Move your mouse back to that edge, and the Dock pops back up.

HINT

Dock Substitutes
The Dock can get crowded if you store everything there. Some users use the Dock as an application switcher, with inactive programs and documents stored in a third-party Dock substitute such as DragThing (**www.dragthing.com**).

Changing the Dock's Size

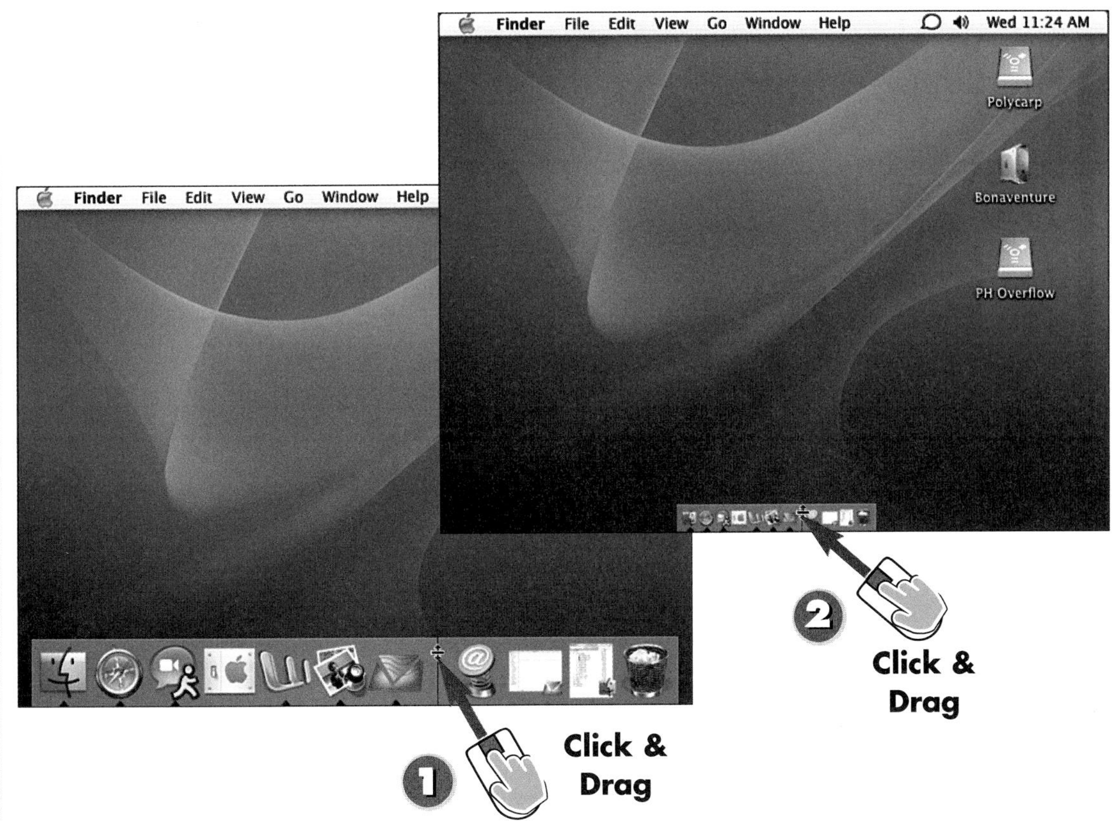

1. Click the line between the two halves of the Dock and drag upward to enlarge the Dock.
2. Drag downward to reduce the Dock's size.

INTRODUCTION

The more stuff you stash in the Dock, the more room it takes up on your screen. If it gets too full, you can shrink it to give you more room onscreen—or, if you prefer, you can make it larger so it's easier to see what it contains.

TIP

There's Always Another Way
You can also use the Dock Size slider in the Dock preferences (choose the **Apple** menu, **Dock**, **Dock Preferences**) if you happen to be going there to change other preferences as well.

Customizing the Dock's Behavior

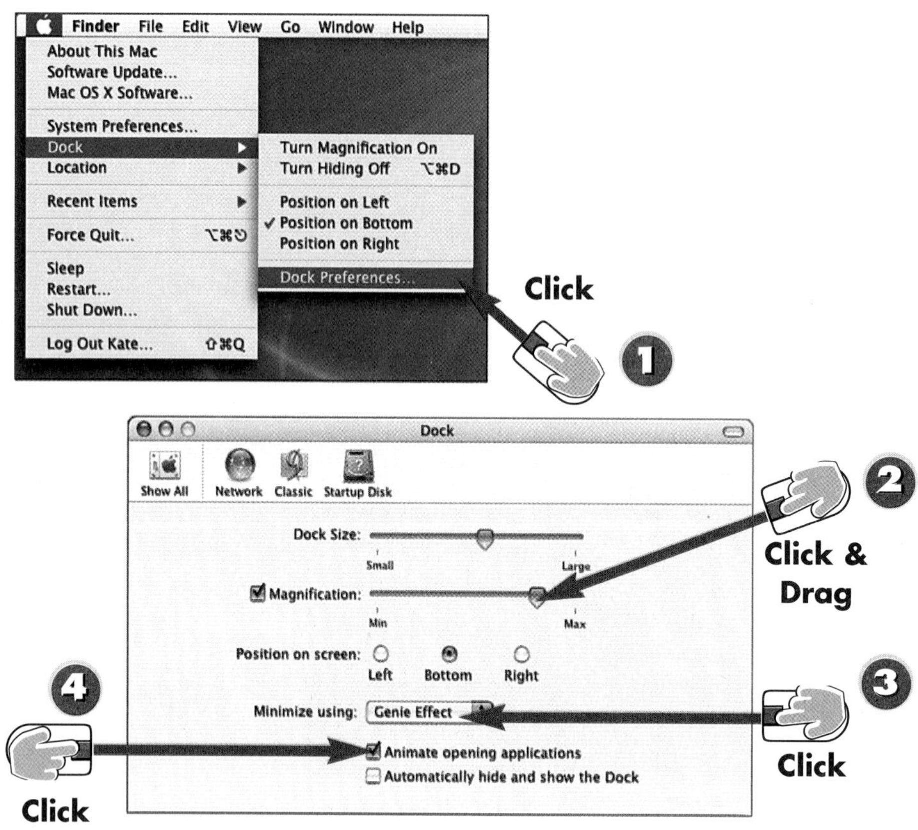

1. Choose the **Apple** menu, **Dock**, **Dock Preferences**.

2. Click and drag the **Magnification** slider toward Max if you want Dock icons to be enlarged as you pass the mouse cursor over them.

3. Choose an option from the **Minimize using** pop-up menu.

4. Click the **Animate opening applications** check box to make Dock icons bounce as their programs start up.

INTRODUCTION

As if moving the Dock around and changing its size weren't enough, there's yet more you can do to make the Dock work just the way you want it to. The Dock preferences enable you to control the way the Dock moves—or, more precisely, the way its icons move and change size and the way windows enter the Dock.

TIP

Dock Behavior in Another Context

You can control Dock Preferences by Ctrl-clicking the dividing line between the halves of the Dock. The contextual menu has controls for magnification, hiding, position, and the minimization effect, as well as a Dock Preferences command.

Changing the Way the Finder Works

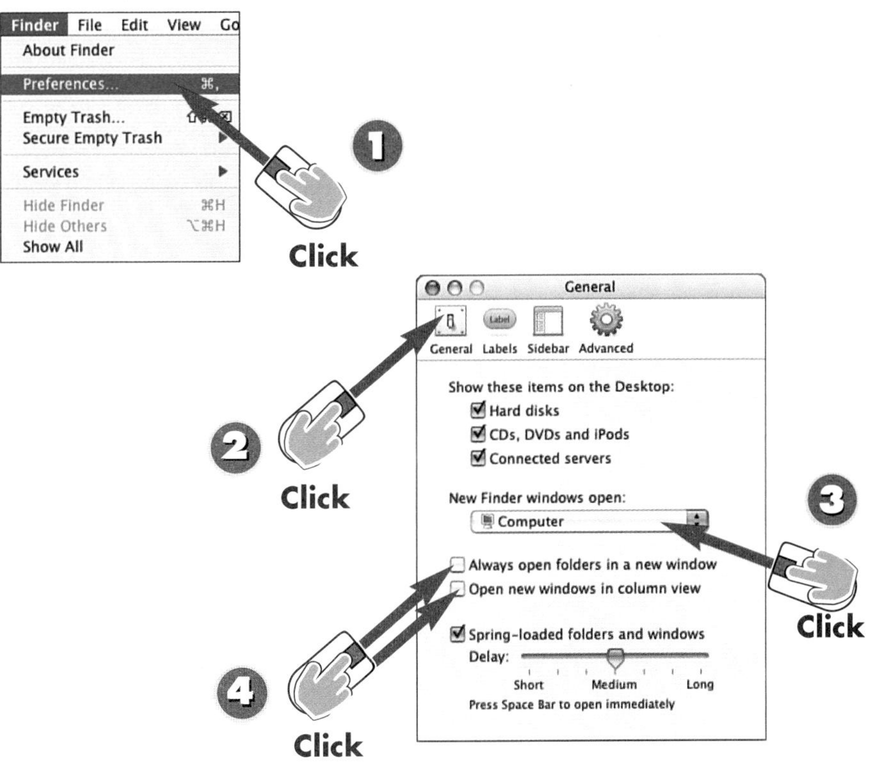

1. In the Finder, choose **Finder**, **Preferences**.
2. Click the **General** button to see basic Finder preferences, and then click check boxes to set the kinds of disks to appear on the desktop.
3. Choose an option from the **New Finder windows open** pop-up menu to determine which folder or disk location appears in new Finder windows.
4. Click the check boxes to set whether each folder generates a new window and whether new windows start out in Column view.

INTRODUCTION

The Finder—the program that generates the desktop and enables you to explore your hard drive and network drives visually via windows—is where you'll spend a lot of time while using your Mac. You have several choices about the way it operates; here's how to set up the Finder to suit your tastes.

TIP

Finding Files with the Finder
The Finder got its name for its capability to find files. To find files in the Finder, choose **File**, **Find** or press **Cmd-F** and type in the search criteria.

Customizing Labels

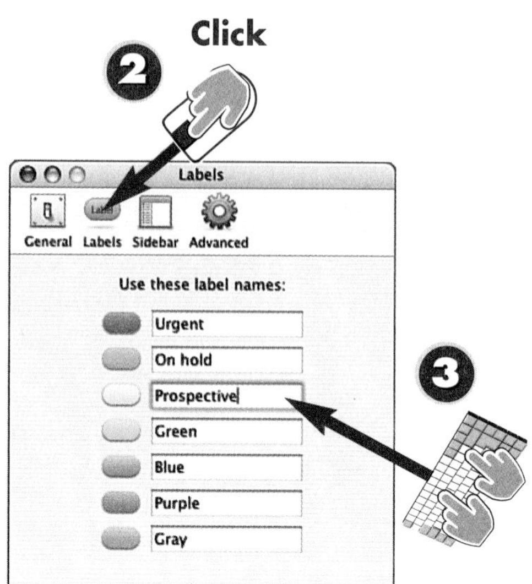

1. In the Finder, choose **Finder**, **Preferences**.
2. Click the **Labels** button to see preferences for labels.
3. Enter more descriptive names for the label colors.

INTRODUCTION

Labels are most useful if you can use them to mean what you want them to mean—such as "urgent job" rather than just "green folder." You can do just that by assigning your custom titles to the various label colors in the Finder's preferences. You can use custom labels to make icons stand out or force lists to sort in a particular way.

TIP

Labels That Do More Than Look Pretty

To sort a list of files and folders by their labels in List view, choose **View**, **View Options** and make sure the Labels check box is checked. Enlarge the window so you can see the Label column and click its column header to change the sort order.

Changing Your Desktop Picture

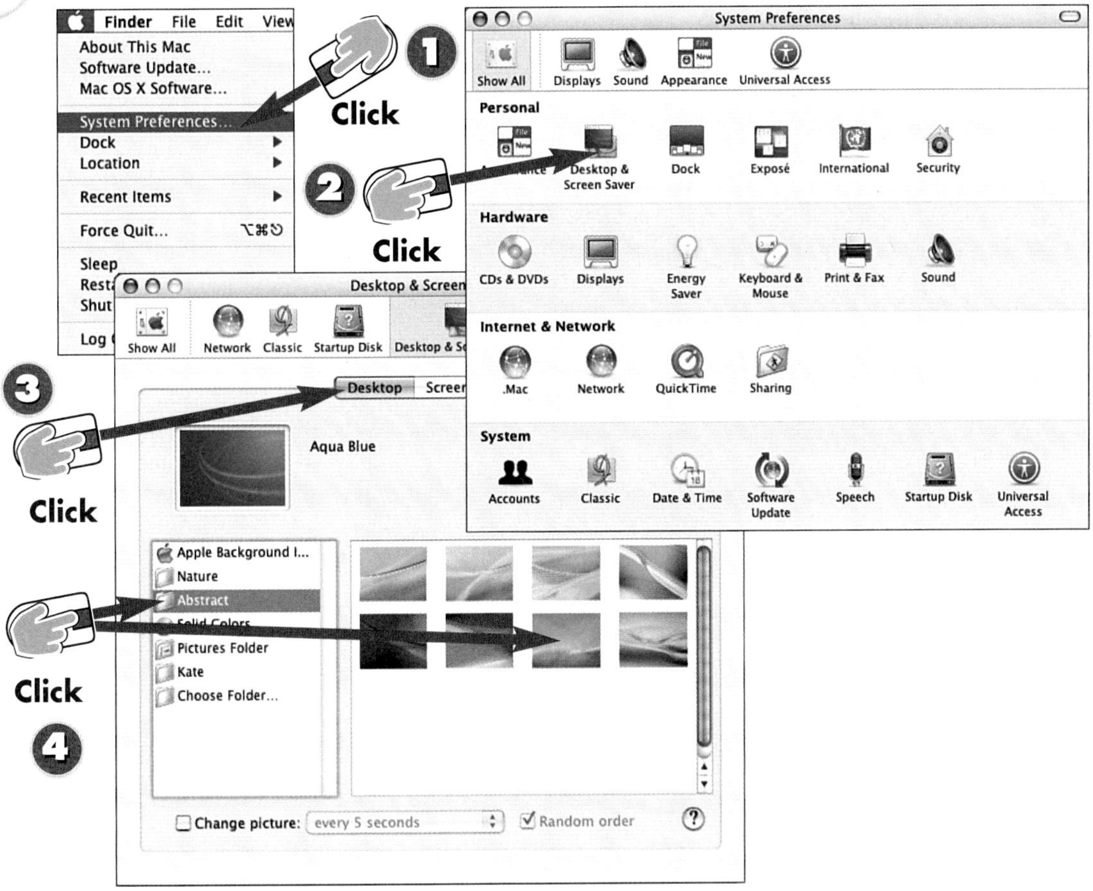

1. Choose **Apple menu**, **System Preferences**.
2. Click the **Desktop & Screen Saver** icon to see your choices.
3. Click the **Desktop** tab.
4. Click a folder and an image from within the folder to apply that image to the desktop.

INTRODUCTION

Every time you sit down in front of your Mac, you're looking at your desktop—or, more specifically, at the picture displayed on it. Why not have some fun with it? You can change the desktop picture any time you like, using any photo, cartoon, or other graphic that catches your fancy.

TIP

Surprise Me

If you want your desktop picture to change automatically, click **Choose Folder** in the Desktop tab and pick a folder full of your favorite images. Then check **Change picture** at the bottom of the Desktop tab and choose a time interval.

HINT

The Mother Lode

Looking for more desktop pictures to relieve your boredom? You can download hundreds of high-quality desktop images at MacDesktops (**www.macdesktops.com**).

Changing Your Login Icon

Click

Click

Click

Click & Drag

Click

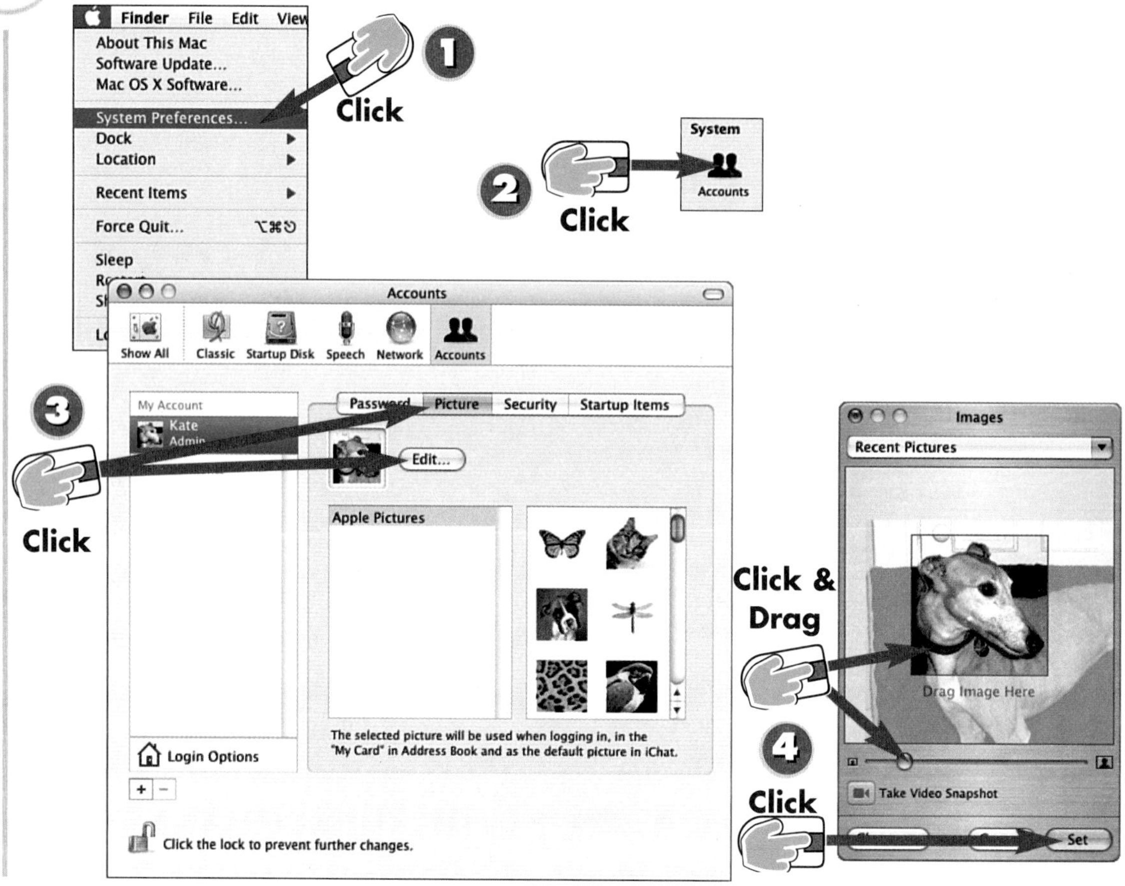

1. Choose **Apple menu**, **System Preferences**.
2. Click the **Accounts** icon to see your choices.
3. Click the **Picture** tab; then click the **Edit** button next to your picture.
4. Drag or paste an image file into the Images window, drag the image and the scaling slider until the square shows the area you want for the icon, and click **Set** to make it your login picture.

INTRODUCTION

Your login item represents your face within the world of your Mac. It's used as your buddy icon for online messaging in iChat, it appears next to your personal information in the Address Book, and you see it every time you log in. You can use one of the built-in pictures, or you can add any picture you like—your photo or anything else.

HINT

Using Your Own Picture

There are some reasons it might not be wise to use your own photo as a login icon. If people you don't know will see the photo—as an iChat icon, for instance—you might want to reconsider using it and substitute a personal logo of some type.

Changing Your Mac's Language

Click

Click

Click

Click & Drag

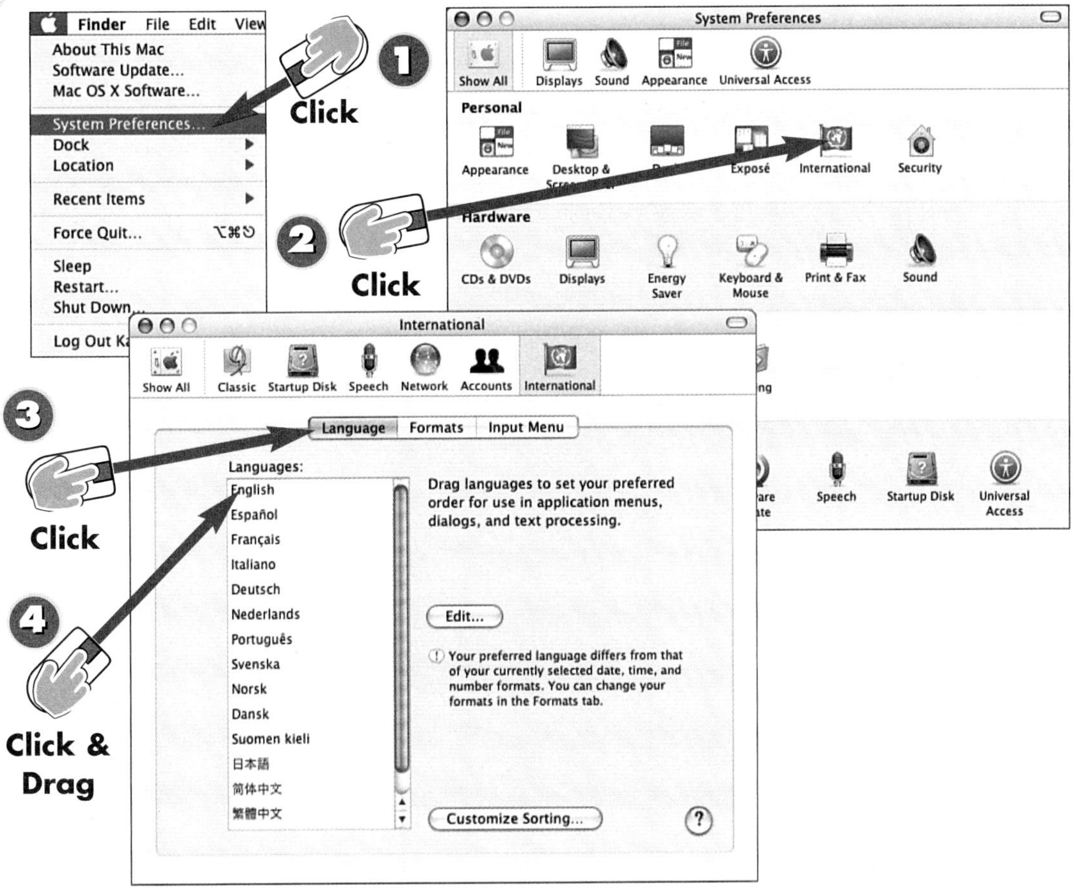

1. Choose **Apple menu**, **System Preferences**.

2. Click the **International** icon to see your choices.

3. Click the **Language** tab.

4. Click and drag your preferred language to the top of the pick list.

INTRODUCTION

You might have thought that you would need to buy a special version of Mac OS X if you want your Mac's interface to use a language other than English. Actually, Mac OS X ships with the capability to display menus, dialog boxes, and other interface elements in a couple dozen languages, including those with special alphabets.

TIP

Making a Menu

When you switch languages, you should also switch keyboard layouts to activate each language's special characters. In the International preferences' Input Menu tab, you can create a menu of the languages you use so you can switch keyboard layouts quickly.

Changing Your Screen Saver

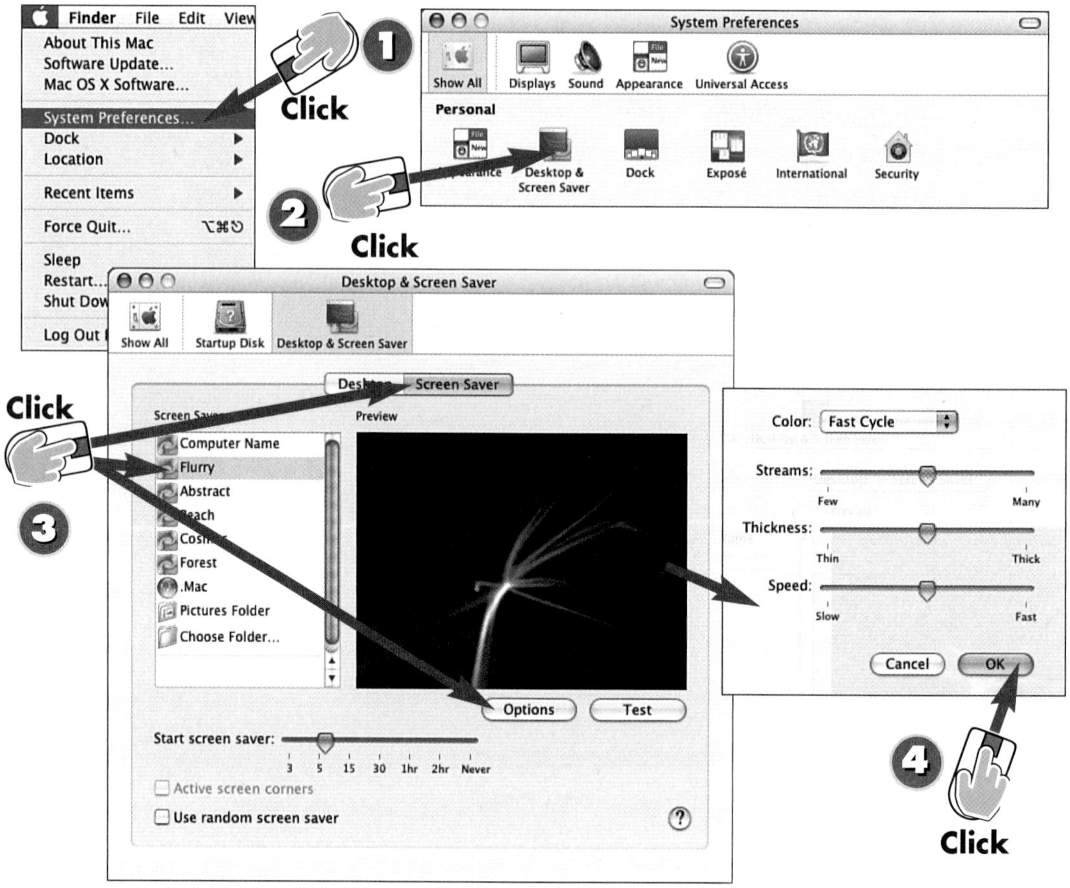

1. Choose **Apple menu**, **System Preferences**.
2. Click the **Desktop & Screen Saver** icon to see your choices.
3. Click the **Screen Saver** tab and then click a screen saver in the list to select it. Click the **Options** button.
4. Use the settings in this dialog box to change settings specific to each screen saver. Click **OK** when finished.

INTRODUCTION

Originally invented to stop the kind of screen burn-in that you see on automatic teller machines, screen savers are actually little more than a pretty entertainment these days. But that shouldn't prevent you from using them; screen savers provide some privacy, shielding your screen from casual observers, as well as being fun to look at.

HINT

Got Savers?

If you're not satisfied with the built-in selection of screen savers—or if you've run through them all and are desperately in need of new ones—check out **www.macscreensavers.com**. There you can download more screen saver modules than you could ever need.

Increasing Your Mac's Security

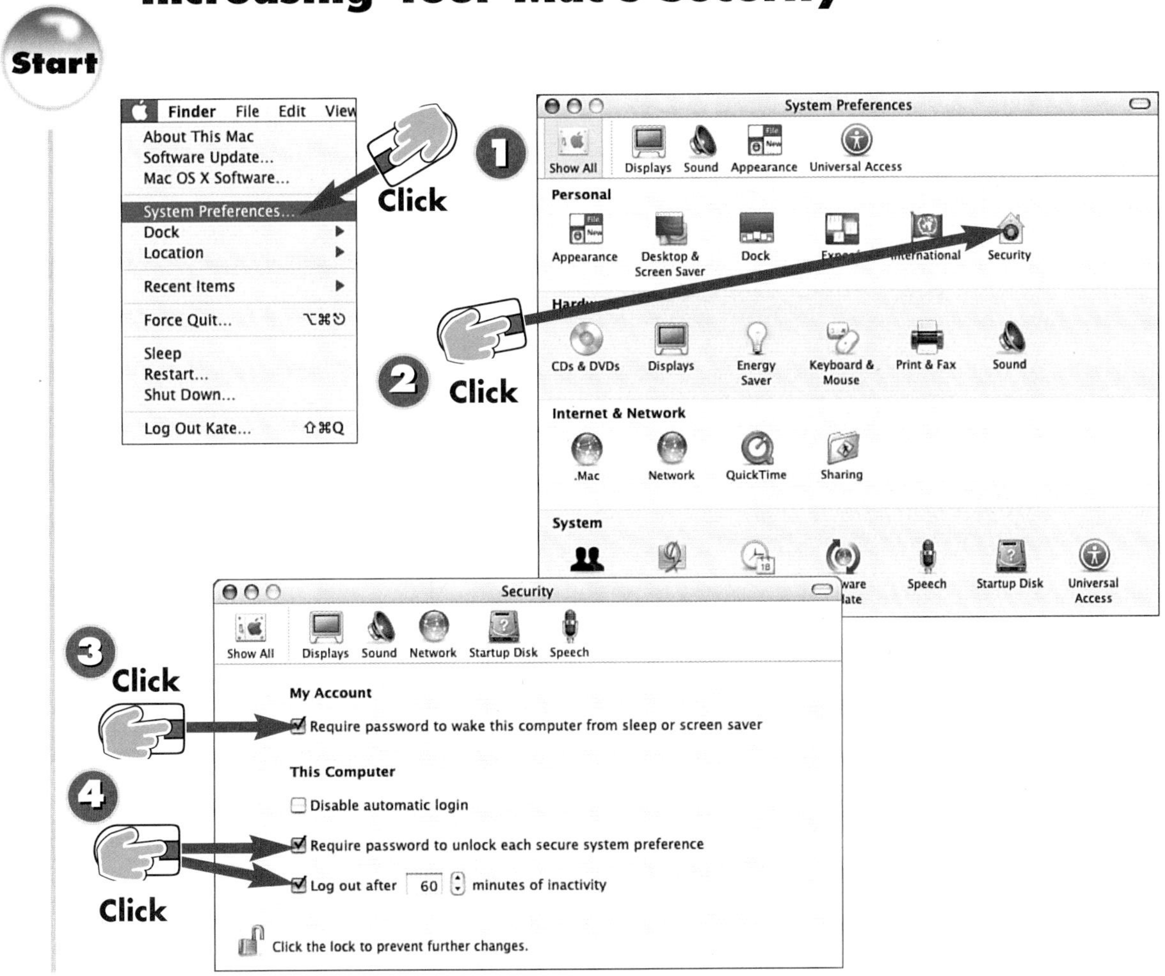

1. Choose **Apple menu**, **System Preferences**.

2. Click the **Security** icon to see your choices.

3. Click the **Require password** check box to make sure that only you can wake the computer up when it's sleeping.

4. Click the check boxes next to the other options to turn them on or off.

INTRODUCTION

Whether these settings are important to you depends on how vulnerable your Mac is to snoopy intruders. If your computer is in a dorm room or an open office, or if it's a PowerBook, you'll probably want to put at least some of these measures in place to ensure that unauthorized people can't use it.

HINT

Learning to Live Together

To learn about ways to get along when you share your Mac with other users, turn to Part 11, "Sharing Your Mac with Multiple Users."

Changing Icons

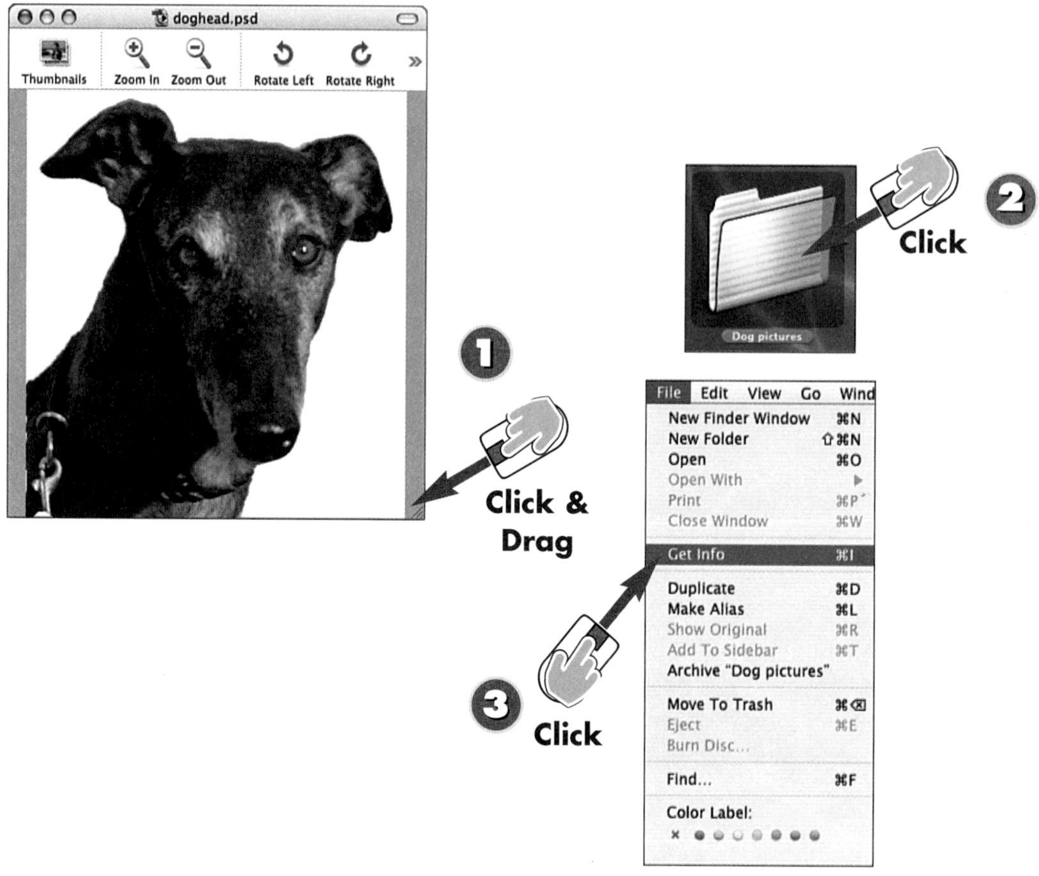

1. In Preview or another graphics program, select part or all of an image to be the new icon. Press **Cmd-C** to copy the selection.
2. In the Finder, click to select the file whose icon you want to change.
3. Choose **File**, **Get Info** to see the file's Info window.

INTRODUCTION

Mac OS X has wonderful graphics; it's a lovely looking operating system, and that's due in large part to its detailed, scalable icons. One of the easiest—and coolest—customizations you can perform on your Mac is to apply the system's dexterity with icons to your own homemade icons. You can turn any picture you like into an icon.

HINT

More Fun with Icons
You can copy and paste existing icons, too. For a great collection of free Mac icons you can download and apply to your files and folders, check out the Iconfactory (**www.iconfactory.com**).

4. Click the icon shown in the Info window.

5. Press **Cmd-V** and the new image is pasted into the icon area.

TIP

For Best Results

The bigger the picture you use to create an icon, the more detailed the icon will be when it's scaled to its largest size. With that in mind, however, remember that at small sizes, simple, clear, less-detailed images are the easiest to identify.

Talking to Your Mac

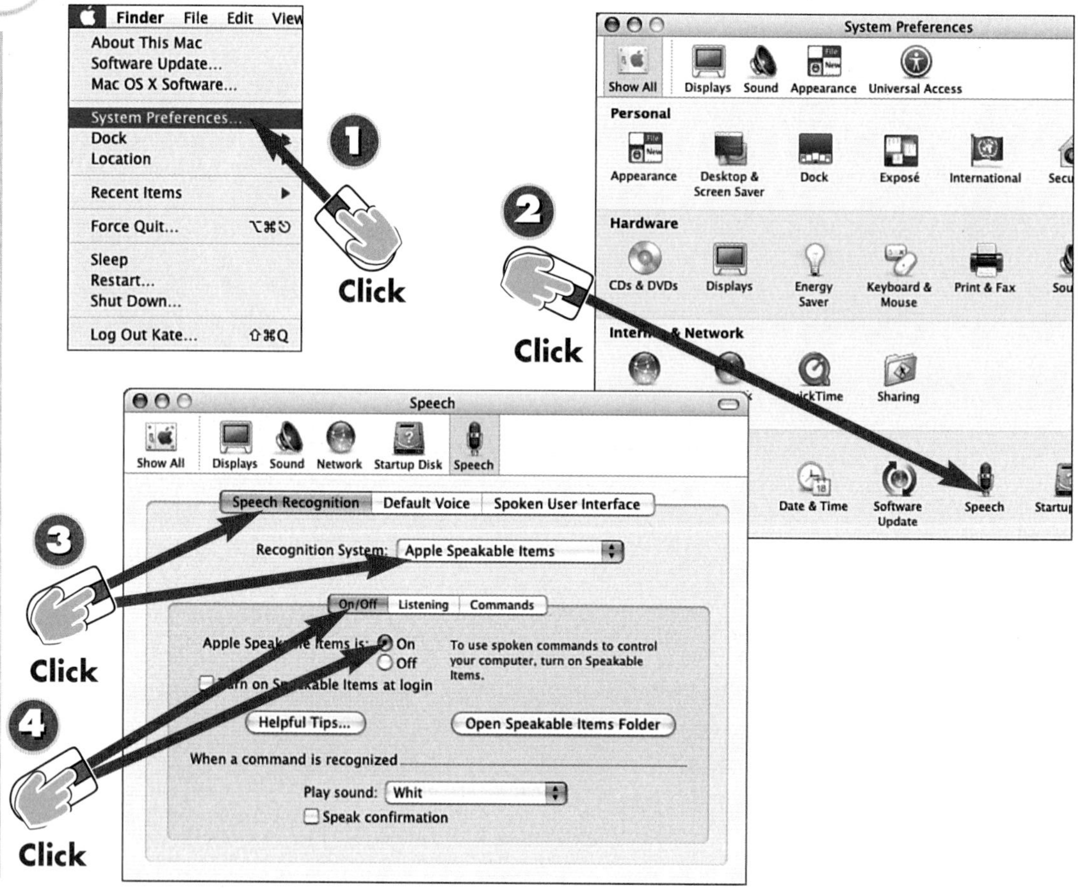

1. Choose **Apple menu**, **System Preferences**.

2. Click the **Speech** icon to see your choices.

3. Click the **Speech Recognition** tab and choose **Apple Speakable Items** from the **Recognition System** pop-up menu.

4. Click the **On/Off** tab, and then click the **On** radio button to activate Speakable Items.

INTRODUCTION

Especially if you work at home or in a real office—as in a room with a door—it's both fun and efficient to teach your computer to respond to spoken commands. Although the Mac doesn't really know English, you can tell it to do a variety of things using just a word or two. Of course, you have to have a microphone connected to the Mac for this to work.

TIP

Keep Talking

Be sure to check the Turn on Speakable Items at login box in the On/Off tab if you want to use speech recognition every time you start up your Mac.

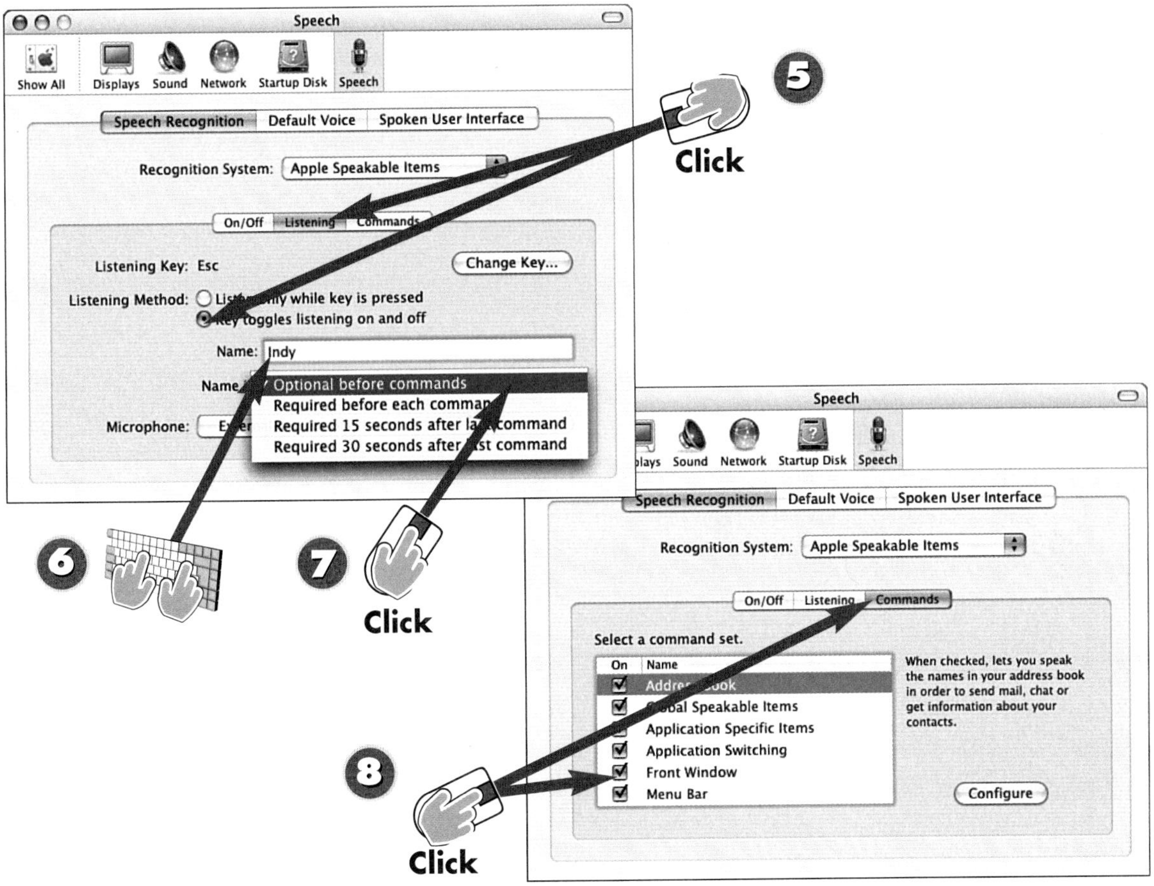

5 Click the **Listening** tab, and then click a **Listening Method** radio button to determine whether the computer listens all the time or only when the Esc key is pressed.

6 In the **Name** field, enter the name by which you want to call your computer.

7 Choose an option from the **Name is** pop-up menu to determine how often you need to say the computer's name to keep its attention.

8 Click the **Commands** tab, and then click the check boxes to choose which spoken commands the computer will recognize.

HINT

Speak into the Microphone

When you're talking to your Mac, speak clearly, but don't shout. If you have trouble getting the Mac to recognize your commands, try moving the microphone to different positions.

TIP

I'm Listening...

If you walk around your office as you work, click the **Key toggles listening on and off** radio button in step 5. This relieves you from having to return to your keyboard to press a key before it will start listening to you.

Making Your Mac Talk Back

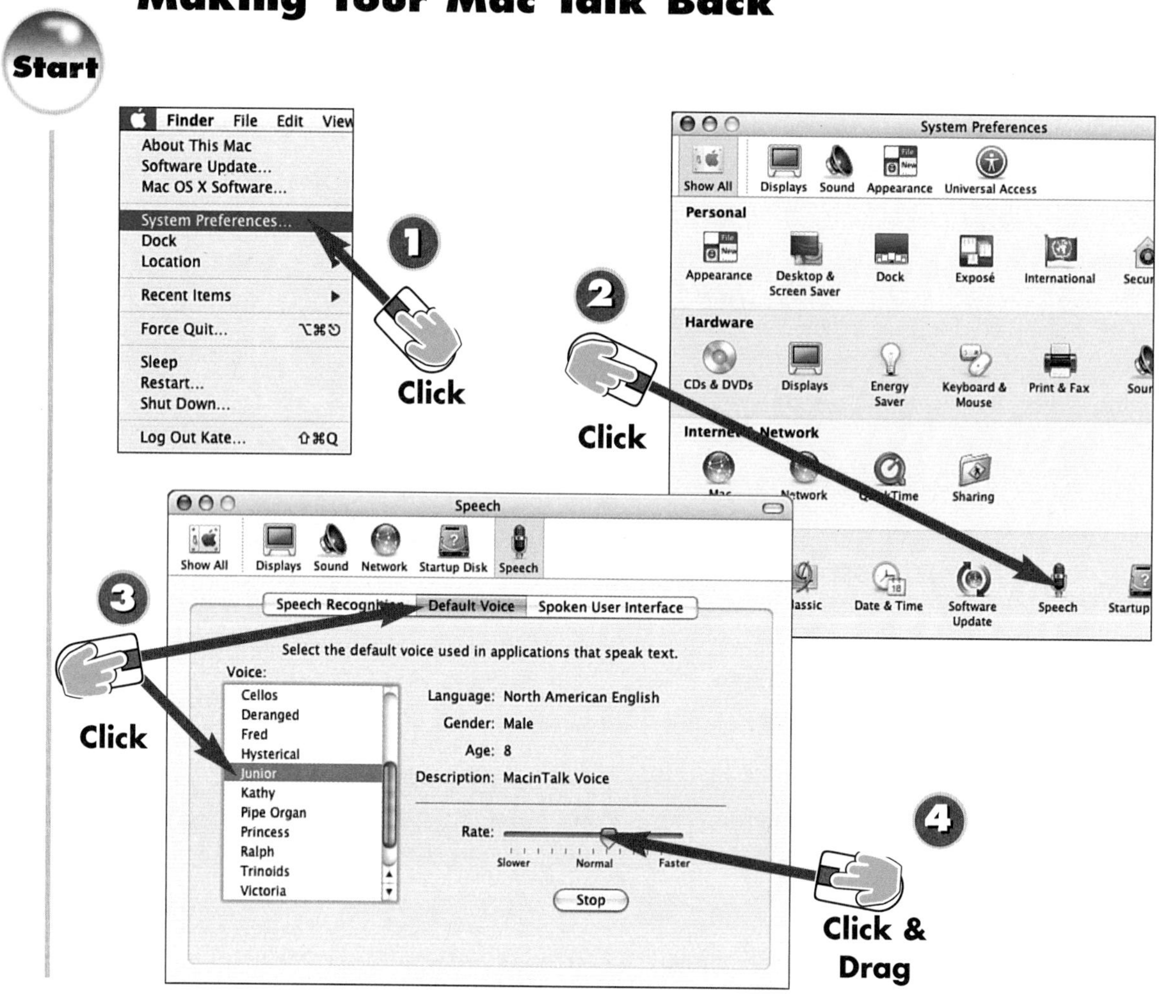

Click

Click

Click

Click & Drag

1. Choose **Apple menu**, **System Preferences**.

2. Click the **Speech** icon to see your choices.

3. Click the **Default Voice** tab and choose a voice from the pick list.

4. Click and drag the **Rate** slider to change the speed at which the computer speaks.

INTRODUCTION

If you want to feel as though you're in an episode of *Star Trek*, *The Jetsons*, or *Buck Rogers*, you absolutely must have a talking computer. With a few preference settings, you can get your Mac to speak alerts instead of waiting for you to notice them, read any text you select, and read you the dialog box labels under your mouse.

HINT

Choosing a Voice
The voices that sound most like real people are the ones with people's names, such as Fred and Kathy. Voices with more unusual names, including Bubbles and Trinoids, tend to sound like something you'd hear on the Cartoon Network.

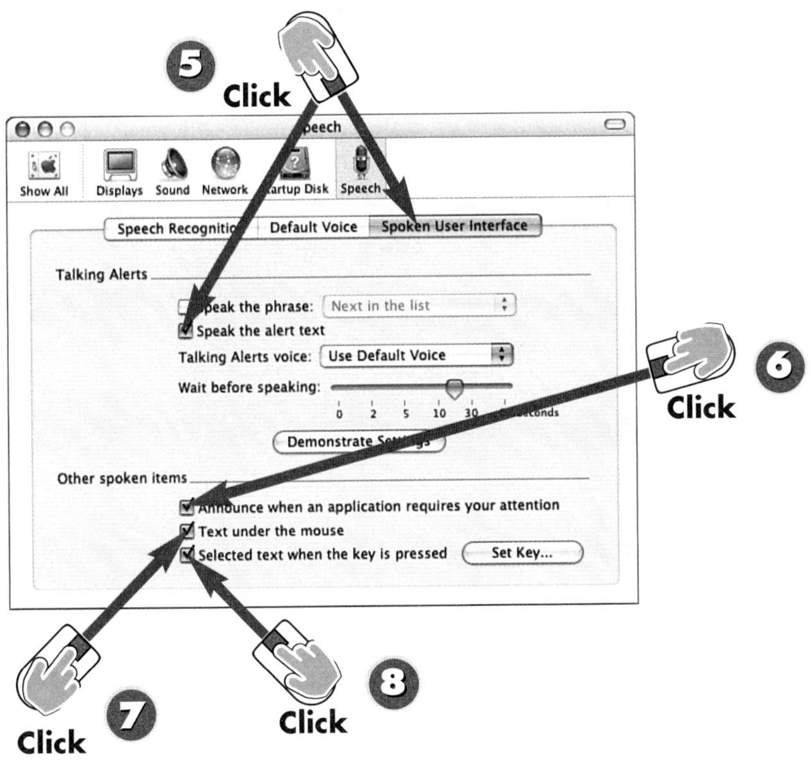

5 Click the **Spoken User Interface** tab and click the **Speak the alert text** check box to have your computer read alert dialog boxes to you.

6 Click the **Announce** check box to hear a spoken alert when a program in the background needs attention.

7 Click the **Text under the mouse** check box to have your Mac read text in dialog boxes when you hold the mouse cursor over the text.

8 Click the **Selected text** check box to have your Mac read the selected text in any program when you press a key.

HINT

It's All About Speed

As you browse through the available voices, be sure to try different speeds using the Rate slider. It's amazing how big a difference speed changes make in how well the various voices work.

TIP

Changes

If you opt to have your Mac read the selected text to you when you press a key, you'll be offered a chance to choose the key when you check the box. To change that key later, click the **Set Key** button.

Creating Custom Network Locations

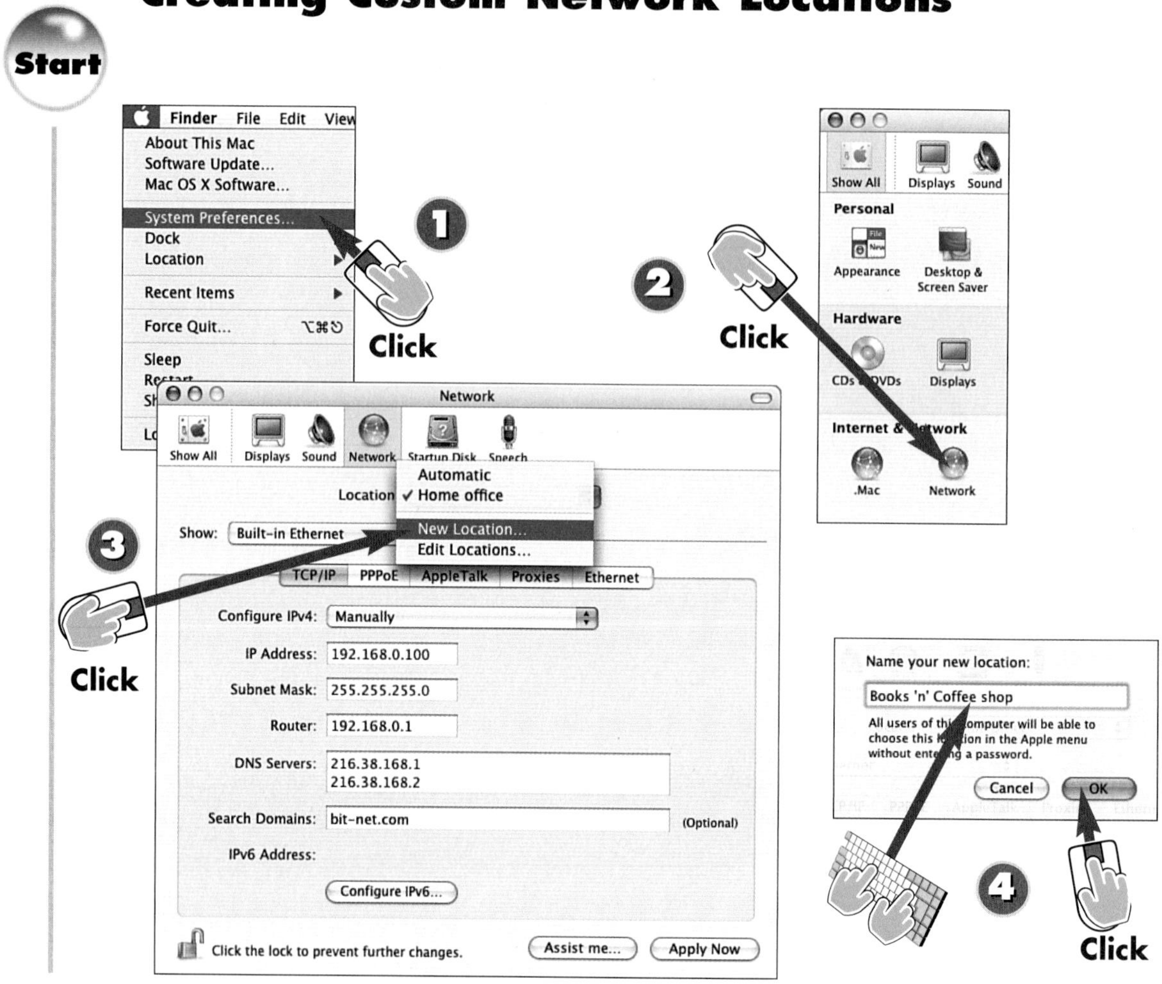

1. Choose **Apple menu**, **System Preferences**.

2. Click the **Network** icon to see your choices.

3. Choose **New Location** from the **Location** pop-up menu.

4. Give the location a descriptive name and click **OK**.

INTRODUCTION

Network locations are groups of network settings, each saved with a descriptive name so you can switch all your settings with a single click and get online or on the local network instantly no matter where you happen to be. After you've created a location, to use it all you have to do is choose it from a pop-up menu.

TIP

A Time and a Place

You can use locations to save settings for different situations as well as different places. For example, if you have both a cable modem and a dial-up account, create a location for each so you can switch to dial-up if the cable connection goes down.

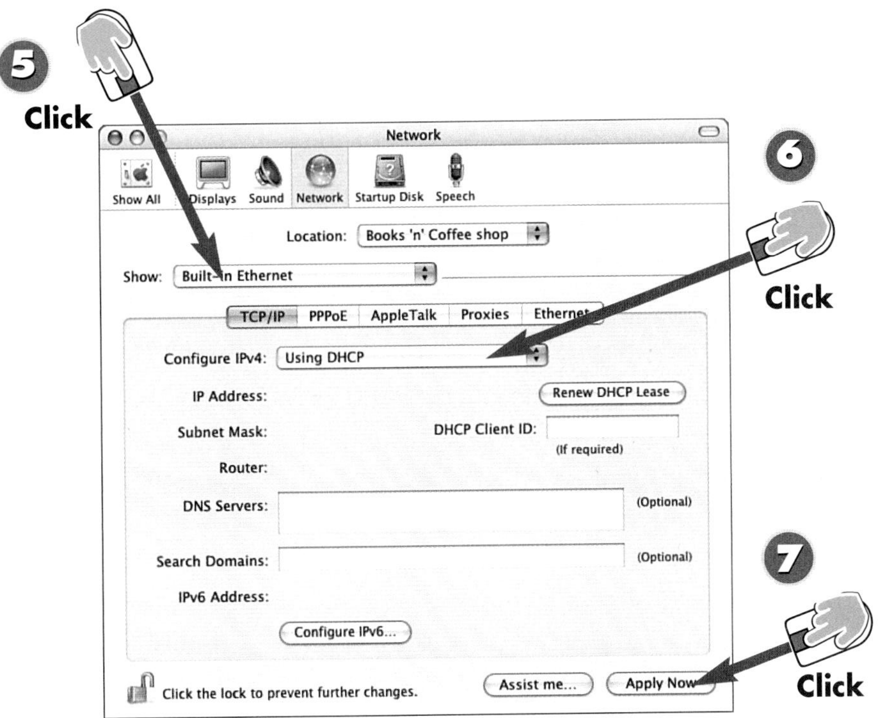

5 Choose the network interface you want to set up from the **Show** pop-up menu.

6 On each tab, make the appropriate settings for that network interface.

7 Click **Apply Now** to switch to the new location.

HINT

Naming Names
Just to be sure we're all on the same page here, a descriptive name (as suggested in step 4) is something like "Joe's office Ethernet," rather than "New Location 4." It tells you where and under what circumstances the location setting is applicable.

TIP

What's in a Name?
To change the names of your locations, choose **Edit Locations** from the pop-up menu instead of New Location. You can also use the Edit Locations command to create a new location based on an existing one; click **Duplicate**.

PART 6

Organizing Your Life

Mac OS X includes several programs that work together to keep you organized: Address Book, iCal, and iSync. Address Book is a contact manager where you can store your friends', family members', and colleagues' names, addresses, and phone numbers along with their modern equivalents of instant messaging IDs, Web sites, and email addresses. iCal keeps track of your appointments and a to-do list, and it can both publish and subscribe to calendars so you can share them with others. And iSync makes sure that all the data in Address Book and iCal is available to your PDA, phone, or other device so you're never without it.

In this part you'll learn how to create and organize contacts in Address Book and how to use the program to view a map of a contact's address. iCal Tasks show how to create appointments and to-do lists and how to invite Address Book contacts to events; how to search calendars; and how to publish, subscribe to, and print calendars. Finally, you'll learn how to use iSync to keep all your information straight across devices and how to find essential information on the Net with Sherlock.

Working with Contacts and Schedules

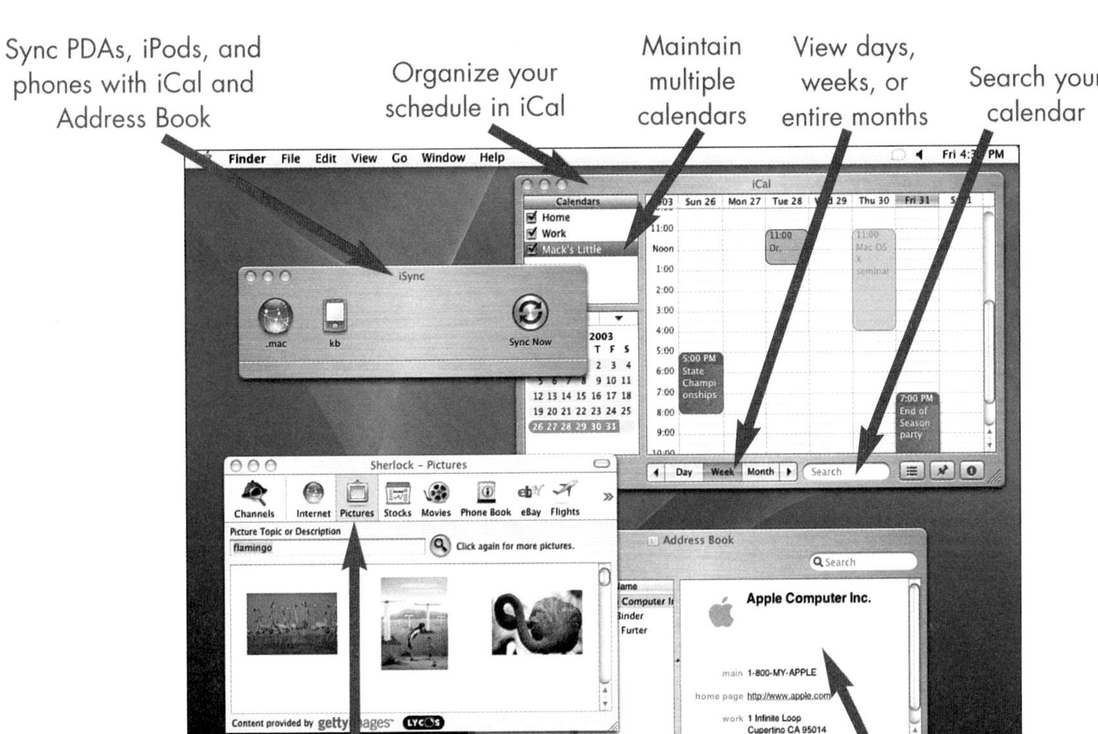

Adding Contacts to Address Book

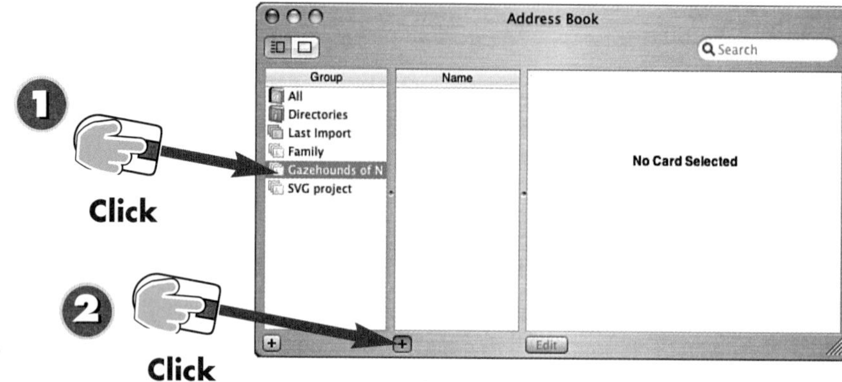

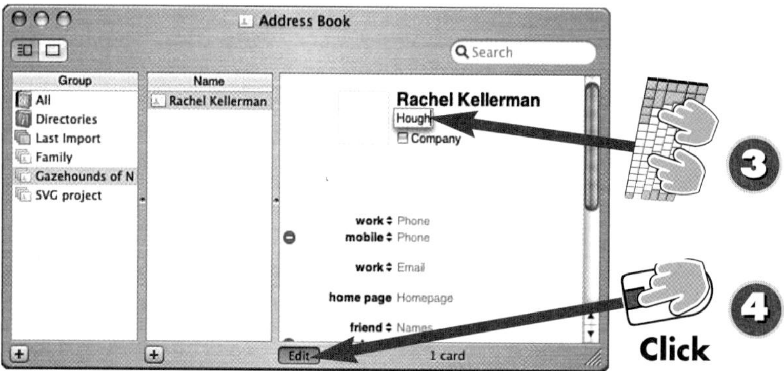

1. Click the group name to which you want to add the contact.
2. Click the **+** button below the list of contacts in that group.
3. Type the person or company's name and other information.
4. Click **Edit** to complete the contact.

INTRODUCTION

Mac OS X's Address Book is accessible systemwide, meaning its information can be used by other programs such as iChat, Mail, and even Microsoft Word. Adding contacts and sorting them into groups is easy, and Address Book has an up-to-date selection of information fields, including places to stash online messaging IDs.

TIP

Edit This

The Edit button is also where you should head (or, more specifically, click) when you want to make changes to an existing Address Book entry. To apply your changes, click **Edit** again, or you can just click another contact or group instead.

Creating Groups of Contacts

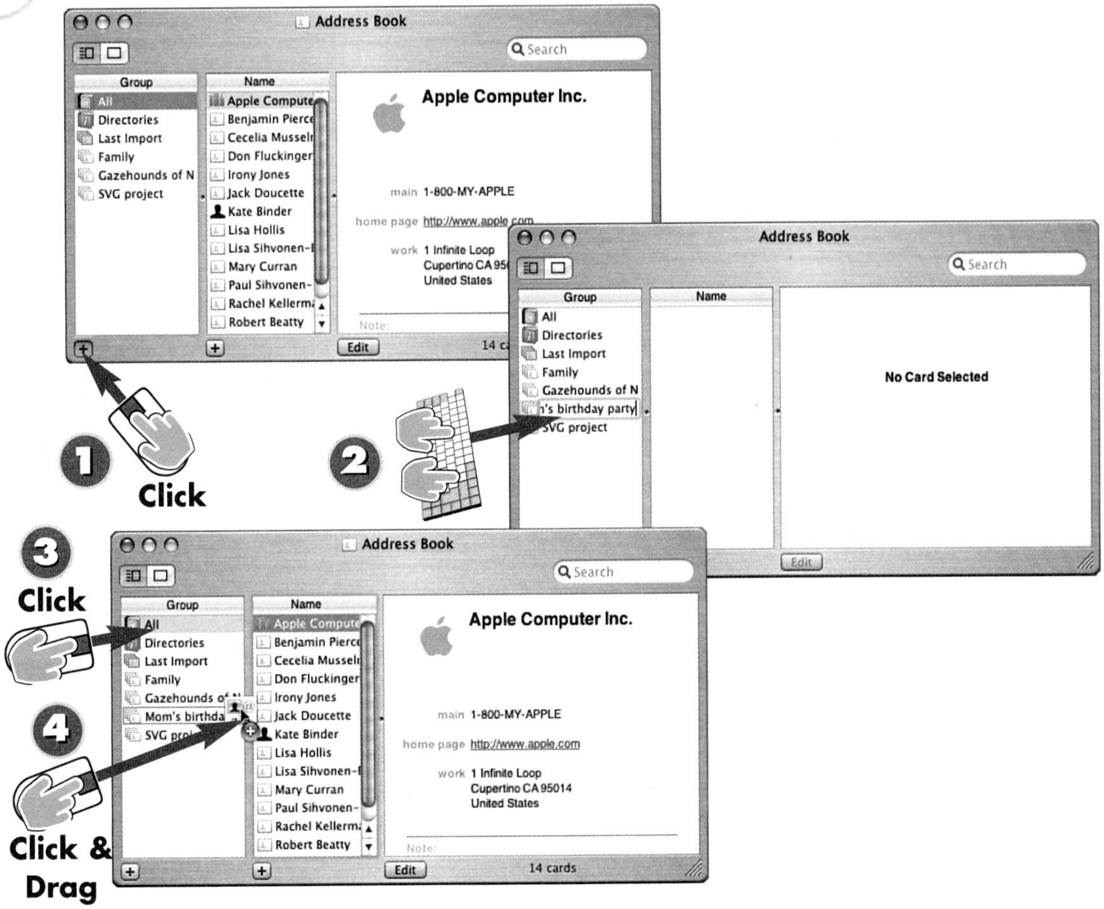

1. Click the **+** button under the list of contacts.

2. Give the new group a name.

3. Click **All** or another group that contains the contacts you want to add to the new group.

4. Drag the contacts into the new group.

INTRODUCTION

You can use Address Book's groups many ways. For example, you can create a group of people working on a current project so you can email them all at once. Or you can create a group of addresses for holiday cards so you can print address labels. Each contact can be in as many groups as you want to put it in.

TIP

A Two-Way Street
Creating a new group can work backward, too. First, **Cmd-click** to select the contacts you want to put in the group; then choose **File**, **New Group from Selection**.

Exporting Contacts As vCards

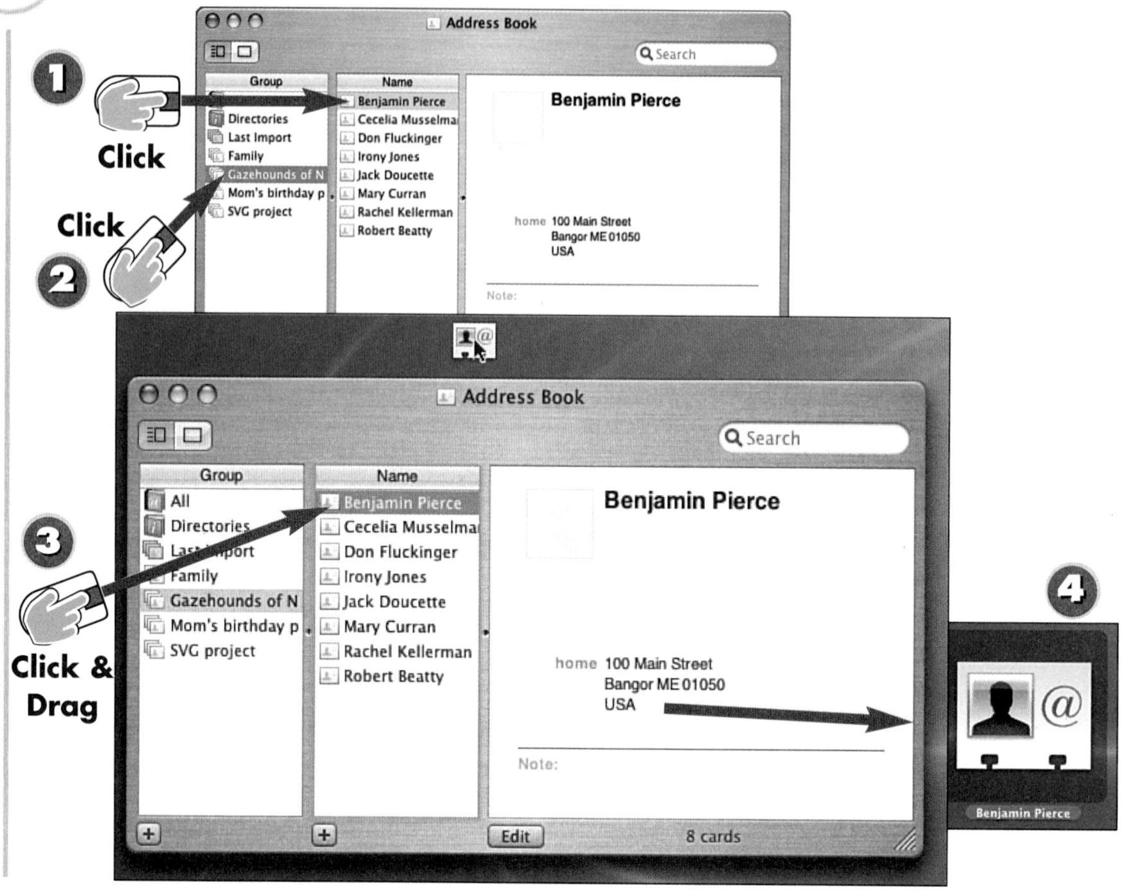

1. Click a name in the contacts column to select a single person, or **Cmd-click** to select more than one person.
2. To create a vCard for an entire group, click the group's name in the first column.
3. Drag the group, contact, or contacts onto the desktop to create the vCard file.
4. The vCard appears on the desktop and can now be attached and sent via email.

INTRODUCTION

Apple has chosen the vCard as its standard method of exchanging contact information among Address Book users as well as between Address Book and other programs. vCards are very small files that you can attach to email messages. Most contact management programs can read them, so they're a good way to send contact information to just about anyone, including Windows users.

HINT

The Express Route
You can find contacts quickly in Address Book by clicking the All group and typing a name, city, or other information into the Search entry field at the upper-left corner of the Address Book window.

Importing a vCard into Address Book

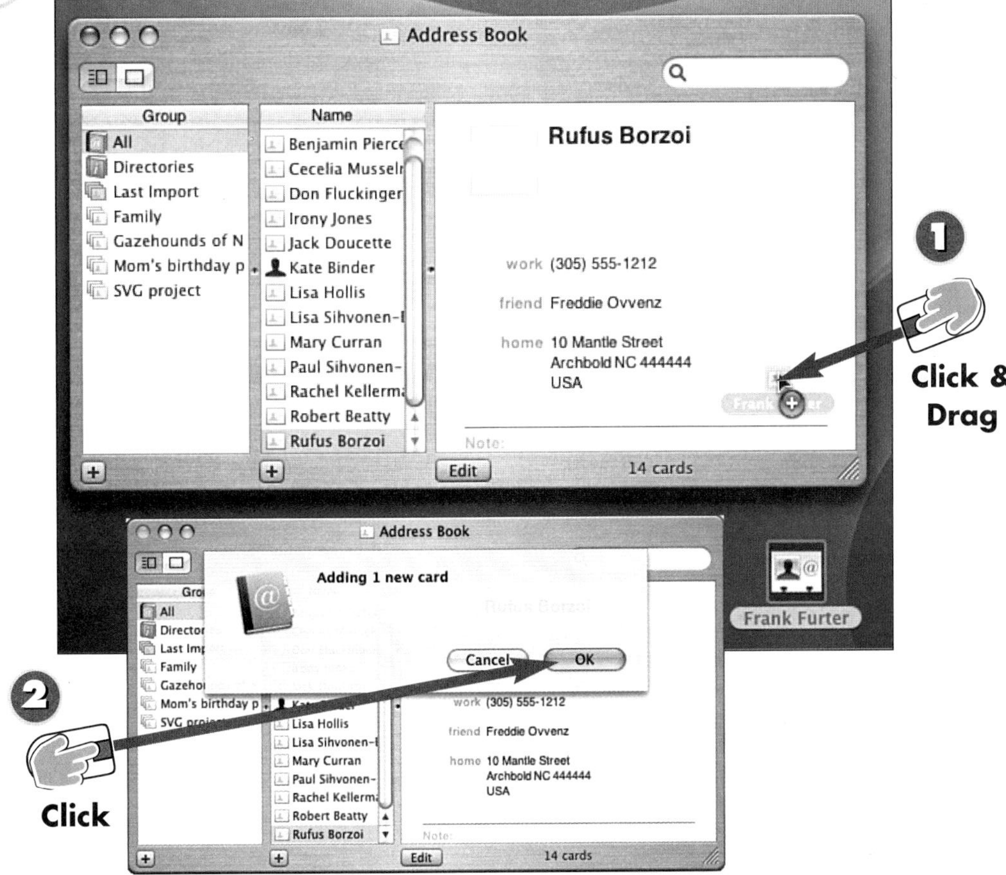

1. Drag the vCard file from the desktop into the Address Book window.

2. Click **OK** in the confirmation dialog box.

INTRODUCTION

Getting vCards into the Address Book is just as easy as getting them out of the Address Book. When you receive a vCard attached to an email as a sort of electronic business card, you need to locate the file in your attachments folder—you'll recognize it because of its **.vcf** filename extension.

HINT

The Case of the Missing Attachment

vCard files typically end up in your email attachments folder—the location and name can vary depending on which email program you use. To get at these files easily, try clicking their names or icons in the email window and dragging them onto the desktop.

Mapping a Contact's Address

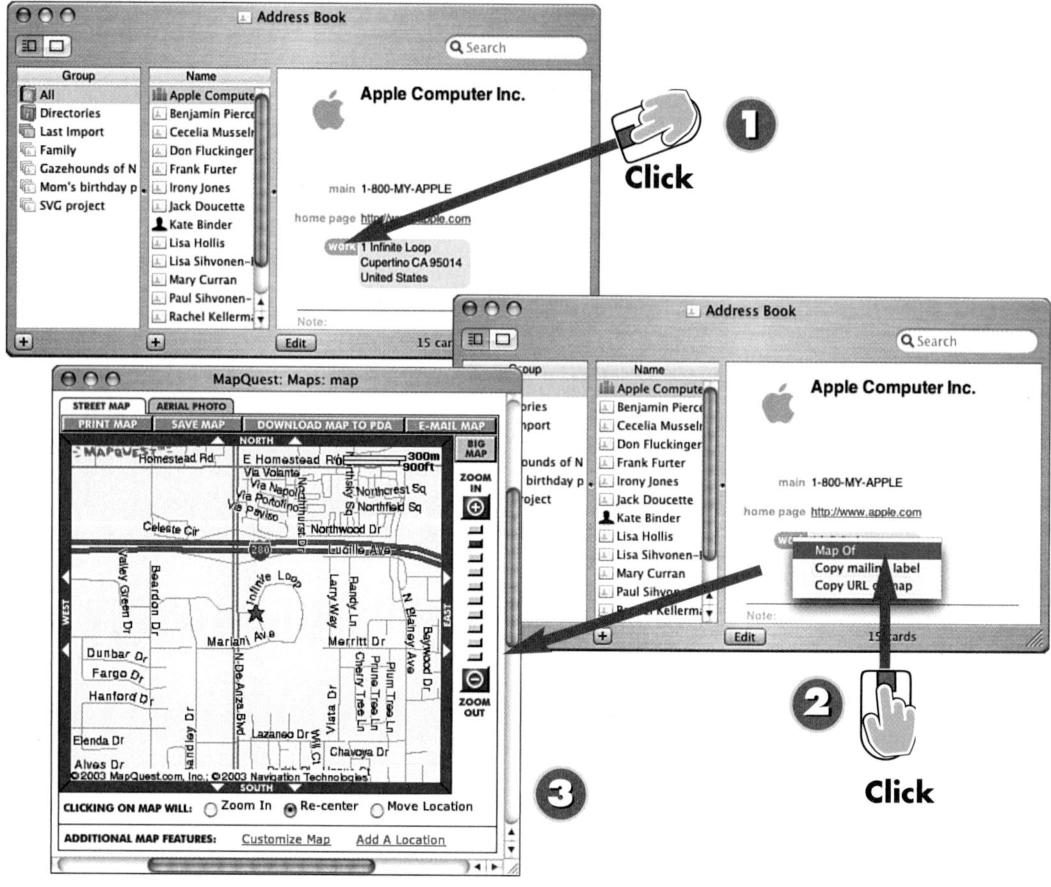

1. Click the address label next to the address to display a pop-up menu.
2. Click **Map Of**.
3. The map is displayed in your Web browser.

INTRODUCTION

If you have an instant-on or constant Internet connection, you're going to love this Address Book feature. You can view a map (and from there, driving directions) for an address in your contact list. It all starts with a simple click to a pop-up menu. Just remember, it won't work if you're not online.

HINT

Just the URL, Please

If you want to pass a map along to a friend, rather than just use it yourself, take advantage of another choice in the address pop-up menu: Copy URL of Map. After you choose this command, click in any text document or email window and press Cmd-V to paste the map's URL so the reader can click it to see the map.

Adding a To-Do in iCal

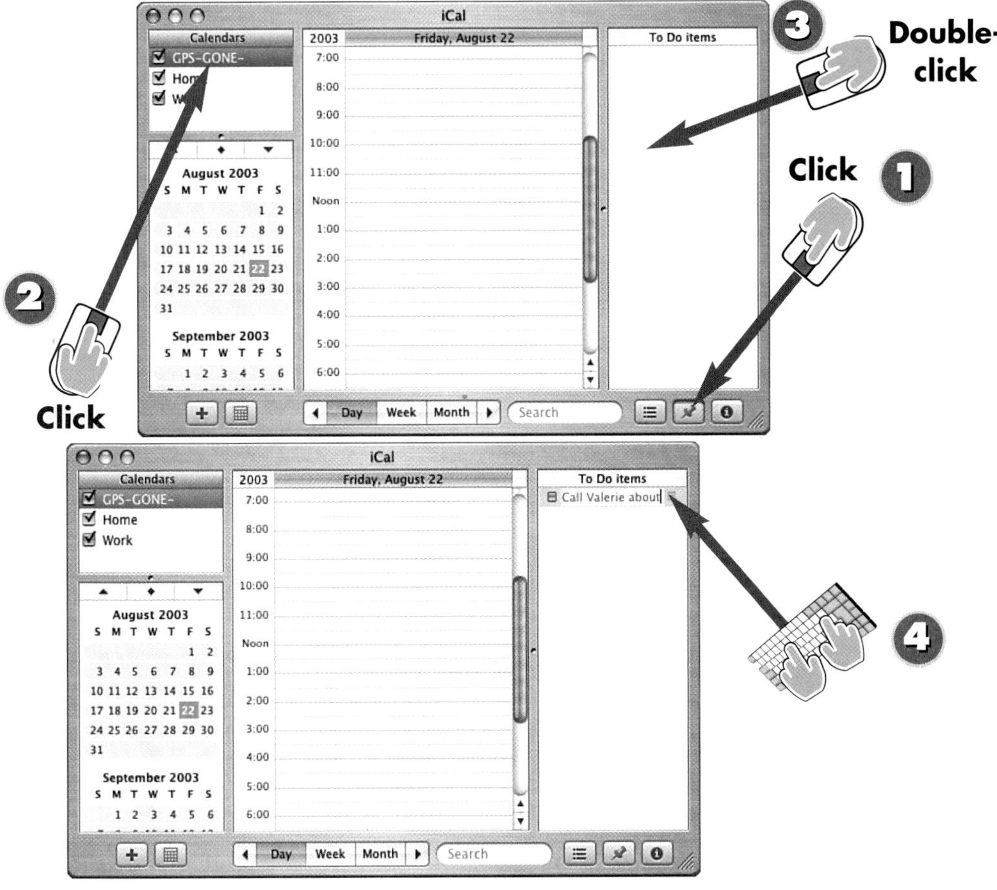

1. Click the **Show/Hide To-Do List** button to display to-do items to the right of the calendar.
2. Click the calendar to which you want to add the to-do item.
3. Double-click in the blank space in the **To Do items** area.
4. Enter the to-do text.

INTRODUCTION

Using a calendar to keep track of events is very important (turn to the next task to see how it works in iCal), but for many people, tracking a to-do list is an even more vital function. In iCal, you can assign each to-do item to a specific calendar, so you can distinguish among work, home, and hobby- or club-related tasks.

TIP

Making To-Do Items Disappear

Choose **iCal**, **Preferences** to change how long items stay on your calendar after they're completed and to determine how to-do items are sorted: by priority, by due date, or alphabetically.

Adding an Appointment in iCal

1 Click

2 Click

3 Click & Drag

4

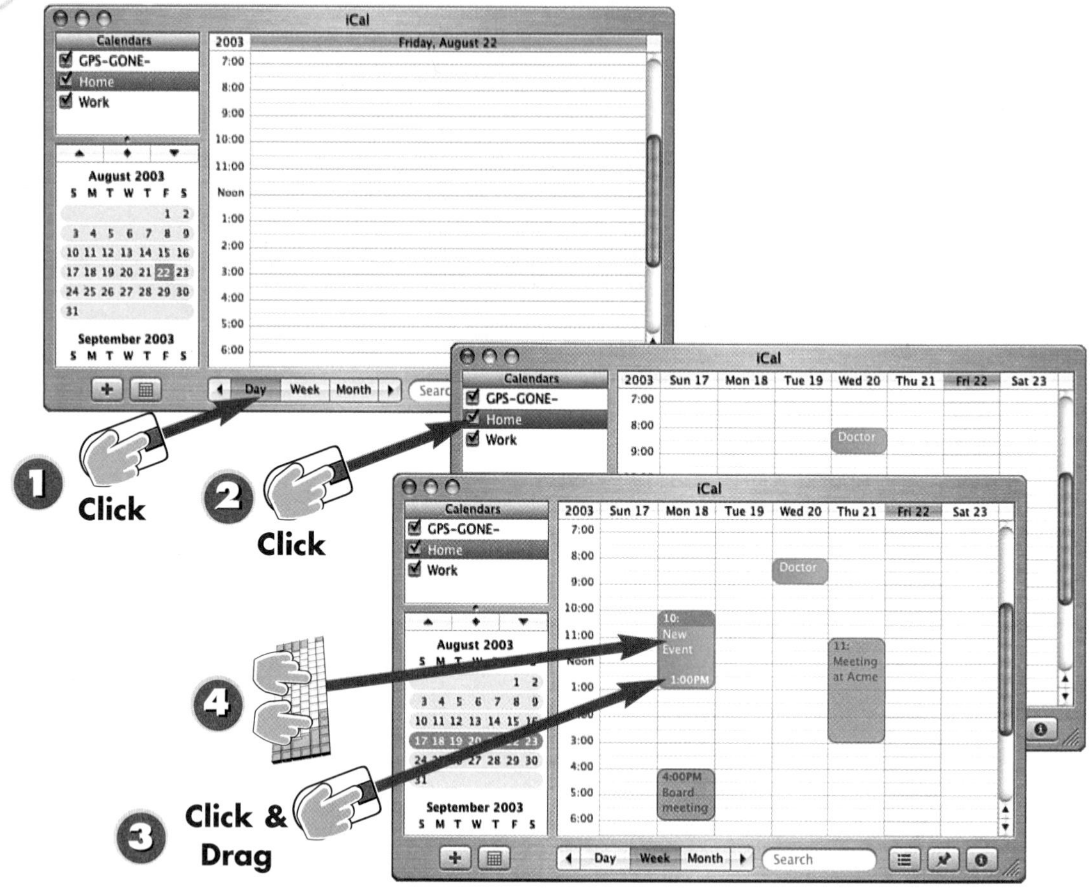

1. Click the **Day** or **Week** button to switch to Day or Week view.

2. Click the calendar to which you want to add the appointment.

3. Click and drag on the hour grid for the day of the appointment to define the time the appointment will last.

4. Type in the appointment text.

INTRODUCTION

iCal is easy to use and compact, but don't underestimate it. This little calendar program has a surprising amount of power. Its primary purpose, of course, is keeping track of your appointments. Adding new ones couldn't be simpler, and reading iCal's neatly color-coded calendar is as easy as it gets.

TIP

Filling in the Details

To refine your appointment entry, click the **Show Info** button at the bottom-right corner of the iCal window. Enter a location, add an alarm notification, set the appointment to repeat regularly, and more. You can also change the event's calendar here.

Switching Calendar Views in iCal

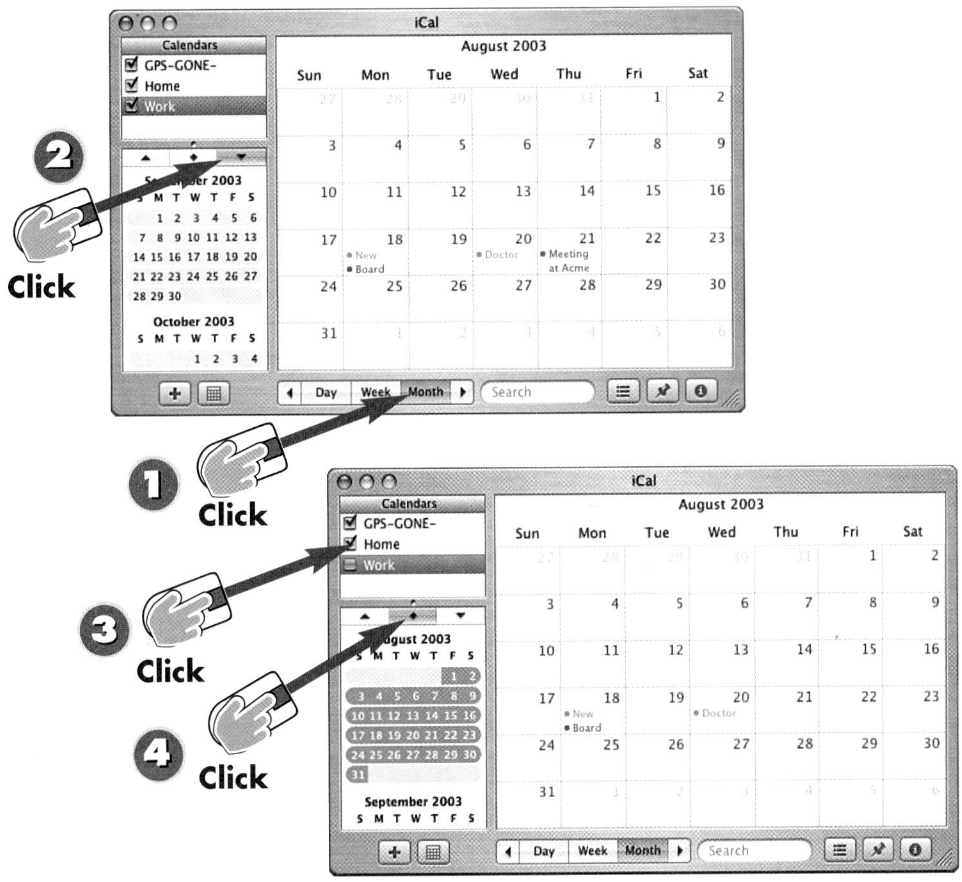

1. Click the **Day**, **Week**, or **Month** button at the bottom of the iCal window to switch views.
2. Click the up and down arrows to view different mini-months at the left side of the iCal window.
3. Click the check box next to each calendar to show or hide its appointments and to-do items.
4. Click the diamond button to return to today.

INTRODUCTION

Whether you want to zero in on each hour of the day or back off and take in a month at a time, iCal can accommodate you. You can view your calendar by the day, week, or month. Meanwhile, mini-months off to the side enable you to keep track of the months surrounding today's date.

TIP

Customizing Day and Week Views

Choose **iCal**, **Preferences** to set the number of days displayed in Week view and choose on which day the week should start. You can also choose how many hours are shown in Day view and set start and end times for each day.

Setting Up an Alarm in iCal

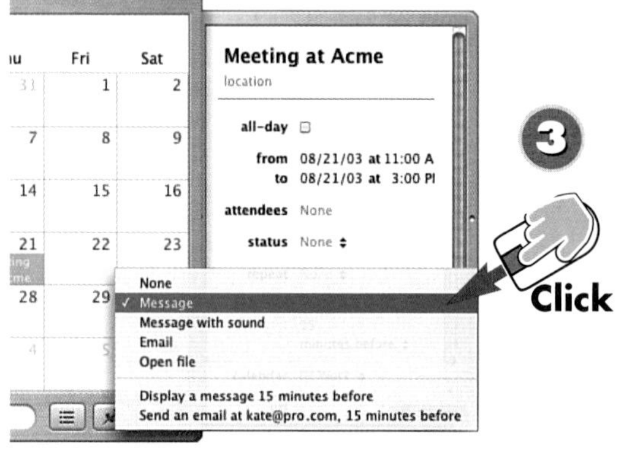

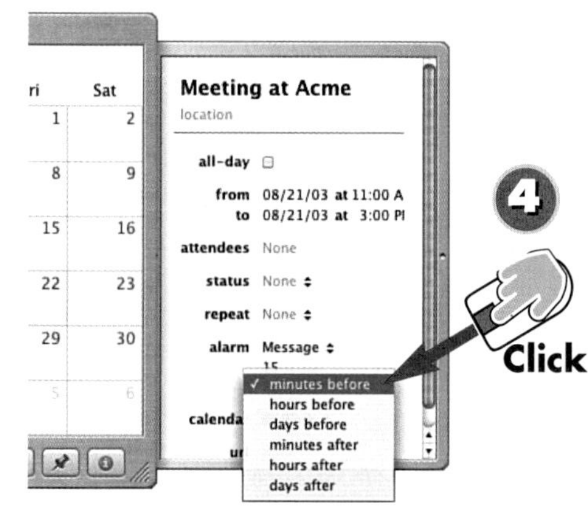

1. Click the appointment to which you want to add an alarm.

2. Click the **Show Info** button.

3. Click next to **Alarm** and choose an alarm type; then specify a sound, a file, or an email address to use, if necessary.

4. Set the time for the alarm to appear.

End

INTRODUCTION

If you want to be reminded before an appointment, you can set up an alarm that will get your attention to let you know the appointment is coming up. iCal alarms take several forms: displaying a dialog box, displaying a dialog box and playing a sound, sending an email, or opening a specified file.

TIP

Hitting the Snooze Button
iCal alarms do have a snooze button—click the small button with the circular arrow in the alarm dialog box and choose a time interval to snooze the alarm. You can snooze an alarm for as little as a minute, a couple of hours, or a day.

HINT

The Missing Drawer
If your iCal window is maximized so it takes up the entire screen, you can't see the Info drawer when it pops out. Reduce the size of the window and move it to the left to see the Info drawer on the right.

Inviting Contacts to Events in iCal

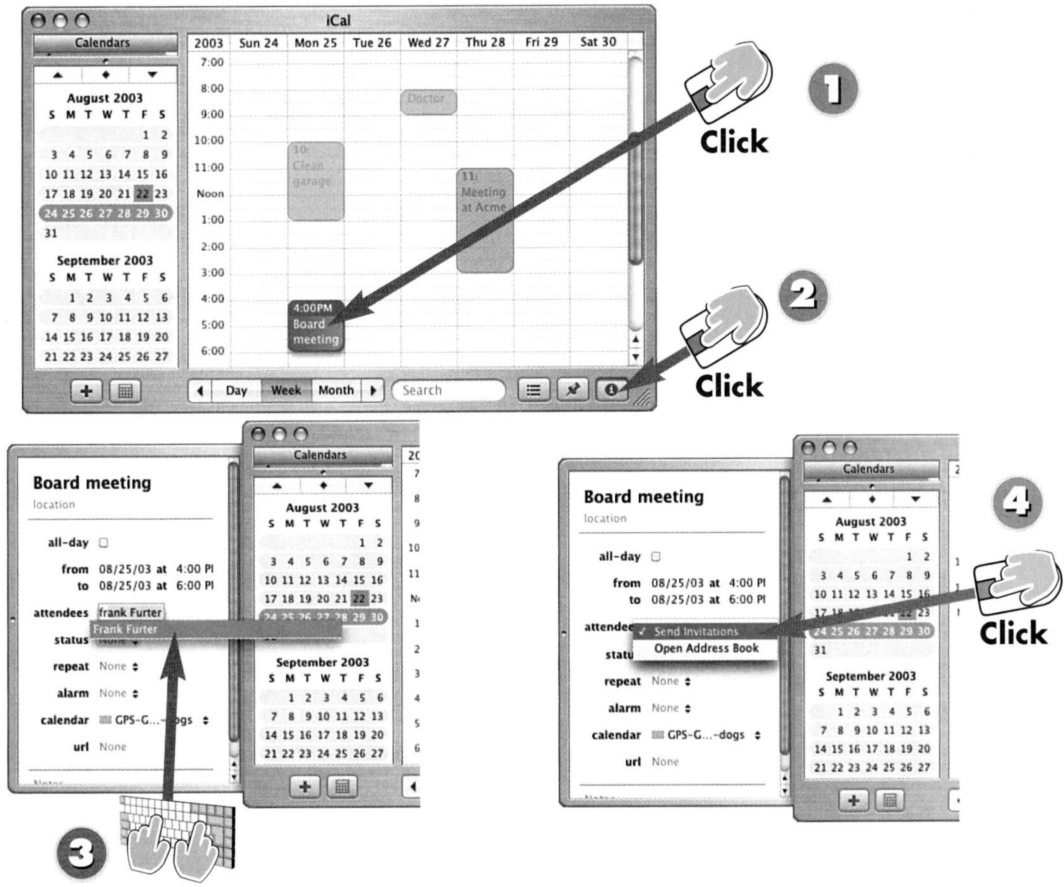

1. Click the appointment to which you want to invite others.
2. Click the **Show Info** button.
3. Click next to **attendees** and type the names of the people you want to invite; iCal fills the names and email addresses in from the Address Book.
4. Choose **Send Invitations** from the **attendees** pop-up menu.

INTRODUCTION

Don't get too excited about this feature; it only works if you are using Apple's Mail for your email program, and you must have the email addresses of the contacts you want to invite. But if you do meet these two requirements, you can use this feature to let your contacts know about an event you've scheduled.

TIP

Getting People in the Door

Another way to add people to the attendees list for an event is to choose **Window, Show People** and drag names from the list to the event's listing in the calendar.

HINT

Separate Names

To invite more than one person to an event, type a comma after each name before you type the next name. Otherwise, iCal isn't sure where one name ends and the next begins.

Searching Calendars in iCal

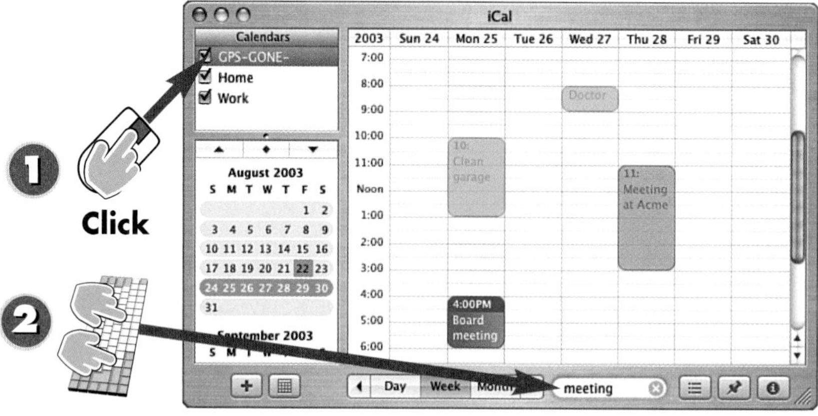

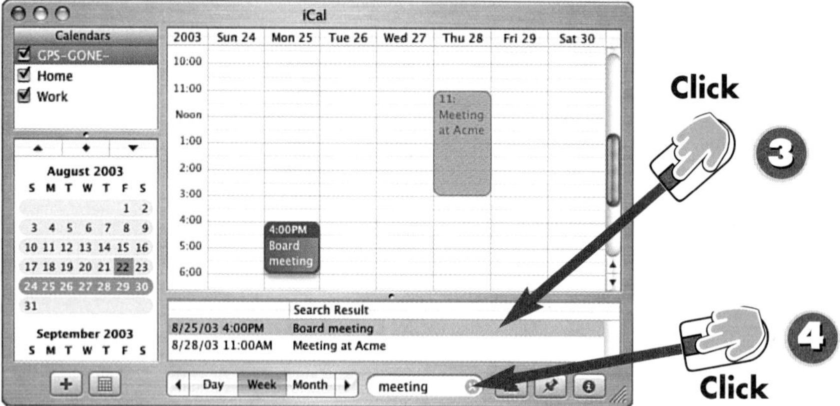

1. Click the check boxes next to the calendars you want to search.
2. Type the text you want to search for in the **search** field.
3. Click an event or to-do in the **Search Result** list to go to it.
4. To clear the search field, click the **X**.

INTRODUCTION

You know you put Aunt Blanche's birthday in iCal, but you can't even remember the month, much less the day. Never fear: iCal will find the date for you. Just search for "Blanche," and your trusty calendar will offer you a list of every event containing her name, including that elusive birthday.

TIP

Searching On-the-Fly

Click **Show/Hide Search Results** in the lower-right corner of the iCal window to see the current results, which, if you haven't entered a search term, is all your entries. Then enter search terms and watch the results filter down to what you're looking for.

Subscribing to an iCal Calendar

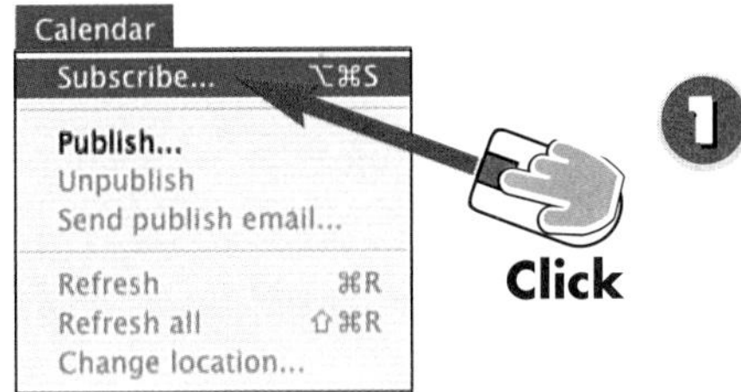

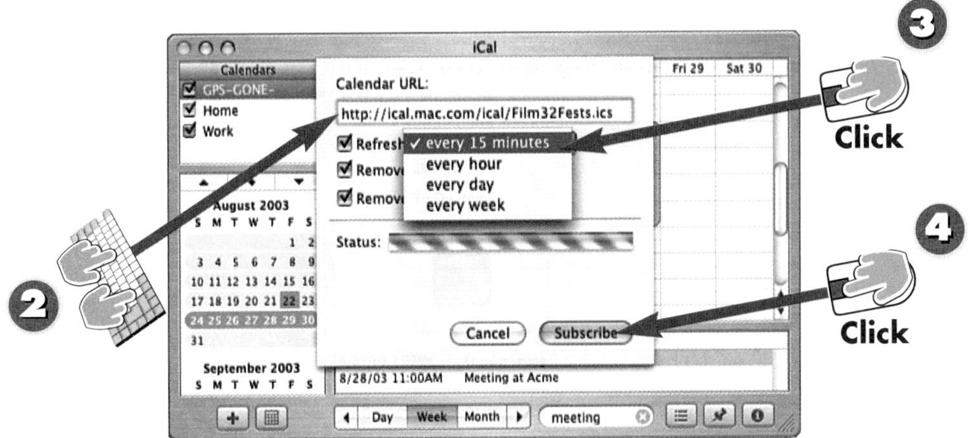

1. Choose **Calendar**, **Subscribe**.
2. Enter the URL for the calendar to which you want to subscribe. The calendar's owner provides this information.
3. Choose a frequency in the **Refresh** pop-up menu for iCal to check the calendar for changes.
4. Click **Subscribe**.

INTRODUCTION

Perhaps iCal's coolest feature is its capability to share calendars online. This means you can subscribe to calendars created by other people, whether of their day-to-day events (your spouse's schedule, perhaps) or of special events (your favorite football team's season schedule, maybe).

HINT

Where to Find Calendars
Apple has compiled a list of carefully selected public iCal calendars on its Web site (**www.apple.com/ical/library/**). Another great site for finding public calendars is iCalShare.com (**www.icalshare.com**).

Publishing an iCal Calendar

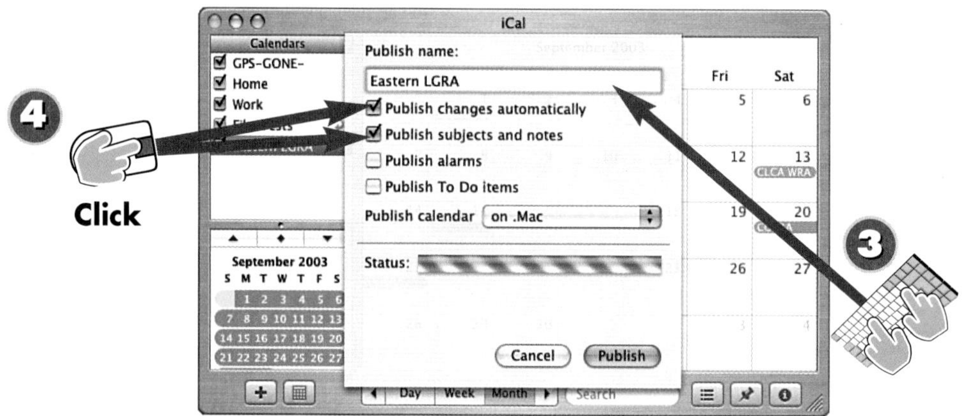

1. Click the calendar you want to publish.
2. Choose **Calendar**, **Publish**.
3. Type a name for the published calendar.
4. Click the check boxes to publish changes automatically and to publish both the title and notes for an event (rather than just its title).

INTRODUCTION

What can you publish? Well, you can choose to share your home or work calendar with your family or colleagues. Or you might decide to be the keeper of the birthdays among your friends and publish a calendar showing everyone's special days. You can use your .Mac account or a free Web service to publish calendars, as you prefer.

HINT

Automatic Updates or Not?

Publishing calendar changes automatically requires a constant online connection. Don't choose this option if you use a dial-up account because you might find your computer dialing in unexpectedly.

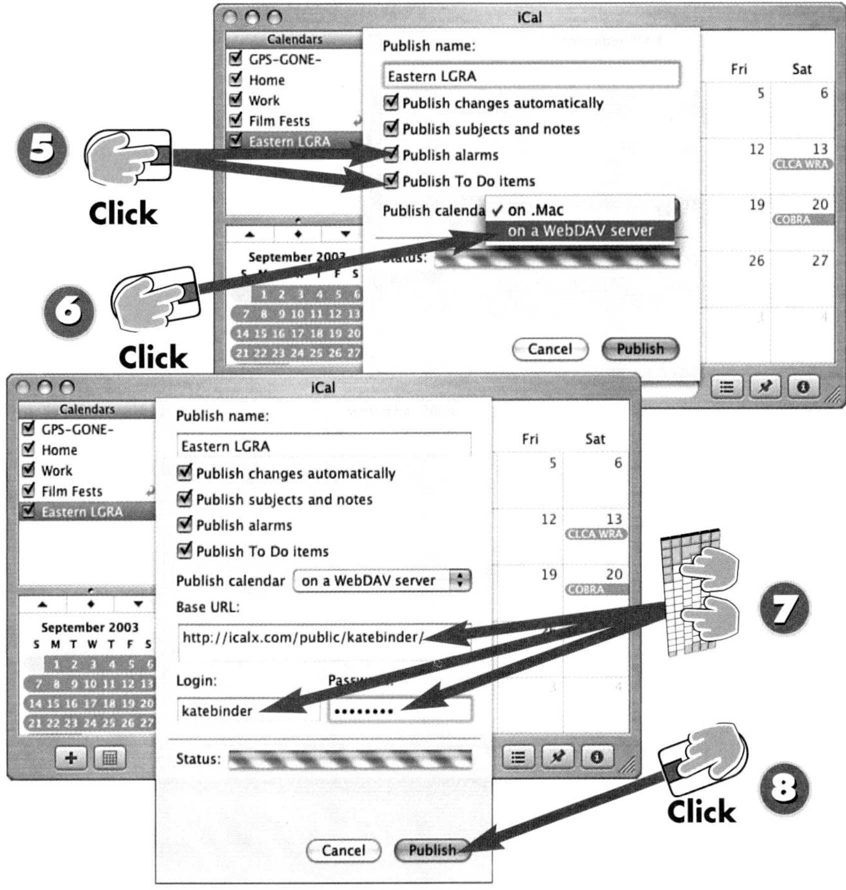

5. Click the check boxes to publish alarms and to-do items.

6. Choose an option from the **Publish Calendar** pop-up menu for where you're publishing the calendar: using .Mac or using an independent server.

7. If you're using a WebDAV server, enter its URL and your login name and password.

8. Click **Publish**.

HINT

Becoming a Publisher

If you want to publish your own calendars but don't have a .Mac account, go to iCalExchange.com (**icalexchange.com**). It offers free access to the WebDAV servers you need to publish calendars.

TIP

Changing Your Mind

If you decide to stop publishing a calendar, click its name in the **Calendars** list, choose **Calendar**, **Unpublish**. iCal warns you that people will no longer be able to subscribe to the calendar; just click **Unpublish** to take your calendar offline.

Printing an iCal Calendar

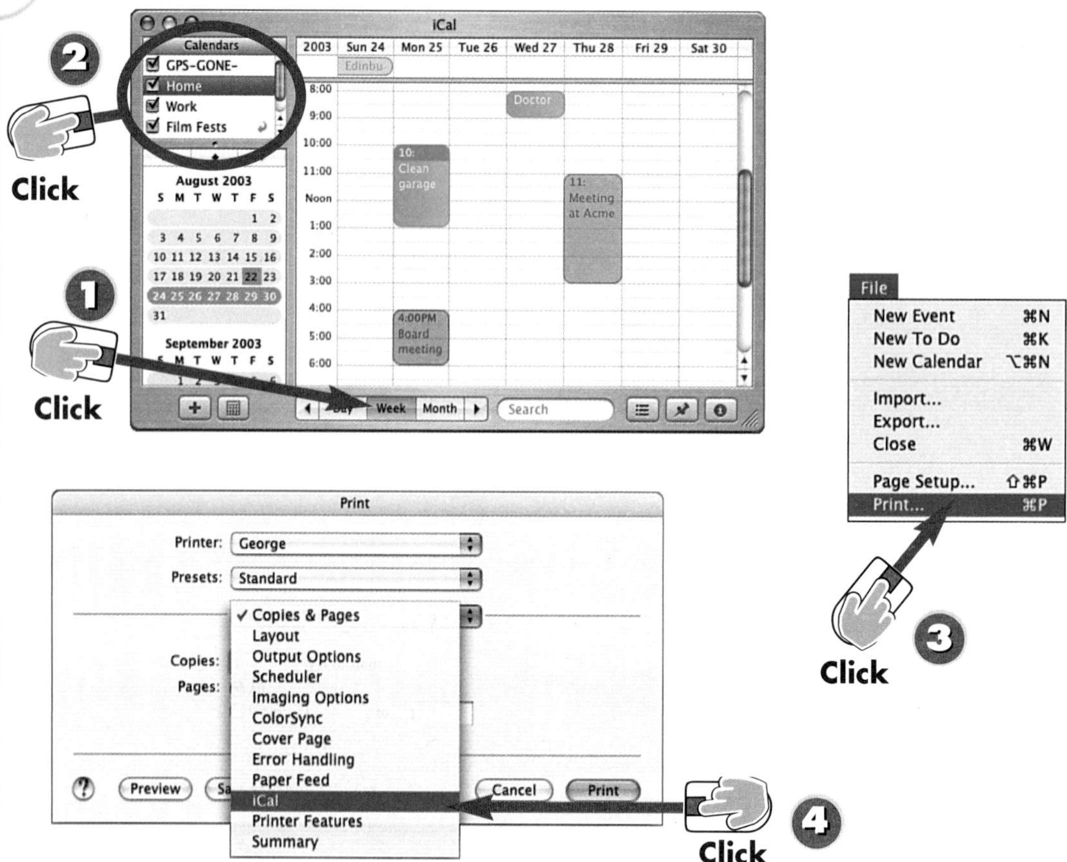

1. Click the **Day**, **Week**, or **Month** button to choose which view you want to print.
2. Click the check boxes to view the calendar(s) you want to print.
3. Choose **File**, **Print**.
4. Choose **iCal** from the pop-up menu to change the iCal-specific settings.

INTRODUCTION

There are always going to be times when we need hard copy, for a variety of reasons. For example, maybe you want to print a club calendar as a handout for your next meeting. Or maybe you want to send your vacation schedule to your parents, but they don't have a computer. Here's how to print daily, weekly, or monthly calendars.

TIP

Hour by Hour
When you're printing a calendar, you can choose the time range you want included in the printout. So, if you never have events scheduled between, say, midnight and 5 a.m., you can leave those hours off your calendar.

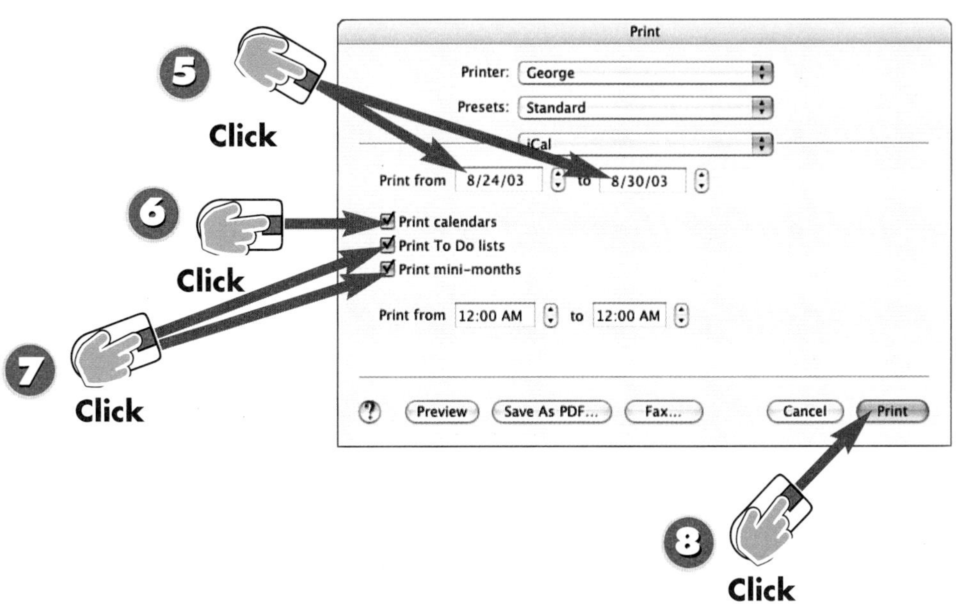

5. Set the start and end dates for the time range you want to print.

6. Click the **Print calendars** check box to list the names of the included calendars.

7. Click the **Print To Do lists** check box to include to-do items and the **Print mini-months** check box to include small month views.

8. Click **Print**.

TIP

Picking Your Colors

If you're printing a calendar on a color printer, you might want to change the color associated with the calendar you're printing. Click its name in the **Calendars** list and click the **Show Info** button to choose a new color from the pop-up menu.

TIP

Make It Easy on Your Readers

When you're printing multiple calendars, events have the same color-coding they have in the iCal window. Be sure to click the **Print calendars** check box to provide a color key that that readers can use to figure out to which calendar each event belongs.

Syncing a PDA, an iPod, or a Phone with Your Mac

Start

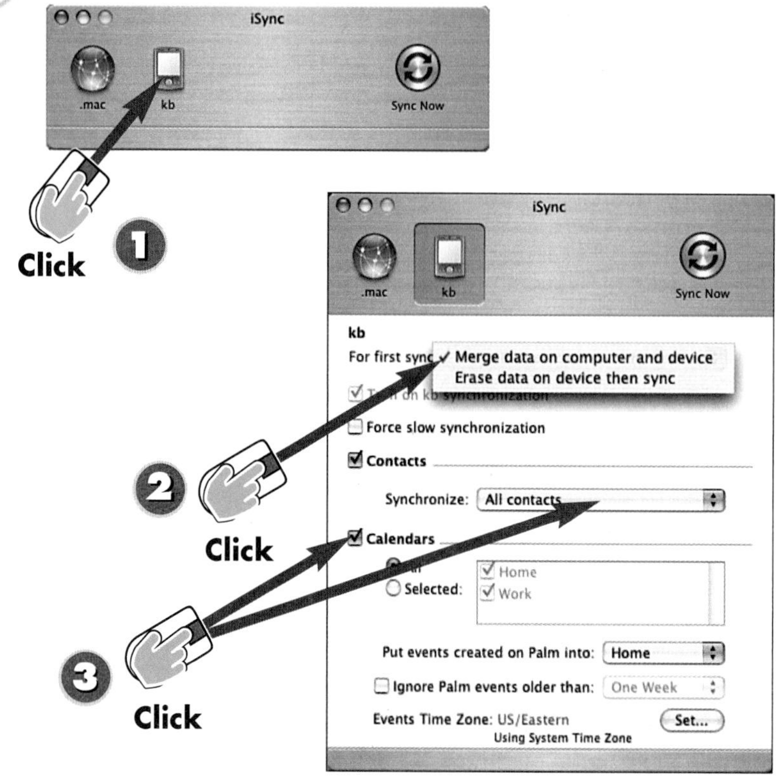

1. Start up iSync (located in the Applications folder) and click the icon for the device you want to sync.
2. If this is the first time you're syncing, click each device icon and choose an option from the **For first sync** pop-up menu.
3. Click the **Contacts** check box to include contacts in the sync, and choose which groups to include from the **Synchronize** pop-up menu.

INTRODUCTION

If you use a Palm or another device that can interact with your Mac, you're definitely going to want to sync that device with iCal and Address Book. The procedure is a bit different for Palms and for devices other than Palms, but in either case it takes only a few steps. Here's how to get started.

TIP

Getting Hooked Up with iSync

You can download iSync at **www.apple.com/isync/**. To add a device to iSync, hook it up to your Mac and start iSync. Choose **Devices**, **Add Device**. Double-click the new device when it appears in the Add Device window.

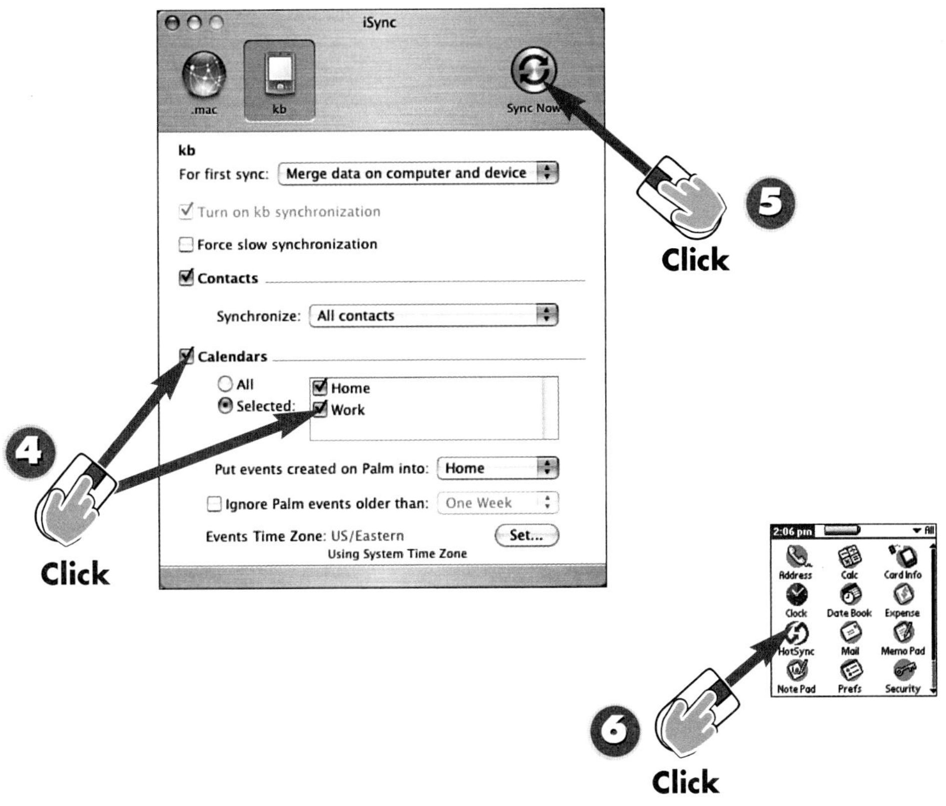

4. Click the **Calendars** check box to include calendars in the sync, and choose which calendars to include.
5. To sync all devices other than a Palm device, click **Sync Now** to begin the sync process.
6. To sync all devices, including a Palm PDA, start a HotSync by pushing the Palm's HotSync button.

TIP

When Little Changes Add Up

If more than 5% of your data is going to be modified by the sync process, iSync lets you know what the percentage of change is and offers you the option of canceling the sync. Choose **iSync, Preferences** to change the percentage that triggers this warning.

Finding Almost Anything with Sherlock

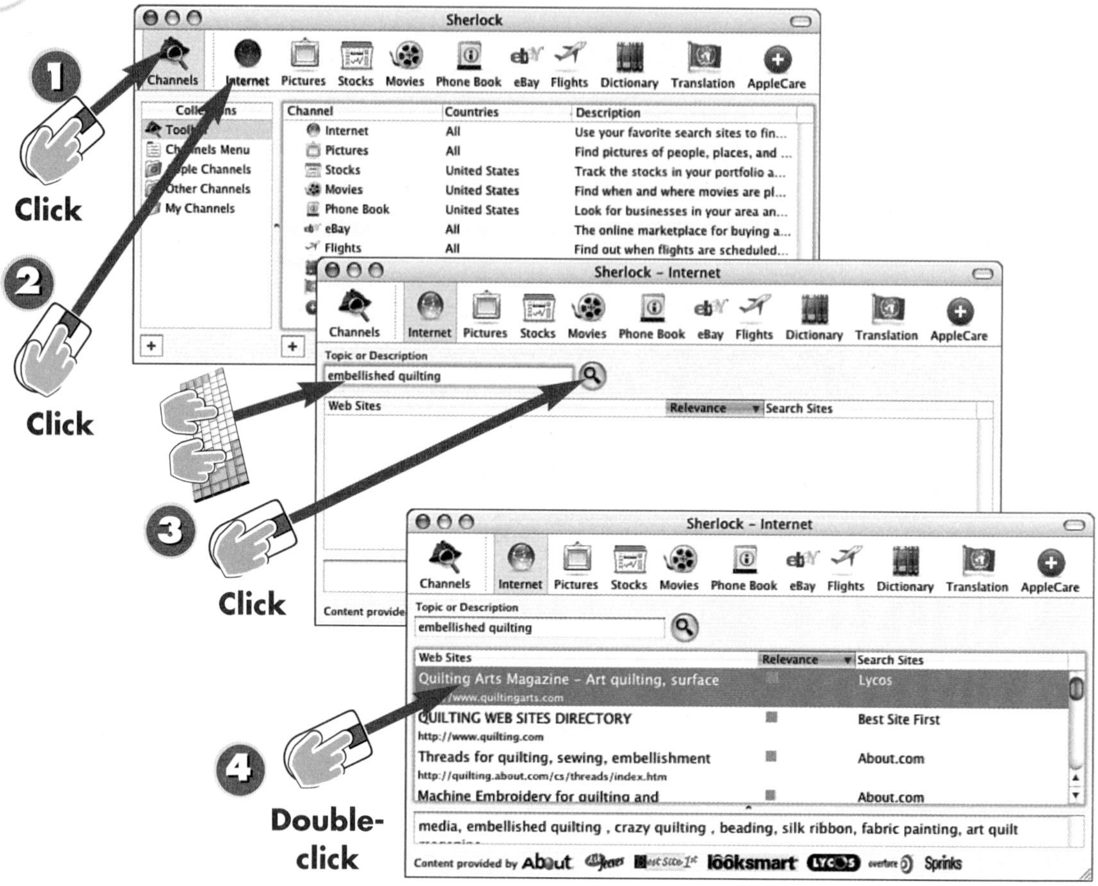

1 Click the **Channels** button to show all; then click the channel you want to use.

2 To search for Web sites, click **Internet**.

3 Type the search terms in the **Topic or Description** field; then click the **Search** button.

4 To go to one of the Web sites shown, double-click its name in the search results list.

INTRODUCTION

Sherlock is a shortcut to some of the most-visited places on the Web. You can use it to look up everything from phone numbers to auction listings on eBay, all without even starting your Web browser. After you've found what you want, a click or two in Sherlock takes you right to that location on the Web.

TIP

Worth the Time?

When you click a Web site name in Sherlock's search results, you see a description of that Web site at the bottom of the Sherlock window. You can use this information to help you decide whether the site is worth visiting.

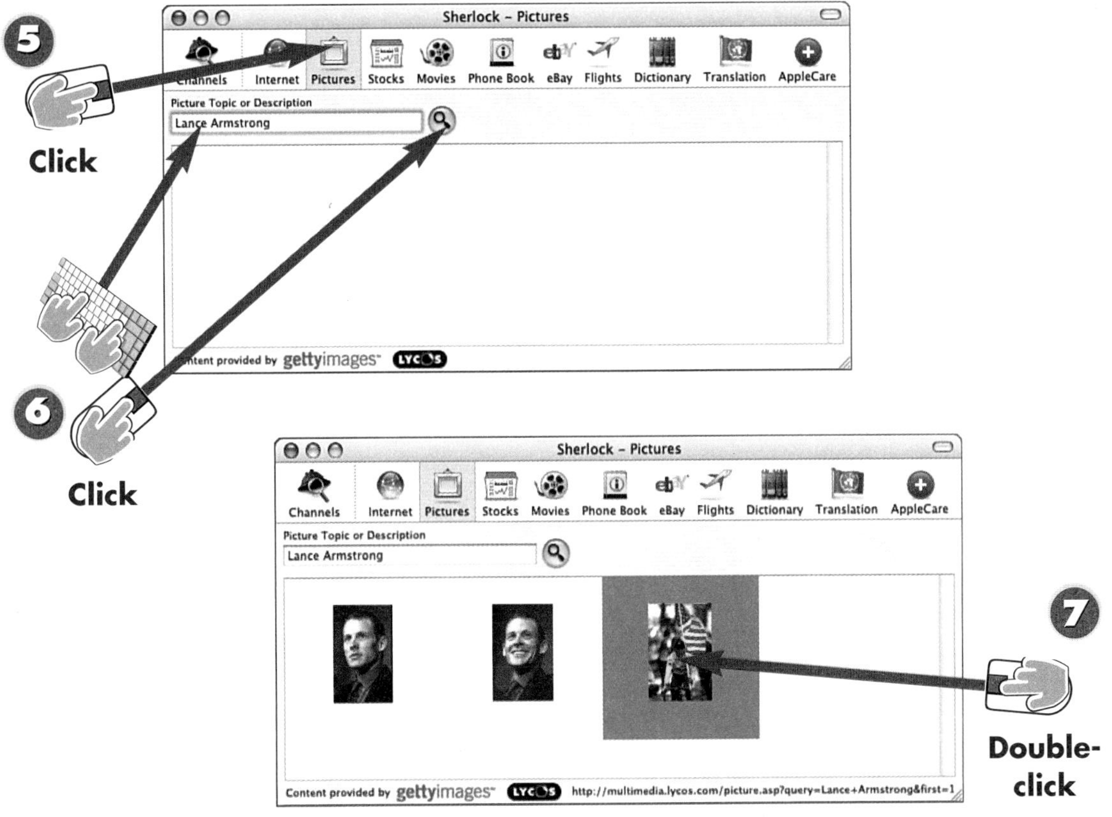

5 To search the Web for images, click **Pictures**.

6 Enter the search terms in the **Picture Topic or Description** field, and then click the **Search** button.

7 To see one of the images in its original context on the Web, double-click its thumbnail.

See next page

HINT

It's the Law
Remember that putting a picture on the Web doesn't mean its creator has relinquished ownership. Respect other people's copyright—don't redistribute their images without permission.

HINT

Good Will Searching
If you don't get enough results when you do a search, remove or change your search terms. If you get too many results and want to narrow them down, add more search terms to get a more specific set of results.

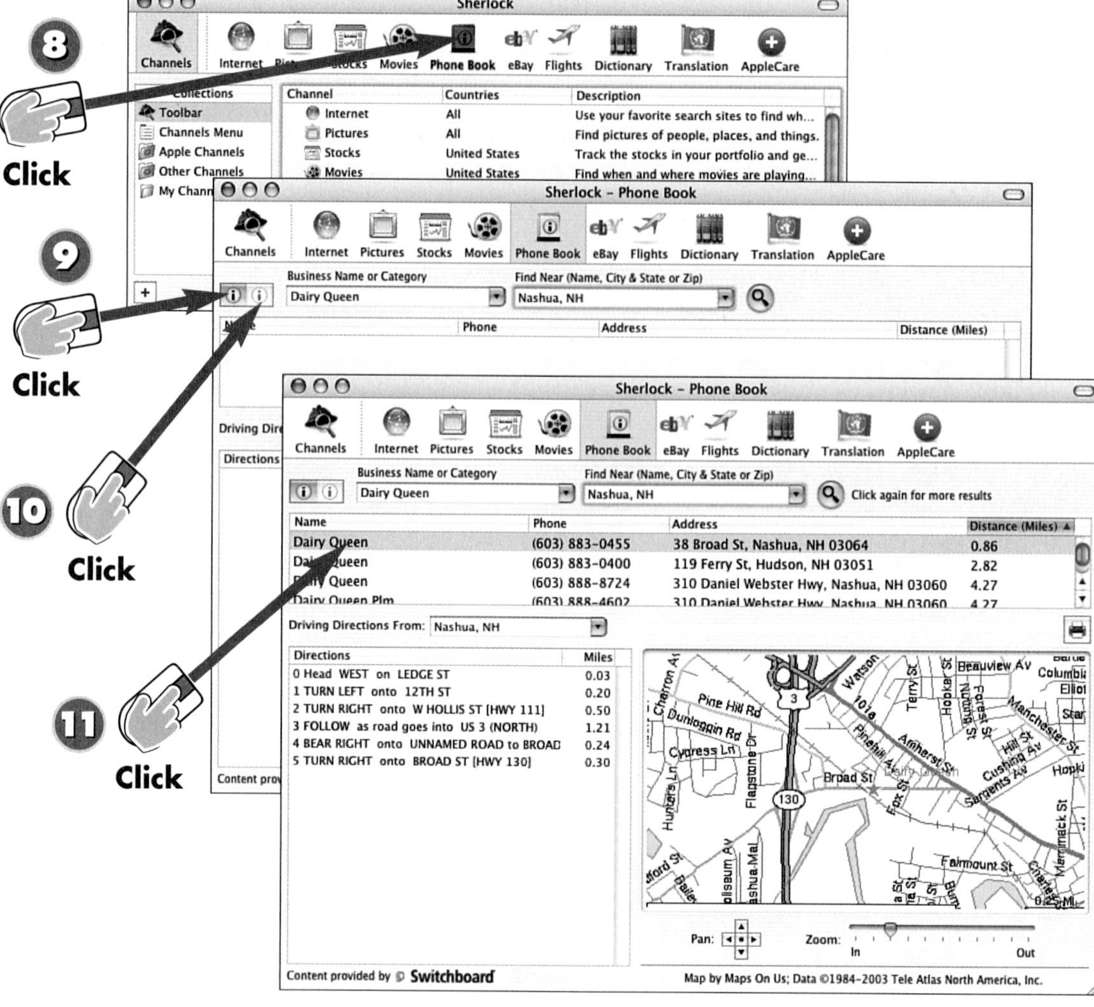

8. To search phone listings, click **Phone Book**.

9. Click the white **Info** button to search for a person; then enter the person's name and click the **Search** button.

10. Click the yellow **Info** button to search for a business; then enter the business's name or a business category and click the **Search** button.

11. Click an entry in the search results list to see a map and driving directions.

INTRODUCTION

Sherlock's talents are especially useful for "quickie" searches. You can look up phone numbers, addresses, word definitions, and more at various Web sites, but with Sherlock all that information is in one place and getting at it is much quicker.

TIP

Getting There from Here

Driving directions need a starting point. You can type a city and a state in the **Driving Directions From** field or type a name from your Address Book. To get directions from your own house, create an Address Book entry for yourself and enter your own name.

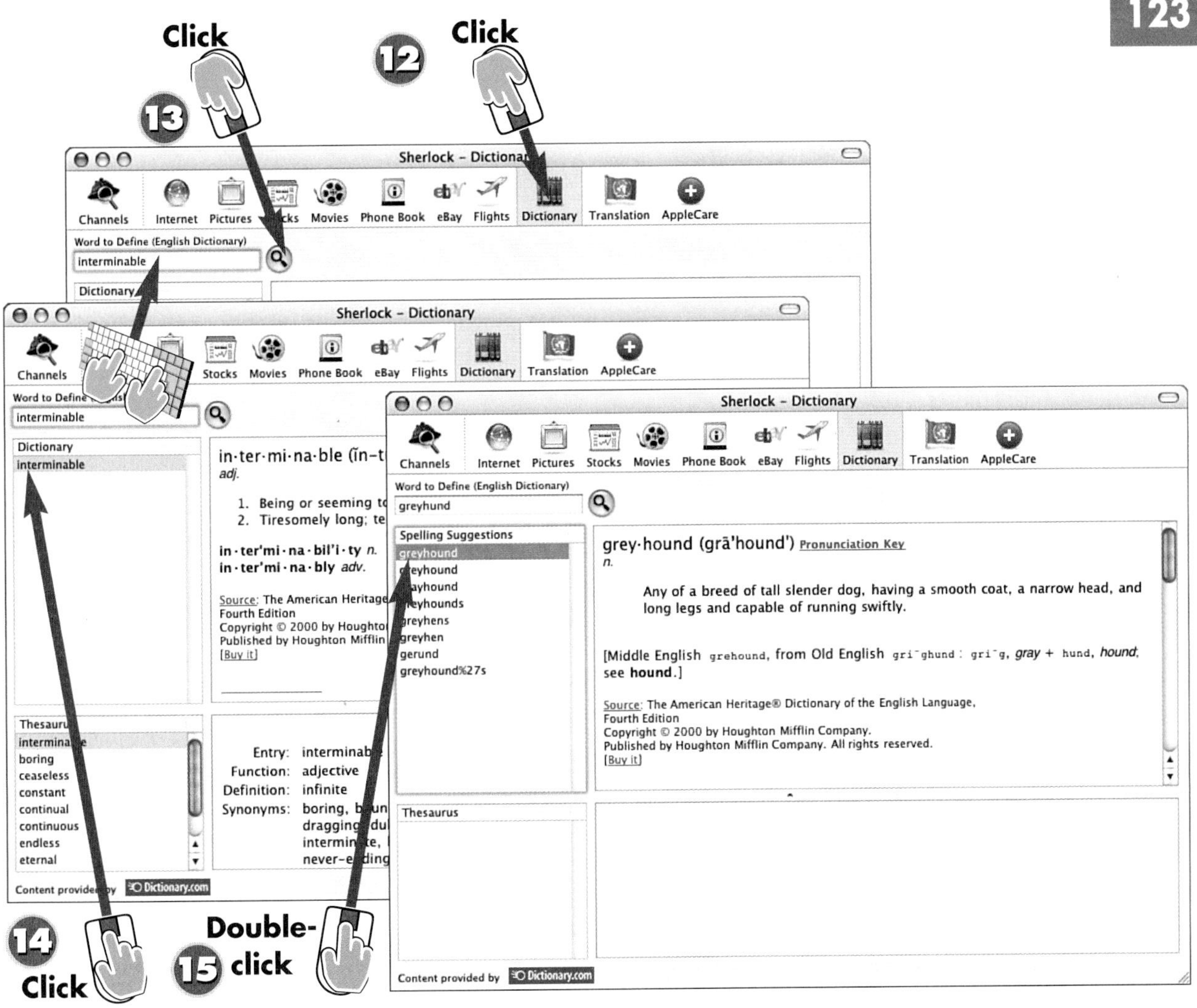

12 To look up a word, click **Dictionary**.

13 Enter the word in the **Word to Define** field, and then click the **Search** button.

14 Click the word in the **Dictionary** or **Thesaurus** area to see its definition or synonyms, respectively.

15 If the word isn't found, double-click one of the alternatives presented in the **Dictionary** area.

HINT

It's All Happening Online

Of course, Sherlock works only when you're online. If you don't have a constant connection to the Internet, remember that searching with Sherlock will trigger a connection attempt on the part of your Mac.

HINT

Finding More Channels

Developers and Mac hobbyists have spent time creating additional channels for Sherlock. You can find one good channel collection at Sherlockers.com (**www.sherlockers.com**). And try a Sherlock Internet search using the keywords "Sherlock channels" to locate more channels.

PART 7

Printing, Faxing, and Scanning

After you've plugged in your printer, fax modem, and scanner, Mac OS X makes them easier to use than ever before. All three functions are now built in to the system, so you don't need to worry about buggy, incompatible software that slows you down when you're trying to get things done. You have lots of options for printing, faxing, and scanning that enable you to get the most from your devices, but if you're in a hurry each function can be accomplished with just a few clicks.

Printing in Mac OS X is as easy as it has ever been, with the option (new in Panther) of using desktop printer icons for quick access to printer features and print queues. You can preview any document before printing it to make sure it looks the way you want it to, and preview documents can be saved as PDFs that you can exchange with others who don't have the software you used to create the document. Faxing happens the same way and in the same place as printing—the Print dialog box—so you can fax any document you can print. And scanning uses your scanner's driver software to determine the device's capabilities, but you can use a small, simple program called Image Capture to get the job done quickly.

Using Printers, Fax Modems, Scanners, and Fonts

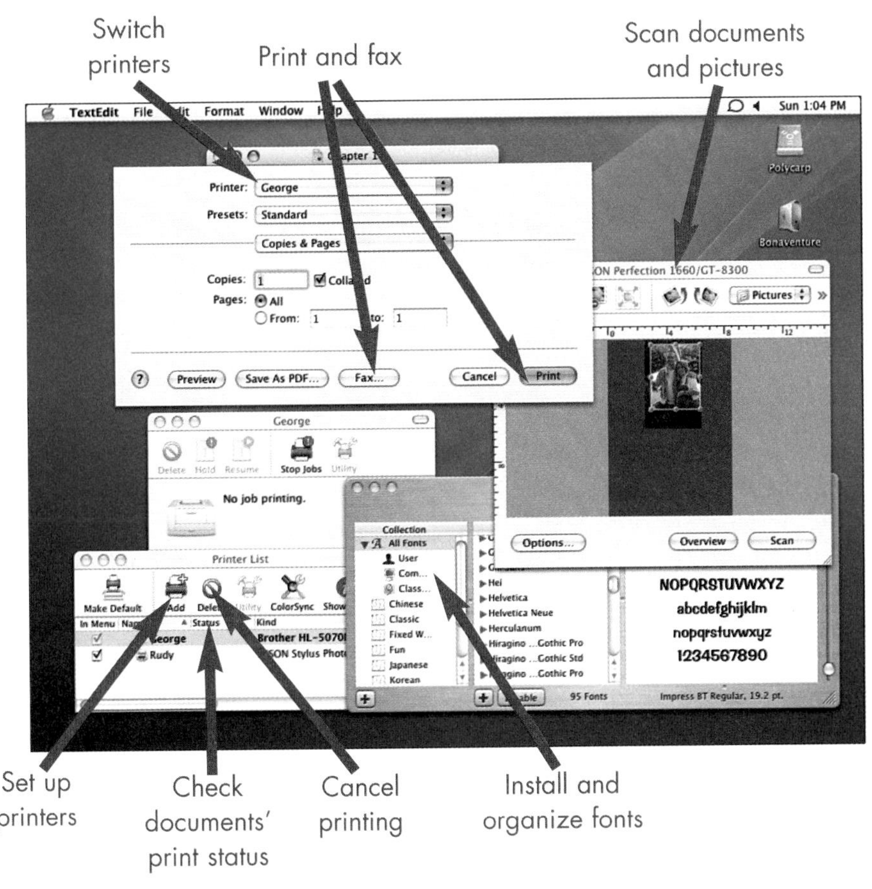

Setting Up a Printer

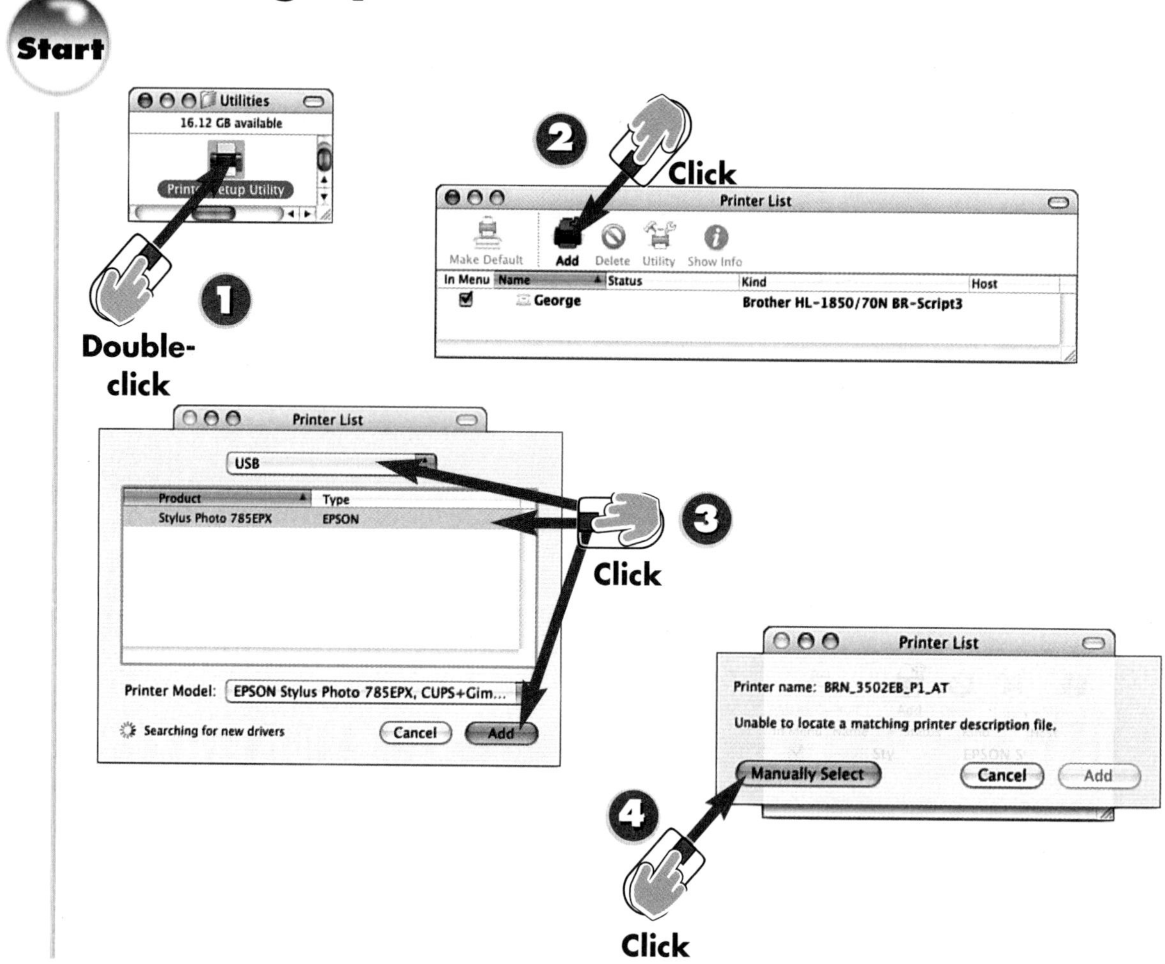

1. Start up **Printer Setup Utility** (in the Utilities folder within the Applications folder).
2. Click the **Add** button on the toolbar.
3. Choose a printer connection type from the pop-up menu at the top of the Add dialog box and choose a printer from the pick list; then click **Add**.
4. If Printer Setup Utility isn't able to figure out which model your printer is, click **Manually Select**.

INTRODUCTION

Before you can print, of course, you have to introduce your Mac to your printer. First, you'll need to know at least one thing about that printer: how it's connected. It might be a USB printer plugged in to the Mac itself, or it could be a network printer. When you get that figured out, the Mac's Printer Setup Utility can go out and find the printer for itself.

HINT

Two for One

If your printer doesn't have its model name and number on the front, check the manual that came with it. Sometimes multiple similar models share a driver, and in that case all the similar models should be listed in the manual.

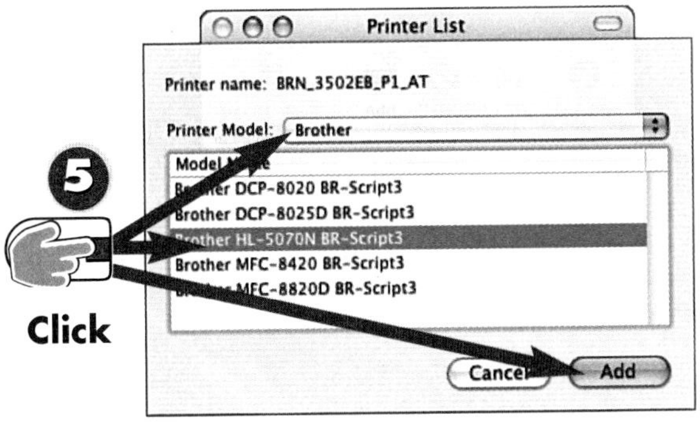

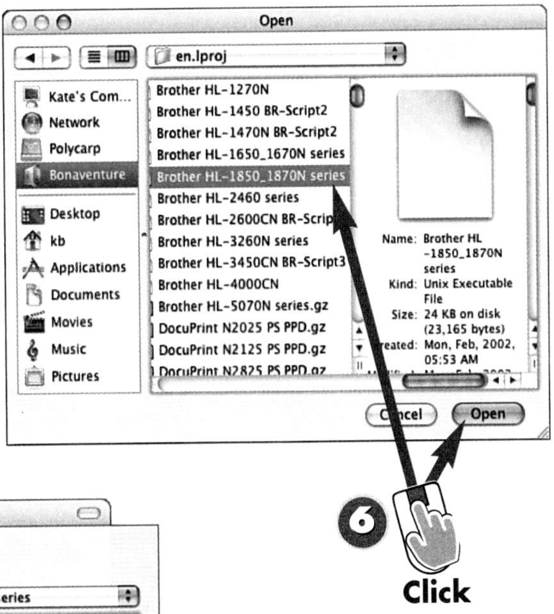

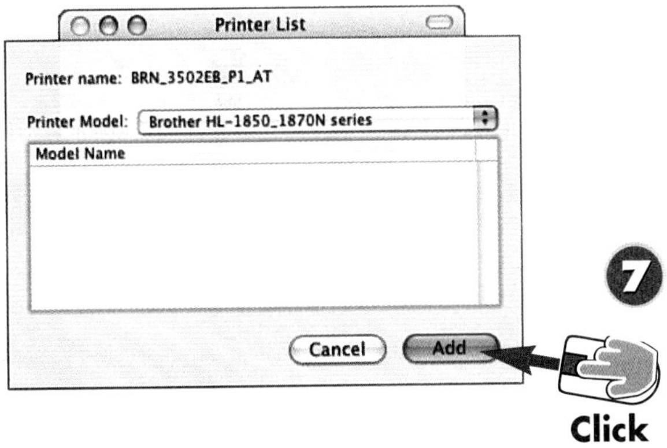

5. Choose a make from the **Printer Model** pop-up menu and a model in the pick list and click **Add**.
6. If you don't see your printer model in the pick list, choose **Other** from the pop-up menu; then navigate to the printer driver that came with your printer and click **Open**.
7. Click **Add**.

TIP

Missing Pieces

To work with your printer, the Mac has to have access to the printer drivers (the software) that came with the printer. If you don't have these, or if they're out of date, visit the printer manufacturer's Web site to download the latest drivers.

HINT

Close Enough

If you don't have the correct printer driver for your printer, you can usually get away with using one that's similar. Just choose the closest model available.

Switching Printers

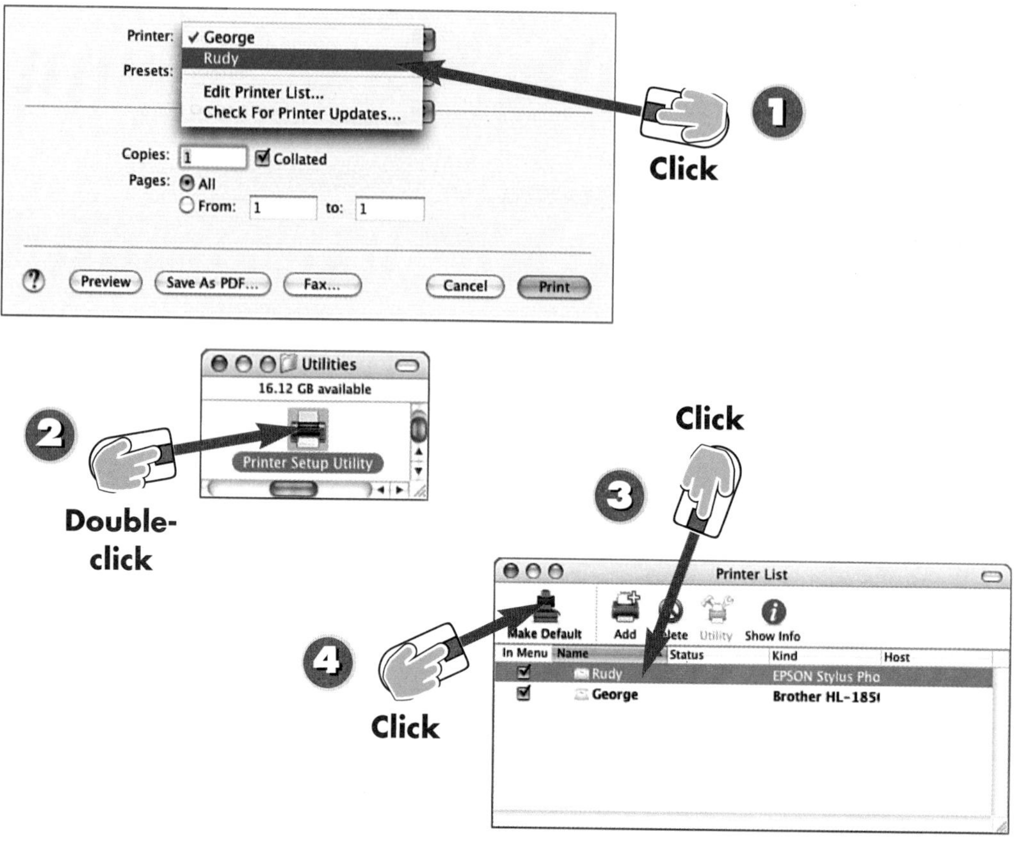

1. To change printers on-the-fly as you prepare to print, choose a different printer from the **Printer** pop-up menu at the top of the Print dialog box.
2. To change default printers ahead of time, double-click the **Printer Setup Utility** to open it.
3. Choose a printer from the pick list.
4. Click the **Make Default** button in the toolbar.

INTRODUCTION

If you have more than one printer, you should make sure you send each document to the right printer. You can choose a printer each time you print, or you can change the default printer to ensure that the next time you click Print the desired printer will be chosen. Start by choosing **File**, **Print** in any program and then follow these steps.

TIP

Keeping Up-to-Date
If you have trouble printing, you might need new drivers to work with your updated software. In the Print dialog box, choose **Check for Printer Updates** from the Printer pop-up menu to search Apple's Web site for updated printer drivers.

HINT

Printing Success
If a friend or family member will be using your computer and you're not confident of that person's ability to select the right printer on-the-fly, set the default printer ahead of time so the right printer is preselected in the Print dialog box.

Viewing Printer Properties

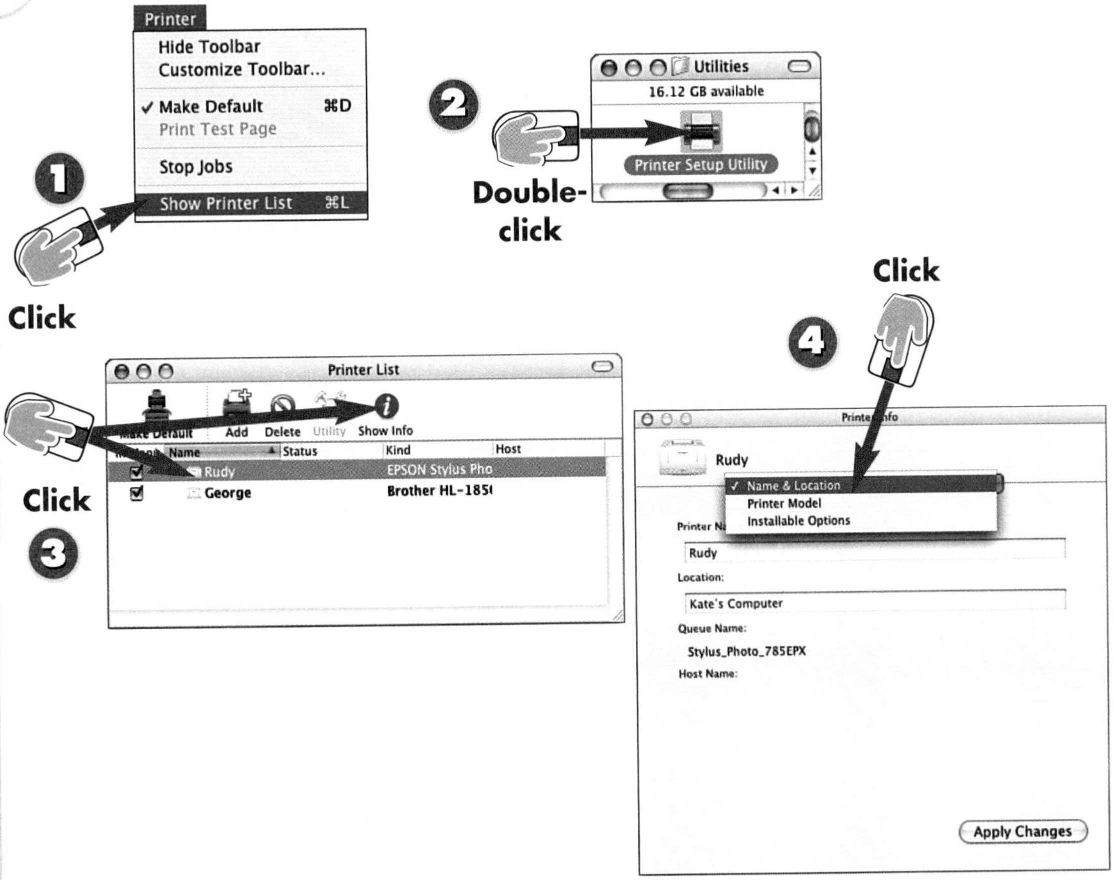

1. If you have a desktop printer icon for your printer, double-click the icon and choose **Printer**, **Show Printer List**.
2. If you don't have a desktop printer icon, double-click **Printer Setup Utility** in the Utilities folder.
3. Click the printer's name in the list and click the **Show Info** button.
4. Use the pop-up menu at the top of the Printer Info window to display different properties and make changes as needed.

INTRODUCTION

Just like any hardware device, each printer has properties that make it unique. Those characteristics include information such as its specs: What resolution can it print at? How much memory does it have? Printer properties also include the printer's name, which you can change to suit yourself.

HINT

What's in a Name?

Keep in mind that you don't have to keep the default printer name. Instead of "EPSON 785EPX," wouldn't it be more fun to call your printer "Rudy"? The name doesn't affect how the printer works, so why not let your imagination rule?

Previewing a Document Before Printing

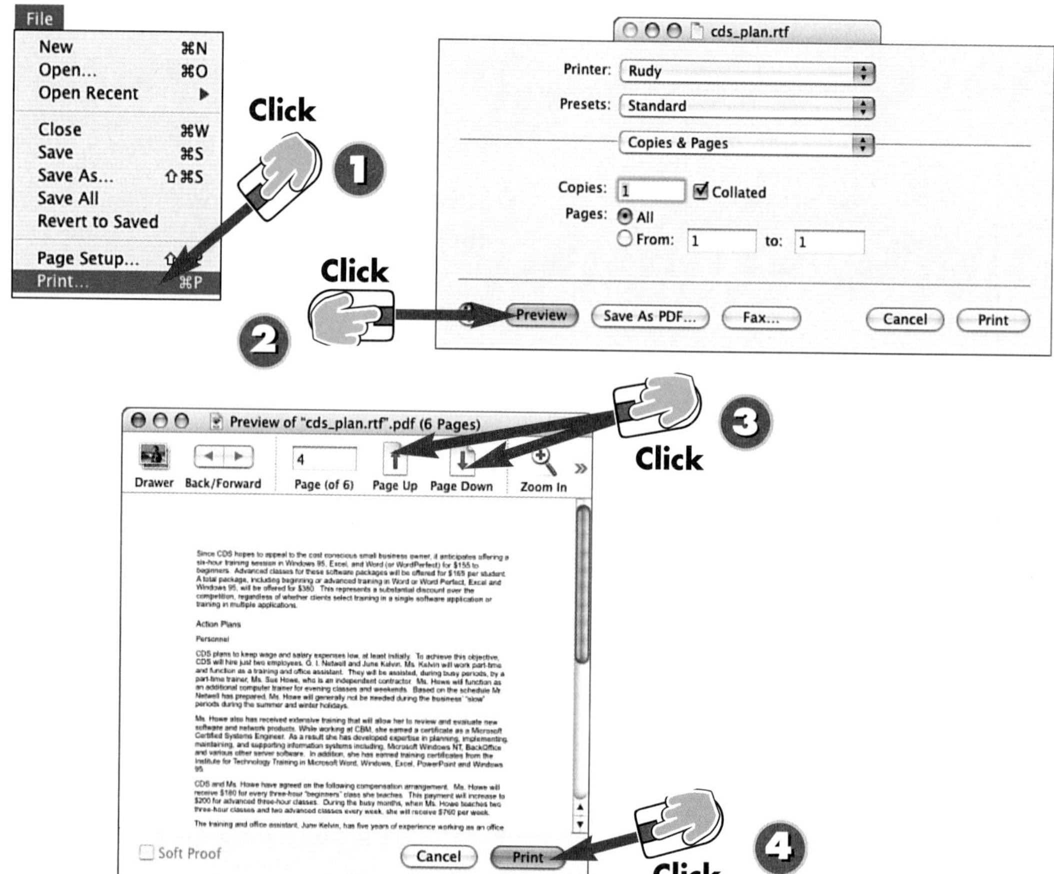

1. Choose **File**, **Print** (or press **Cmd-P**) to display the Print dialog box.
2. Click the **Preview** button; the system creates a PDF of the document and opens the PDF in the Preview program.
3. Scroll through the document in Preview using your keyboard or by clicking the **Page Up** and **Page Down** buttons on the toolbar.
4. Click the **Cancel** button to return to the original application, or click **Print** to print the document.

INTRODUCTION

Mac OS X's printing system lets you easily see what a document will look like when it's printed before you commit it to paper. Although some programs have this feature built-in, many don't, but now you can preview any document you can print, right from the Print dialog box.

HINT

Spreading the Wealth

When you click Preview, Mac OS X creates a new document from your original and opens it in Preview. You can save the preview document in PDF format, which also opens in Adobe Reader, to share with others who don't have the program you used to create it.

Printing a Document

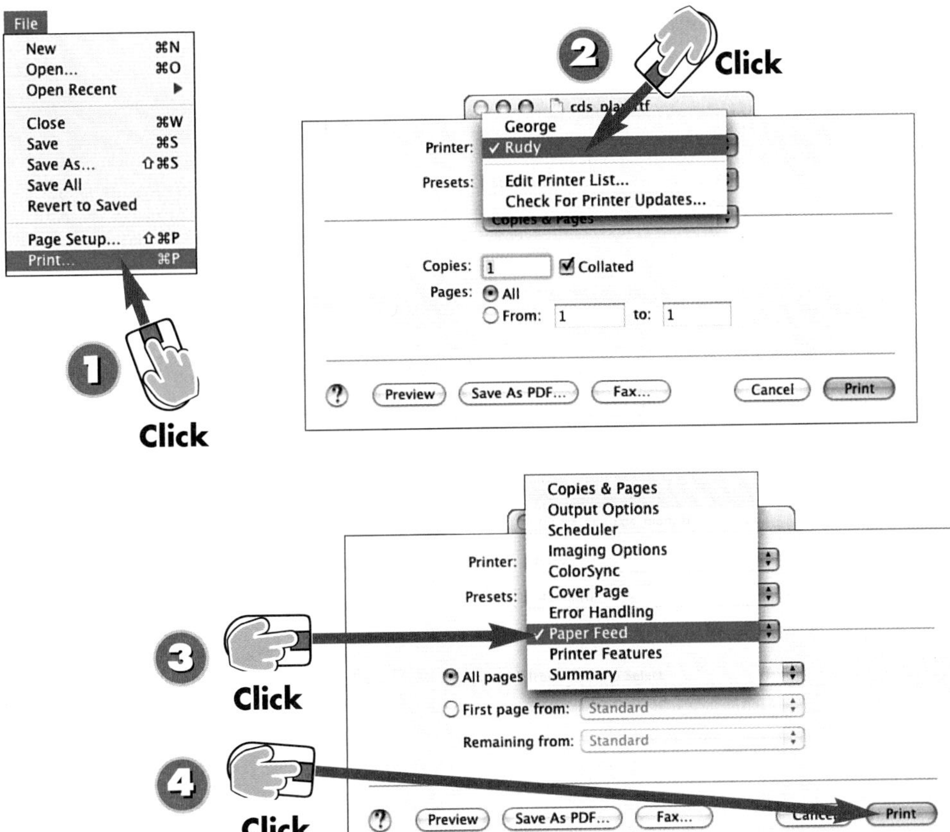

1. Choose **File**, **Print** (or press **Cmd-P**) to display the Print dialog box.
2. Choose a printer from the **Printer** pop-up menu.
3. Check the settings in each pane of the Print dialog box using the third pop-up menu and make changes as needed.
4. Click **Print**.

INTRODUCTION

For all practical purposes, the actual process of sending a document to the printer works the same in Mac OS X as it has in previous generations of the Mac OS. You can exert greater control if you want by inspecting each pane of the Print dialog box and adjusting the settings you find there, or you can just click Print and go.

HINT

The Print Dialog Box
The Print dialog box's panes vary according to the printer, but they always include Copies & Pages (the number of copies to print and the page range), Paper Feed (which paper tray the printer should use), and one for program-specific features.

Viewing the Print Queue

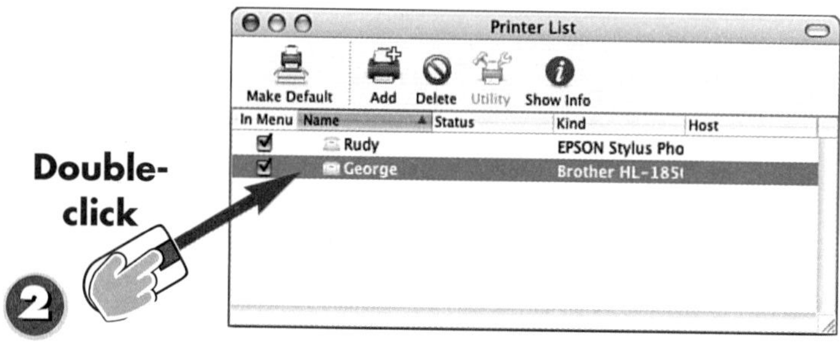

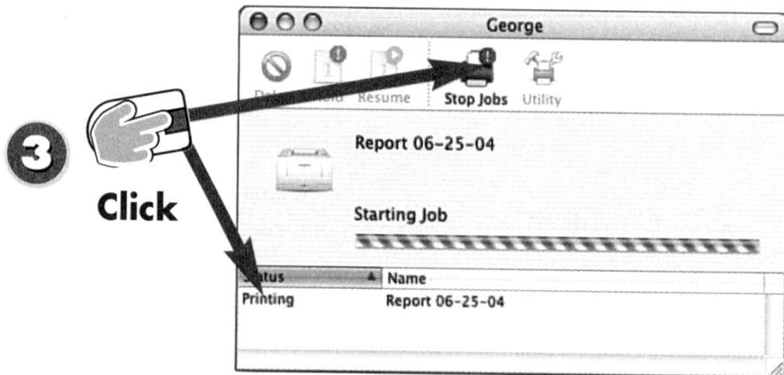

1. Double-click your desktop printer icon, or start the Printer Setup Utility to see the queue for that printer.
2. In the pick list, double-click a printer name to see its queue.
3. Click **Stop Jobs** to pause the print queue; click **Start Jobs** to restart the queue.

INTRODUCTION

Printing has a twist, though, that would certainly come in handy at the theater: the ability to specify a higher priority for a document when you send it to the printer, enabling it to jump to the head of the queue.

TIP

Sort List By...
When you're looking at a print queue, you can click the Status or Name column head to re-sort the current print jobs. This doesn't change the order in which they'll print, just the order in which you can read them.

TIP

Line Jumping
Choose **Scheduler** from the Print dialog box's third pop-up menu to set the time you want the document to print and choose a priority for it. If the document's priority is higher than other jobs queued for the same printer, it's printed before them.

Canceling a Print Job

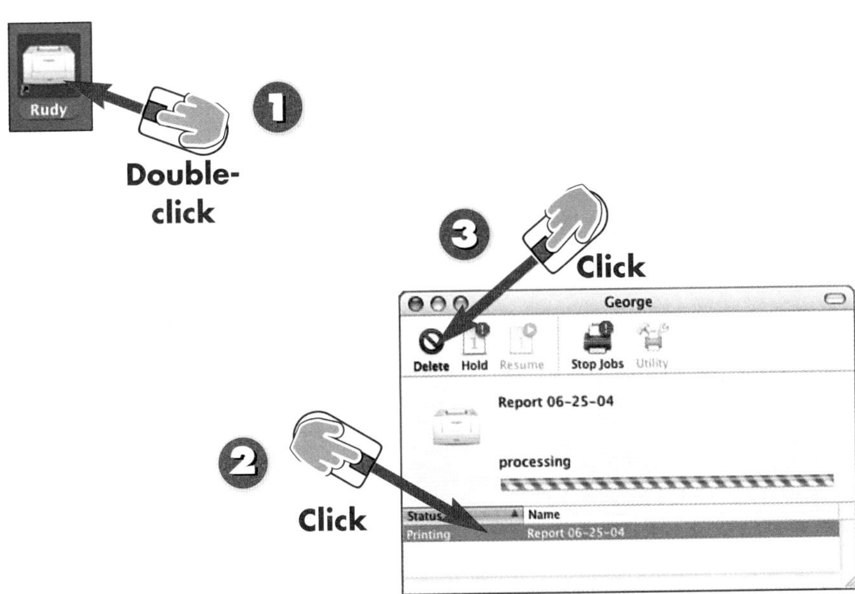

1. View the printer's print queue, either by double-clicking the desktop printer icon or by starting up Printer Setup Utility.
2. Click the job you want to cancel.
3. Click the **Delete** button in the toolbar.

INTRODUCTION

It happens to the best of us: You send a received fax or a rough draft of your term paper to the printer, only to realize that you're printing the document on $1/page glossy photo paper. Cancel that print job—now! Here's how.

TIP

Not Now, But Later
If you want to stop a job from printing now but you plan on allowing it to print later, don't delete it from the queue. Instead, click the **Hold** button in the print queue's toolbar to put it on hold. When you're ready to restart printing, click **Resume**.

Sending a Fax

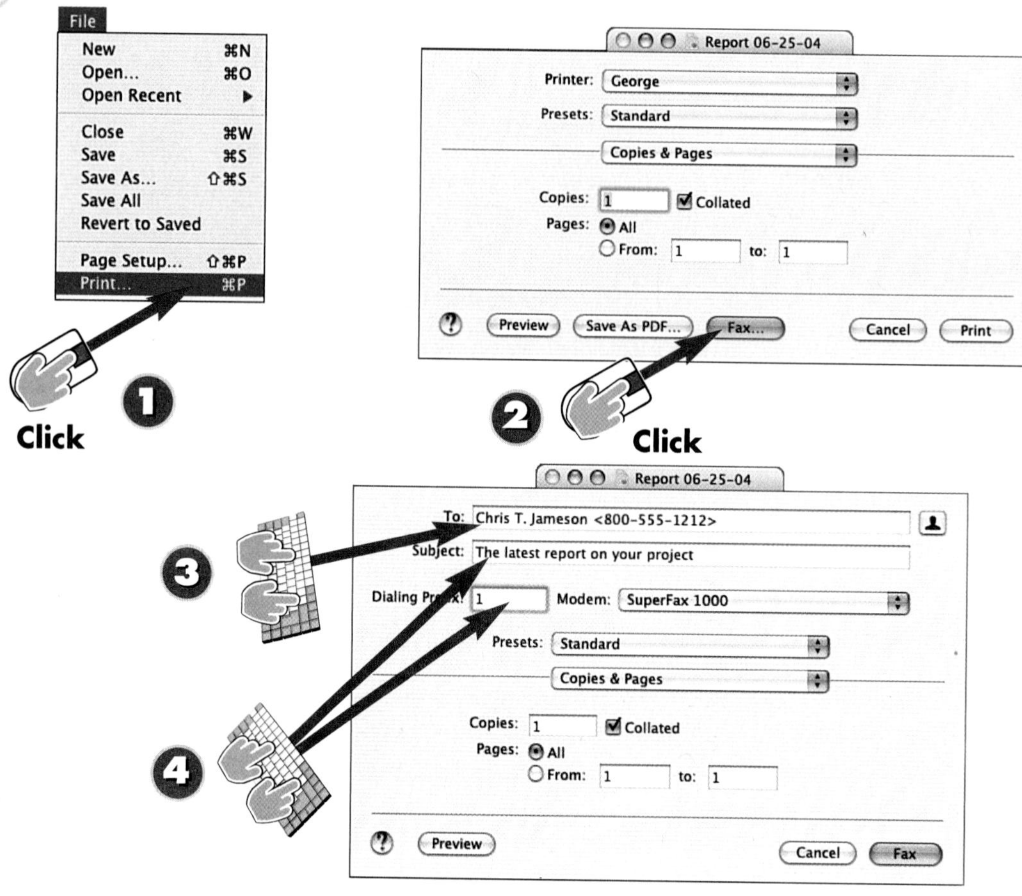

1. Open the document and choose **File**, **Print**.
2. Click the **Fax** button.
3. Type the name and fax number of the person you want to fax. If the fax recipient's name is in the Address Book, the fax number is filled in automatically.
4. Type a subject for the fax and a dialing prefix (such as 1 for long distance or a long distance access code).

INTRODUCTION

If you have a fax modem, you've probably spent some time wrestling with third-party fax software, which never seems to work right with either the system software or all the programs from which you want to fax. Those days are over; fax sending capability is built in to Mac OS X, and it's as close as the Print command.

TIP

Choosing Fax Recipients

To select fax recipients from your Address Book, click the **Address Book** button to the right of the To field. A small dialog box appears in which you can click to select a single person or Cmd-click to select multiple people.

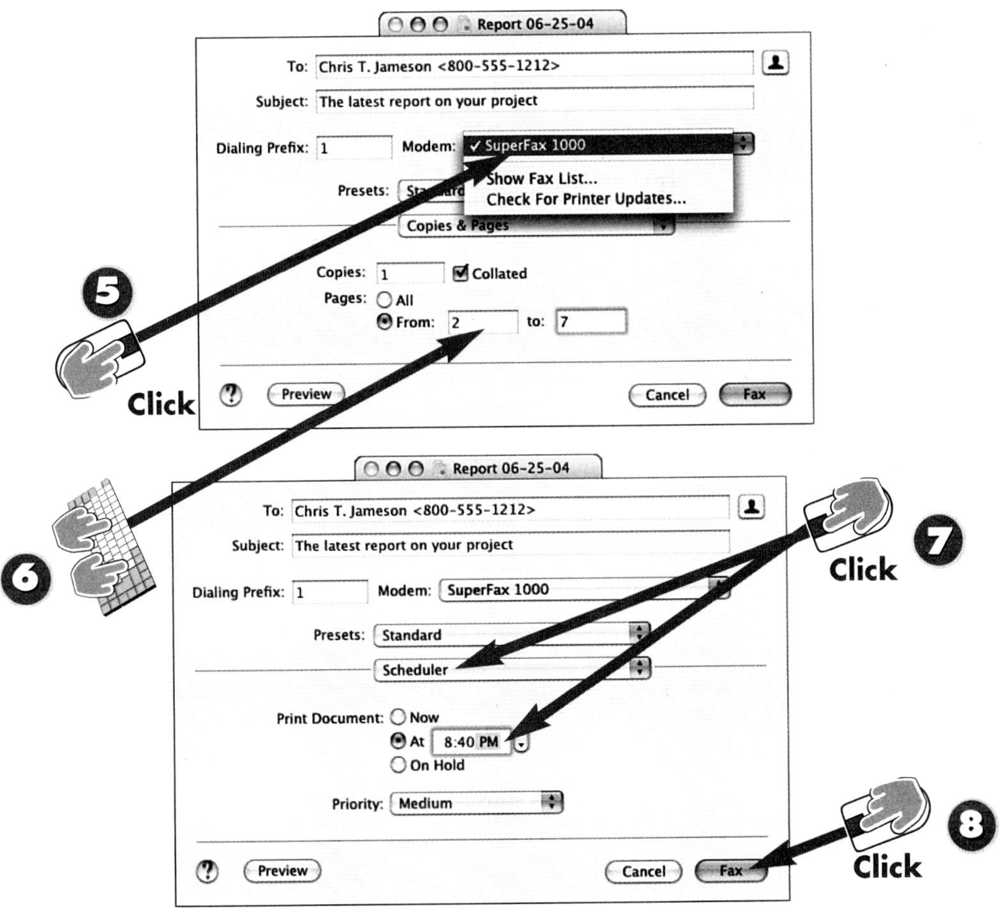

5 Choose your fax modem from the **Modem** pop-up menu.

6 Type the range of pages you want to include in the fax.

7 Choose **Scheduler** from the third pop-up menu and enter the time you want the fax to start.

8 Click **Fax**.

TIP

What Goes Out Can Come In, Too

To receive faxes on your Mac, choose **Apple menu**, **System Preferences**; then click **Print & Fax**. Click the **Faxing** tab and click the check box labeled **Receive faxes on this computer**. Then type your fax number and set options for what your Mac is to do when a fax is received.

Using a Scanner

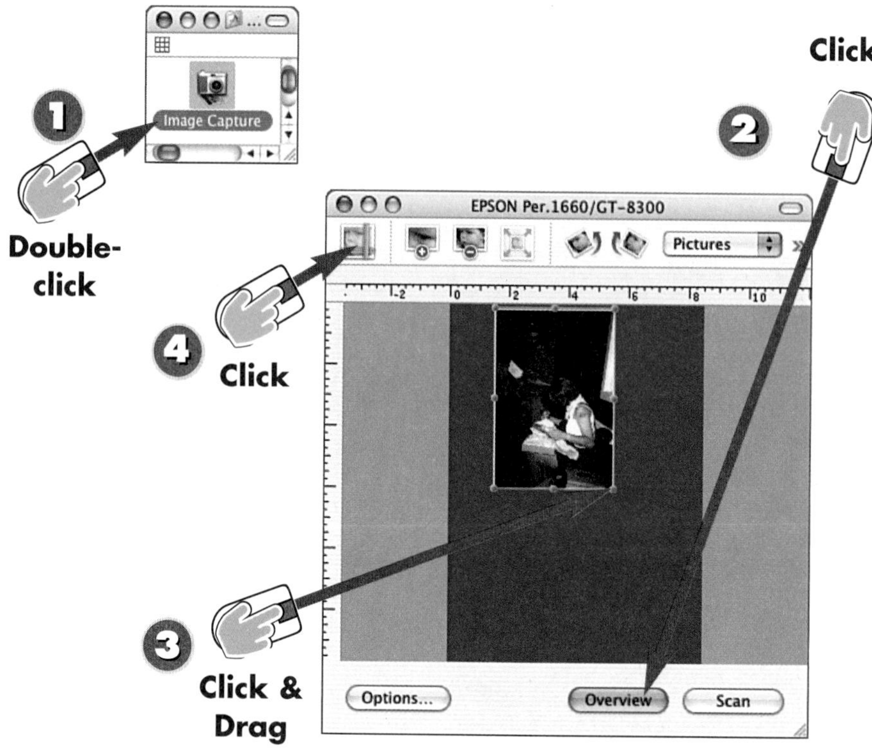

1. Double-click **Image Capture** in the Applications folder.
2. Click **Overview** to see a quick scan of the entire scanner bed.
3. Click and drag in the window to select the portion of the image you want to scan.
4. Click the **Scan Setup** button to open the Scan Setup Drawer.

INTRODUCTION

Your scanner is the way to get pictures inside your Mac, whether you need to copy a document, email a photo, or produce a Web image of a flat item you're selling at auction online. First, install the scanner and its software according to the instructions that came with it. Then you're ready to get scanning.

HINT

Sticking to the Safe Side
You should be conservative in selecting the scan area. If you scan a larger area than you need, you can trim it when you edit the image in Adobe Photoshop or another program. If you don't scan enough, you'll have to rescan the image.

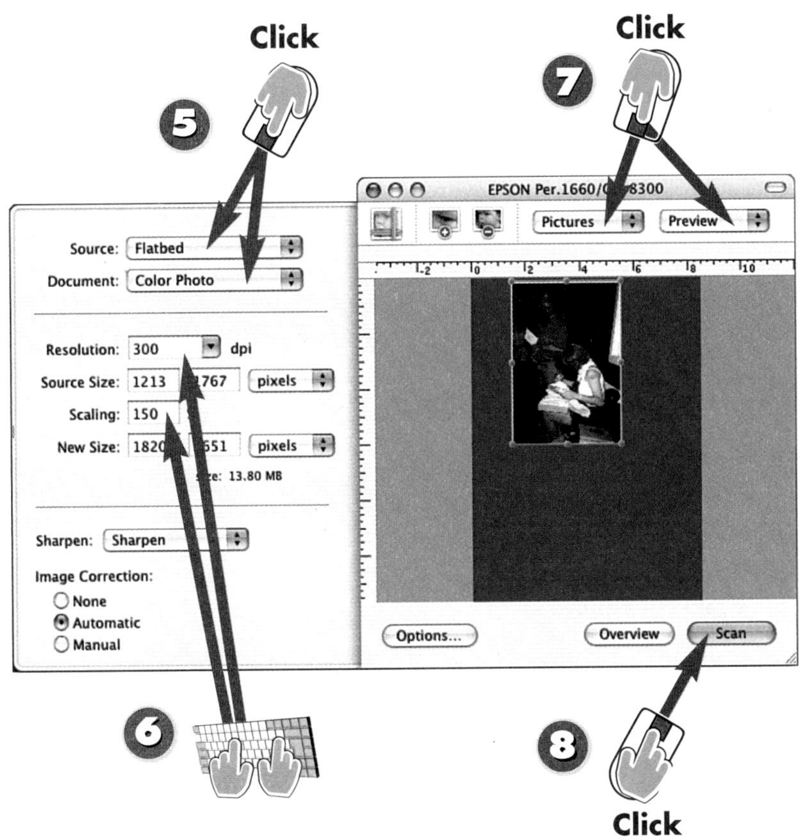

5 Use the **Source** and **Document** pop-up menus to choose a scan source and a document type.

6 Set the **Resolution** and the **Scaling** percentage.

7 Choose a location for the image file and a program in which to open it from the pop-up menus.

8 Click **Scan**. The image opens in the selected program and is saved in the selected folder.

HINT

To Each Its Own

The controls you see for functions such as sharpening and image correction vary depending on what type of scanner you have. Check your scanner manual to find out how to work with the scanner's settings.

TIP

More Scanner Options

Click **Options** to change some of the scanner's global settings, such as the resolution at which it makes overview scans and which programs start up when you press the buttons on the front of the scanner.

Adding Fonts

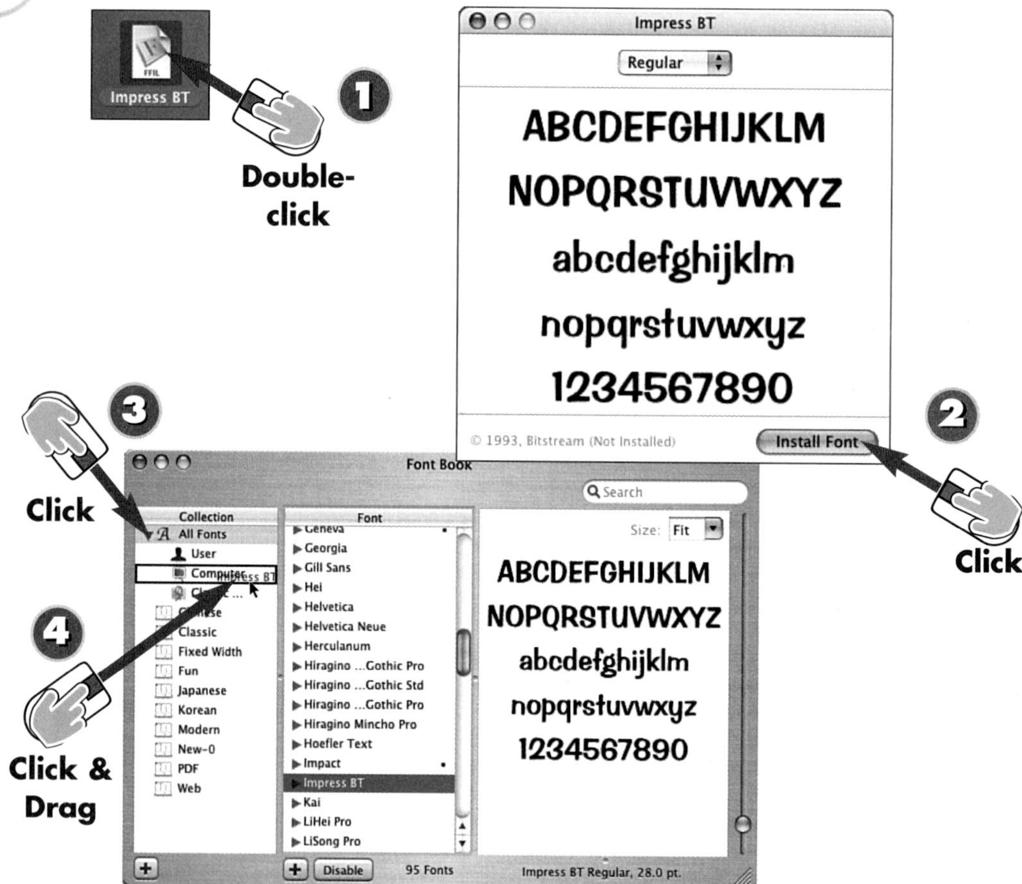

1. Double-click the font's icon. Font Book starts up and displays the font.

2. Click **Install Font**. The font is installed in your home folder's Library folder.

3. To install the font so that all your Mac's users can use it, click the disclosure triangle next to **All Fonts** in the **Collection** column.

4. Click and drag the new font to the **Computer** folder.

INTRODUCTION

There's no such thing as a font collection that's too big. Don't take that the wrong way—using all the fonts you have in one document is usually a very bad move, design-wise. But having a lot of fonts to choose from when you're creating graphics or printed documents is a luxury that's available to anyone with a Mac.

TIP

Shopping Time

Where do fonts come from? One place to start is Apple's Macintosh Products Guide (**www.guide.apple.com**). Click **Productivity & Utilities** in the left navigation bar on the Web page and click the **Fonts** radio button; then click **Find Products** in the subsequent page.

Organizing Fonts

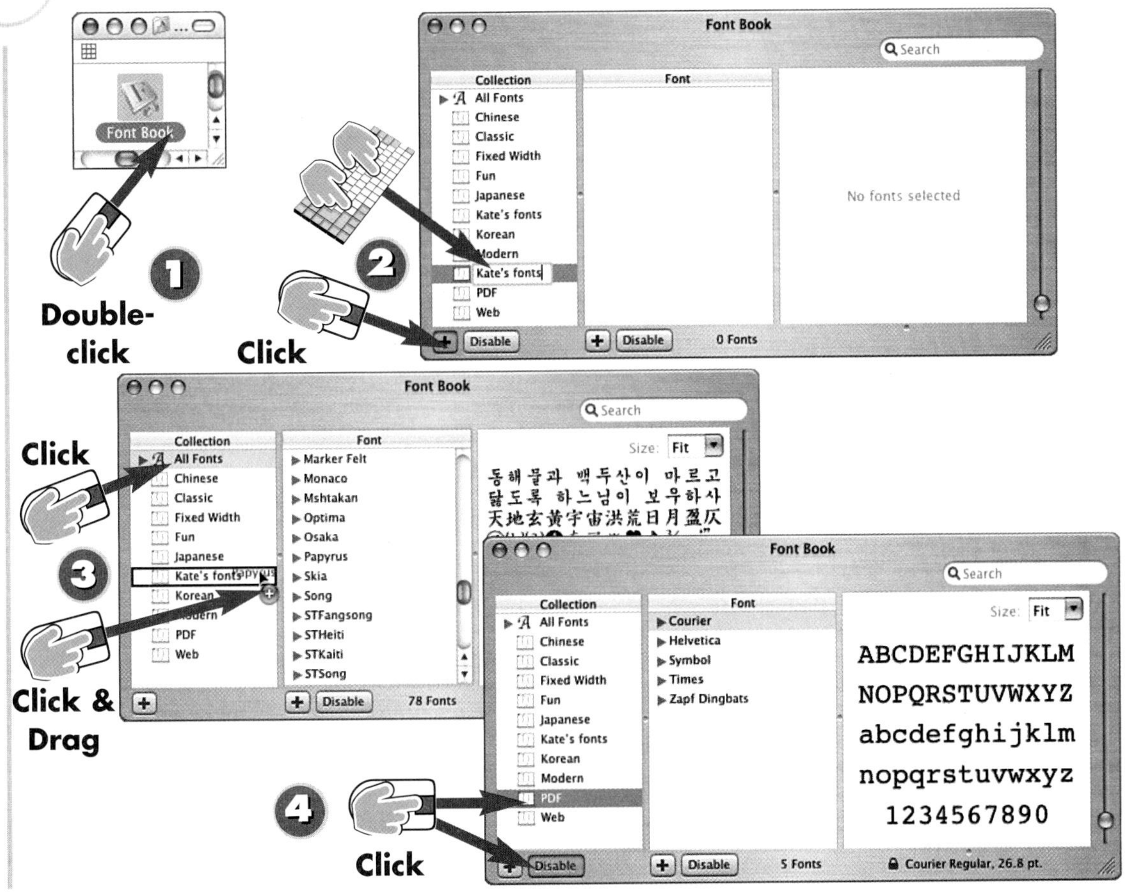

1 Double-click **Font Book** in the Applications folder.

2 Click the **+** button below the Collection column to create a new collection; then type in a name.

3 Click **All Fonts** in the Collection column and drag a font from the Font column into the new collection.

4 Click a collection name or a font name and click **Disable** to remove that font from the Font panel. If you see a confirmation dialog box, click **Disable** again.

INTRODUCTION

If your font collection has been growing, you'll love the ability to group the installed fonts into collections. Collections keep your fonts organized so you can quickly apply the fonts you're using for a given project. Mac OS X comes with a few predefined collections, but feel free to create as many collections as you want.

TIP

Putting Fonts Back on the Menu

Disabling a font doesn't delete it—you can always return to Font Book, select the font from the All Fonts collection, and click Enable to make the font available again.

PART 8

Getting Online

Before you can do anything online, you have to actually get online. Fortunately, with Mac OS X getting online couldn't be easier. In fact, your Mac might have completed some of these tasks already based on the information you gave it when you first started up Mac OS X. If not, though, don't worry—nothing here will take you more than a couple of minutes to complete, and then you'll be ready to go.

In this part you learn how to set up an Internet connection and how to get online using those settings. Although the details vary somewhat depending on your connection type, the setup process is similar no matter how you connect. Don't be intimidated by the techie terminology—after you have your settings in place, you won't need to worry about any of the details again. You might need to get some information from your Internet service provider, but if that's the case, you'll receive this information when you sign up with the provider.

You'll also learn about Mail accounts: how to set them up and use them to send and receive email. And you'll learn ways to keep your email spam-free, organized, and easy to deal with—no matter how much email you receive each day. You can even automate some organizational tasks so Mail takes care of them for you, such as filing your email in the proper mailboxes according to sender, recipient, or subject; this part shows you how.

Setting Up an Internet Connection and Your Email

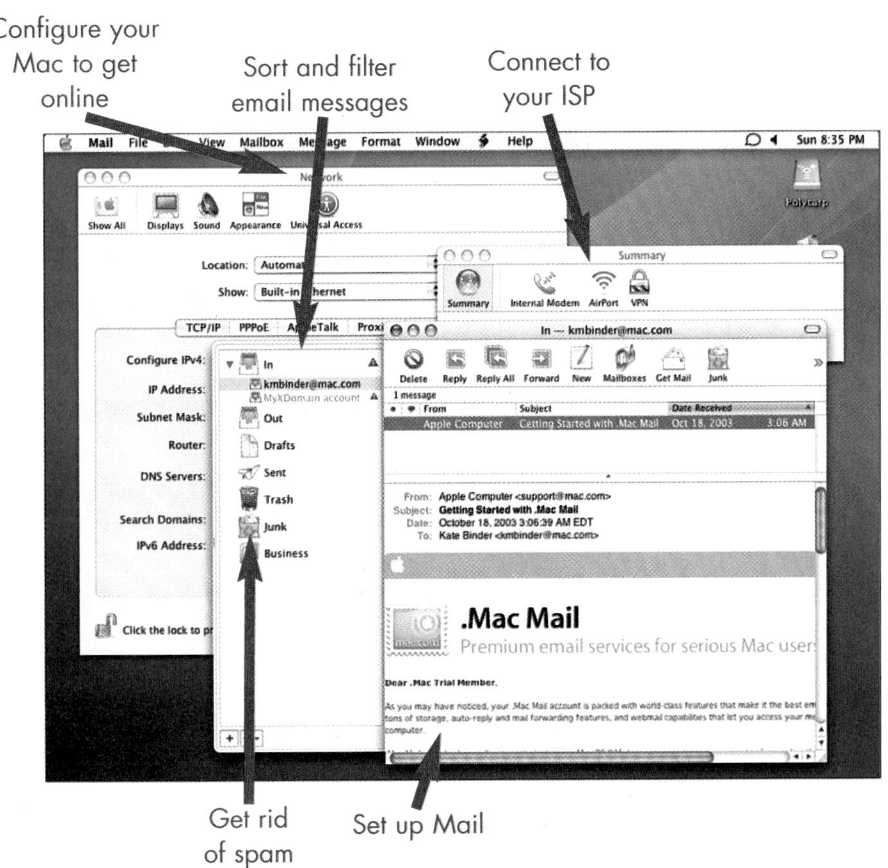

Setting Up Your Connection

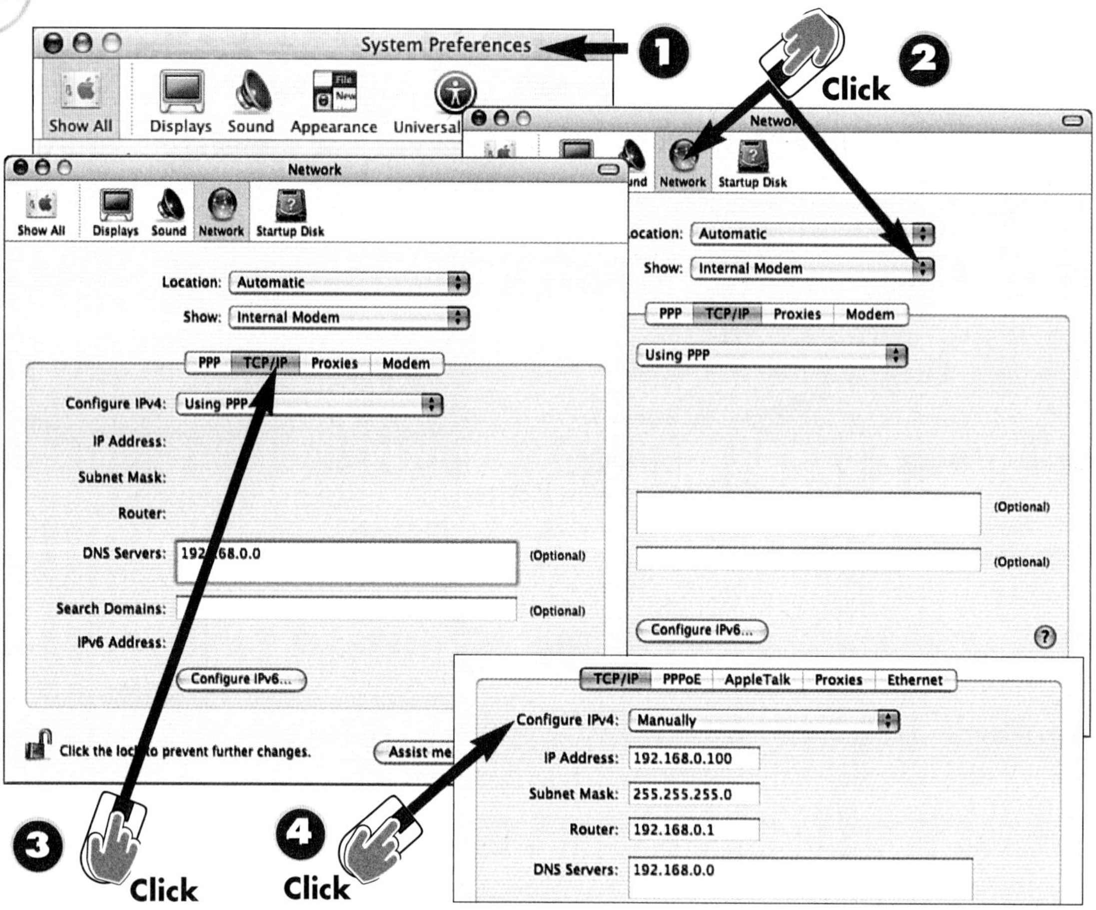

1. Choose **Apple menu**, **System Preferences**.
2. Click the **Network** icon to see your connection settings and choose your connection type from the **Show** pop-up menu.
3. Click the **TCP/IP** tab if it's not visible.
4. Choose your ISP's configuration method from the **Configure IPv4** pop-up menu: usually **Using PPP** for phone modems, **Manually** for LAN connections, or **Using DHCP** for cable and DSL modems.

INTRODUCTION

To set up your Internet connection, you'll need to find out a few things from your Internet service provider (ISP): your login name and password, possibly the ISP's DNS server addresses, and definitely the preferred configuration method.

HINT

Talk to Me

The Transmission Control Protocol/Internet Protocol (TCP/IP) is the language in which your Mac communicates with the other computers on the Internet. The choices in the Configure IPv4 menu are different ways of setting up a TCP/IP connection. PPP (Point-to-Point Protocol) is used for phone line connections, and DHCP (Dynamic Host Configuration Protocol) is used for broadband connections and internal networks. With DHCP, your ISP's server makes most of your TCP/IP settings for you. If your ISP doesn't use DHCP, you need to make those settings manually.

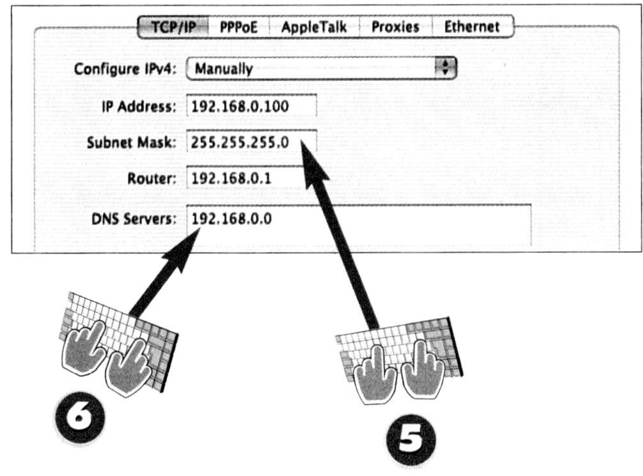

5 If your configuration method is Manually, enter your IP address, the subnet mask, and the router address for your network.

6 Enter your ISP's DNS server in the **DNS Servers** field.

HINT

Getting Help When You Need It
If any of these settings don't make sense to you, get in touch with your ISP's tech support people. It's their job to give you the information you must have to make the connection, so stick with it until you have what you need.

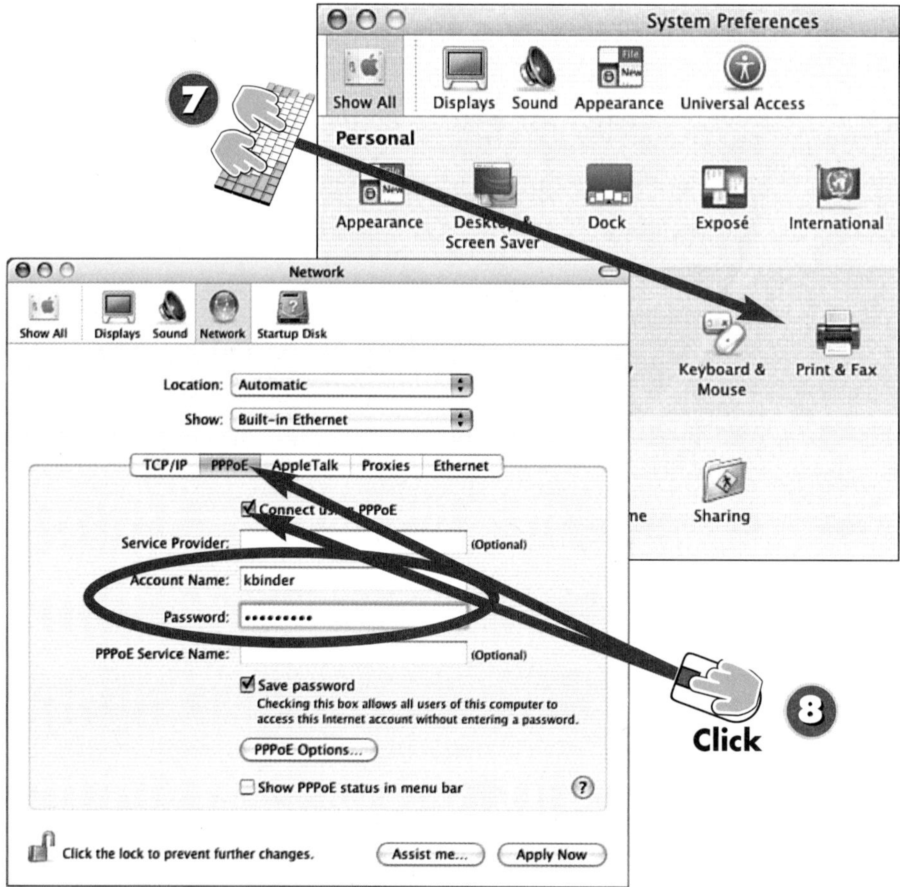

7 If your configuration method is Using DHCP and your ISP requires it, enter your DHCP Client ID.

8 If you have DSL and your ISP uses PPPoE, click **PPPoE**, choose **Connect using PPPoE**, and enter your account name and password.

INTRODUCTION

You might notice different tabs in the Network preferences pane as you switch interfaces, but don't worry—that's normal. For example, when you're configuring Ethernet, you see a PPPoE pane that doesn't appear when you're configuring a phone modem—because phone modem connections don't use PPPoE.

HINT

If Your Mac Is a PowerBook
If you connect using different methods in different places, you should definitely look into creating custom locations so you don't have to change all these settings every time you switch connections (see Part 5, "Customizing the Mac").

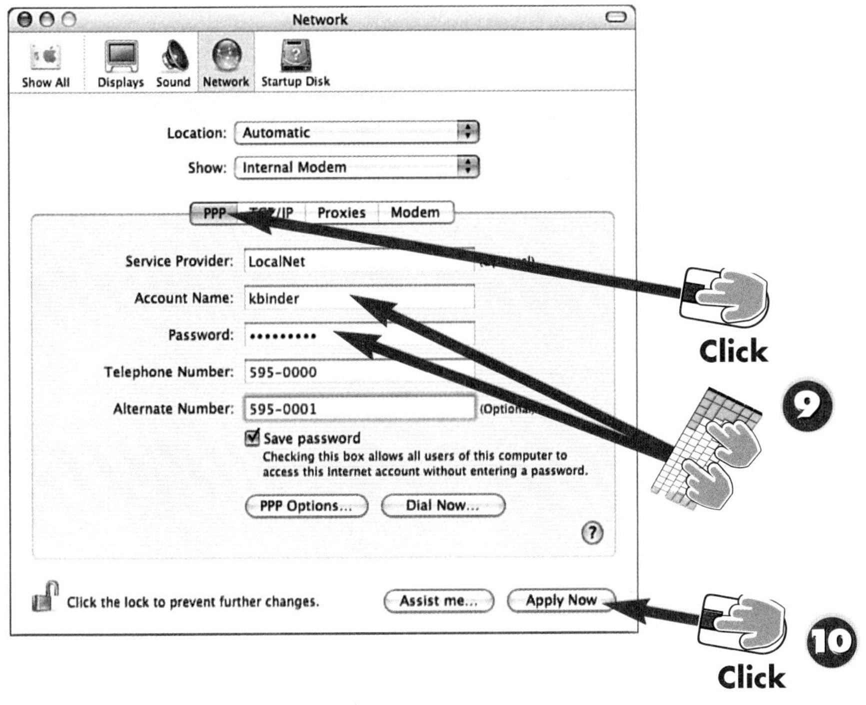

9 If you're connecting via phone modem using PPP, click **PPP** and enter your account name, password, and your ISP's dial-up access number.

10 Click **Apply Now**.

HINT

Don't Worry, Be Happy

You might notice different tabs in the Network preferences pane as you switch interfaces, but don't worry—that's normal. For example, when you're configuring Ethernet, you see a PPPoE pane that doesn't appear when you're configuring a phone modem because phone modem connections don't use PPPoE.

Connecting to Your ISP

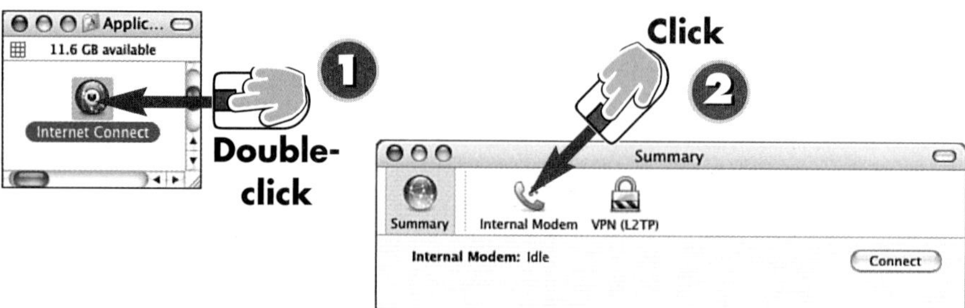

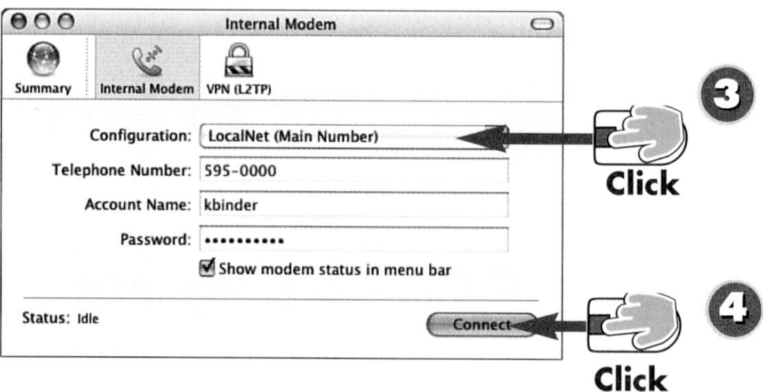

1. Open the **Applications** folder and double-click **Internet Connect**.
2. Click to choose a connection method in the toolbar.
3. Choose a configuration from the **Configuration** pop-up menu.
4. Click **Connect**.

INTRODUCTION

To connect to your ISP, you use a small program called Internet Connect. You can store more than one configuration, in case you connect in different ways at home, at work, and on the road. Internet Connect remembers the last connection you made, so most of the time you can get online with a single click.

TIP

Getting Offline
Don't forget that you need to disconnect when you're done surfing and checking your email. Go back to Internet Connect and you'll find that the Connect button has changed to a Disconnect button. Click that and you're offline again.

TIP

Status Symbol
In Internet Connect, check the box labeled **Show modem status in menu bar** to add a Modem Status menu to your menu bar. And in the Modem Status menu, choose **Show time connected** to display how long you've been online.

Setting Up Your Main Mail Account

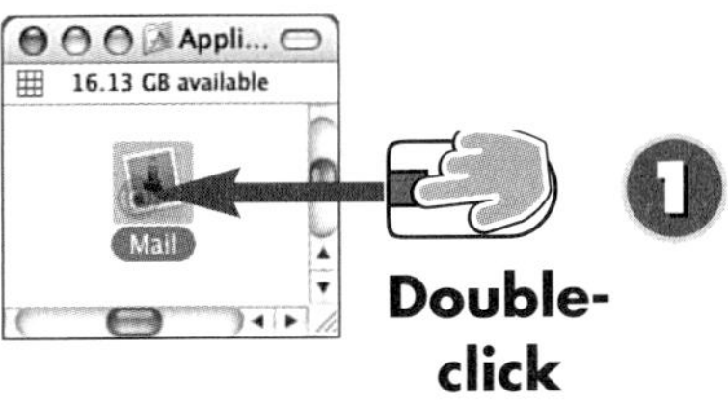

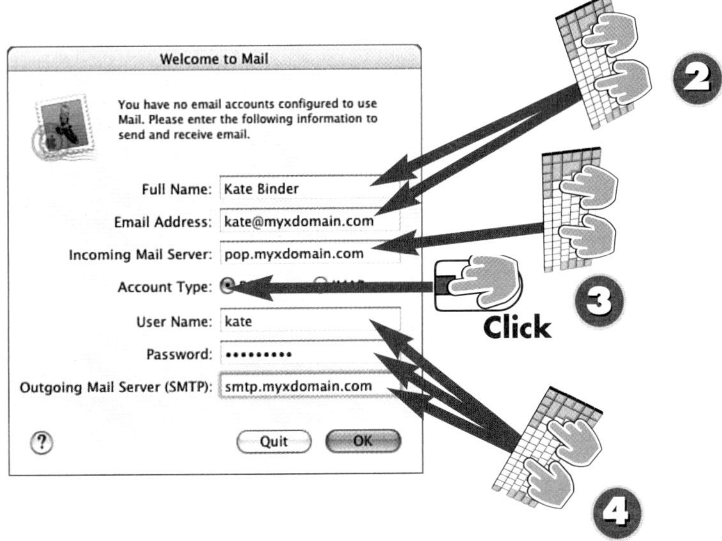

1. Open the **Applications** folder and double-click **Mail**. If you haven't created any accounts in Mail yet, you'll see the Welcome to Mail dialog box.
2. Type your name and email address in the corresponding fields.
3. Type your incoming mail server (often something like **pop.your-ISP.com**) and choose an account type; use POP for most ISP email and IMAP for some corporate email (check with your system administrator).
4. Type your username and password and your outgoing mail server; then click **OK**.

INTRODUCTION

The first time you set up an account in Mail, the program presents a welcome dialog box in which you can enter your settings. You need to know the account type (POP or IMAP), your user-name and password, and your incoming and outgoing mail servers.

HINT

Surprise!
If you signed up for a .Mac account when you first set up your Mac, or if you've already entered your .Mac information in System Preferences at a another time, your .Mac email account is already set up in Mail when you start the program.

Setting Up Additional Mail Accounts

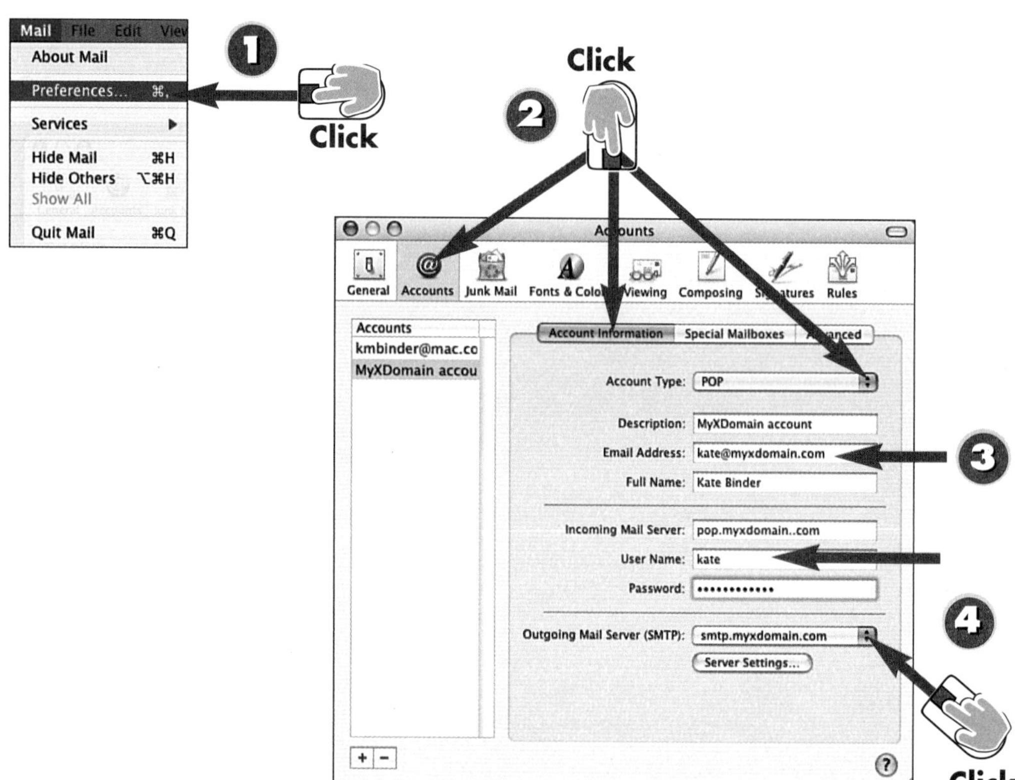

1. In Mail, choose **Mail**, **Preferences**.
2. Click **Accounts** and the **Account Information** tab. Then choose an account type.
3. Give this account a name in the **Description** field and type your name and email address in the corresponding fields.
4. Type your incoming mail server and your username and password, and choose your outgoing mail server (often something like **smtp.your-ISP.com**); then click **Close**.

INTRODUCTION

If you have more than one email account—maybe you have a .Mac account as well as email through your ISP—you need to use Mail's preferences to set up the additional email accounts. The settings are the same as in the Welcome to Mail dialog box, but the preferences dialog box looks a little different.

HINT

More Fun with Mail Accounts

You can set up as many Mail accounts as you have email addresses. Mail automatically filters your incoming email into a separate mailbox for each address, so you can keep your messages organized.

Working with Email in Mail

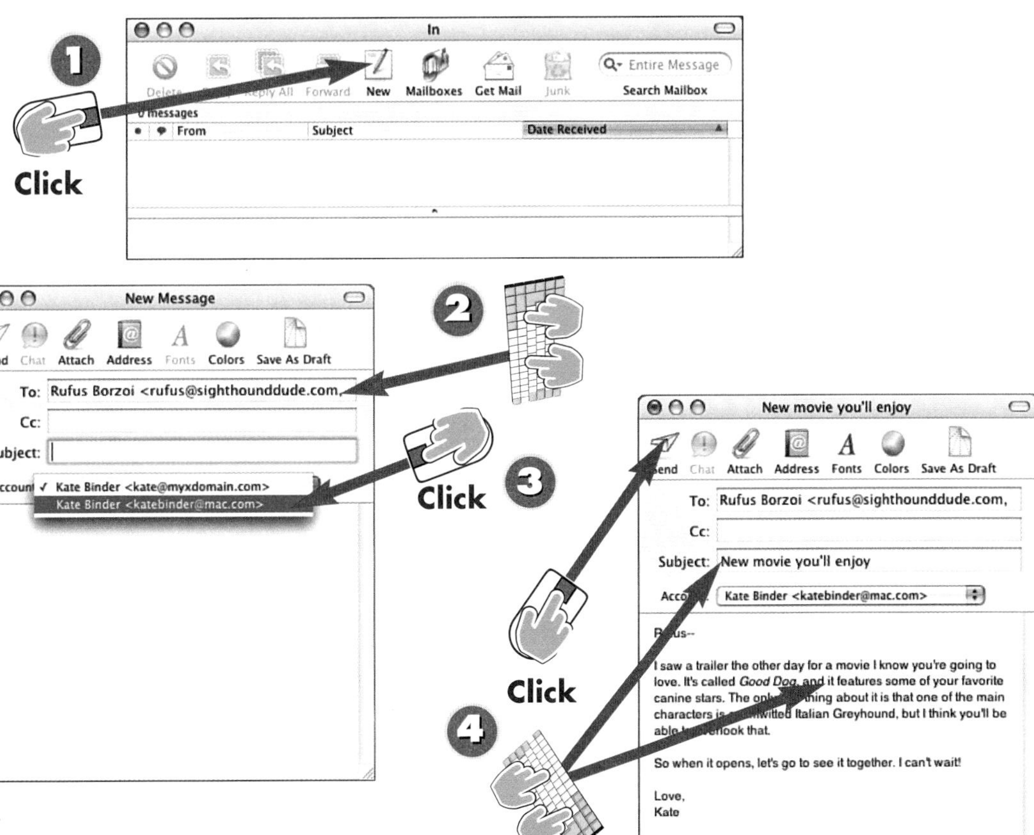

1. Click the **New** button in the toolbar.

2. Type the name of the person you want to email. If his email address doesn't appear automatically, type his email address after the name.

3. If you've set up multiple email accounts, choose the one from which you want to send in the **Account** pop-up menu.

4. Type a subject in the **Subject** line and your message in the message area. Click **Send**.

INTRODUCTION

Sending email works the same whether you're composing a new message or forwarding or replying to a received message. The steps given here assume you want to start from scratch with a new message. If you click a received message in one of your mailboxes, you'll see toolbar buttons for replying and forwarding.

TIP

Jazzing Up Your Emails
To attach a file, click the **Attach** button in the toolbar and navigate to the file you want to attach. To make your email text colored, click the **Colors** button and choose a color in the Colors panel.

TIP

It's Better to Receive
To see email others have sent you, click **Get Mail** in the Mail toolbar. Or, you can schedule automatic mail pickups by choosing **Mail**, **Preferences**. Click **General** and choose an option from the **Check for new mail menu**.

Organizing Mail's Mailboxes

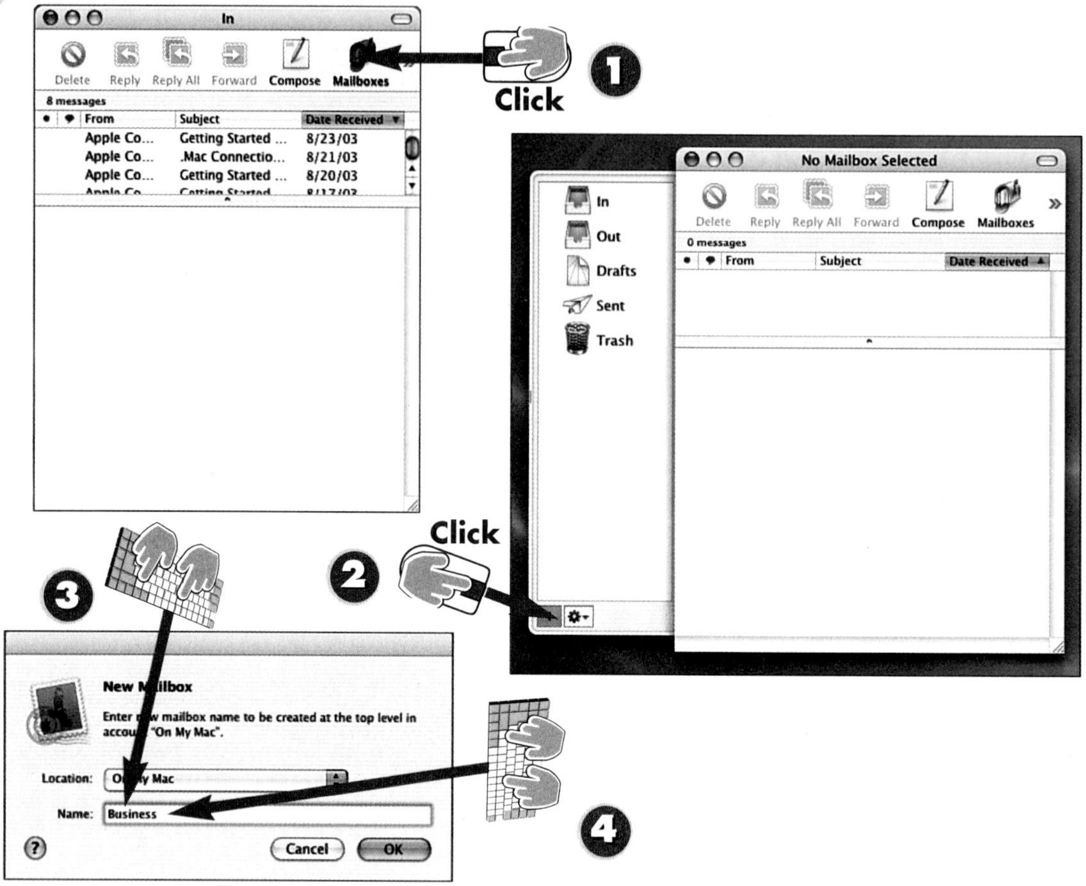

1. In Mail, click the **Mailboxes** button in the toolbar to open the Mailboxes drawer.
2. Click the **+** button at the bottom of the drawer to create a new mailbox.
3. Enter a name for the mailbox and click **OK**.
4. To create a mailbox inside another mailbox, type the name of the existing mailbox, then a slash, and then the new mailbox name. Then click **OK**.

INTRODUCTION

If you get a lot of email, you'll quickly find your In box filling up. Creating a system of mailboxes in which you can file all that email will save you time in the long run because it makes finding what you want when you need it easier. You can nest mailboxes within other mailboxes to set up as complex a system as you need.

HINT

Like Parent, Like Child
If a mailbox is selected when you click the + button, the new mailbox is created as a child of the selected mailbox—in other words, it is within the selected one.

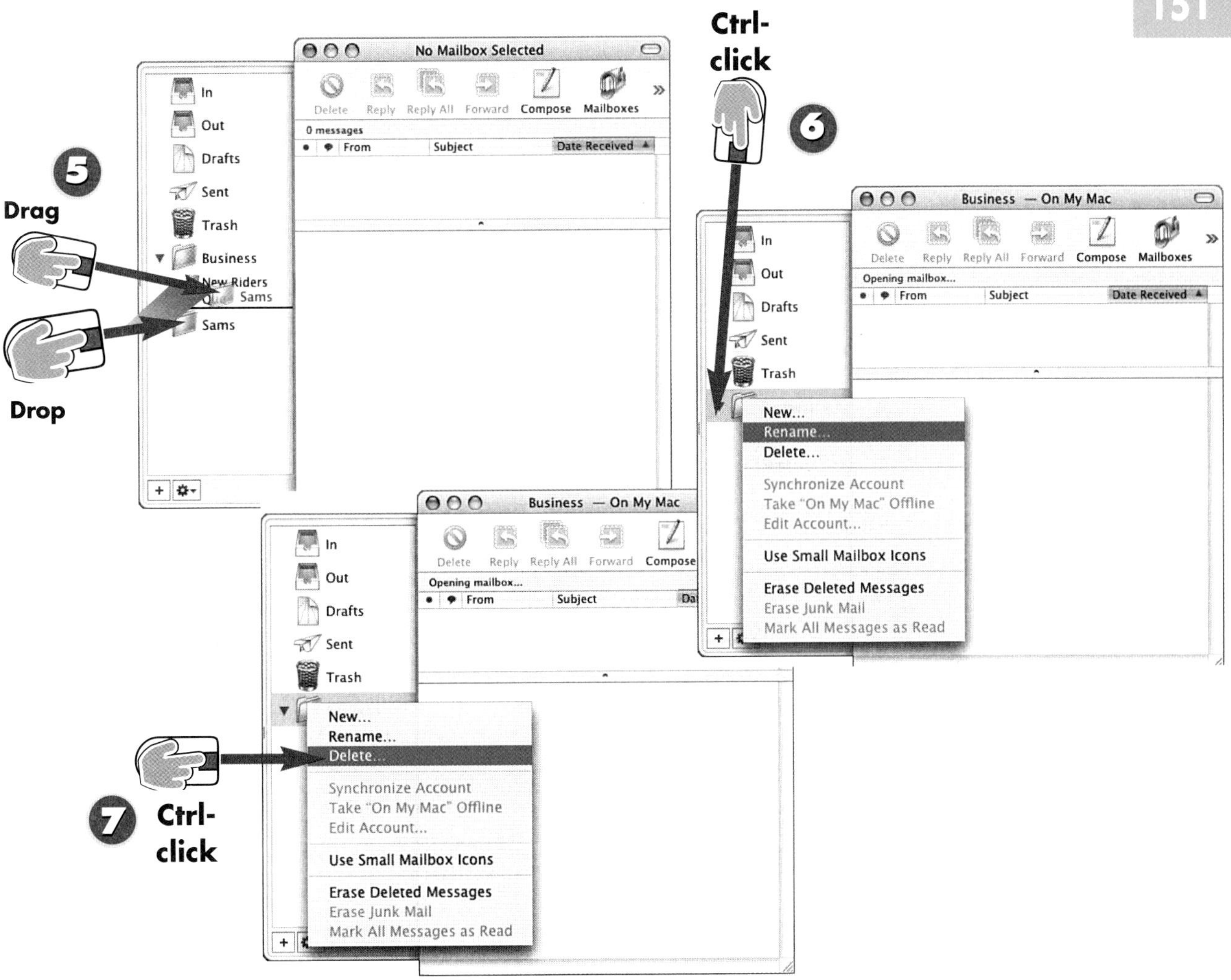

5 Drag Drop

6 Ctrl-click

7 Ctrl-click

5 To move a mailbox or submailbox inside a different mailbox, drag and drop it into position. A black line shows you where it will end up when you release the mouse button.

6 **Ctrl-click** a mailbox and choose **Rename** from the contextual menu to change its name.

7 **Ctrl-click** a mailbox and choose **Delete** from the contextual menu to remove it.

TIP

Another Way to Get There

The same commands you see in the contextual menu are available in the Action menu at the bottom of the Mailbox drawer—click the button next to the + button to see the menu.

HINT

You Can't Go There

You can't add mailboxes inside the default mailboxes (In, Out, Drafts, and Sent). However, Mail automatically creates mailboxes within your In box to segregate mail received at different email addresses.

Filtering Email in Mail

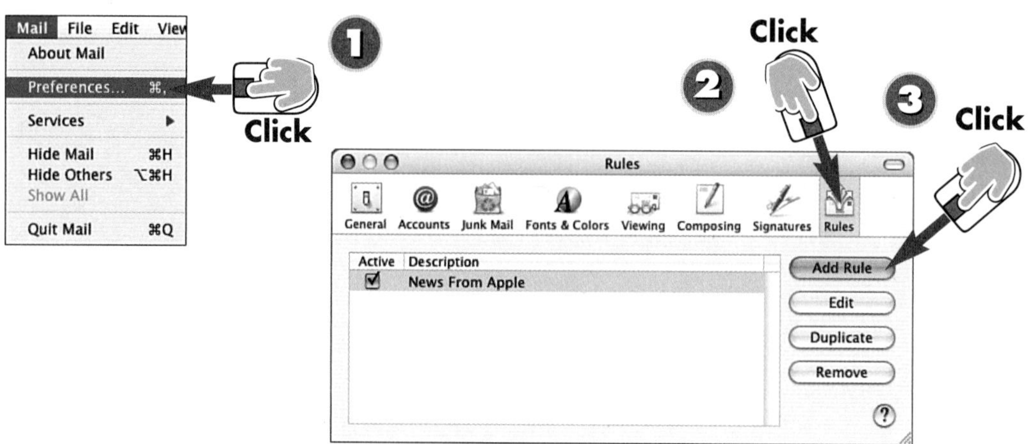

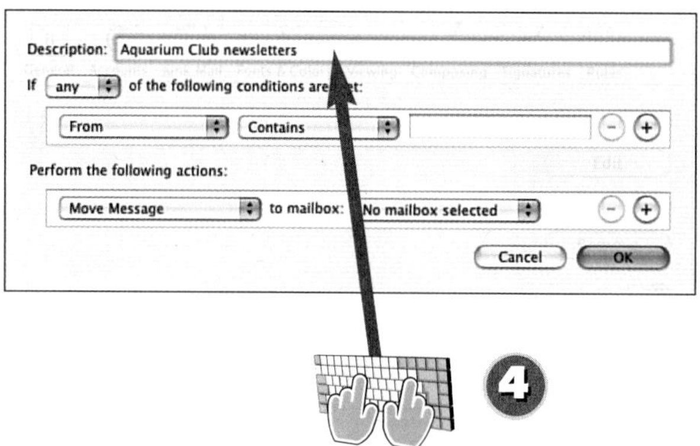

1. In Mail, choose **Mail**, **Preferences**.
2. Click the **Rules** button to see the filtering options.
3. Click **Add Rule**.
4. Give the rule a name in the **Description** field.

INTRODUCTION

The more email you get, the more you'll appreciate having Mail help you with the filing. Mail can analyze each message you receive based on who sent it, where it was addressed, what it says, or several other criteria, and it can file that message in the appropriate mailbox. Mailboxes with unread messages are shown in bold type.

TIP

Excluding Messages from Rules
You can make a set of rules that acts on all email messages but a particular group. First, create a rule that filters the group you don't want to act on into the Trash or a mailbox. Then create another rule to apply your action to Every Message; this rule acts on all the messages remaining after the first rule is executed.

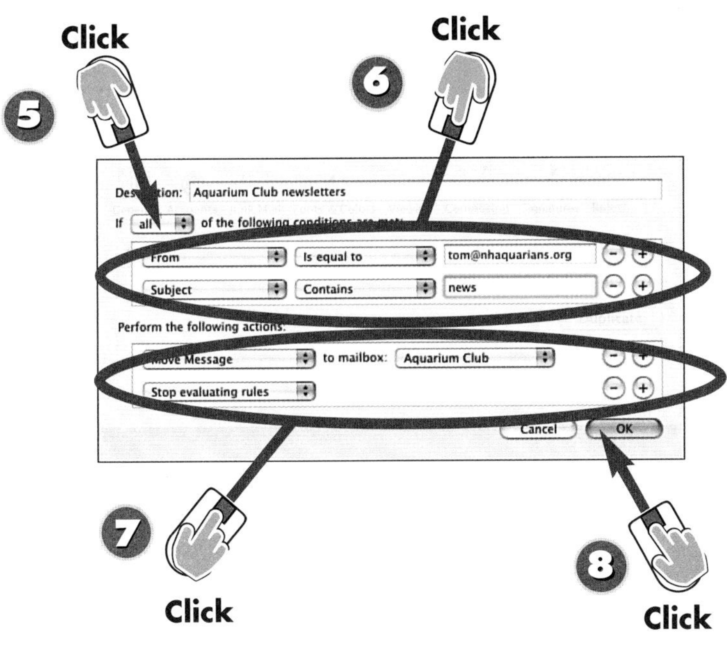

5. Choose **any** or **all** from the pop-up menu; with any, the rule is activated if one or more condition is met, and with all it's activated only if they're all met.

6. Set up the condition you want to filter on; click the **+** button to add more conditions.

7. Set up the action to be invoked if the conditions are met; click the **+** button to add more actions.

8. Click **OK**.

HINT

Explore Your Options
There are many ways you can select messages for special treatment. For example, you can tag all messages sent to a particular address with a red label, or you can put messages from anyone in an Address Book group into a specific mailbox.

TIP

Watching for Rule Interactions
The last action step in most rules should be Stop evaluating rules. That way, a message properly filed according to one rule won't be refiled by another. You can also drag and drop rules within the list to determine what order they're executed in.

Intercepting Spam in Mail

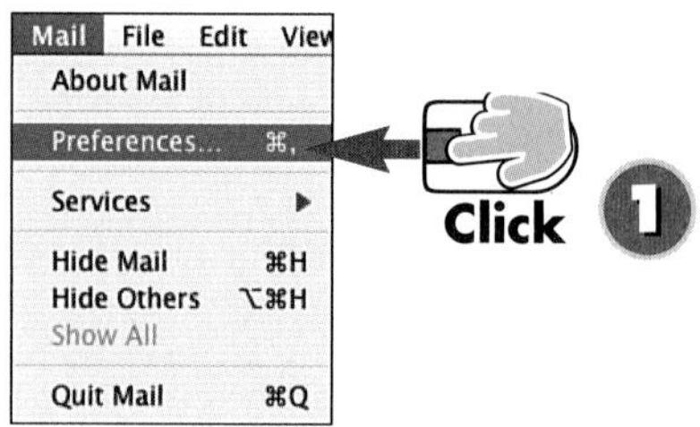

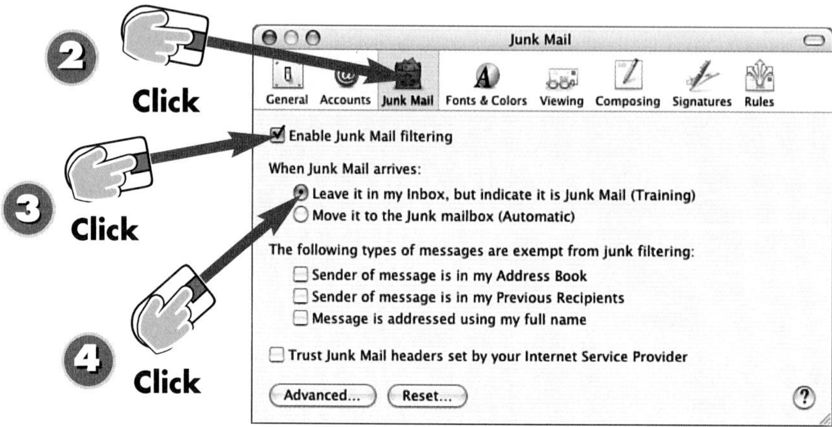

1. In Mail, choose **Mail**, **Preferences**.
2. Click the **Junk Mail** button to see the spam options.
3. Click the **Enable Junk Mail filtering** check box.
4. Click a radio button to tell Mail what to do with junk mail it receives.

INTRODUCTION

Spam (or junk mail, or unsolicited commercial email) is everywhere, and it's increasing by the moment. Email users are constantly looking for new ways to deal with the deluge, and Apple has done its part by including a built-in, smart junk mail filter in Mail. With your help, the filter learns to better recognize spam day by day.

TIP

How Does It Work?
Mail recognizes junk mail using what Apple calls "latent adaptive semantic analysis." The program scans email messages for certain word patterns—not typical spam keywords such as "make money," but speech patterns spammers tend to use.

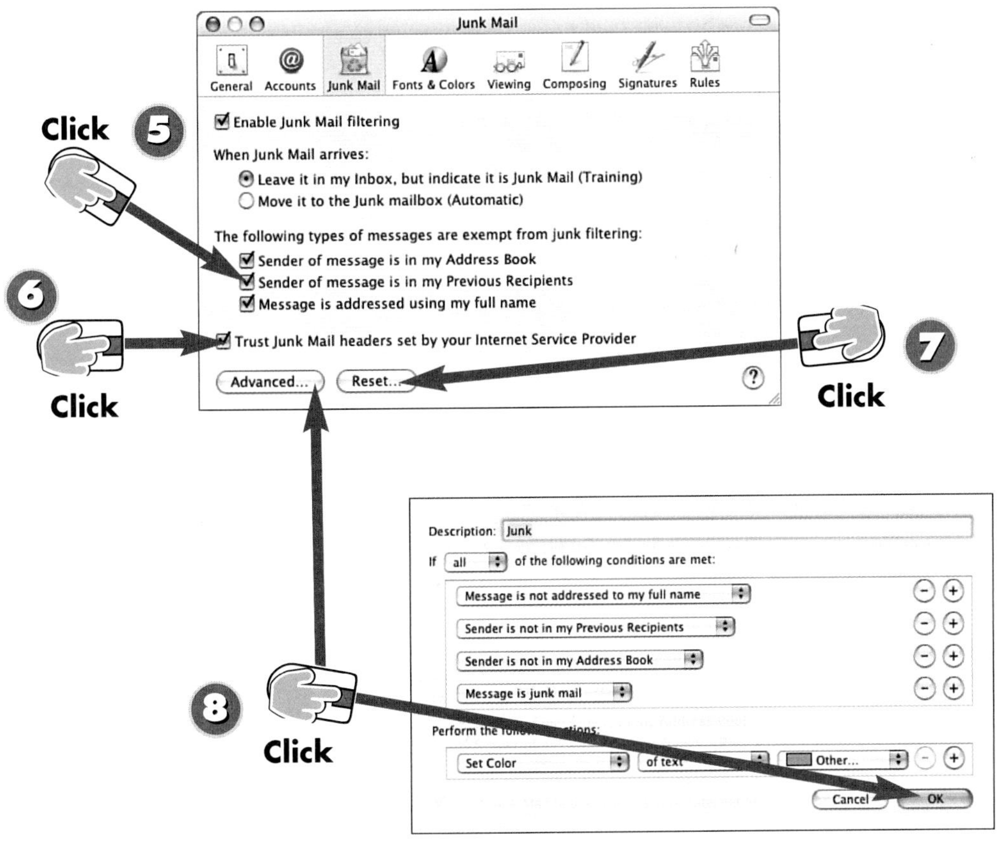

5. Click the check boxes to indicate which types of email shouldn't be considered spam.

6. Click the check box to take advantage of junk mail prefiltering done by your ISP.

7. Click **Reset** to make Mail forget the list of known junk mail senders and subjects it has compiled.

8. Click **Advanced** to create your own junk mail filter (see the task "Filtering Email in Mail" for more information); then click **OK** when you're done creating the filter.

TIP

Teaching Mail More About Spam
Mail marks junk mail with a brown label. If a message is brown but isn't spam, click it and choose **Message, Mark As Not Junk Mail**. If you get spam that's not labeled brown, choose **Message, Mark As Junk Mail**. This trains Mail to recognize spam better.

TIP

Where to Put Spam
To put all your junk mail in a special mailbox, choose **Mail, Preferences** and click **Junk Mail**. Click **Move it to the Junk mailbox (Automatic)**. You can get rid of all the spam you've received by choosing **Mailbox, Erase Junk Mail**.

PART 9

Living Online

So much of modern life happens online. Despite some people's complaints that community is disappearing, it's thriving on the Internet. That's what the World Wide Web is all about—a network of people sharing a network of information—and Safari is your passport to that network. Instant messaging, too, is a great way to keep in touch with others, and iChat brings it right to your Mac OS X menu bar.

In this part you learn how to set up iChat and begin exchanging messages with others. iChat works with AOL and .Mac screen names, but if you don't have a screen name already you'll learn how to create one for free. With iChat, you can set up your own chat rooms in which multiple people can exchange messages; in this part you learn how to create a chat room and how to take advantage of iChat's video and audio chat features to actually talk with your buddies or even see them over a video feed. For those features, of course, your Mac must have a microphone and a FireWire Webcam (a small digital video camera).

Other tasks introduce you to surfing the Web with Apple's very own Web browser, Safari—a fast, compact browser that you'll quickly learn to love. You'll learn how to create bookmarks and use the History so you can return to your favorite sites, as well as how to keep those bookmarks organized and accessible. And you'll see how to download files, save a Safari Web page, and enable Safari to automatically fill out Web forms for you—a great time-saving feature if you do a lot of online shopping.

Getting Online

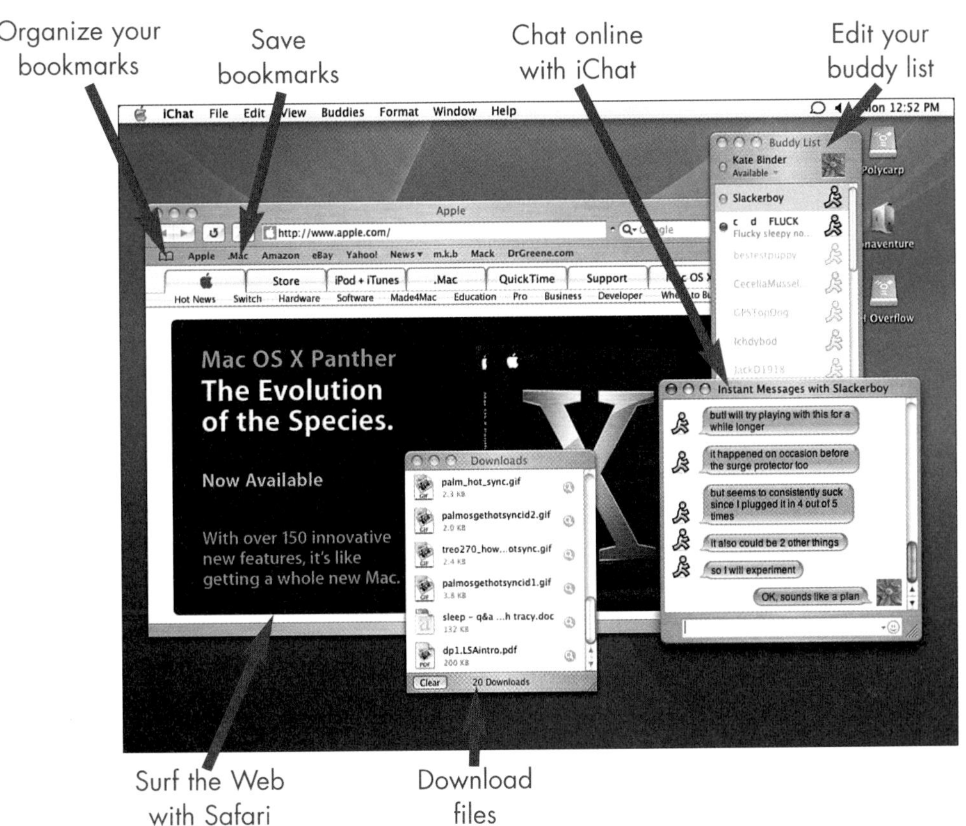

Start

Putting Contacts, Bookmarks, and Calendars Online

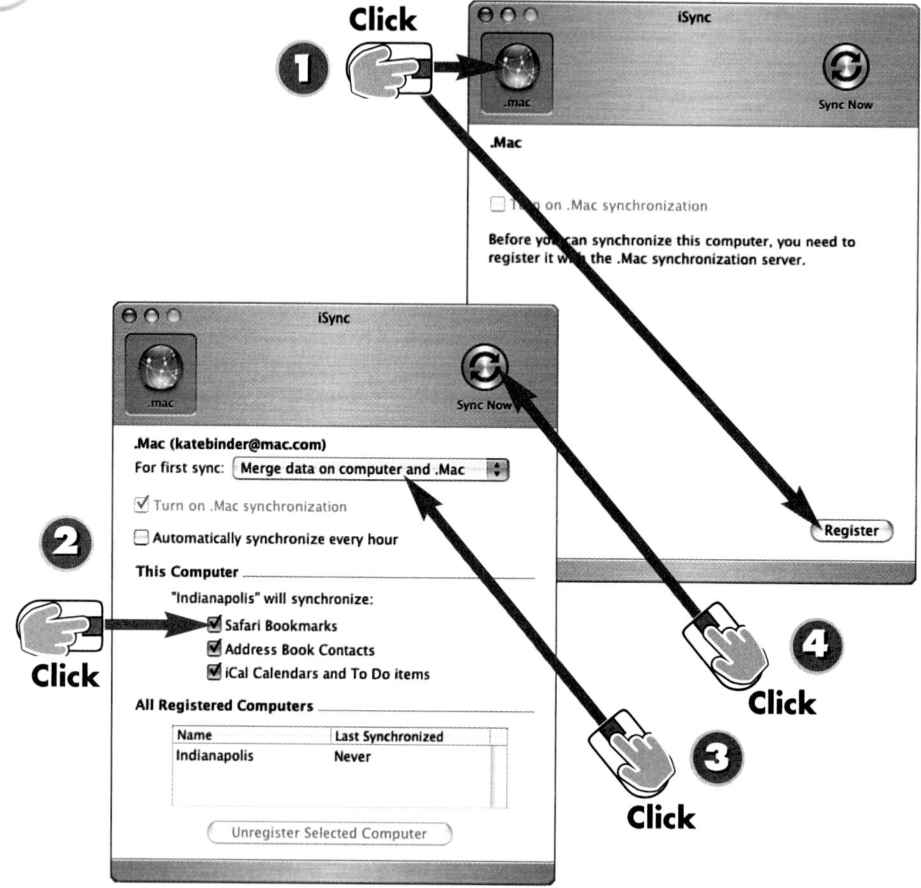

1. Start iSync (located in the Applications folder) and click **.Mac** at the top of the window; click **Register** if you haven't done so before.
2. Click the check boxes next to the data you want to sync.
3. The first time you sync, select an option from the pop-up menu to determine which information takes precedence.
4. Click **Sync Now**.

INTRODUCTION

With Mac OS X, you can sync the data on your computer with your .Mac account and back the other way, so you can keep your contacts, bookmarks, and calendars identical on more than one Mac. If you sync Address Book with .Mac, you can access contact information from the .Mac Web site.

TIP

Going Both Ways
Syncing—short for *synchronizing*—your other computers with .Mac follows the same procedure outlined here. But don't select Erase data on .Mac then sync from the For first sync pop-up menu.

HINT

More Fully Apple
Syncing with .Mac requires you to use Apple's iCal, Address Book, and Safari programs. If you're ready to switch, you'll be glad to hear that these programs can import data from similar programs, such as Internet Explorer bookmark lists.

Setting Up an iChat Account

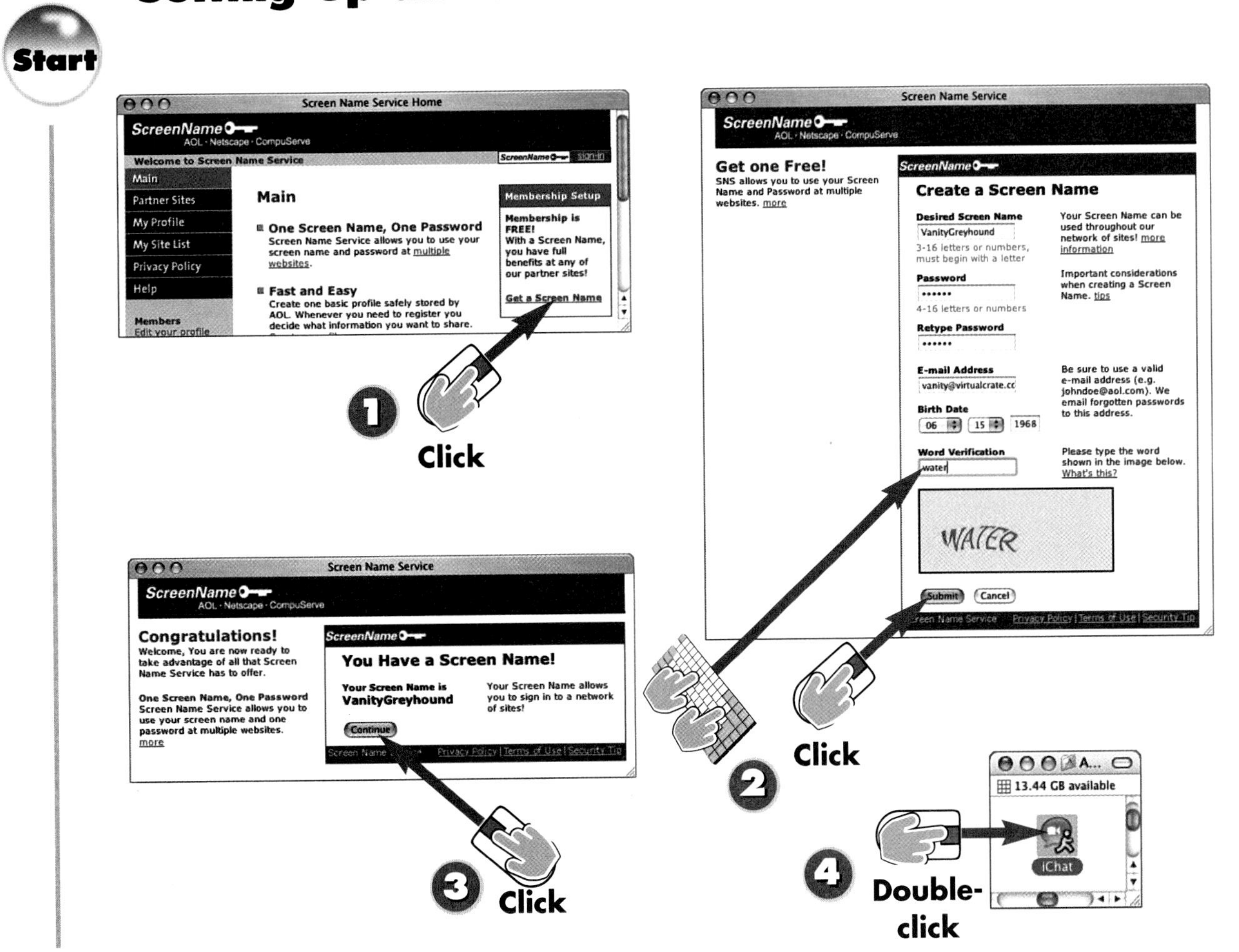

1. If you need to get an AIM screen name, go to the AIM Web site (**my.screenname.aol.com**). Click the **Get a Screen Name** link.
2. Enter the requested information and click **Submit**.
3. Click **Continue** in the confirmation screen (or, if you're told that the screen name you chose isn't available, go back and try another one).
4. Open the Applications folder and double-click **iChat**.

See next page

INTRODUCTION

iChat works with either your .Mac username or an America Online Instant Messenger (AIM) screen name. If you don't have either, use the AIM screen name—it's free. The steps below walk you through getting a screen name and then entering your name and password in iChat so you can get online and start chatting.

HINT

What's in a Name?
When choosing a screen name, think about how you want to appear. If you'll be using iChat with clients and colleagues, you probably don't want to choose "FluffyBunny." And if you'll be chatting mainly with friends, "AcmeInc" isn't the best choice.

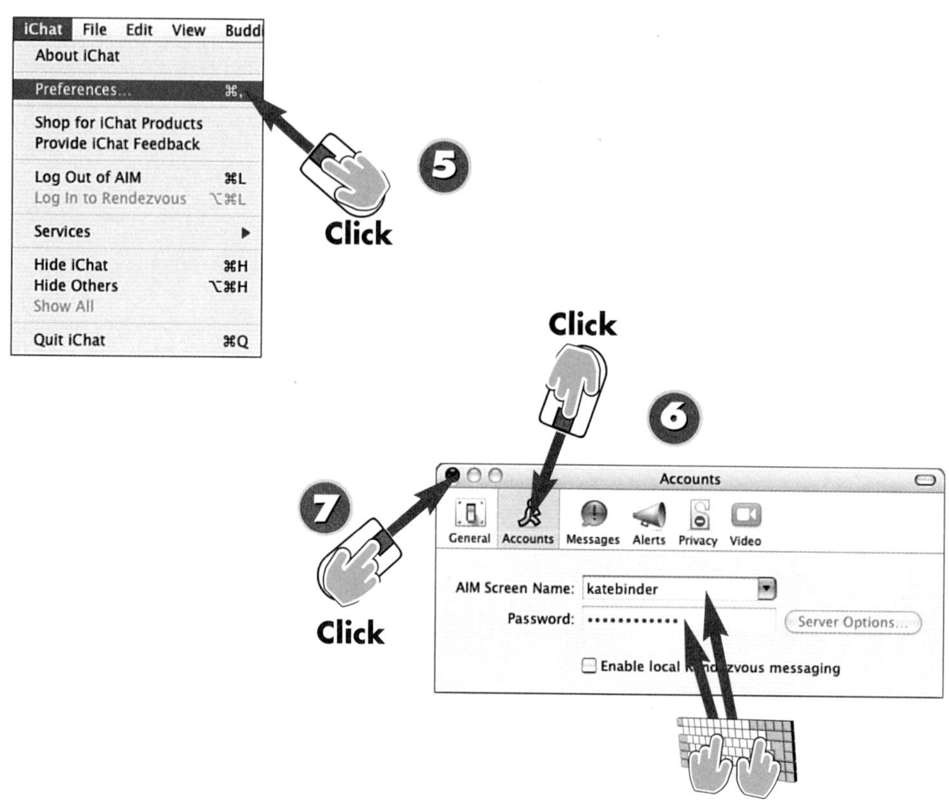

5 Choose **iChat**, **Preferences**.

6 Click the **Accounts** button and enter your AIM screen name and password, or, if you have a .Mac account, choose **Use my .Mac account** from the pop-up menu.

7 Click the **Close** button to save your changes.

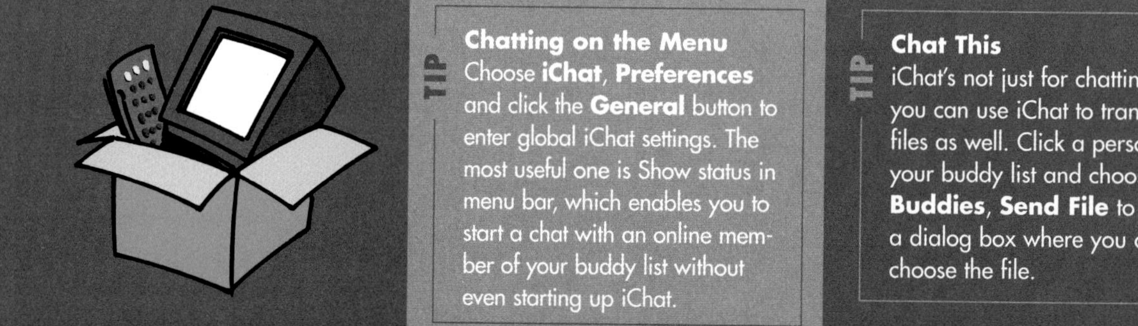

TIP

Chatting on the Menu
Choose **iChat**, **Preferences** and click the **General** button to enter global iChat settings. The most useful one is Show status in menu bar, which enables you to start a chat with an online member of your buddy list without even starting up iChat.

TIP

Chat This
iChat's not just for chatting—you can use iChat to transfer files as well. Click a person in your buddy list and choose **Buddies**, **Send File** to open a dialog box where you can choose the file.

Messaging with iChat

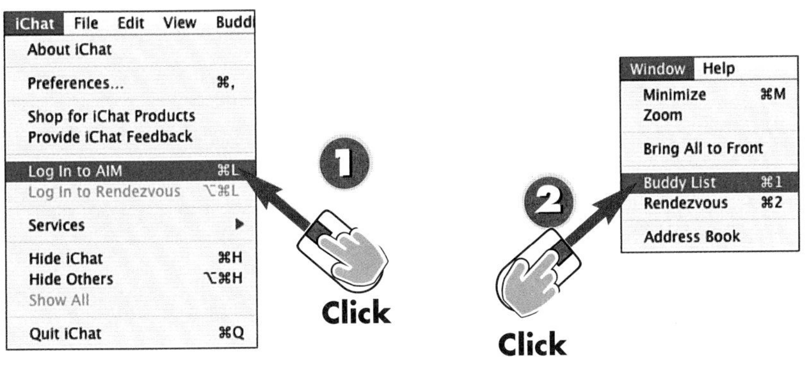

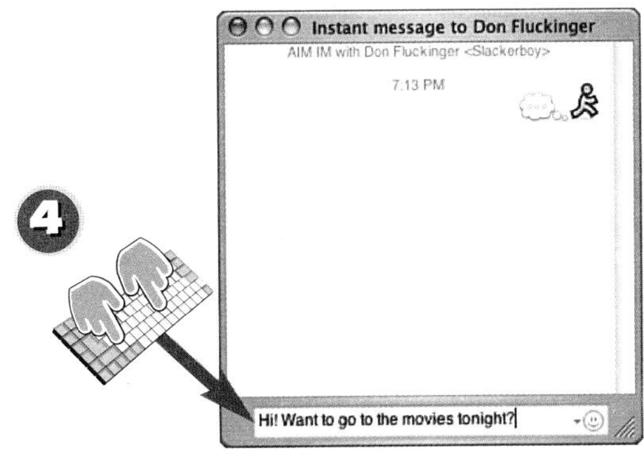

1. Open iChat from the Applications folder and choose **iChat**, **Log In to AIM**.
2. Choose **Window**, **Buddy List** if your buddy list isn't visible.
3. Double-click the name or screen name of the person to whom you want to send an instant message.
4. Enter your message at the bottom of the message window and press **Return** to send the message.

INTRODUCTION

Chatting with iChat requires two things: You must sign on to AIM with iChat and know the screen name of the person you want to reach. Conveniently enough, your buddy list is stored on AOL's servers, so it follows you around—you'll always see your own buddy list even if you log in on a computer other than your own.

TIP

On the Record

You can save transcripts of iChat conversations: Choose **iChat**, **Preferences** and click the **Messages** button. Click **Automatically save chat transcripts**. Click the **Open Folder** button to go to the folder of saved transcripts.

HINT

A Two-Way Street

You don't have to be an AOL member to use iChat. Whether you use an AOL screen name or a .Mac one, iChat works the same. However, you can use an AOL screen name with AOL Instant Messenger, but you can't use a .Mac name with AIM.

Talking over the Internet in iChat

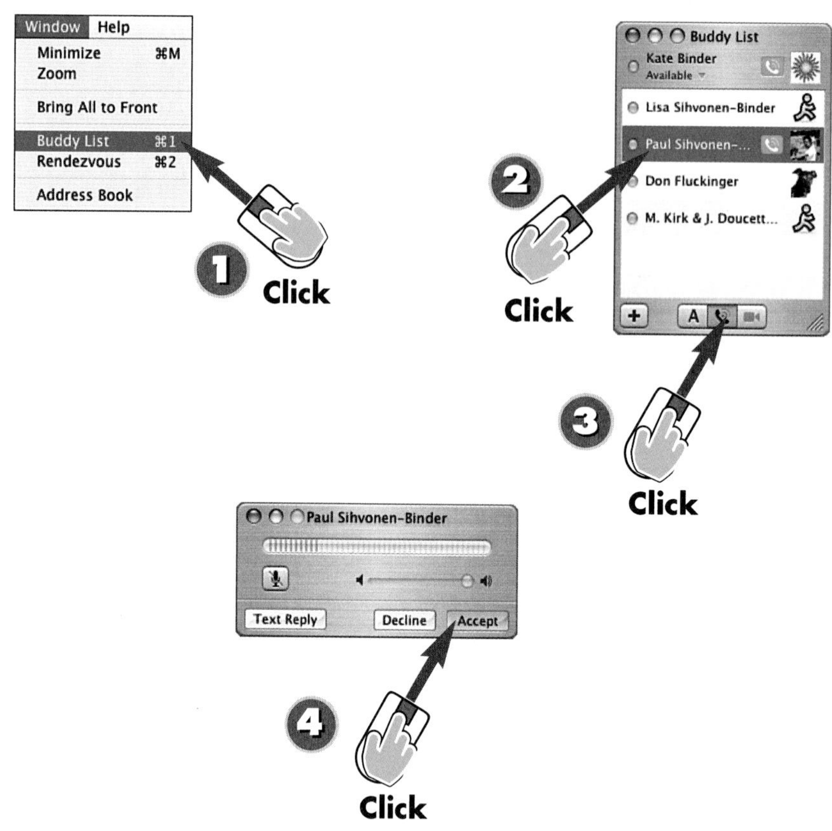

1. In iChat, choose **Window**, **Buddy List** if your buddy list isn't visible.
2. Click the name or screen name of the person to whom you want to talk.
3. Click the **Start Audio Chat** button at the bottom of the Buddy List window.
4. If you receive an audio chat invitation, click **Accept** to begin the conversation.

INTRODUCTION

With iChat AV (the version that comes with Mac OS X 10.3) and a microphone, you can enjoy voice conversations over the Net with anyone similarly equipped. All PowerBooks and iBooks have built-in microphones, and mics for other Macs are very inexpensive—so it's time to say hello to iChat AV and goodbye to your long-distance phone bill.

HINT

Going One Way

If the person you want to talk to has iChat AV but no microphone, you can still have one-way audio along with two-way text. This feature is great for calling up your microphone-less friends via iChat and singing "Happy Birthday" to them.

Sending Video over the Internet in iChat

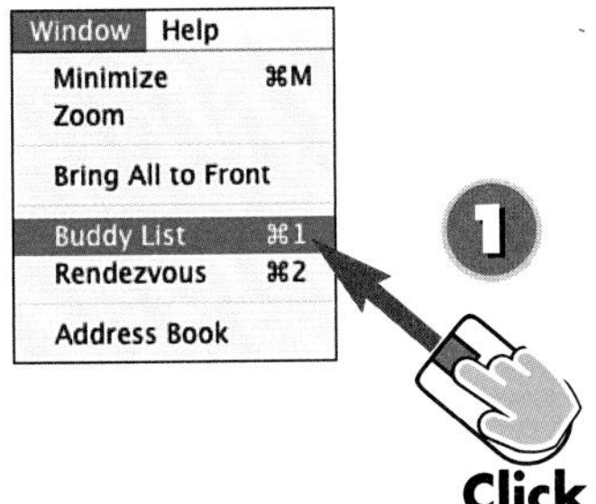

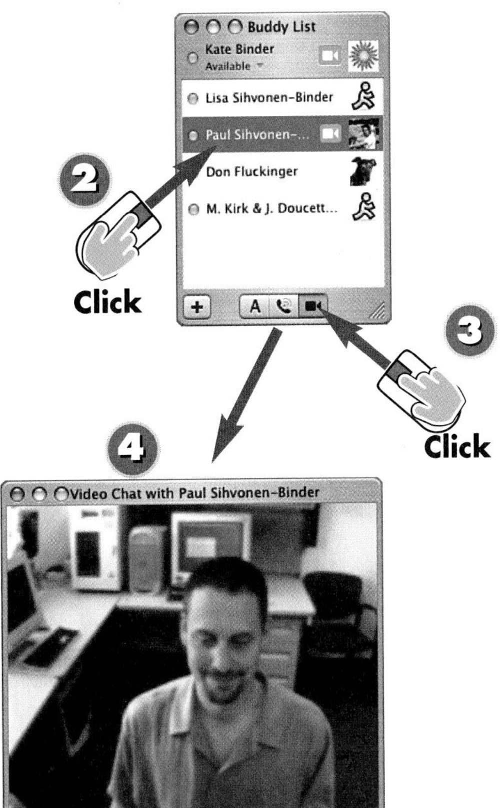

1. In iChat, choose **Window**, **Buddy List** if your buddy list isn't visible.
2. Click the name or screen name of the person to whom you want to talk.
3. Click the **Start Video Chat** button at the bottom of the Buddy List window.
4. The video window opens and you can see the person with whom you are chatting.

INTRODUCTION

Who needs a videophone? You don't—you have your Mac. If you also have a broadband connection (such as DSL or a cable modem) and a FireWire Webcam, you're good to go. First, make sure your camera is plugged in to your Mac and working correctly. Then check your iChat preferences to ensure iChat realizes it's there.

HINT

Where to Find a Cam

Most Webcams use USB interfaces. Some FireWire Webcams to check out are the PYRO 1394 (**www.adstech.com**), the iSight (**www.apple.com**), and the iBOT (**www.orangemicro.com**).

TIP

Knock Knock

If someone initiates a video or audio chat with you, you see a dialog box telling you so. As soon as you've combed your hair, you can click Accept to begin chatting.

Editing Your iChat Buddy List

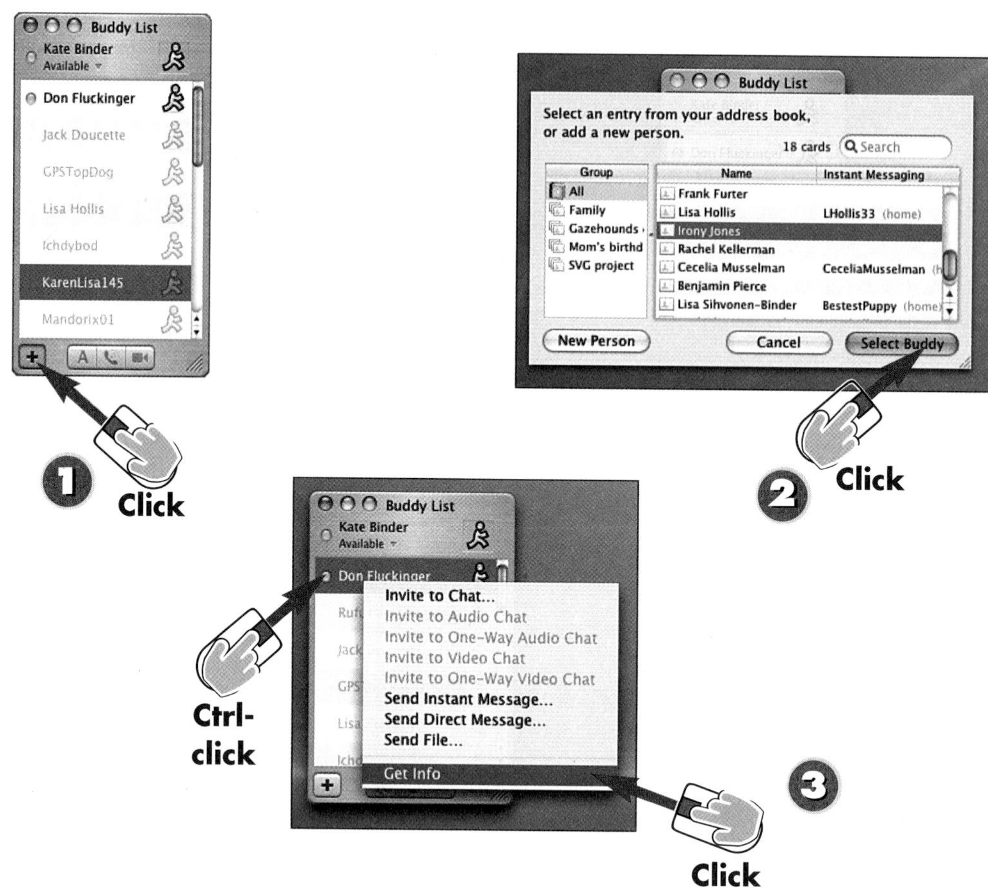

1. To add a buddy in iChat, choose **Window**, **Buddy List** and click the **+** button.
2. Choose a listing from your Address Book and click **Select Buddy**, or click **New Person** to add someone who's not in your Address Book.
3. To change a buddy's screen name or other information, **Ctrl-click** the name and choose **Get Info** from the contextual menu.

INTRODUCTION

If iChat finds your buddies' screen names in your Address Book, it can attach their real names to them and display those in the Buddy List window. The most convenient thing you can do with the buddy list is set it to show only buddies who are online at the moment.

TIP

Nice to Meet You

If you're adding a completely new person to your buddy list, you must enter the screen name. If you want, you can also add the person's first and last name and email address. When you're done, click **+**.

TIP

Bye-Bye

To remove a buddy, click to select the name and choose **Buddies**, **Remove Buddy**.

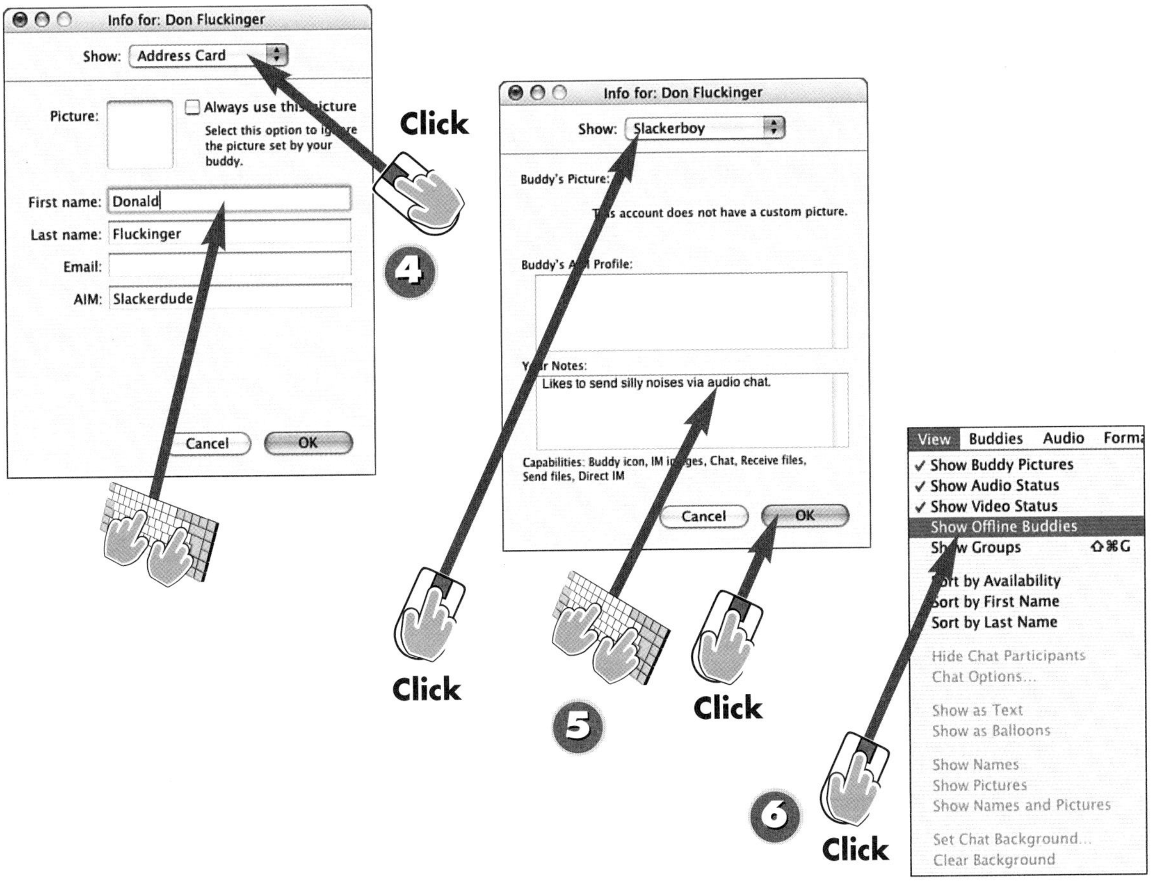

4. Choose **Address Card** from the **Show** pop-up menu and make your changes.
5. To make notes about the person, choose the screen name from the pop-up menu and enter the information in the **Your Notes** field; then click **OK**.
6. To show only buddies who are currently online, choose **View**, **Show Offline Buddies** to remove the check mark next to it.

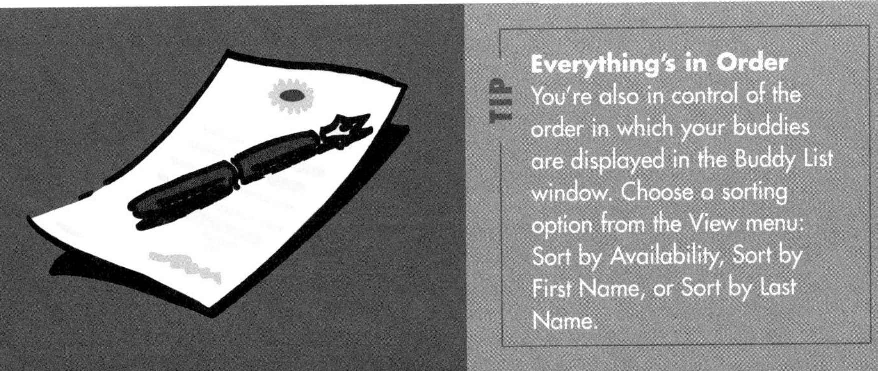

TIP

Everything's in Order

You're also in control of the order in which your buddies are displayed in the Buddy List window. Choose a sorting option from the View menu: Sort by Availability, Sort by First Name, or Sort by Last Name.

Setting Up .Mac

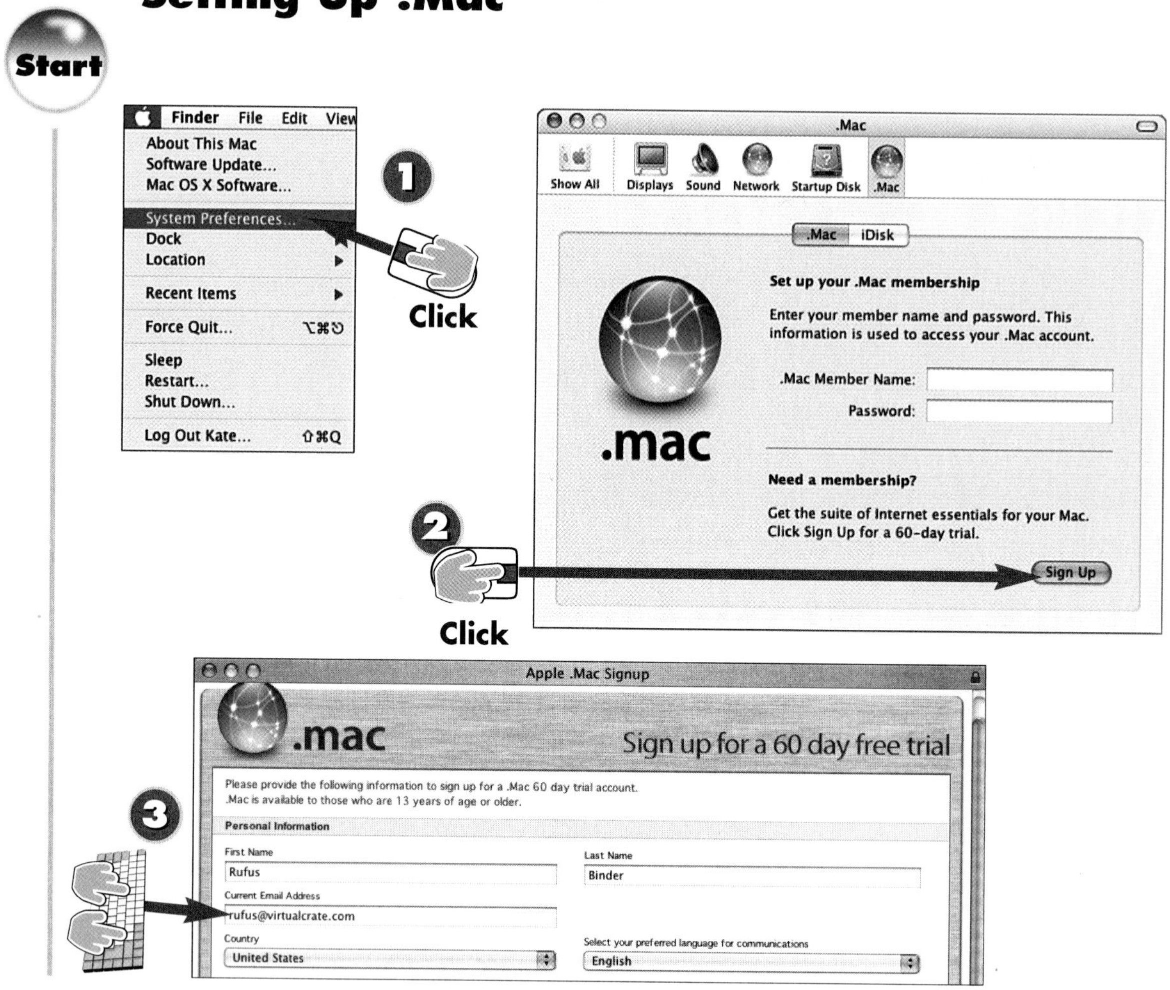

1. Choose **Apple menu**, **System Preferences**, and click the **.Mac** icon.
2. Click **Sign Up** to go to the .Mac Web page.
3. Click the **Free Trial** button to see the sign-up page. Enter the requested information and click **Continue**.

INTRODUCTION

.Mac is Apple's own set of Web services, including email, a custom Web site, online storage space (iDisk), e-cards, and more. It costs $99 per year, but the first two months are free—so why not give it a try? Many .Mac services are accessible directly from your Mac desktop—such as file storage on your iDisk—and others are based on the .Mac Web site.

HINT

What's an iDisk?
An iDisk is your hard drive on the Internet. It's storage space on an Apple server that belongs just to you. You can use it to store pictures for your .Mac Web page, for backing up your important files, or to hold anything you want.

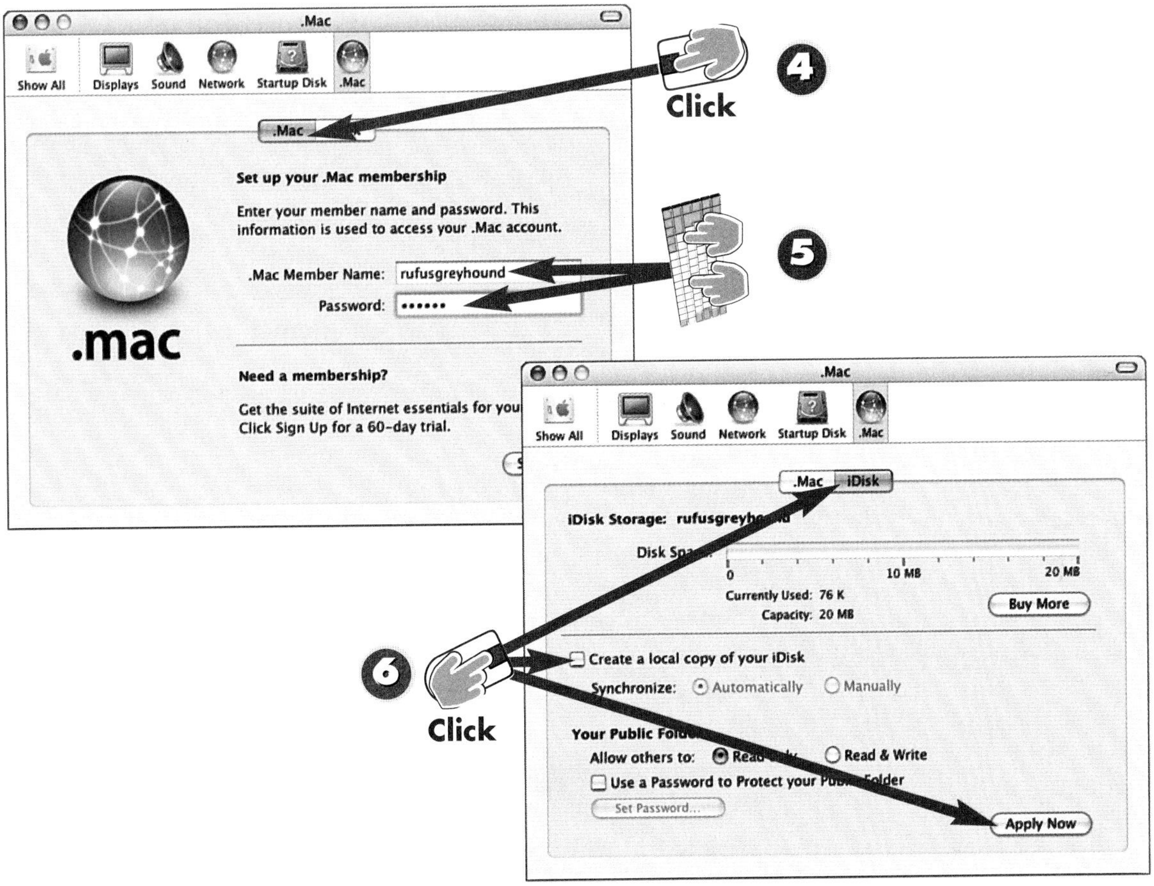

4. Make a note of your account settings; then return to System Preferences and click the **.Mac** tab in .Mac preferences.

5. Enter your new .Mac username and password.

6. Click the **iDisk** tab and click to check or uncheck the **Create a local copy of your iDisk** box; then click **Apply Now**.

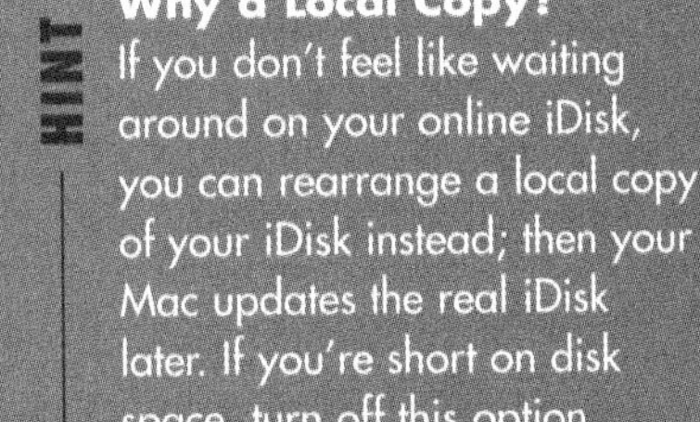

HINT

Why a Local Copy?
If you don't feel like waiting around on your online iDisk, you can rearrange a local copy of your iDisk instead; then your Mac updates the real iDisk later. If you're short on disk space, turn off this option.

TIP

I Just Don't Remember
If you've forgotten your .Mac password, go to the .Mac Web site (**www.mac.com**) and click **Log In**. On the login page, click **Forget your password** and follow the directions to get your password back.

Surfing in Safari

Double-click

Click

Click

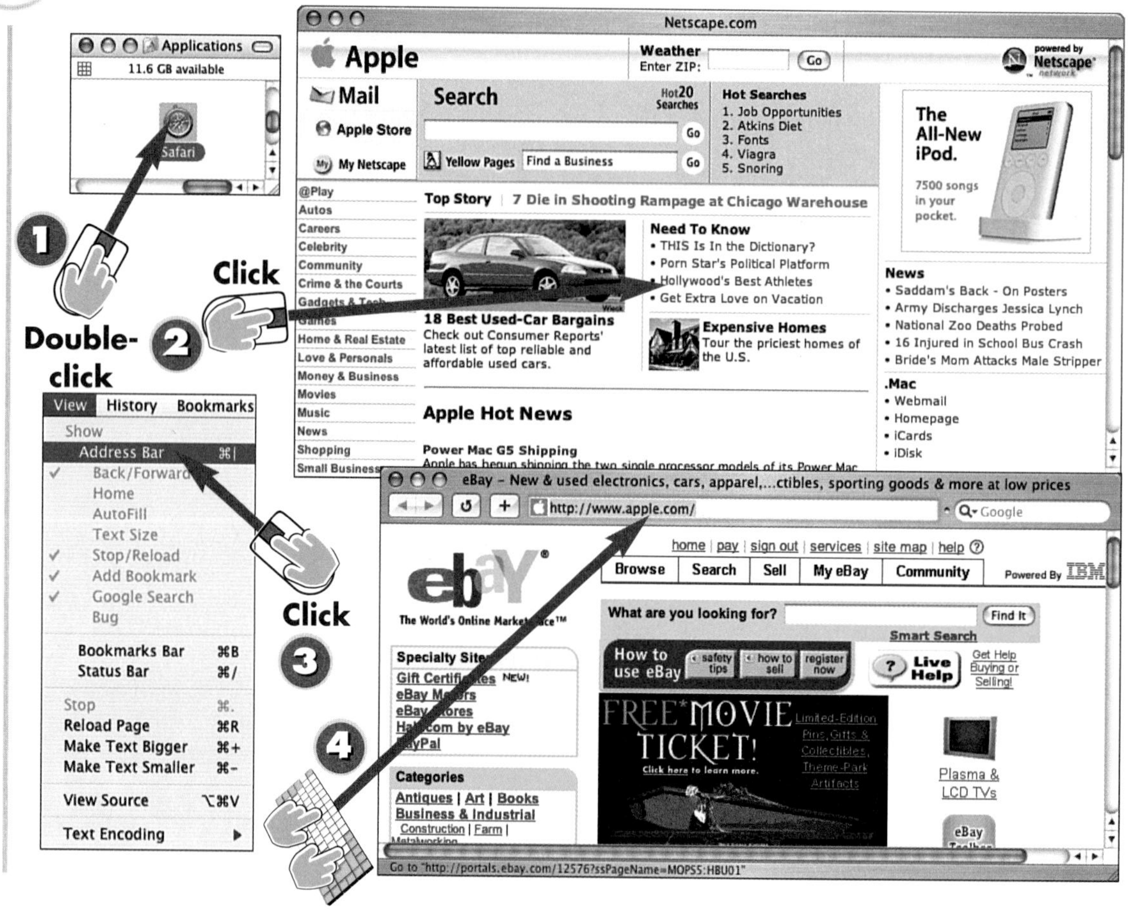

1. Start up Safari (in the Applications folder).

2. Click a link on your home page to go to another page.

3. Choose **View**, **Address Bar** if the address bar isn't already visible.

4. Type the URL in the address bar for the site you want to visit.

INTRODUCTION

For many years, Mac Web surfers had a simple choice of Web browsers: Netscape or Internet Explorer. Now Apple has decided to trump everyone with its very own, Mac-only browser, Safari. It's fast, it's smooth, and—best of all—it's designed from the ground up to work the way a Mac should.

TIP

Two for the Price of One

If you want to view a new Web page without getting rid of the one you're looking at now, press **Cmd-N** or choose **File**, **New Window** to begin surfing in a new window while leaving the current window open in the background.

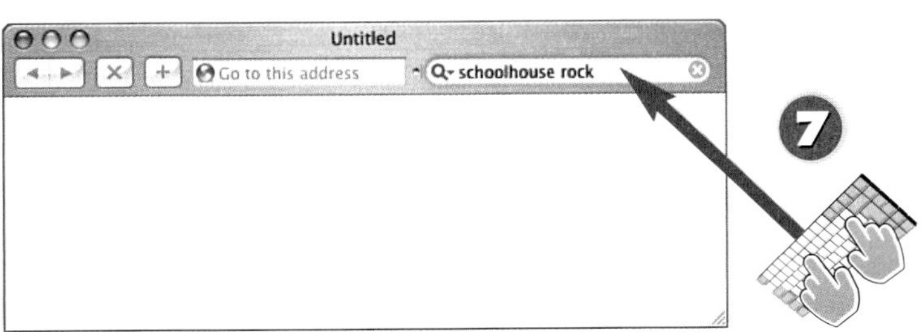

5 Click the **Previous Page** and **Next Page** buttons to go back and forward through the Web pages you've visited.

6 Click **Reload** to have Safari redisplay the page from scratch; this is how you can update pages that change every few minutes, such as online auction listings.

7 Type search terms in the **Google Search** field and press **Return** to go to the Google site and initiate the search.

TIP

Browsing with Tabs
You can view different Web pages in a single window, switching views by clicking a tab showing the page's name. Choose **Safari**, **Preferences** and click the **Tabs** button; then click to check the box marked **Enable Tabbed Browsing**.

TIP

Successful Surfing
To go back or forward, respectively, press **Cmd-[** or **Cmd-]**. To reload a page, press **Cmd-R**. And to see your bookmarks, press **Cmd-Option-B**.

TIP

Checking Your Status
Safari's Status bar shows you when it's contacting a Web server, and it shows you the URL behind any link you hold the mouse cursor over. To see the Status bar, choose **View**, **Status Bar**.

Making a Bookmark in Safari

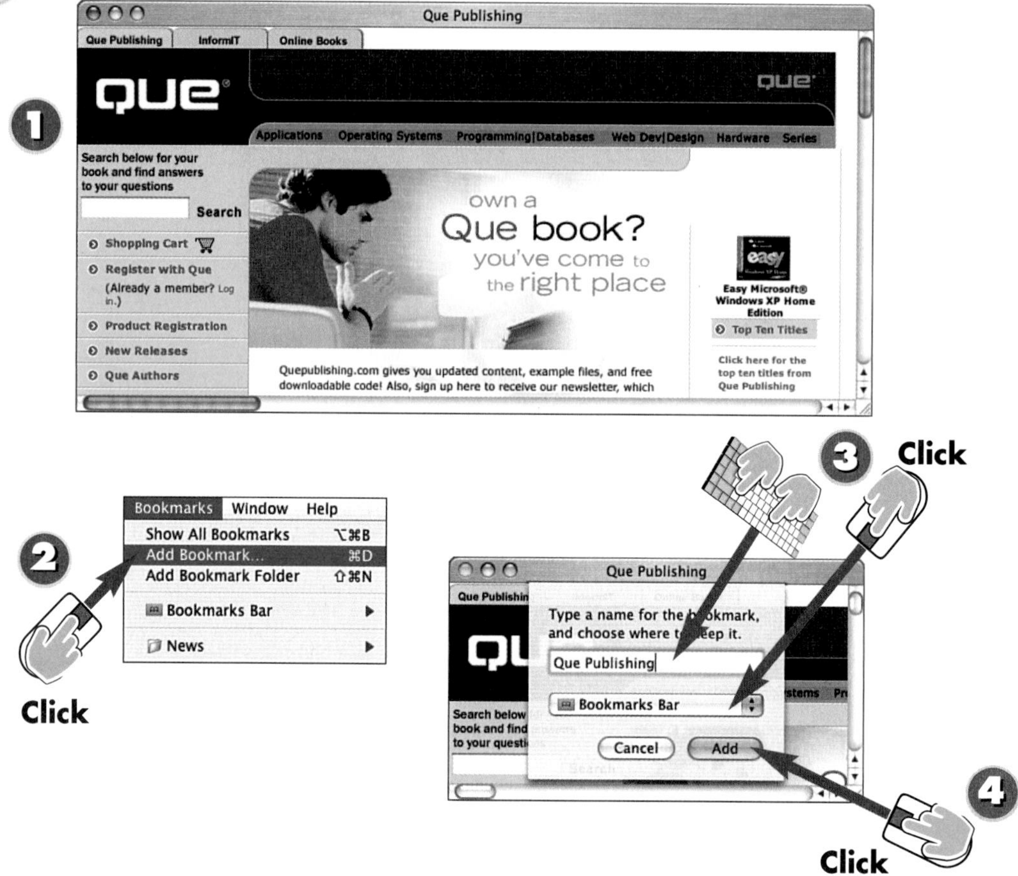

1. Open Safari (in the Applications folder) and go to the site for which you want to create a bookmark.
2. Choose **Bookmarks**, **Add Bookmark** (or press **Cmd-D**).
3. Enter a name for the bookmark (the page title is inserted by default) and choose a location for it.
4. Click **Add**.

INTRODUCTION

Whether you're used to calling them *bookmarks* or *favorites*, they mean the same thing: Your Web browser notes a Web site's address so it can get you there again the next time you ask for that page. Bookmarks have two components: the Web address (called a *URL*) and a name.

TIP

Bookmarks Here, There, and Over There

Safari stores bookmarks in three places: the Bookmarks menu, the Bookmarks bar, and its main Bookmarks collection. If you create a bookmark but don't put it in the Bookmarks menu or bar, go to your Bookmarks collection to find the bookmark.

Saving a Clickable Bookmark File

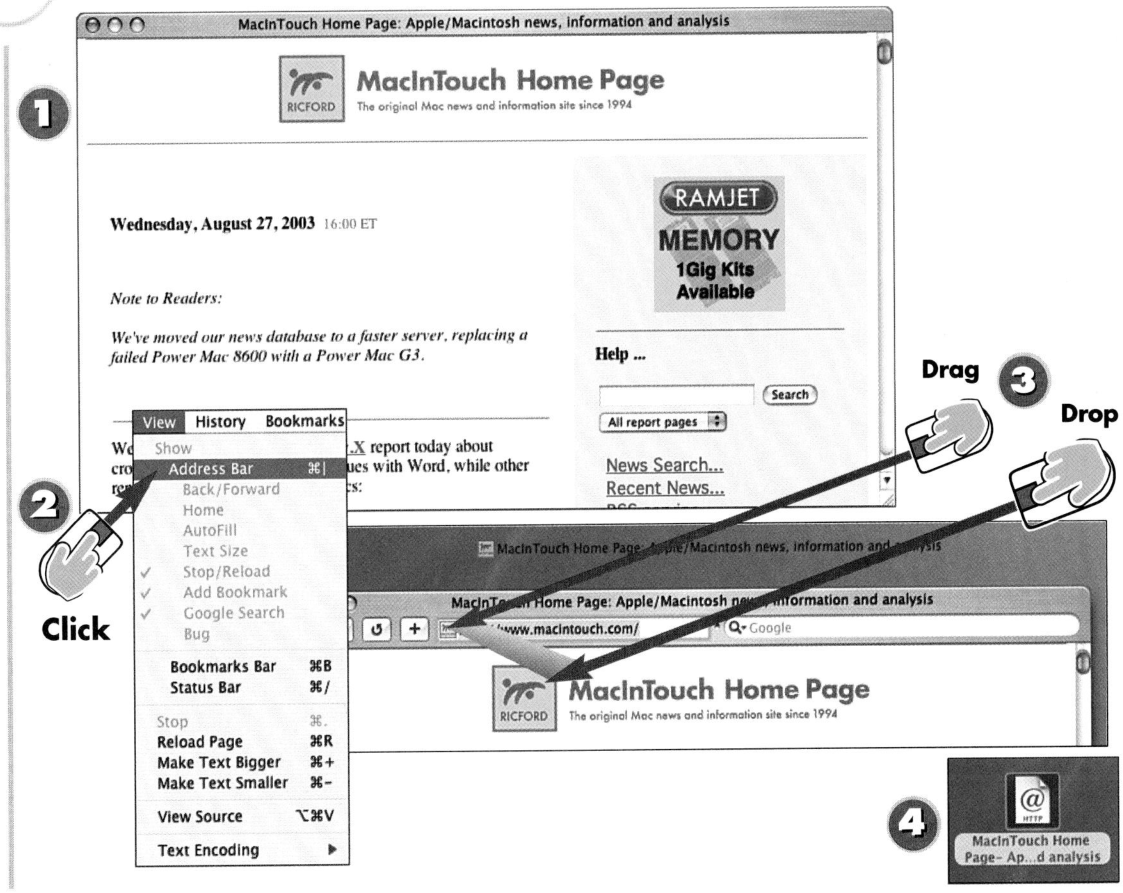

1. Start up Safari (in the Applications folder) and go to the site for which you want to create a clickable bookmark file.
2. Choose **View**, **Address Bar** if the address bar isn't already visible.
3. Click the icon to the left of the Web site's URL and drag it onto your desktop.
4. The clickable bookmark is now available on your desktop.

INTRODUCTION

When you're in a hurry to get to your favorite Web page—so much so that you don't even want to start up Safari first, you can double-click a bookmark file. Safari starts up or comes to the front (if it was already running) and opens that page in a new window. It doesn't interfere with any windows you already have open.

HINT

Where and How

Bookmark files are useful when you're working in the Finder. For quick surfing when you're using other programs, drag the files into the Dock so you can jump to your favorite sites with a single click in the Dock.

HINT

Click the Mark

You can use bookmark files to open your favorite Web pages every time you log in to your Mac. Put the files in your Documents folder, and then add them to your Login Items (turn to Part 11, "Sharing Your Mac with Multiple Users," to learn how).

Organizing Bookmarks

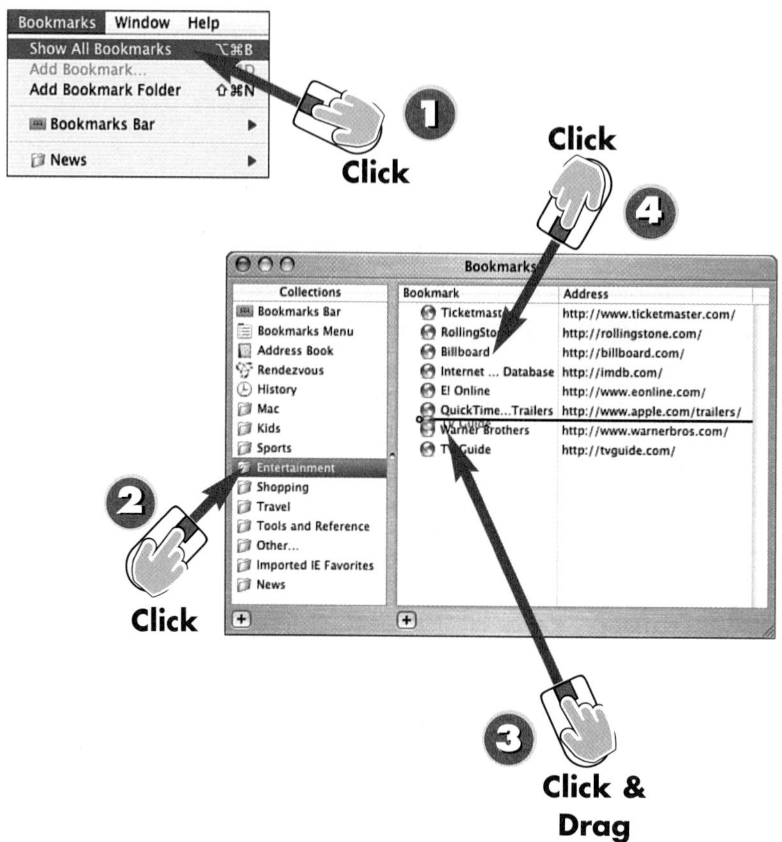

1. Choose **Bookmarks**, **Show All Bookmarks** (or click the **Bookmarks** button in the Bookmarks bar).
2. Click a collection in the **Collections** column to see the bookmarks it contains.
3. Drag bookmarks up or down to change their order.
4. Click a bookmark and press **Delete** to remove it.

INTRODUCTION

Some people never bookmark anything. Others are sensible enough to bookmark only sites they know they'll need again. And still others—naming no names here—bookmark just about everything. If you're in that third group, chances are you could stand to spend some time organizing your bookmarks.

HINT

More Bookmarks

You can fit a lot more bookmarks in the Bookmarks bar by using submenus. Create a folder for each bookmark category, and then drop your bookmarks inside. Back in the main window, click a category name to see the submenu of bookmarks.

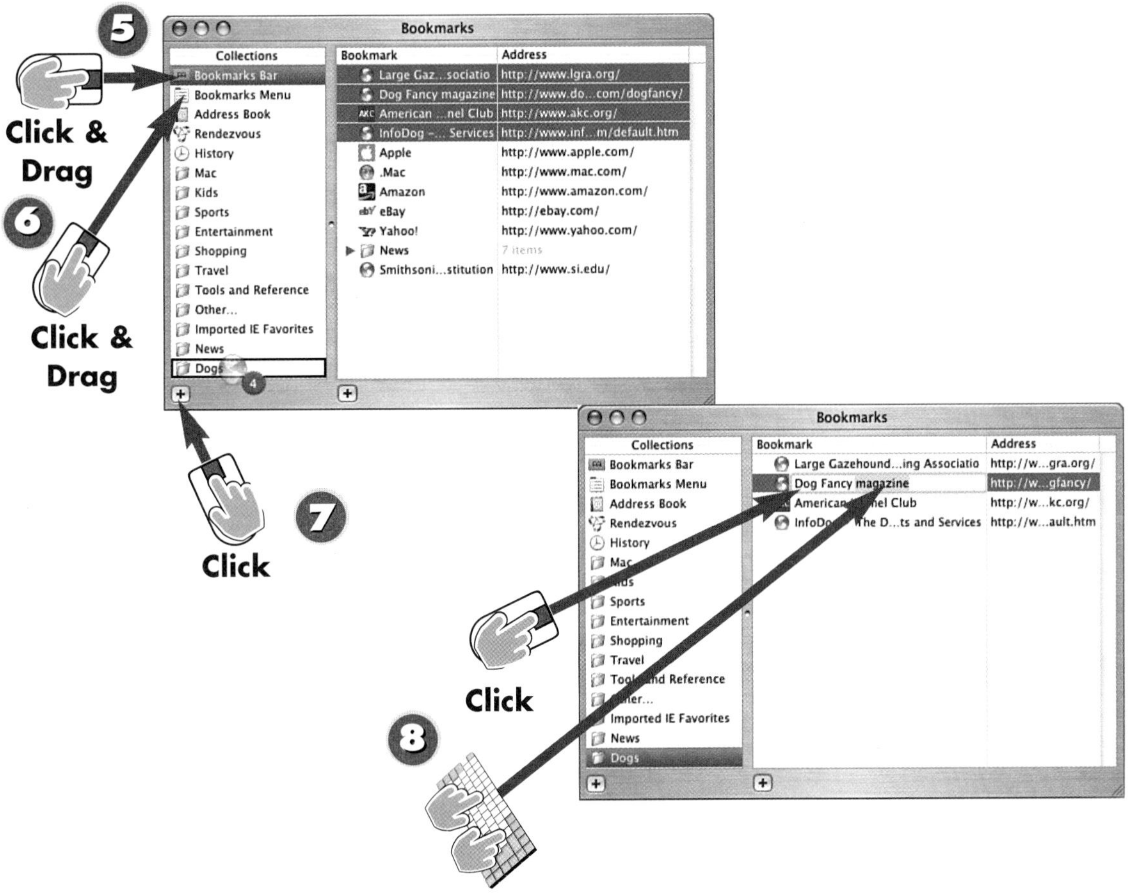

5 To add a bookmark to the Bookmarks bar, drag it into the **Bookmarks Bar** collection.

6 To add a bookmark to the Bookmarks menu, drag it into the **Bookmarks Menu** collection.

7 To make a submenu, add a folder by clicking the **Add** button at the bottom of the **Bookmark** column, give it a name, and then drag bookmarks into the folder.

8 To change the name of a bookmark or folder, click it, type the new name, and press **Return**.

TIP

More Address Book Integration

If you keep your contacts' URLs in the Address Book, you can add them to the Bookmarks bar or menu automatically. Choose **Safari**, **Preferences** and click the **Bookmarks** button; then click the appropriate check box to add Address Book items.

Using the History in Safari

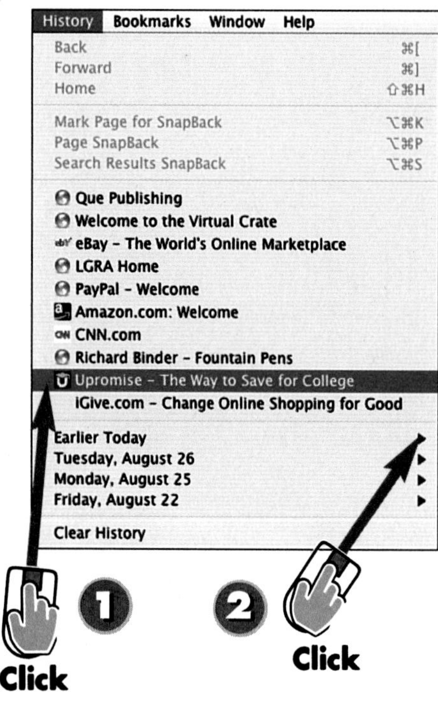

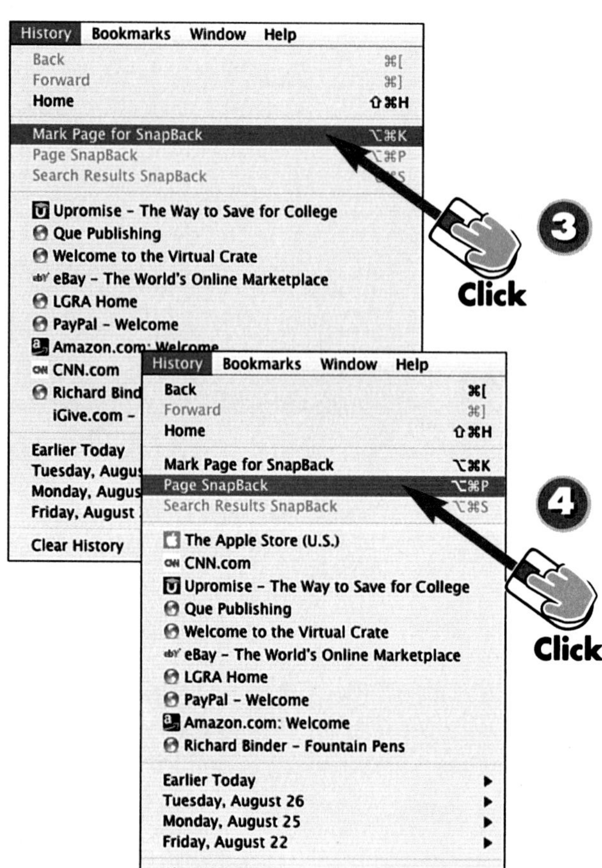

1. To return to one of the last 10 pages you've visited, click the **History** menu in Safari and choose the page's name.
2. To go back to an earlier page, click the **History** menu and choose the appropriate submenu; then choose the page's name.
3. To mark a specific page you know you'll want to return to, choose **History**, **Mark Page for SnapBack**.
4. To return to a marked page, choose **History**, **Page SnapBack**.

INTRODUCTION

Safari's History listing is just what you need when you need to go back to a Web site you visited recently but forgot to bookmark. It keeps track of the last several days of your surfing exploits, neatly listing the Web sites you visited in folders labeled by date.

TIP

A Fresh Start for History
If you've been surfing a lot and you're finding the History list a bit too crowded to let you find what you want, choose **History, Clear History** to start over with a blank History.

TIP

Automatic SnapBack
When you use Safari's Google search field, search results are automatically marked for SnapBack. When you click to view a page in the results, click the orange **SnapBack** button in the search field to return to that page.

Downloading Files

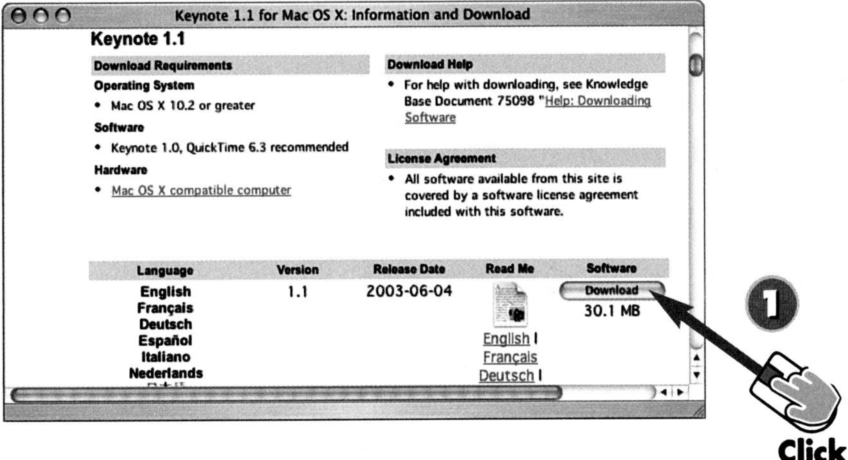

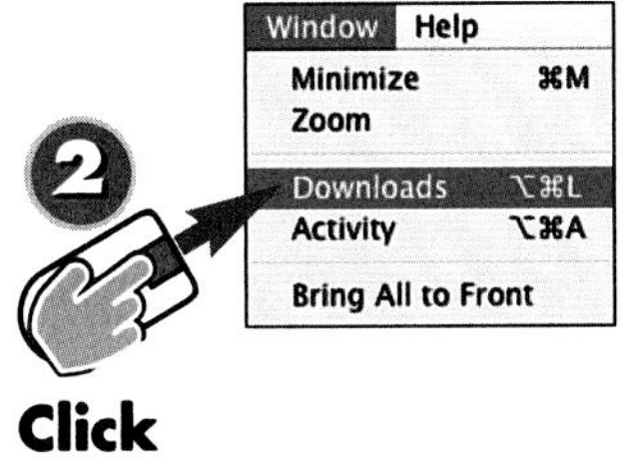

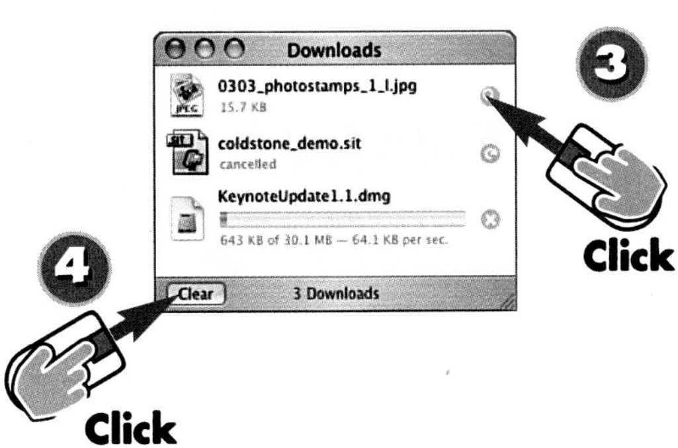

1. Click a Web page link to download a file.

2. To watch the download's progress, choose **Window**, **Downloads**.

3. To go to a previously downloaded file, locate it in the Downloads window and click the **Show in Finder** button next to its name.

4. Click the **Clear** button to remove all downloaded files from the Downloads window. This deletes Safari's record of the download, not the file itself.

INTRODUCTION

Surfing the Web isn't just about looking and reading; it's also about downloading—copying files from their homes on the Web to your Mac's hard drive. Using the Downloads window, you can monitor the status of files you're downloading now, find out what you've downloaded in the past, and locate downloaded files in the Finder.

TIP

Download with Care

Virus scanning software is a good investment if you transfer files from other computers. Check out Norton AntiVirus (**www.symantec.com**), Sophos Anti-Virus (**www.sophos.com**), Virex (**www.drsolomons.com**), and VirusBarrier X (**www.intego.com**).

Saving a Web Page in Safari

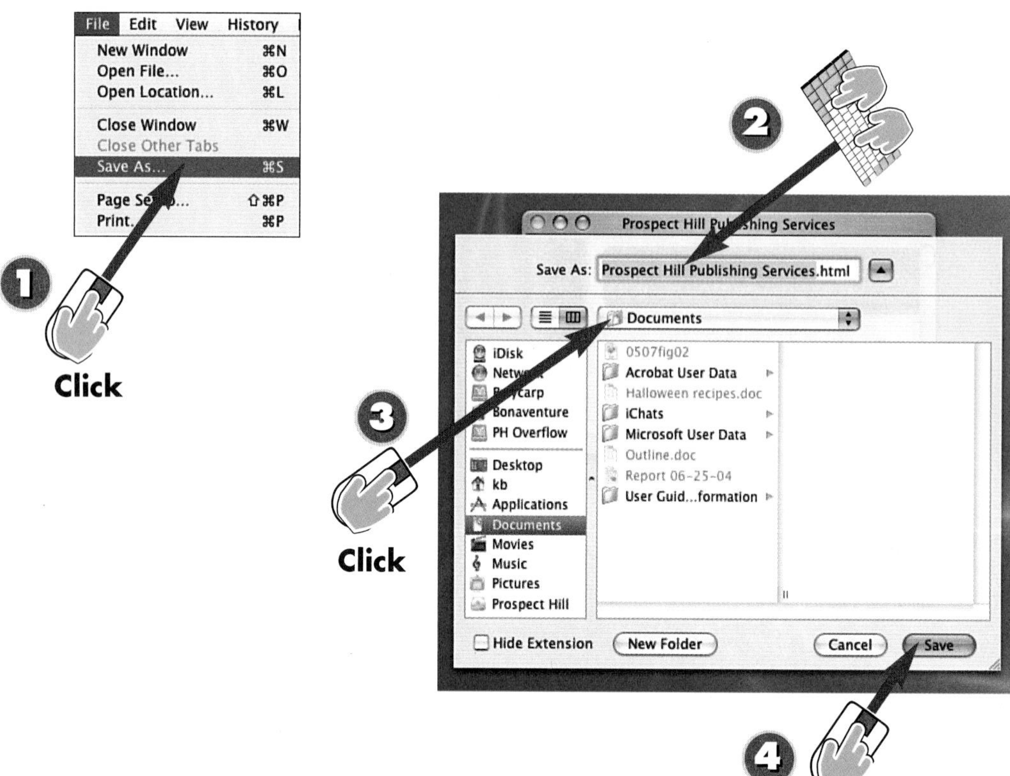

1. In Safari, choose **File**, **Save As**.
2. Enter a name for the file.
3. Choose a location to save the file.
4. Click **Save**.

INTRODUCTION

Safari can save Web pages in their original formats (HTML coding) so you can view them even when you're not online. Another reason to save Web pages is so you can look at how their code is constructed and copy cool techniques for your own Web pages. Remember that saving a Web page doesn't save the graphics.

TIP

What to Do with a Saved Page

To view a Web page saved from Safari, double-click its icon—it opens in Safari. If you are connected to the Internet, the graphics show up as well as the page. To look at a page's coding, start up TextEdit and open the file using the Open command. Or choose **View**, **View Source** in Safari—you can't edit the source in Safari, but this command is good for a quick look.

Automatically Filling Out Forms

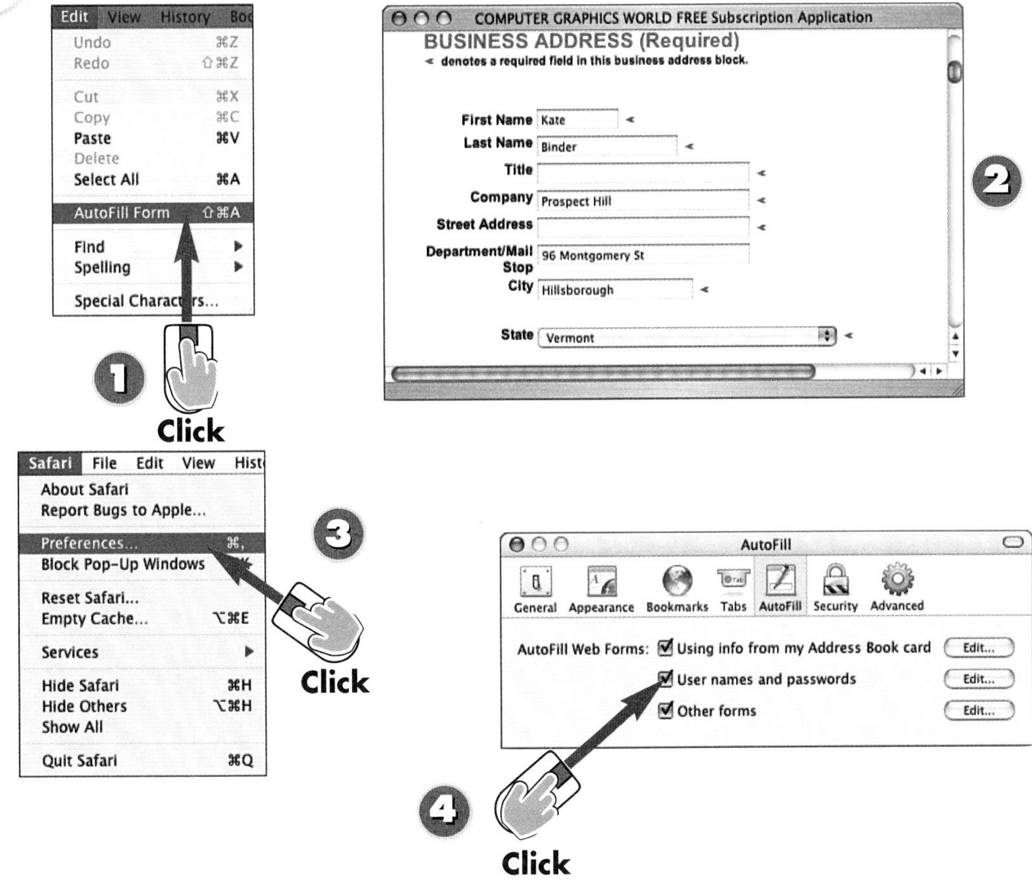

1. On a page with a form that requires this information, choose **Edit**, **AutoFill Form** (or press **Cmd-Shift-A**).

2. The information is automatically filled in.

3. To enable AutoFill to work with other types of forms, choose **Safari**, **Preferences**.

4. Click the **AutoFill** button and check **User names and passwords** and **Other forms**.

INTRODUCTION

Every time you buy something from a Web store, create a new account with a Web site, or sign up to receive some service from a Web site, you have to input the same information. Wouldn't it be nice if Safari could remember that information and type it in for you? Guess what? It can.

TIP

When Safari Gets It Wrong

Safari tints the fields yellow where it's inserted information. If Safari guesses wrong and inserts incorrect data, just click in the field and type the correct information to fix it.

HINT

First Things First

Before using AutoFill, make sure your address, phone numbers, fax number, and other information are correct in your Address Book (which you'll find in the Applications folder).

Backing Up to Your iDisk

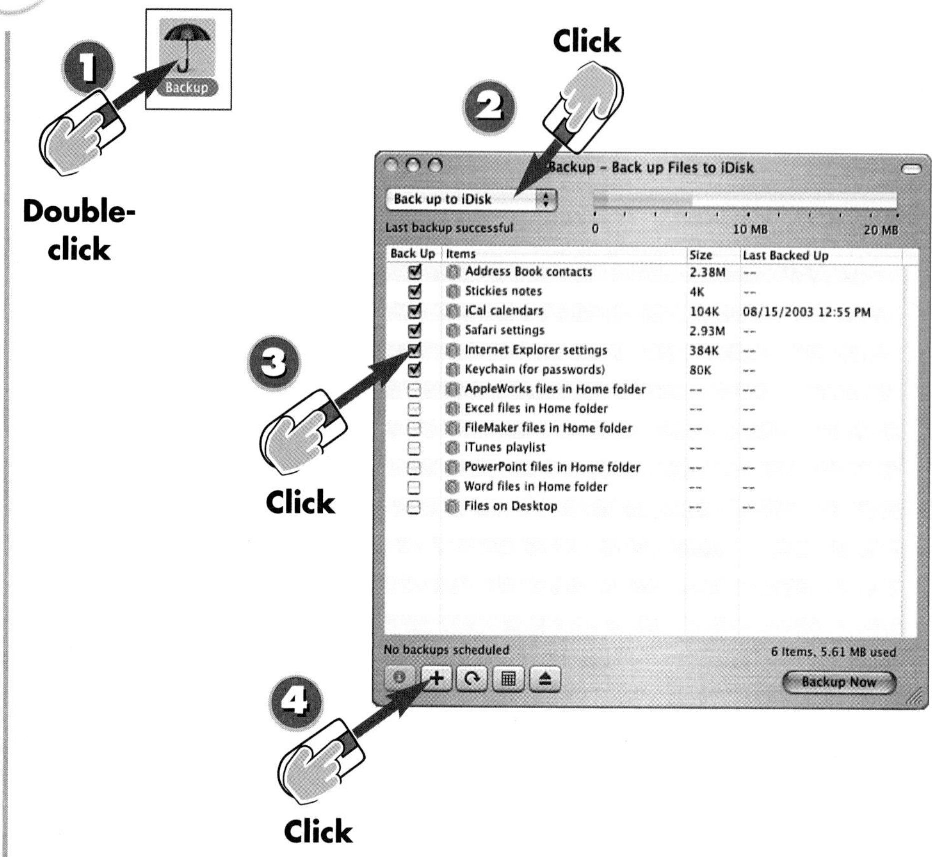

1. Copy Backup from the Software folder in your iDisk to your Applications folder and double-click it to open it.
2. Choose **Back up to iDisk** from the pop-up menu.
3. Click check boxes to select the files you want to back up. The total size of those files appears at the bottom of the window.
4. Click the **Add** button to include other files in the backup.

INTRODUCTION

Backing up your important files is a good thing, but you won't appreciate how good it is until you need that backup someday. In the meantime, take the experts' word for it—set up a backup routine and stick to it. You can automate backups to your iDisk with Apple's own Backup software.

HINT

When to Upgrade

Backup is great for home users or very small businesses that don't need to back up a lot of data. If you need to back up your entire hard drive daily, however, you should look into an industrial-strength backup program such as Retrospect (**www.dantz.com**).

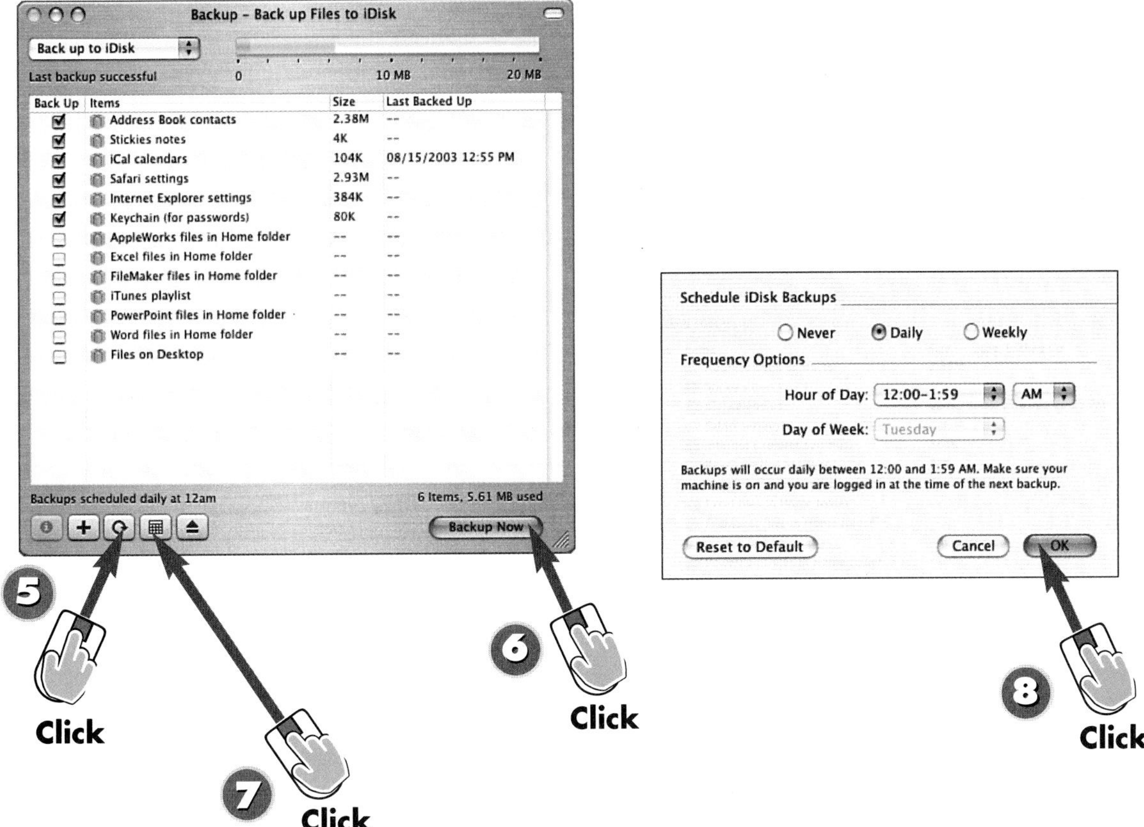

5. Click the **Update** button if you've made changes to your files since you started Backup.

6. Click **Backup Now** to begin moving files to the iDisk.

7. Click the **Schedule** button to set a schedule for automatic backups.

8. Select a frequency, time, and day and click **OK**. Backup starts automatically at that time and backs up the files currently selected.

HINT

Backing Up the Big Files

If you have a built-in CD-R drive, CD-RW drive, or SuperDrive, you can back up to CDs. They hold more information than your iDisk, and backups go more quickly. Insert a blank disc after you start Backup, and the Back up to CD menu option becomes available.

HINT

For the Stubborn Ones

Still not backing up? Remember, you're the one with the most to lose if your hard drive crashes irretrievably. And statistics show that a major crash will happen to every computer user sometime in his life.

Creating a .Mac Home Page

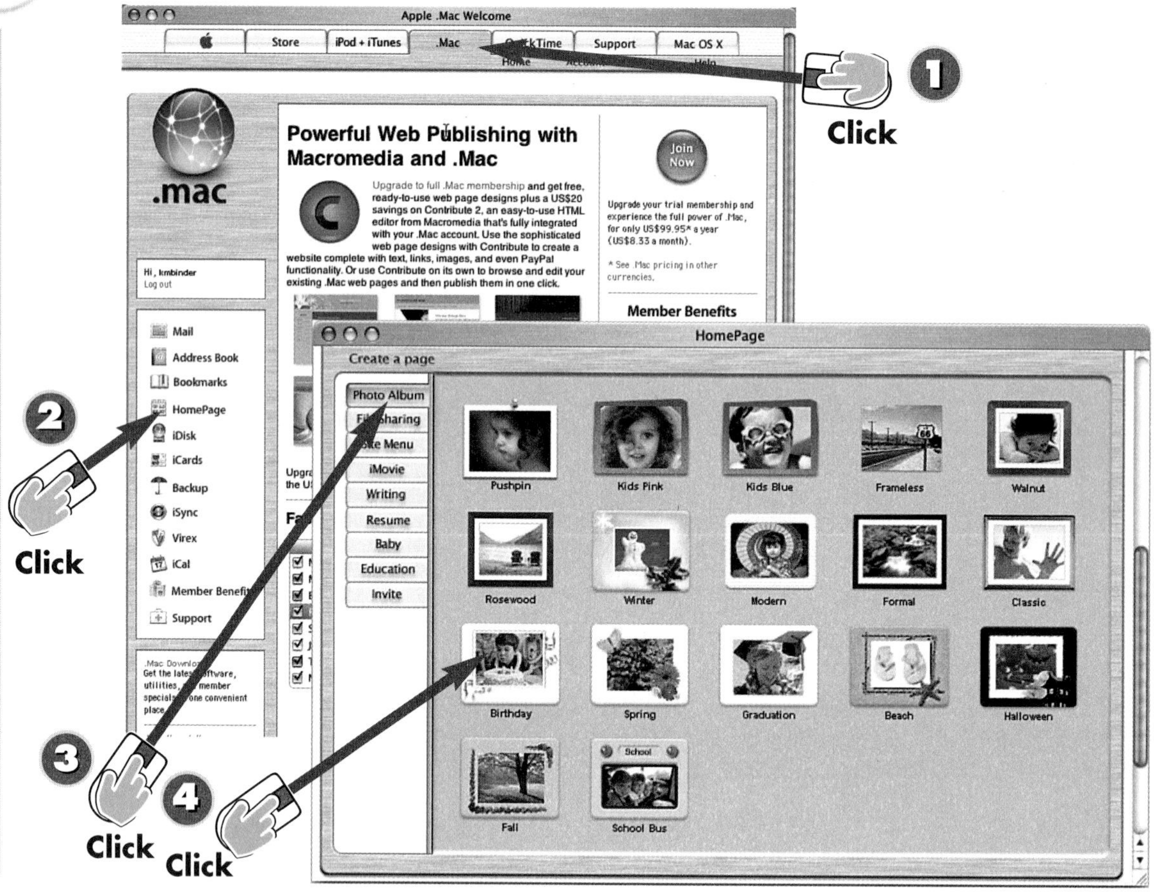

1. Use your Web browser to go to Apple's Web site; then click the **.Mac** tab and sign in.
2. Click **HomePage** in the column on the left side of the page.
3. Click a page category on the left side of the page.
4. Click the right side of the page to choose a page from the category.

INTRODUCTION

HomePage features built-in templates for photo albums, file sharing, iMovies, résumés, new baby announcements, invitations, and more—each category comes with anywhere from a few to a couple dozen page templates you can customize to suit your needs.

TIP

Rolling Your Own

If you're already a Web wizard, you can create your own Web pages in any program. Just drop them into the Sites folder on your iDisk and make sure the main page is called **index.html**; your pages will be published just like ones created in HomePage.

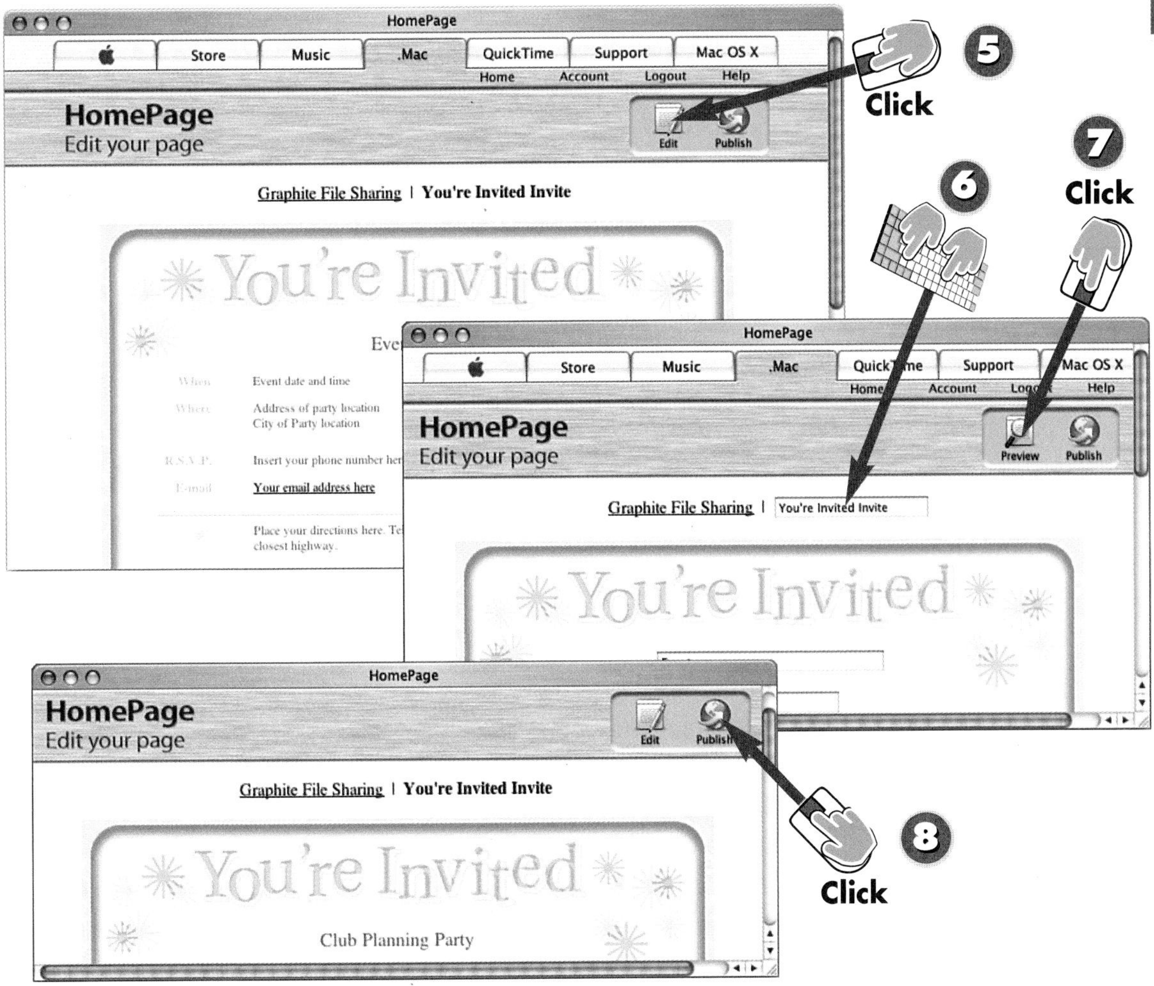

5 Click **Edit** at the top of the page to make changes to the basic template.

6 Type your changes in the text entry fields and click the buttons to insert photos from the Pictures folder on your iDisk or add Web links.

7 Click **Preview** to see how the page looks.

8 Click **Edit** if you want to make more changes, or click **Publish** if you're satisfied.

TIP

Letting the World Know

If you want to let your friends know about your new Web site, click the **Announce Site** button at the top of the page that appears after you click Publish. You'll be guided through creating an e-card that will be emailed to your friends to publicize your new home on the Web.

PART 10

Getting an iLife

iLife is Apple's name for its collection of four *i* programs: iPhoto, iTunes, iMovie, and iDVD. This software represents the company's effort to empower Mac users to create and control their own entertainment media. With iLife, you can manage and share your digital photos; acquire and mix music; produce digital movies; and create professional-looking DVDs that combine movies, music, still images, and more.

In this part you'll learn how to get your pictures into iPhoto and organize them into albums. When you have albums, you can print your photos, share them on the Web, and design real coffee-table-style books of photos. You'll also learn how to import music from your CD collection into iTunes, create custom mixes called *playlists*, and burn your own CDs. With a visit to the iTunes Music Store, you'll pick and choose from the latest tunes on the market—at 99¢ a pop.

With iMovie, you'll learn how to import video from your camcorder, add scene transitions and fun special effects, and save the final result so you can share it with your friends and family. Finally, you'll be introduced to iDVD; with this program, you'll create a new DVD project, add video and other elements to it, preview it to make sure it's just the way you want it, and then burn it to a DVD disc so you can play it in your DVD player.

Managing Photos, Video, and Music

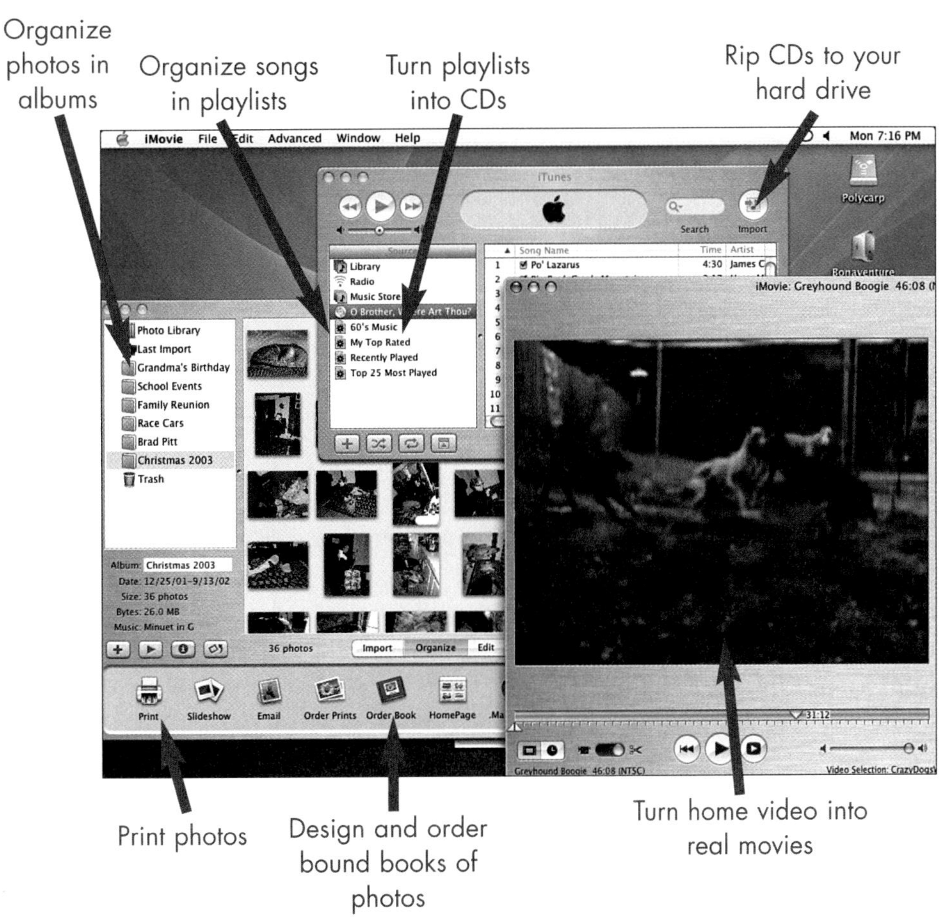

Importing Photos into iPhoto

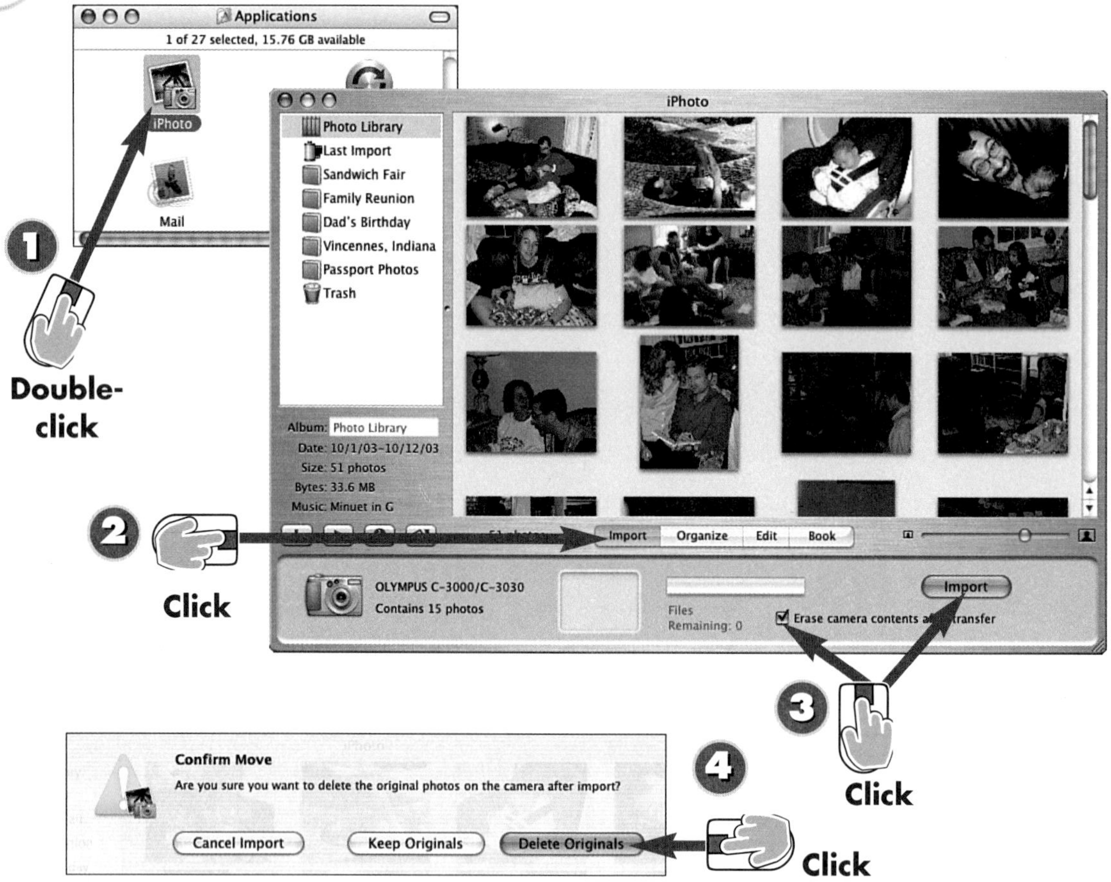

1. Plug your camera in to your Mac's USB port, turn it on, and start up iPhoto (in the Applications folder).
2. Click the **Import** tab.
3. Check the **Erase camera contents after transfer** box to erase the camera's storage media after transferring files to your Mac; then click **Import**.
4. Click **Delete Originals** if you're deleting the original images from the camera. iPhoto imports the photos and switches to the Organize tab to display them.

INTRODUCTION

iPhoto can do a lot of things, but its most important function is simply providing a place to keep all your digital photos. Think of it as a super-duper photo album, or maybe a filing cabinet for your photos (if you take a lot of them). So, the first step in doing anything with iPhoto is getting your photos into its database.

TIP

You Can Get There From Here

To import image files from your hard drive, a removable disk, or camera media you've mounted on the Desktop, drag and drop the files directly onto the Photo Library entry in the Albums list.

HINT

Found, Not Lost

If you can't find the latest photos you brought into iPhoto, check out the Last Import album. That's where the most recent group of images you imported is always stored.

Creating iPhoto Albums

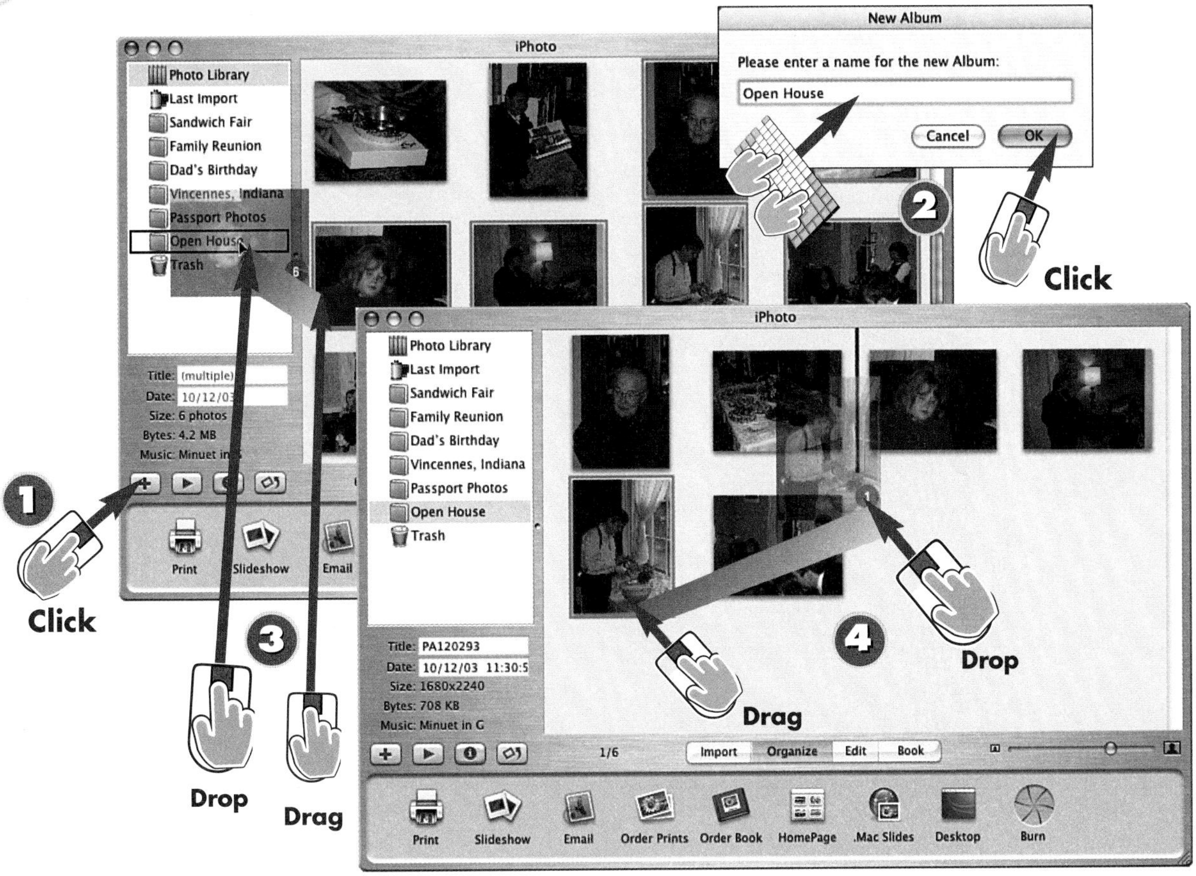

1. In iPhoto, click the **Add Album** button.

2. Type a name for the new album and click **OK**.

3. Add photos to the new album by dragging and dropping them from the preview area to the album's name.

4. Click the album's name and drag and drop the album's photos in the preview area to change their order.

INTRODUCTION

Rather than being exactly parallel to a real-word photo album, an iPhoto album is really just a way to group photos together so iPhoto knows which photos you want to print, display, or export. Albums are the way you organize your photos so you can find the ones you want. Creating an album is also the first step in creating a book or Web page.

TIP

Information Please

You can add descriptive information to the photos in your albums. Click the **Show Info** button below the Album column to display Title, Comments, and Date fields that you can fill out.

Printing Photos

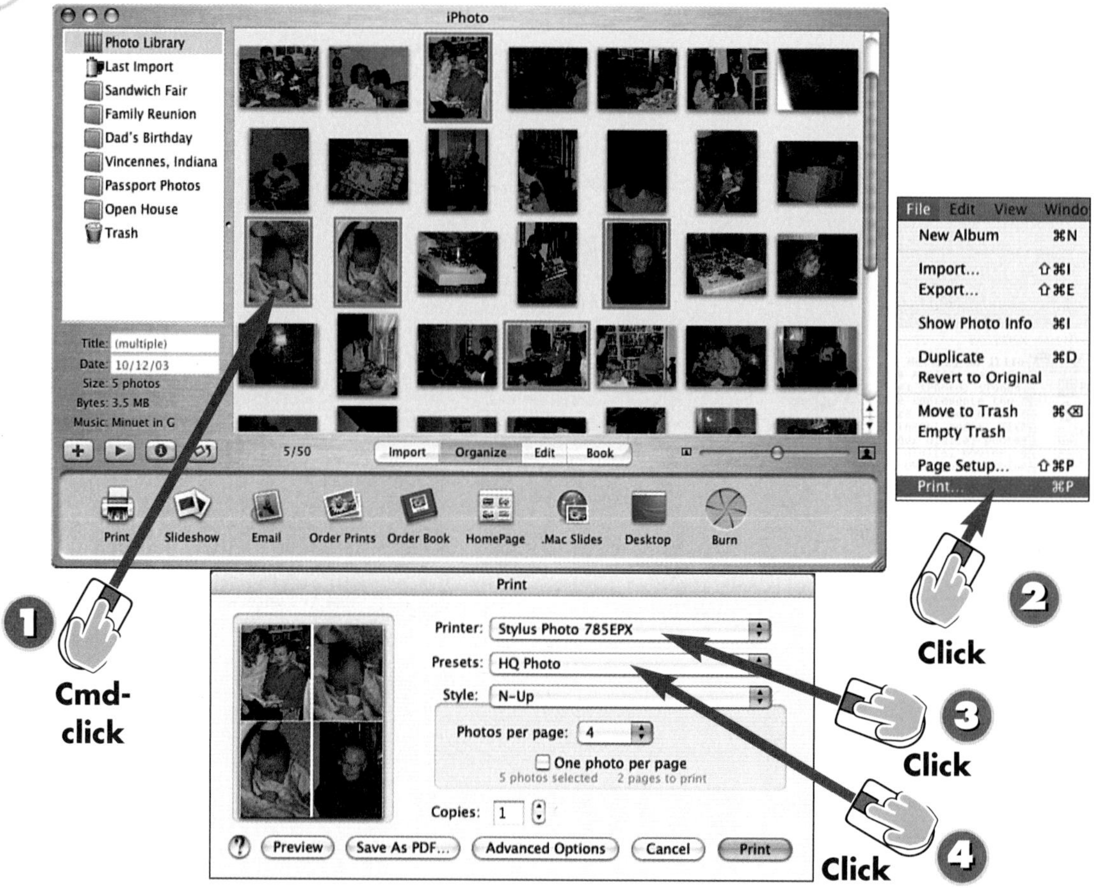

1. Click an album to print all its photos, or Cmd-click in the preview area to select individual photos.
2. Choose **File**, **Print**.
3. Choose a printer from the **Printer** pop-up menu.
4. If available, choose an option from the **Preset** pop-up menu to set the output type.

INTRODUCTION

It's not a paperless world yet, so you're bound to want to print your photos at some point. iPhoto offers several printing layouts so you can create standard prints, picture packages like the ones photo studios offer, or just plain printouts in your choice of size and number.

TIP

Fine-Tuning Print Settings
Although your printer driver probably includes presets for photo and plain paper, you'll need to fine-tune the settings for your printer. Click **Advanced Options** to get to a Print dialog box with the usual options, including color and media.

TIP

Cutting Paper Costs
If you're printing the Contact Sheet layout, check the **Save Paper** box to put the photos closer together; depending on the number of photos in your selection, this could save one or more sheets of paper.

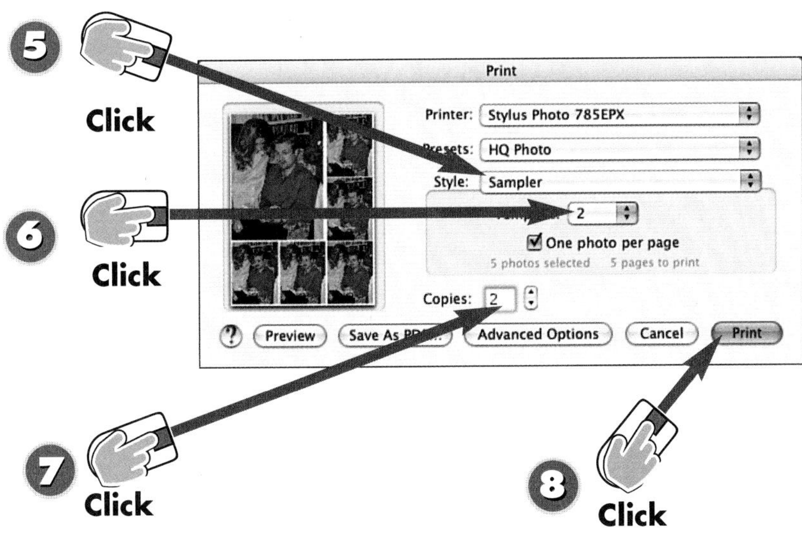

5. Choose a **Style** option.

6. Make the style's settings, such as the number of prints per page.

7. Enter the number of copies you want to print.

8. Click **Print**.

HINT

Proxy Preview

The proxy preview area in iPhoto's Print dialog box shows you how your printouts will look with the selected printer's paper size and the selected Style option. The proxy preview updates on-the-fly as you change the settings for the selected style.

TIP

Printing Mini-Pictures

If you want to print several copies of a photo and the exact size of each print isn't important, choose **N-Up** from the Style pop-up menu. To print multiple copies of a single image, click the check box labeled **One photo per page**.

Sharing Photos on the Web

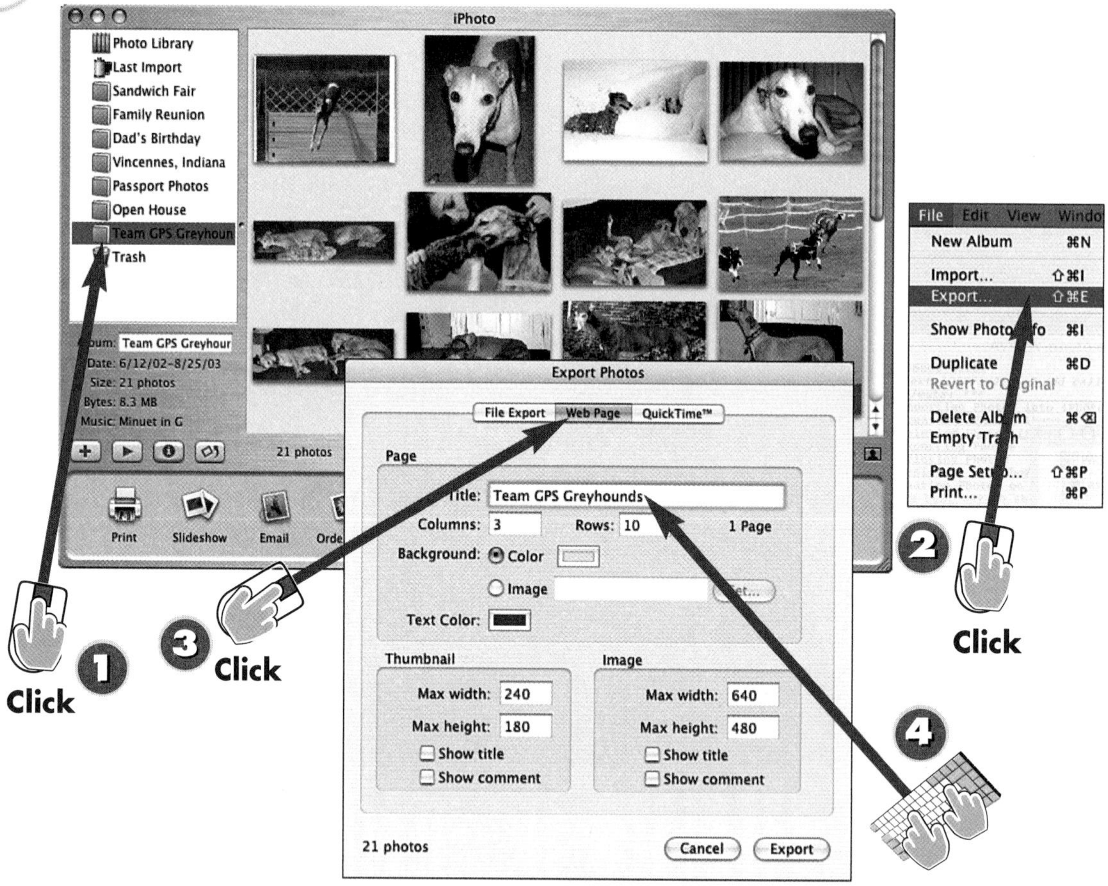

1 Click the album you want to share on a Web page.

2 Choose **File**, **Export**.

3 Click the **Web Page** tab in the Export dialog box.

4 Type a name for the Web page and specify options for the page's layout.

INTRODUCTION

The best way to share your photos with friends and family all over the country or the world is to put them on the Web. iPhoto makes creating a Web picture gallery easy. To share pictures, all you have to do is put the files that iPhoto generates on your .Mac home page or any other Web space available and let everyone know the URL.

HINT

Color Sense

You might be tempted to get creative with the photo gallery's background and text colors, but be sure to pick a contrasting pair. White on black, black on white, or similar high-contrast colors are much easier to read than, say, light blue on soft gray.

HINT

What's in a Name?

iPhoto inserts the album's name in the Title field, but you can change the page title to anything you want. Because it's visible at the top of the document window, you have a little more room to work with than in the Album list in iPhoto's window.

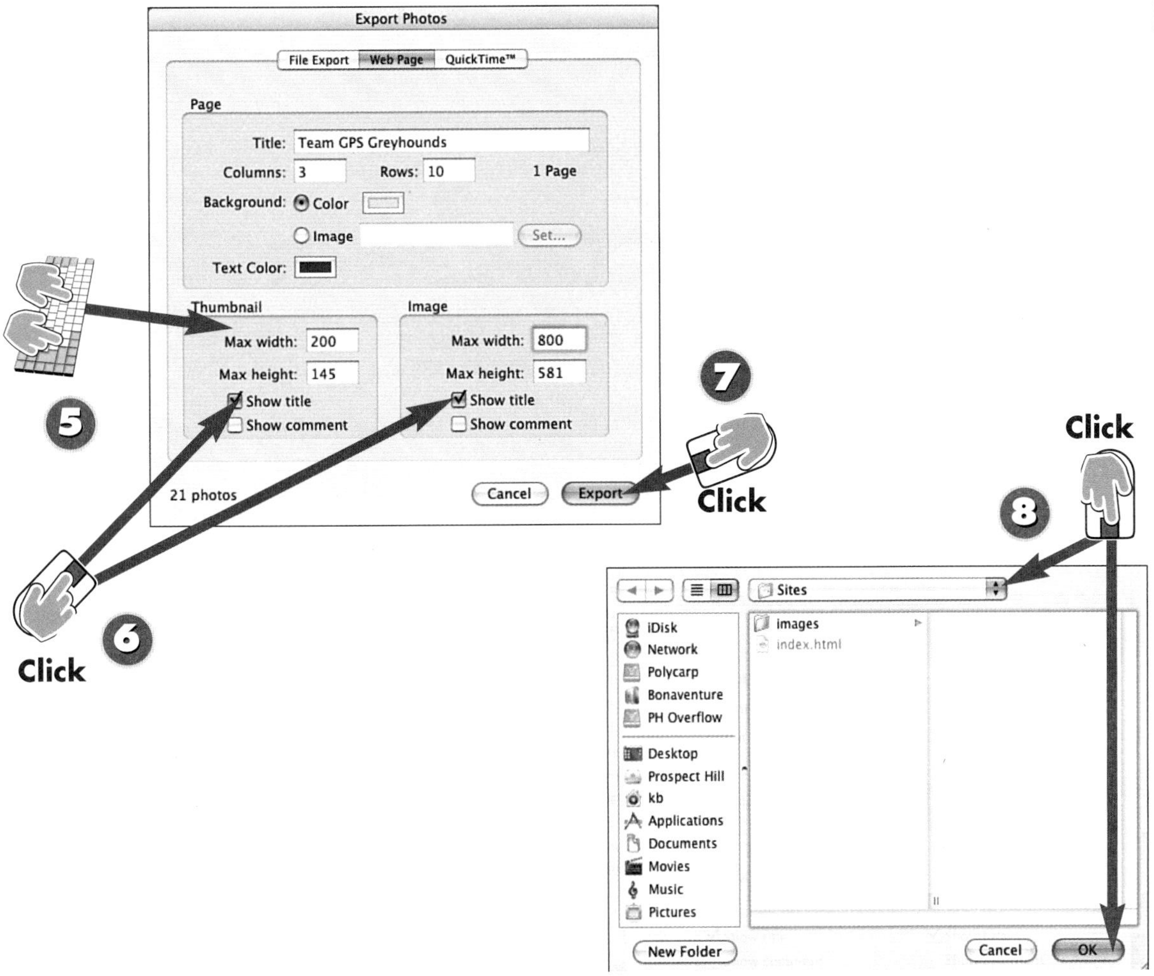

5 Type the dimensions in pixels for thumbnail and full-sized images.

6 Click **Show Title** or **Show Comment** in the Thumbnail and Image areas to display text with the images.

7 Click **Export**.

8 Navigate to the location where you want to save the files; then click **OK**.

HINT

Big and Little

iPhoto creates all the full-size and thumbnail images your Web album needs, but you must specify sizes. Thumbnail images are small versions of the photos on which viewers can click to see the full-size versions.

TIP

Taking Your Photos Home

If you have a .Mac account (see "Setting Up .Mac" in Part 9, "Living Online"), you can publish your photos on your .Mac HomePage Web site. Click the **HomePage** button at the bottom of the **Organize** pane and follow the prompts.

HINT

Measuring in Pixels

Pixels—the dots of light that make up the picture on your Mac's screen—are the unit in which onscreen objects are measured. Most monitors have 72 pixels to the inch, which means that a 640 pixel by 480 pixel photo measures 8.9"×6.7".

Ripping Songs from a CD

1

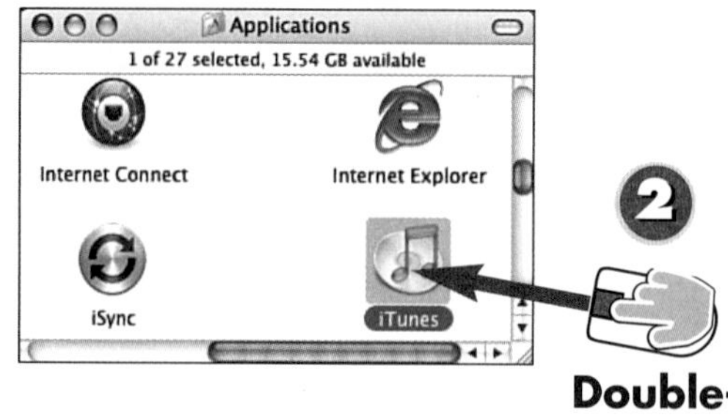

2

Double-click

3 Click

4 Click

1. Insert the CD.
2. Open the Applications folder and double-click to start up iTunes.
3. Click to remove the check marks next to any songs you don't want to add to your library.
4. Click **Import**.

INTRODUCTION

You'll be amazed at how much more use you get from your CD collection after you get the music off CDs and into iTunes. The songs on CDs are already digital files; *ripping* them consists of transferring them to your hard drive and resaving them in MP3 format.

TIP

The Sounds of Silence
iTunes plays songs while it's importing them, but if you don't want to listen to them, you can click Pause to stop the playback. iTunes continues importing the songs.

TIP

Mind the Gap
If you want consecutive songs to play with no pause between them, choose **Advanced**, **Join CD Tracks** before clicking Import.

Making a New Playlist

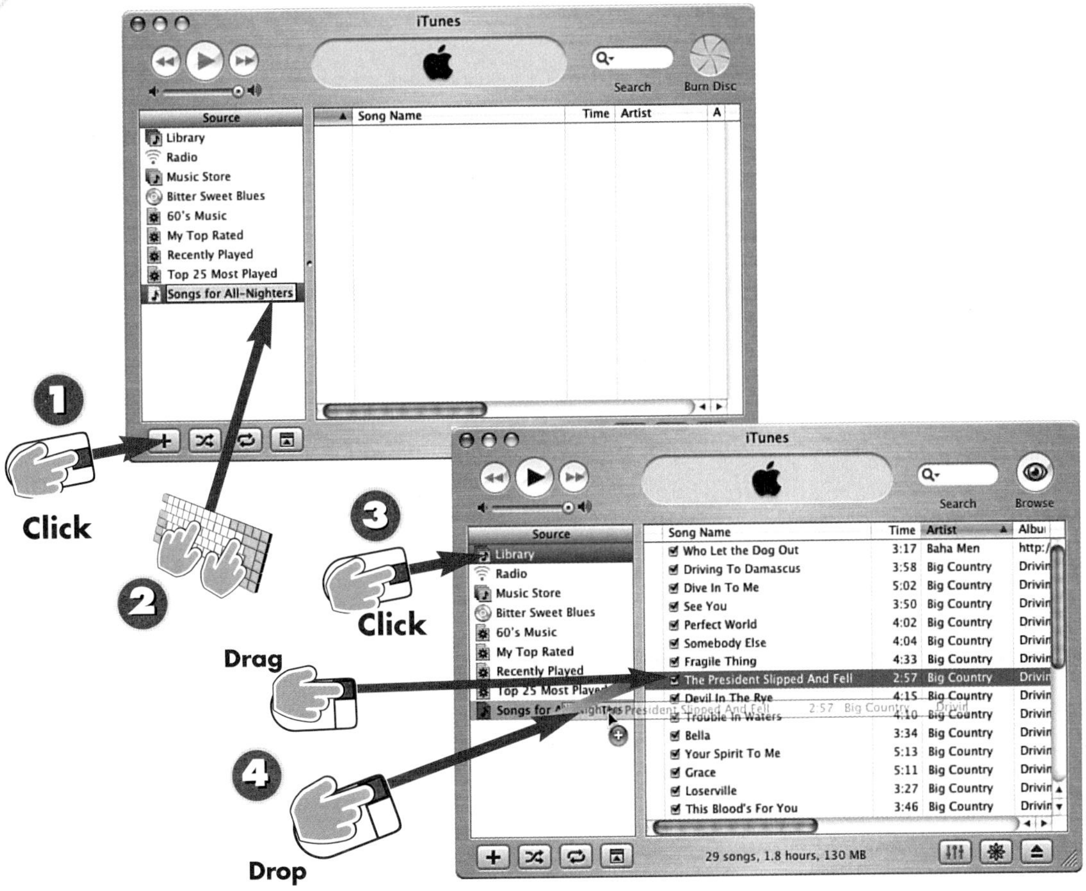

1. In iTunes, click the **Create Playlist** button.

2. Type a name for the playlist.

3. Click the **Library** entry in the **Source** column to see all your songs, or click the name of another playlist.

4. Drag songs from the **Song** column and drop them into the new playlist.

INTRODUCTION

Playlists are simply groups of songs, containing just one song or hundreds. You can use them to create party mixes, plan mix CDs, or categorize your music by genre or any other criterion. Building playlists is a simple drag-and-drop operation.

TIP

Finding What You Want

To locate a specific song in the Library or in a playlist, click in the **Search** field and type part of the song name. As you type, the list of songs shortens to include only the songs that match your search term.

TIP

Changing Your Mind

To remove a song from a playlist (but not from your Library), click to select it and press **Delete**.

Burning a Music CD

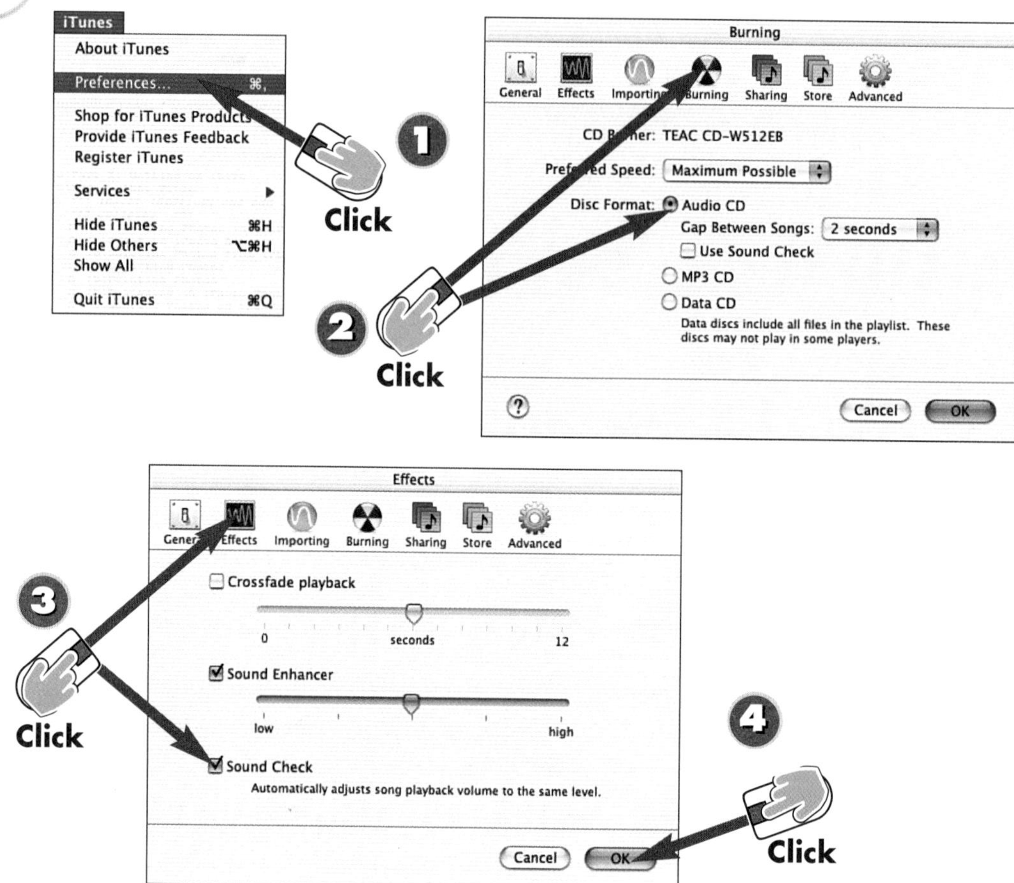

1. In iTunes, choose **iTunes**, **Preferences**.
2. Click the **Burning** button at the top of the window; then choose **Audio CD** as the Disc Format.
3. Click the **Effects** button and click the check box to turn on **Sound Check**.
4. Click **OK**.

INTRODUCTION

You can take your music with you in the form of custom mix CDs for parties, for gifts, or just to use in the car. Before you burn a CD, you need to create a playlist containing the songs you want to use on the disc. And, of course, you need to have a CD drive that can write CDs as well as play them.

TIP

Fair Warning
If any of the songs in your playlist were bought at the iTunes Music Store, you'll be able to burn that particular playlist only 10 times. That's part of Apple's agreement with the record labels that supply songs for the Music Store.

TIP

The Right Media
Make sure you use CD-R media, rather than CD-RW media, if you plan to play your CD in a regular CD player (meaning, on your stereo) rather than in a computer CD drive.

5. Click to select the playlist you want to make into a CD.

6. Click the **Burn Disc** button.

7. Insert a blank CD-R disc and click **Burn Disc** again.

INTRODUCTION

If you include too many songs in the playlist to fit on the CD, iTunes lets you know that they won't all fit. You'll have the option of burning the songs to an MP3 CD instead or creating a disc that contains as many songs as will fit.

TIP

Stop Right There

To stop the CD burner after you click Burn Disc, click the **X** next to the progress bar. You can use your CD drive again immediately, but the CD you canceled is no longer usable.

TIP

Avoiding a Small Annoyance

If you insert a blank CD before clicking Burn Disc in the iTunes window, your Mac asks you what you want it to do with the CD. Clicking Burn Disc before putting the CD-R in the drive bypasses this dialog box.

Buying New Songs Through iTunes

1. In iTunes, click **Music Store** in the Source column.

2. Click **Sign In**.

3. Type your Apple ID and password and click **Sign In**.

4. If you haven't bought songs before, a dialog box tells you that this ID hasn't been used with the Music Store; click **Review**.

INTRODUCTION

The iTunes Music Store offers thousands of tunes in all genres at very reasonable prices. You can download entire albums or one song at a time. Your purchases are charged to your credit card, and the songs are downloaded directly into iTunes, where you can play them on your computer, transfer to them to an iPod, or burn them to a CD.

TIP

Getting an iTunes Account

If you already have an Apple ID, you're all set—just enter that username and password to sign in to the iTunes Music Store. If you have a paid subscription to .Mac, use that username and password for the Music Store. If you don't have either, follow the Music Store's prompts to create a new ID and supply your credit card information for purchases.

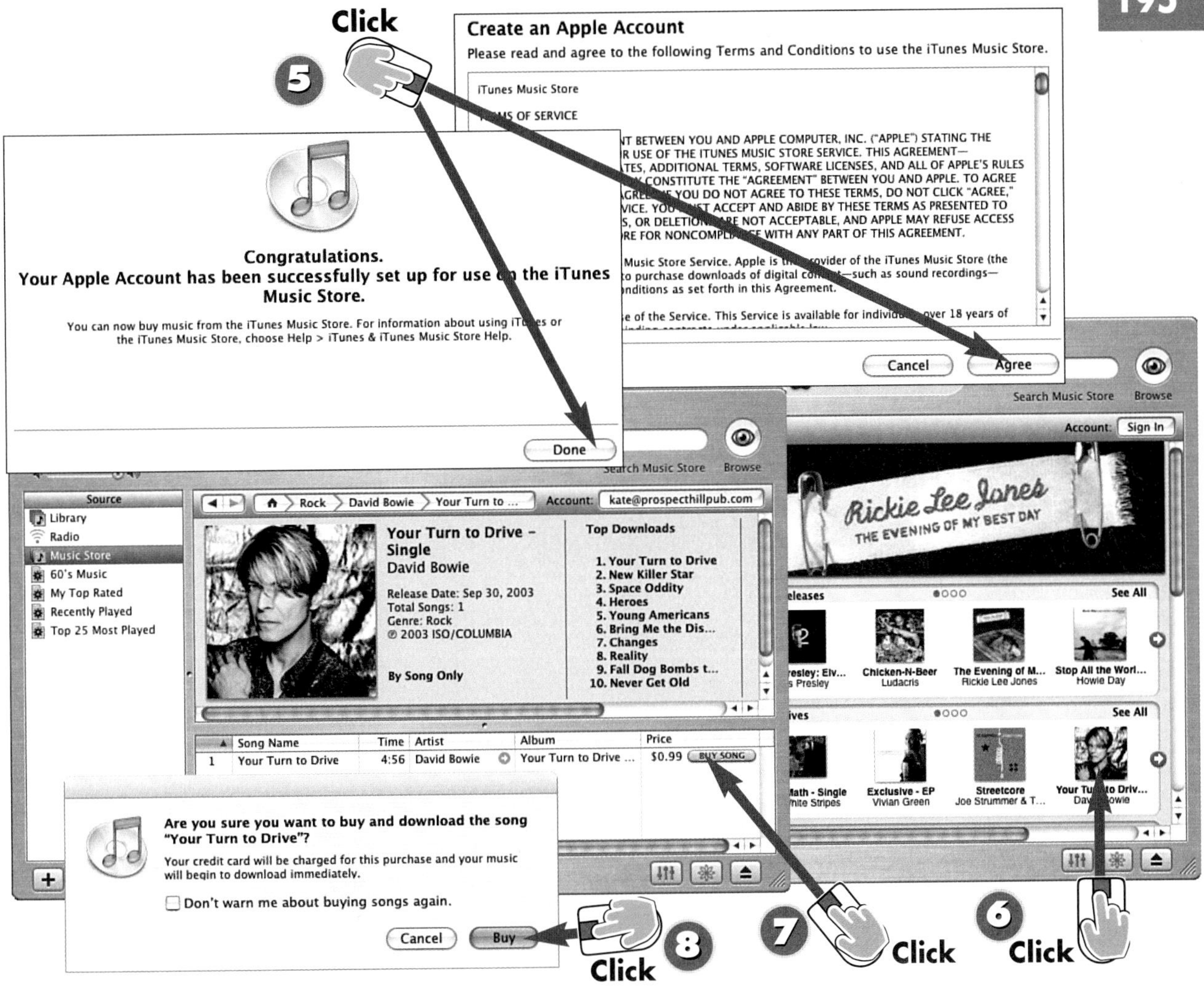

5 Read the Terms and Conditions and click **Agree**; then click **Done**.

6 Click a song or album title to see more information about it.

7 Click **Buy Song** or **Buy Album** to purchase music.

8 Click **Buy**. The song downloads into iTunes and appears in a new playlist called Purchased Music.

INTRODUCTION

The Music Store appears in iTunes, but it works similarly to a Web page. Click a song, an album title, or an artist's name to see items for sale. Use the pop-up menu to choose a genre, or click **Power Search** to look for an artist or song title.

TIP

Just a Taste

When you're browsing the iTunes Music Store, click iTunes' **Play** button to hear a high-quality, 30-second snippet of a selected song.

TIP

Quick and Clean Searching

You can search the Music Store quickly for any text by entering the search text in the regular iTunes search field at the top of the iTunes window. Type the song or artist name you want to look for and press **Return**.

Importing Video Footage into iMovie

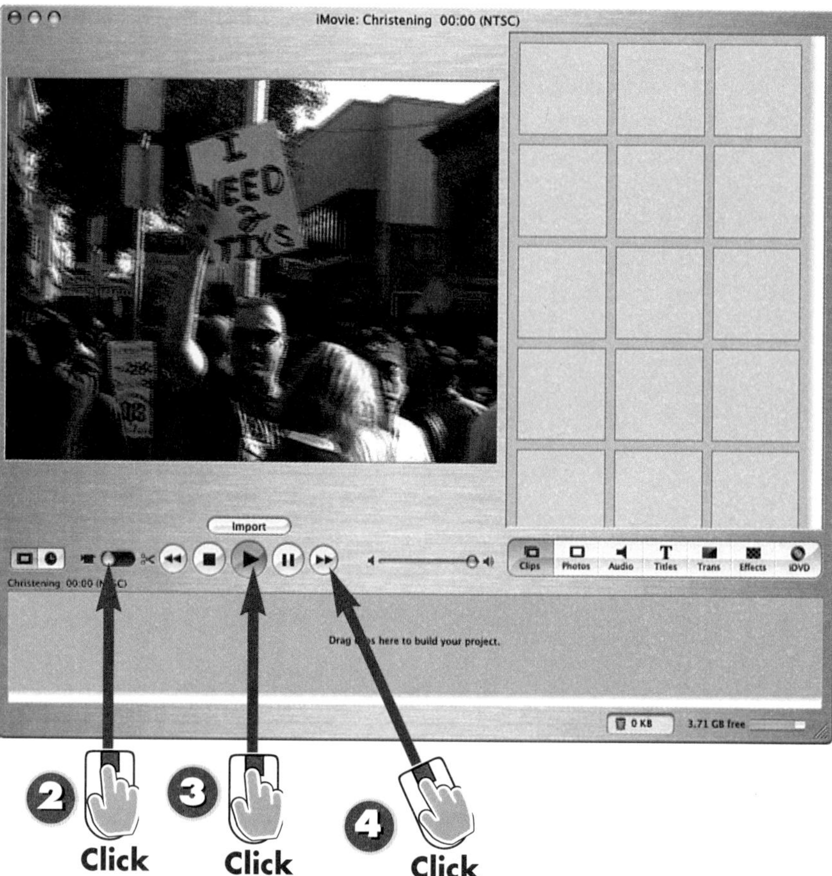

1. In iMovie, choose **File**, **New Project**.
2. With your camera connected to the Mac and turned on, click iMovie's **Camera** switch so that it is in Camera mode.
3. Click **Play** below the monitor area to begin viewing the tape in the camera.
4. Click **Fast Forward** to move the tape to the section you want to import.

INTRODUCTION

With iMovie, your home movies will reach new heights. You can add titles and credits, special effects, music and sound effects, and more. Then you can save your finished creations as small QuickTime files for emailing, high-quality DVD movies, or anything in between. The first step is to bring video from your video camera into iMovie. iMovie can control your camcorder so you can get to the right place on the tape to locate the footage you want. The playback controls work just like the buttons on the camera itself or on your VCR. When iMovie is in camera mode, you can use the controls to play, pause, stop, rewind, and fast-forward the tape in the video camera.

HINT

Trouble in iMovie Paradise

Can't seem to get the camera to respond to iMovie's controls? Check to make sure the camera is in playback mode (VTR or VCR mode) rather than recording mode.

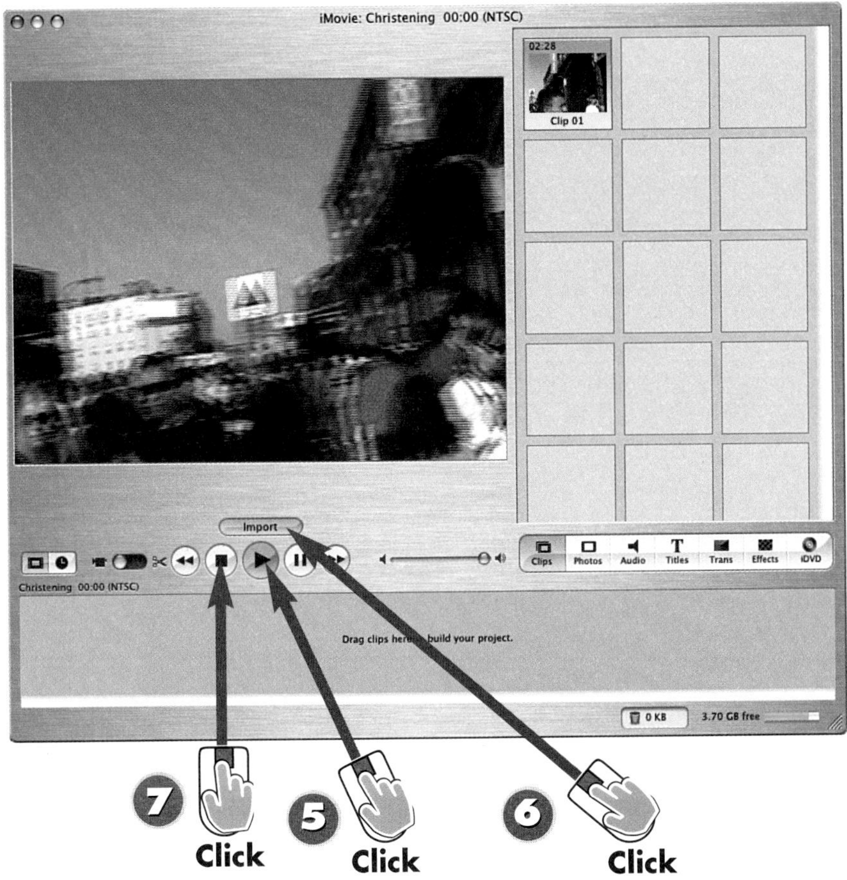

5. Click **Play** again to begin viewing the footage you want to import.

6. Click **Import** to start importing footage.

7. Click **Stop** when you've imported the footage you want. The video is added to the Clip Shelf.

HINT

On the Safe Side

Be conservative when importing video—always import a bit extra on either end of the section you want. You can trim extra footage in iMovie to end up with just the right scene, but if you cut off the scene you'll need to import it again.

TIP

Camera Tips

Here are a few words of wisdom regarding your camera. First, if you have a power adapter, use it while importing video to your Mac, rather than running down your batteries. And second, be sure to turn off the camera while connecting its FireWire cable.

TIP

Sound and Vision

Drag the slider next to the playback controls to adjust the volume level of the tape's audio while you watch it import. Doing this doesn't affect the recording level on the tape or in the final movie.

Inserting Transitions and Effects

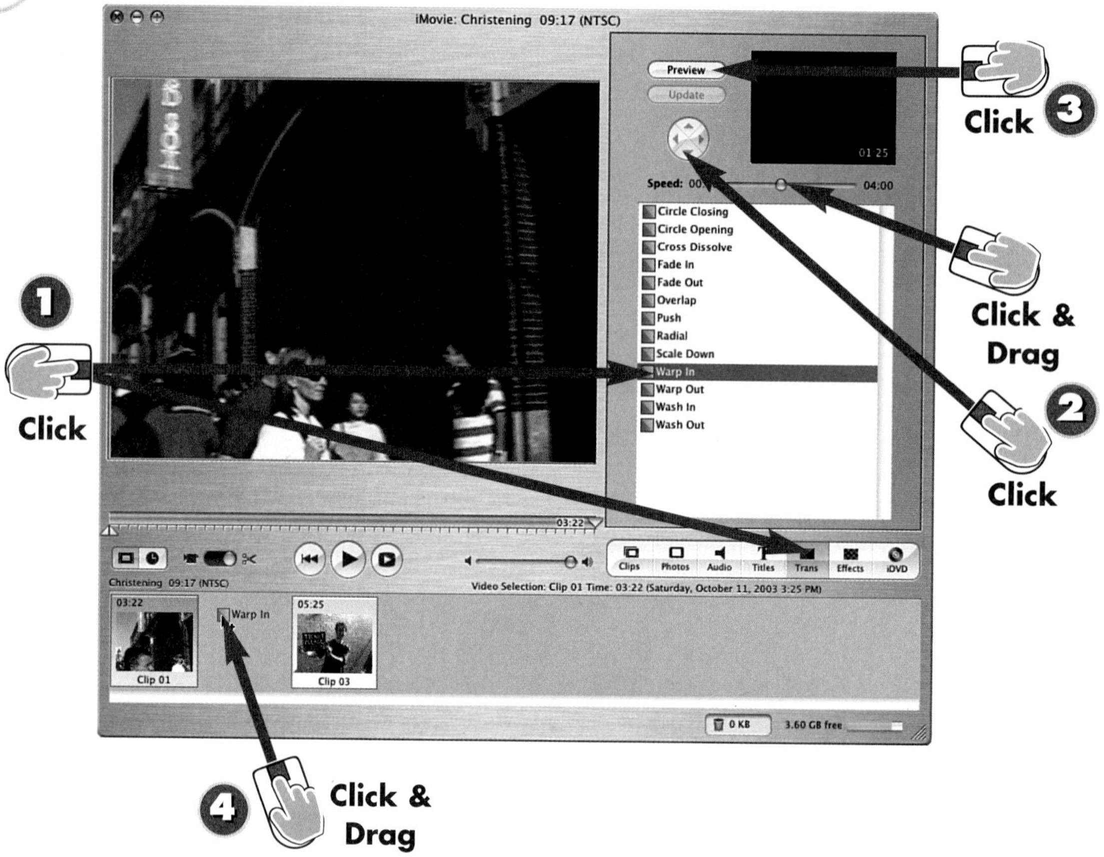

1. To add a transition between two clips, click **Trans** and choose a transition style.
2. Set the duration and direction of the transition.
3. Click **Preview** to play the transition.
4. Drag the transition to the Clip Viewer and drop it into the point in the movie where you want it.

INTRODUCTION

After you've assembled your movie's raw footage by dragging clips from the Clip Shelf into the Clip Viewer, you can spice up the production by adding *transitions* between clips and applying special effects.

TIP

Controlling Transitions
Most transitions have just one control: Speed, or the amount of time the transition takes. Push, in which the new scene slides in from one side of the screen, also has a direction control that enables you to determine which way the scene moves.

HINT

The Story Continues...
There's not nearly enough room to show you all the wonders of iMovie in this book! If you want to learn more about how to use iMovie, check out the iMovie chapter in *Special Edition Using Mac OS X Panther*.

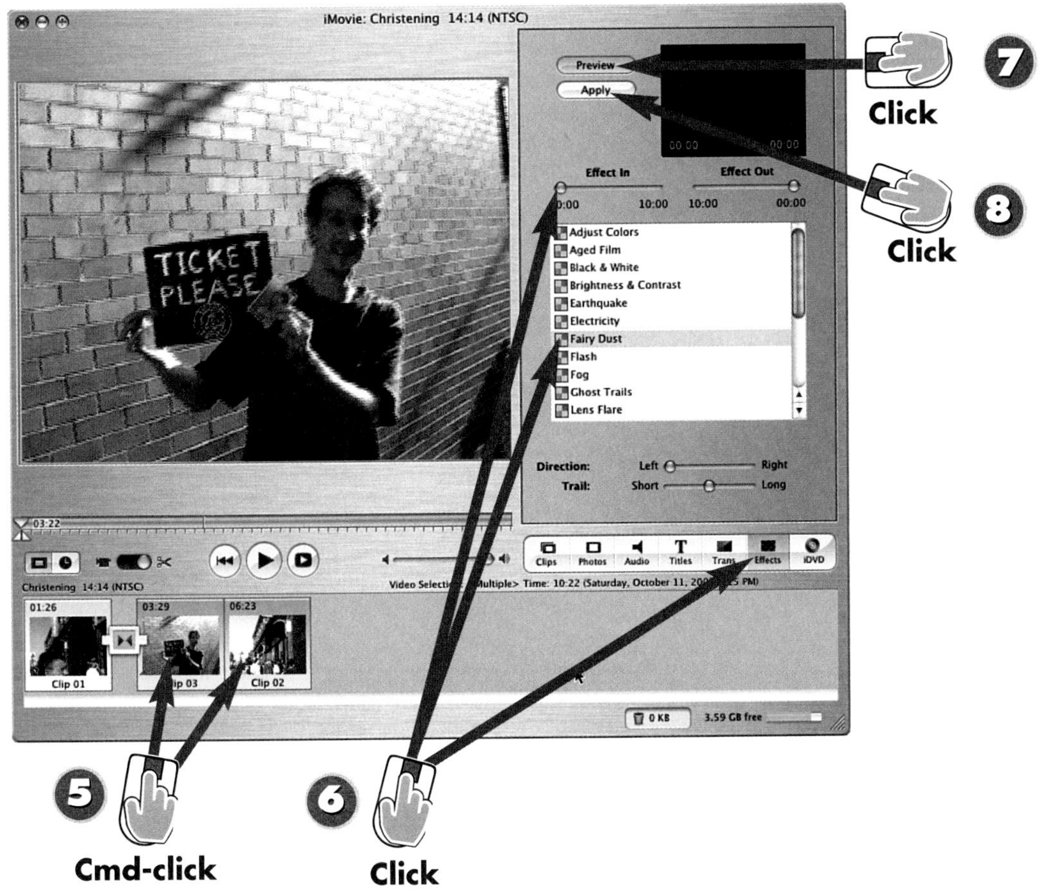

5. To apply a special effect, **Cmd-click** to select the clips you want to apply it to.

6. Click **Effects** and choose an effect; then set the effect's options.

7. Click **Preview** to see how the effect looks.

8. Click **Apply**.

HINT

Creative Transitioning

You're not restricted to using one transition between each pair of clips—you can combine as many transitions as you like to create the effect you're looking for. You can also use transitions before and after titles, photos, and other elements.

TIP

Moving Pictures

For that zippy public television documentary look, drop in some still photos (click **Photos** to see the contents of your iPhoto Library) and apply the Ken Burns Effect. This effect zooms and pans on a photo, giving the impression of motion.

HINT

Transition Timing

As you drag the Speed slider, the total time the transition occupies is displayed in the lower-right corner of the transition thumbnail preview. Keep an eye on that time; quick transitions are okay, but 5-minute ones are a bad idea.

Saving a Movie

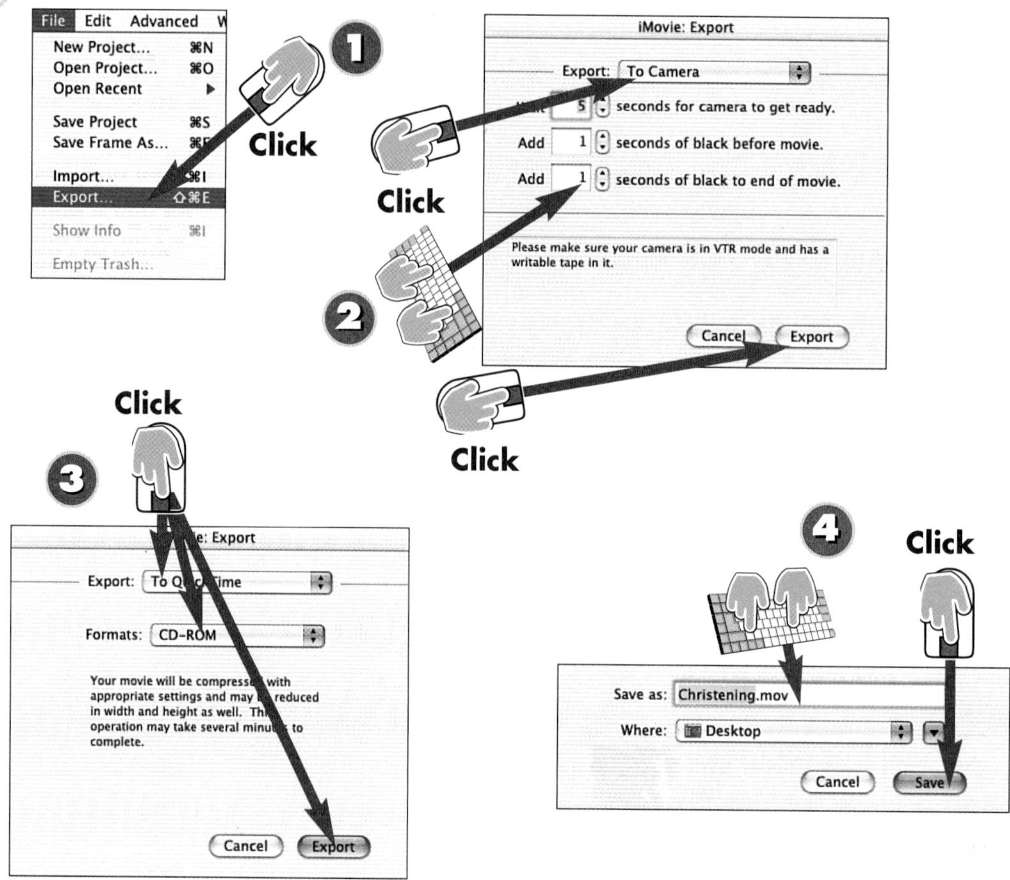

1. Choose **File**, **Export**.

2. To save the movie to a videotape, choose **Export**, **To Camera**; then enter the appropriate time settings to accommodate the camera and click **Export**.

3. To save the movie to a QuickTime document, choose **Export**, **To QuickTime**. Choose an option from the **Formats** pop-up menu and click **Export**.

4. Choose a location to save the file, enter a name, and click **Save**.

INTRODUCTION

When your magnum opus is complete—or at least when you're ready to share it with the outside world—you'll need to export it to a tape or to QuickTime movie. This is an easy process, with only a few options to set.

TIP

Doing a DVD
To turn your movie into a DVD, rather than a video, choose **File**, **Export** and then choose **To iDVD** from the pop-up menu. Then click **Export**. iDVD opens immediately, with the movie already incorporated into an iDVD project.

TIP

Saving Your Work
Choose **File**, **Save Project** to save your movie as an iMovie project—in other words, a work in progress. You don't need to export the movie until you're done working on it.

Creating a New iDVD Project

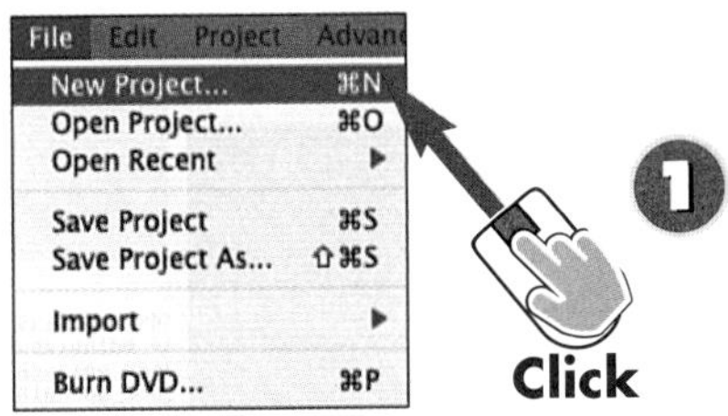

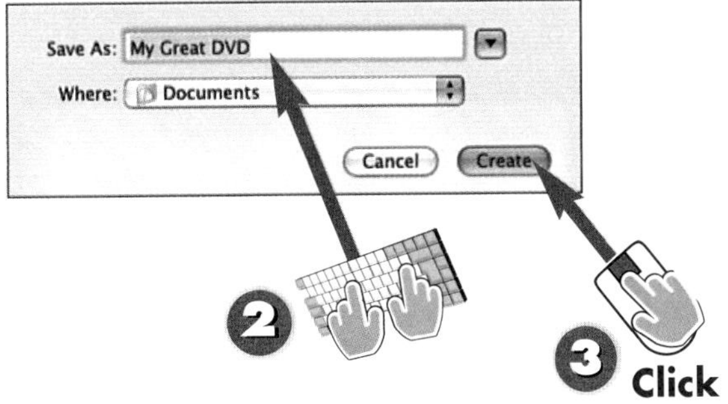

1. Start iDVD or, if it's already running, choose **File**, **New Project**.
2. Enter a name for your DVD project.
3. Navigate to the location where you want to save the project and click **Create**.

INTRODUCTION

Like iMovie, iDVD always opens the last project you worked on. You can open another project by choosing File, Open, or you can begin a new project from scratch. Here's how to do that.

HINT

Where to Stash Projects
Using the folders that Mac OS X creates for certain purposes makes remembering where you put things much easier. In the case of iDVD, the default folder in which to save your projects is the Documents folder within your home folder.

Adding Elements to a DVD

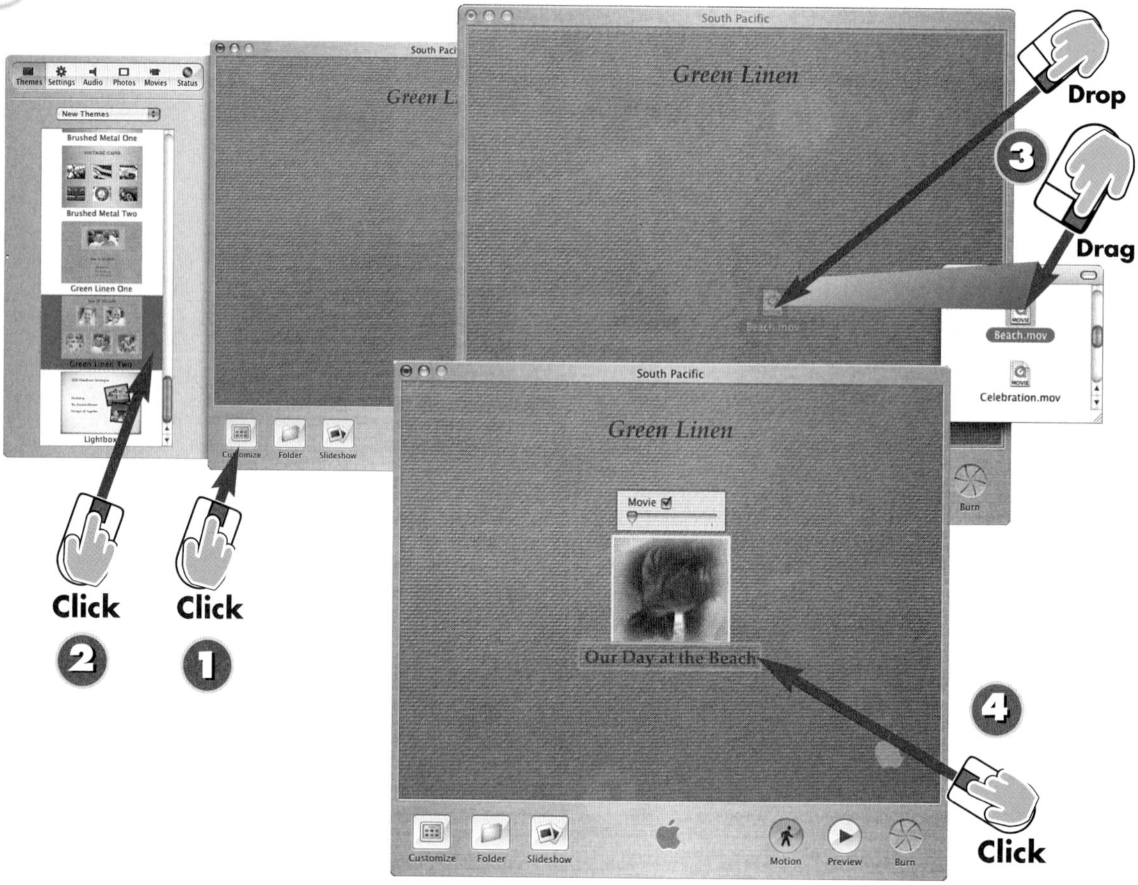

1. In iDVD, click **Customize** to open the drawer at the side of the window.
2. Choose a theme from the list.
3. Click and drag a movie file into the preview area that shows the main menu of your DVD. iDVD creates a button for that movie.
4. Click the button's name to change the text.

INTRODUCTION

DVDs have three types of elements: content, in the form of movies, photos, or other documents; navigation, in the form of folders that open to reveal menu screens; and interface, in the form of background images, sound effects, and the like. Adding these elements is incredibly easy in iDVD.

HINT

More Theme Choices
If iDVD's built-in themes aren't to your liking, you can purchase more themes online. A good place to start is **www.idvdthemepak.com**, where you'll find a selection of very cool iDVD ThemePAKs.

HINT

Supersizing Your DVDs
If your content won't fit on a 60-minute DVD, you can tell iDVD to create a 90-minute DVD instead. But to see this option, you have to add all your content at once so iDVD sees that it won't fit in 60 minutes.

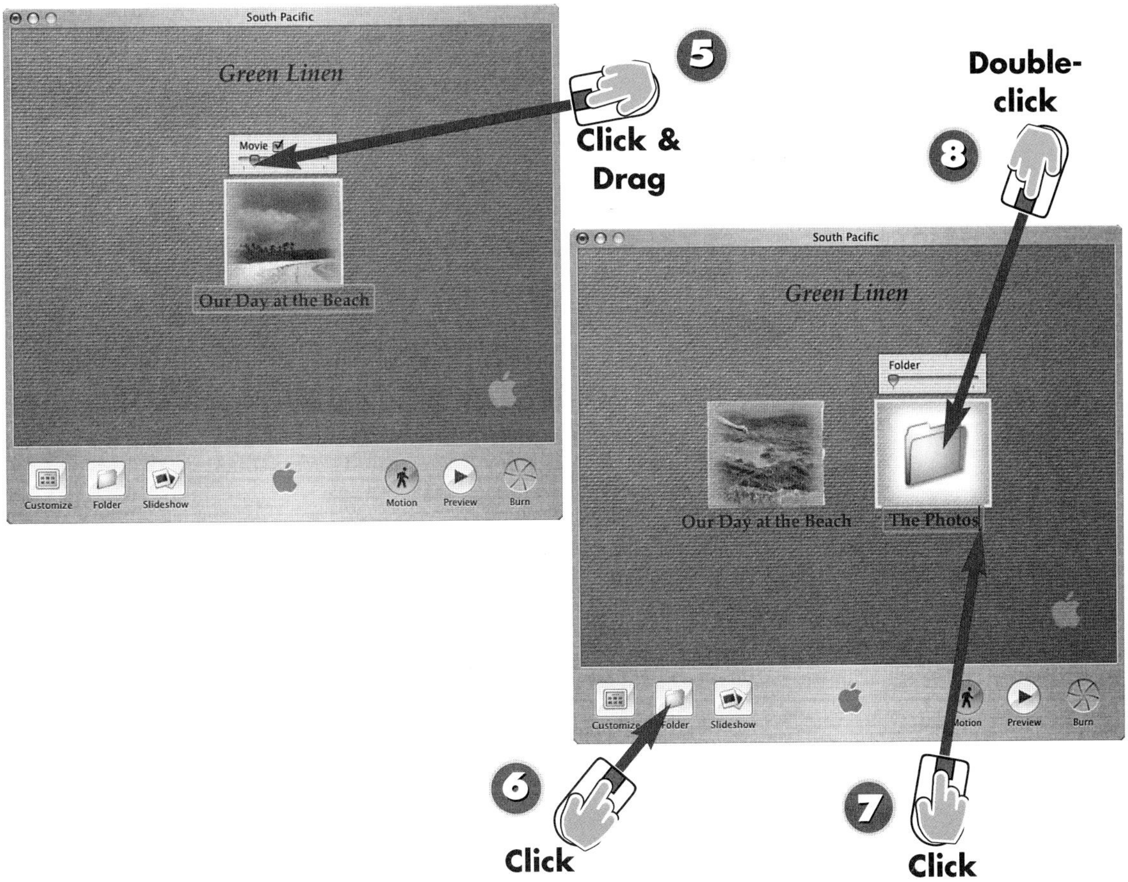

Click & Drag

Double-click

Click

Click

5 If the current theme includes video buttons, click and drag the slider above the button to change the video frame that appears on the button.

6 Click **Folder** to add a folder.

7 Click the folder's name to change the text.

8 Double-click the folder's icon to view the submenu it represents.

HINT

The theme you choose for your DVD project determines the placement of buttons and whether they're text buttons or video buttons. You can experiment with applying different themes at any point during the creation process.

TIP

iDVD Assistance

Apple's free helper program, iDVD Companion, is a useful tool for iDVD users. With it you can move quickly to menus and slideshows, place buttons and titles precisely, and change menu layouts. Learn more at **www.apple.com/applescript/idvd/idvd_companion/**.

Previewing a DVD

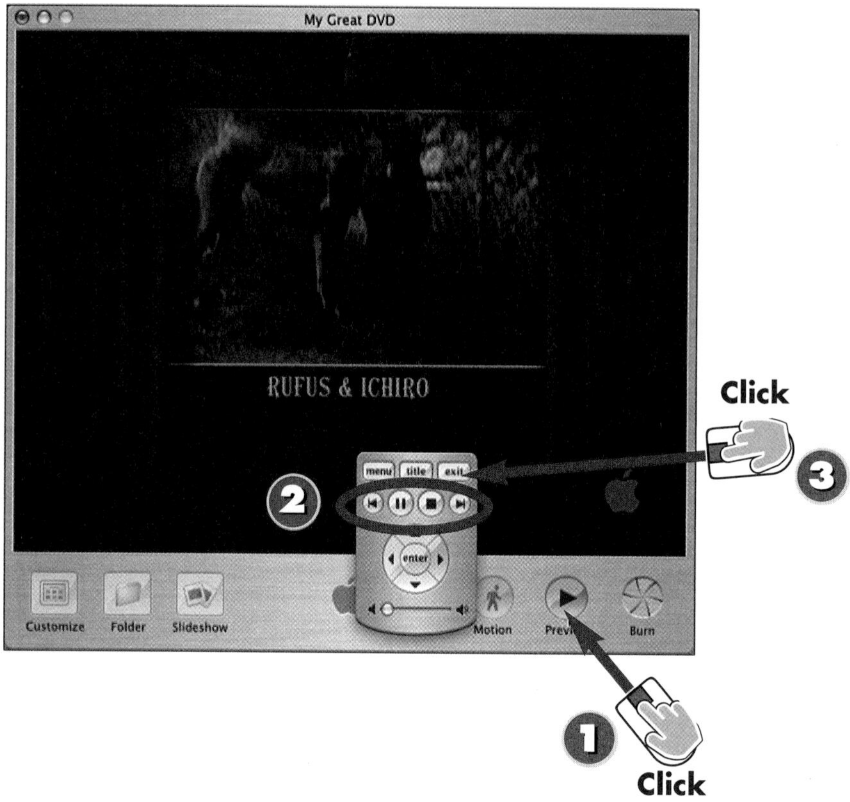

1. Click **Preview** to play the DVD.
2. Click buttons on the remote control to test the way the DVD will work on a TV.
3. Click **Exit** to leave preview mode.

INTRODUCTION

It's a well-known fact that creative projects don't always turn out the way they're envisioned. It's far better to catch mistakes and make tweaks before you've burned a DVD than after. That's where iDVD's Preview function comes in handy. Always preview your projects before burning them to disc.

TIP

Menus in Motion

Some iDVD themes include animated menu backgrounds called *motion menus*. To see these backgrounds in action when you preview the DVD, make sure the Motion button at the bottom of the iDVD window is green. If it's not, click it.

TIP

Playing It Safe

To be sure the DVD's elements won't extend off the edge of the screen, choose **Advanced**, **Show TV Safe Area** before you click Preview. This command places a rectangle on the screen that defines the boundaries of older TV screens.

Burning a DVD

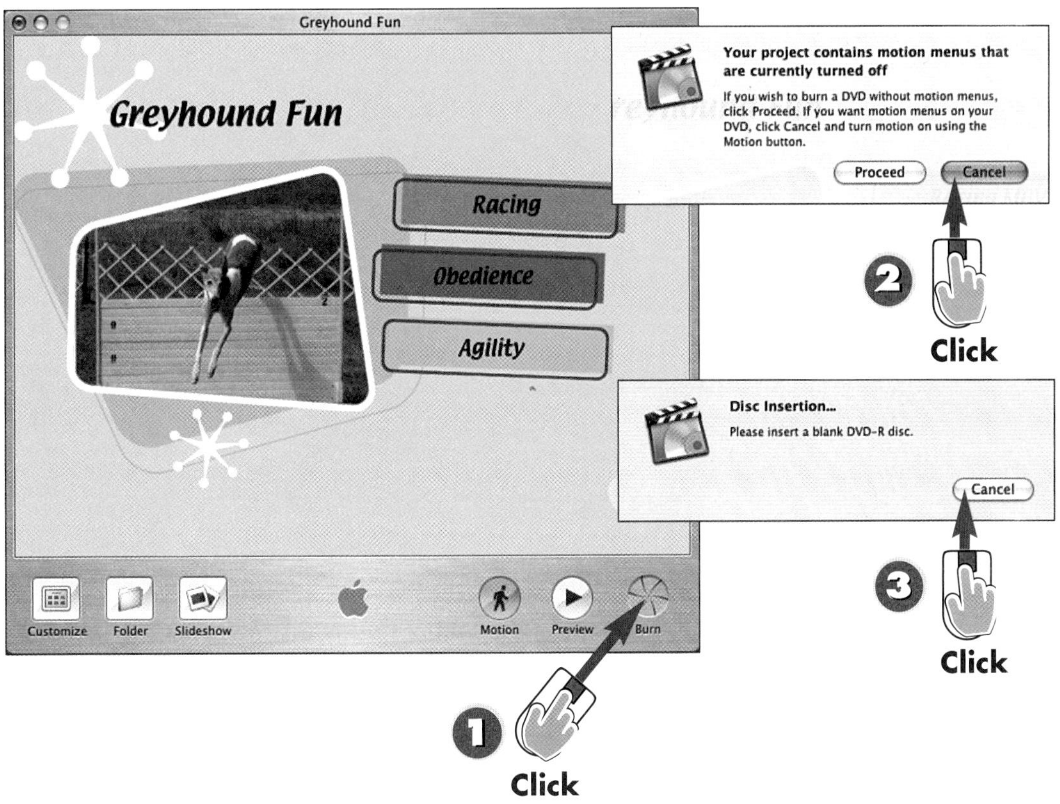

1. In iDVD, click the **Burn** button twice.
2. If motion is turned off, click **Cancel** and turn it on; then go back to step 1.
3. Insert a blank DVD disc.

INTRODUCTION

After your DVD project is set up the way you want it and you've confirmed this by using the Preview feature, it's time to burn an actual DVD disc. You must have a Mac with a built-in SuperDrive to accomplish this with iDVD.

HINT

Make Way for DVDs

You should quit all other programs while you're burning a DVD. This ensures that no other program will take over the computer while the DVD is being created, which might cause an error in the DVD.

HINT

iDVD Without the Burn

Previously, iDVD wouldn't even install if your Mac was SuperDrive-less, but with iDVD 3.0.1, you can create iDVD projects on a Mac that doesn't have a SuperDrive. To burn a project, copy it to a SuperDrive-equipped Mac.

PART 11

Sharing Your Mac with Multiple Users

Mac OS X is designed to be a multiuser operating system, meaning each user of a single Mac has his own account. Along with each account comes a login icon, a name and password, a home folder, and a set of capabilities that determines how extensively that user can affect the way the Mac works. Each user is either a standard user or an admin user; admin users can change preferences, install programs, and modify files—all changes that affect all users rather than just the user who implements them.

Your account can be customized with your choice of name, password, and login picture (used both in the login dialog box and for Internet messaging with iChat). You also get your very own home folder, named with a shortened version of your login name. Your home folder is where you can put all your documents, music, pictures, and so on, and you can keep other users from reading, moving, or even seeing what files are in your home folder. When you do want to share files, you can put them in specific places where other users have access to them. Because customizations—such as the desktop picture, screen saver module, monitor resolution, and clock settings—apply only to the user who sets them up, you can also use user accounts to create different configurations of your Mac for specific purposes, rather than for different people.

In this part, you'll learn how to create user accounts and change their attributes, as well as how to log in and log out. You'll also learn how to add startup items—programs and files that open when you log in—and how to manage security with passwords and the FileVault feature.

Account and Security Setup

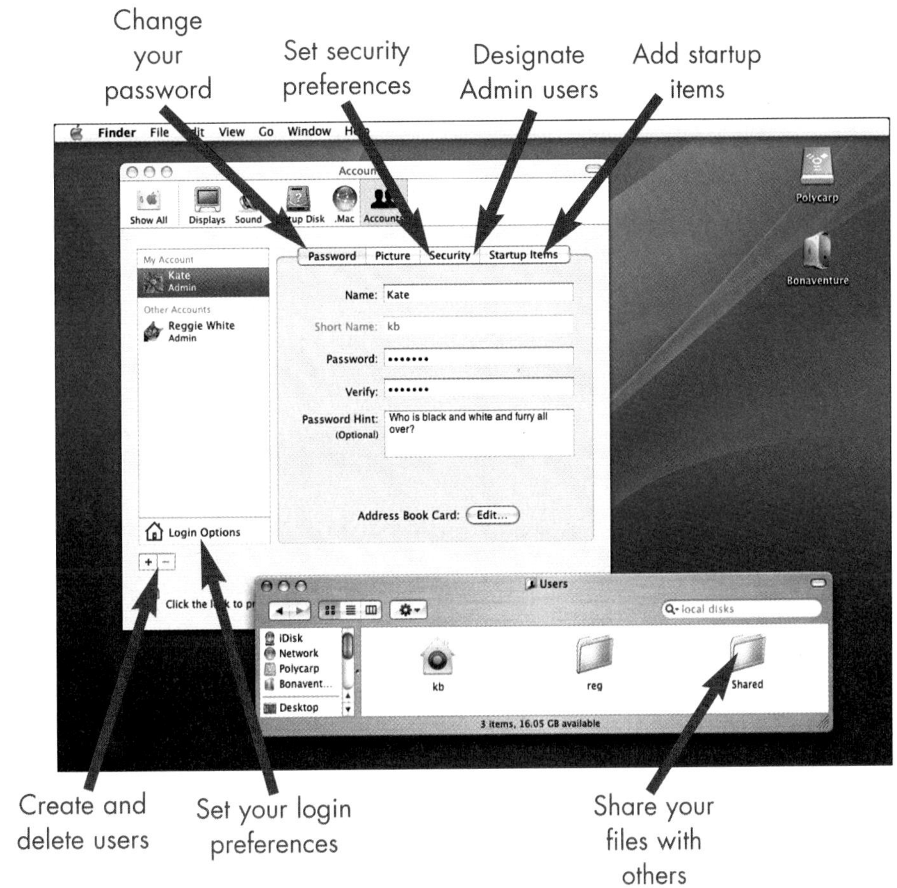

Creating and Deleting Users

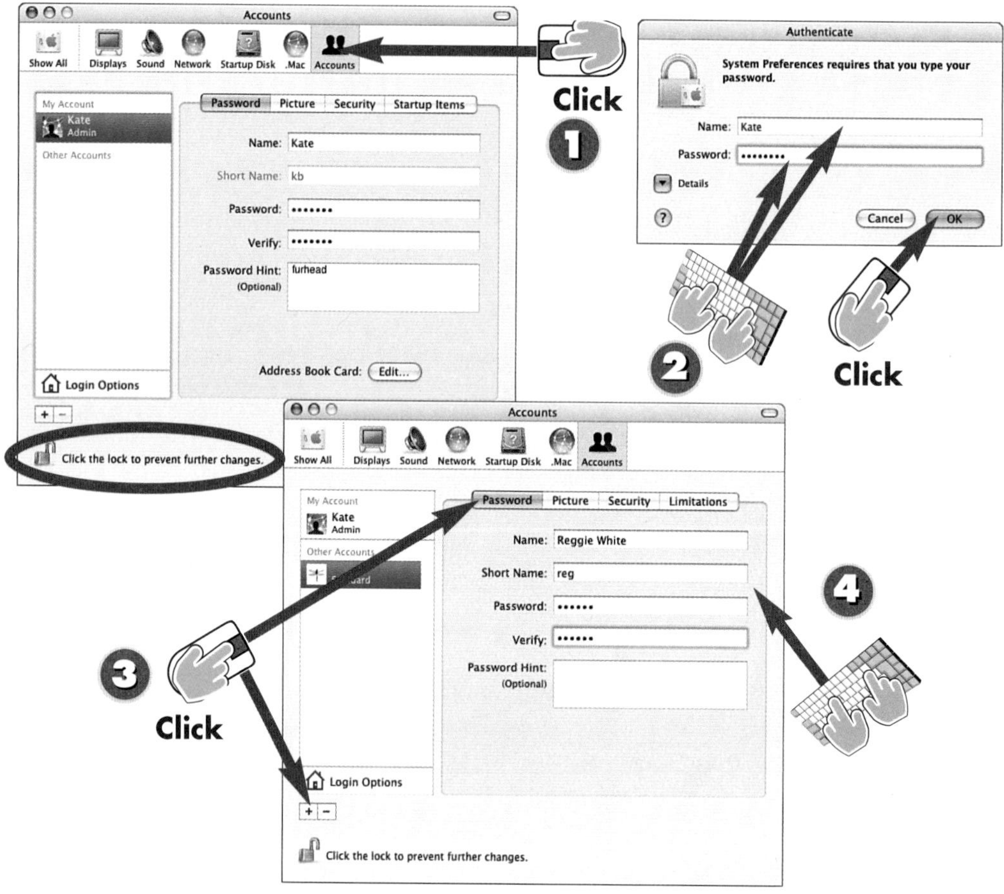

1. Choose **Apple menu**, **System Preferences**, and click **Accounts** to see the accounts preferences.
2. If the preferences are locked, click the closed padlock button to unlock them; then enter an admin name and password and click **OK**.
3. To create a new user, click the **Add User** button and then click the **Password** tab.
4. Enter the new user's name, a short version of her name (such as initials), and a password.

INTRODUCTION

Each user of a Mac gets her own account, with separate preferences, home folder, and login identity. You can also create accounts for different uses of your Mac—one that's all business, another for weekends that starts up your favorite game on login, and so on. Each account can have a customized level of access to system functions.

TIP

Setting Limits

When you create a new standard user account, you can determine how much access that user has to system functions. In the **Accounts** pane, click **Limitations** and choose **No Limits**, **Some Limits**, or **Simple Finder**. With Some Limits, you can specify functions such as burning DVDs that the user may or may not perform. Simple Finder removes all Finder functionality other than locating and opening files.

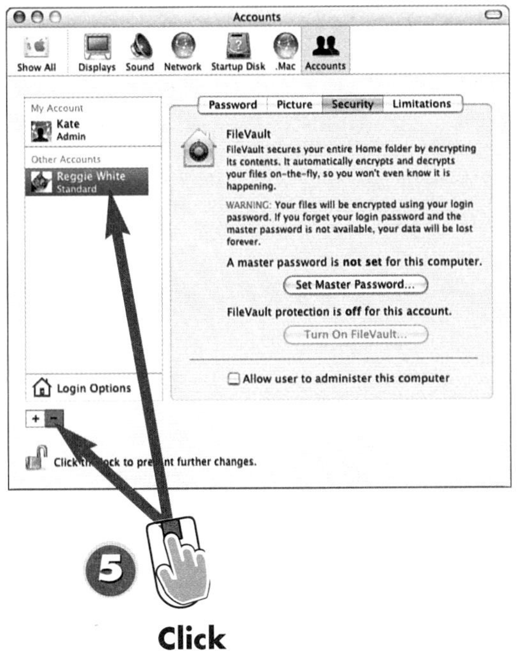

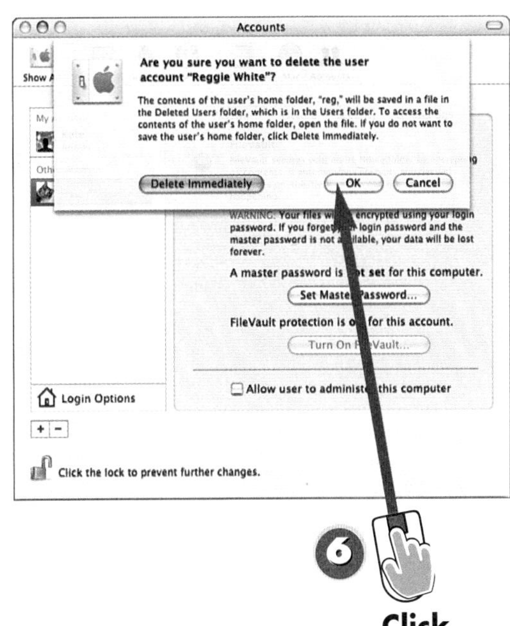

5 To delete a user, click a username in the list and then click the **Delete User** button.

6 Click **OK** in the confirmation dialog box.

TIP

The Stuff They Leave Behind

When you delete a user, you can save the user's files as a disk image that's placed in the Deleted Users folder in the Users folder. Double-click the disk image to see the saved files. If the user was using FileVault (see "Keeping Your Secrets," later in this part, to learn about FileVault), enter the user's password. FileVault or no FileVault, drag the disk image file to the Trash to delete the files. If you don't want to save the user's files in the first place, click **Delete Immediately** instead of OK in step 6.

Making a User an Admin

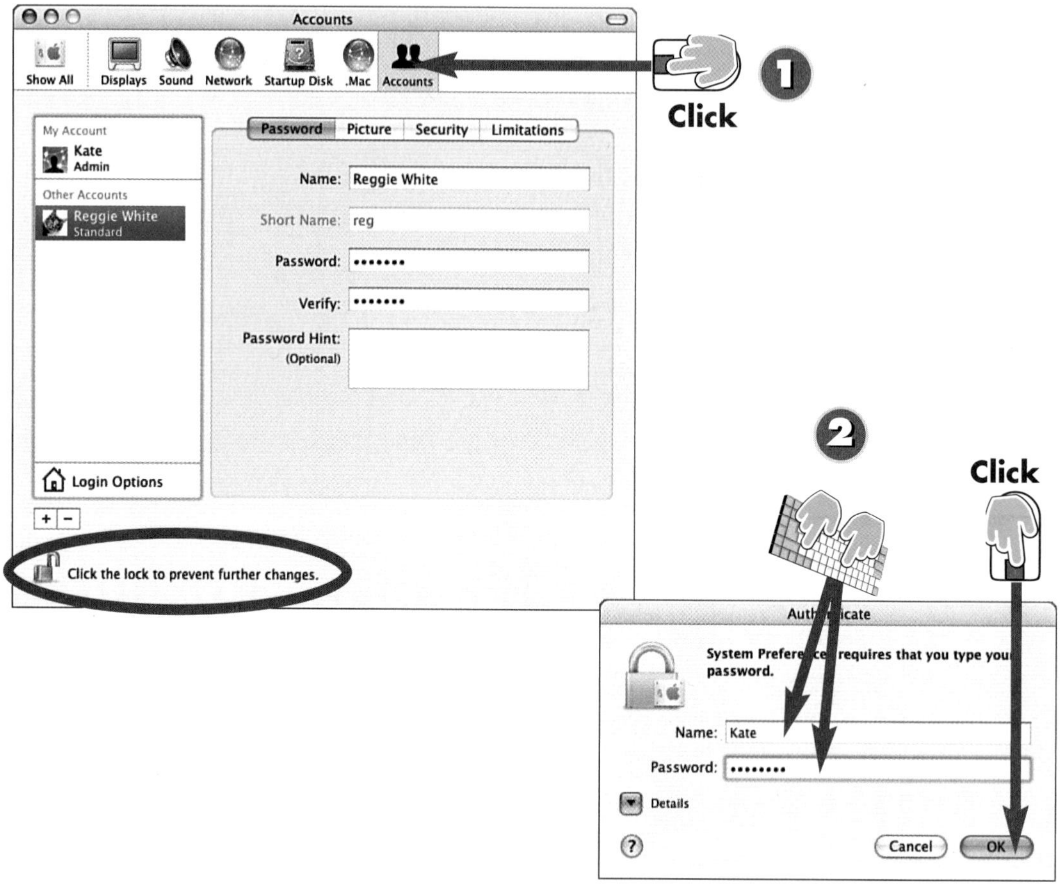

1. Choose **Apple menu**, **System Preferences**, and click **Accounts** to see the accounts preferences.
2. If the preferences are locked, click the closed padlock button to unlock them; then type an admin name and password and click **OK**.

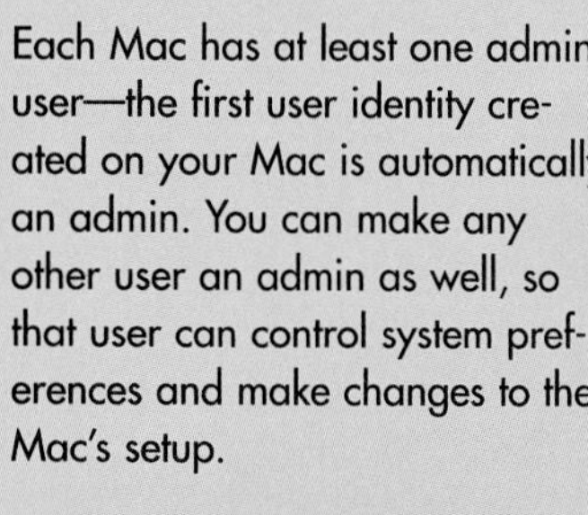

INTRODUCTION

Each Mac has at least one admin user—the first user identity created on your Mac is automatically an admin. You can make any other user an admin as well, so that user can control system preferences and make changes to the Mac's setup.

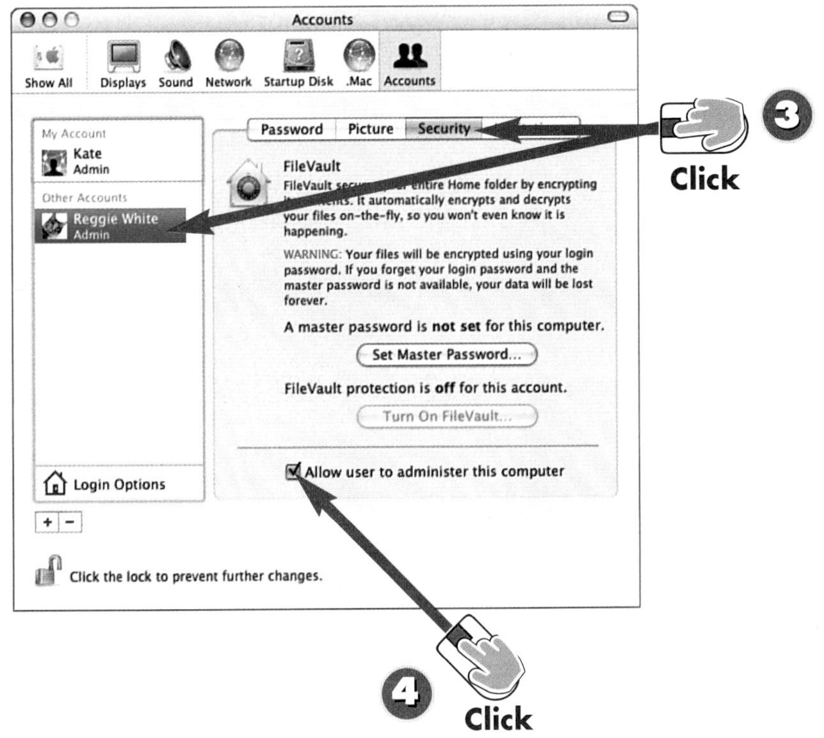

3. Click a username in the account list and then click the **Security** tab.

4. Click the **Allow user to administer this computer** check box.

Admins Beget Admins

Only admin users can create other admin users. If you're not an admin user, you'll need to have someone who is already designated as an admin on your Mac to give you that status.

Wherefore Admin, Anyway?

To home users the term *admin user* can seem strange. It's a result of Mac OS X's emphasis on accommodating multiple users of a single Mac. In most multiuser situations, such as computer labs, only authorized administrators should be able to change the Mac's setup.

Logging In and Out

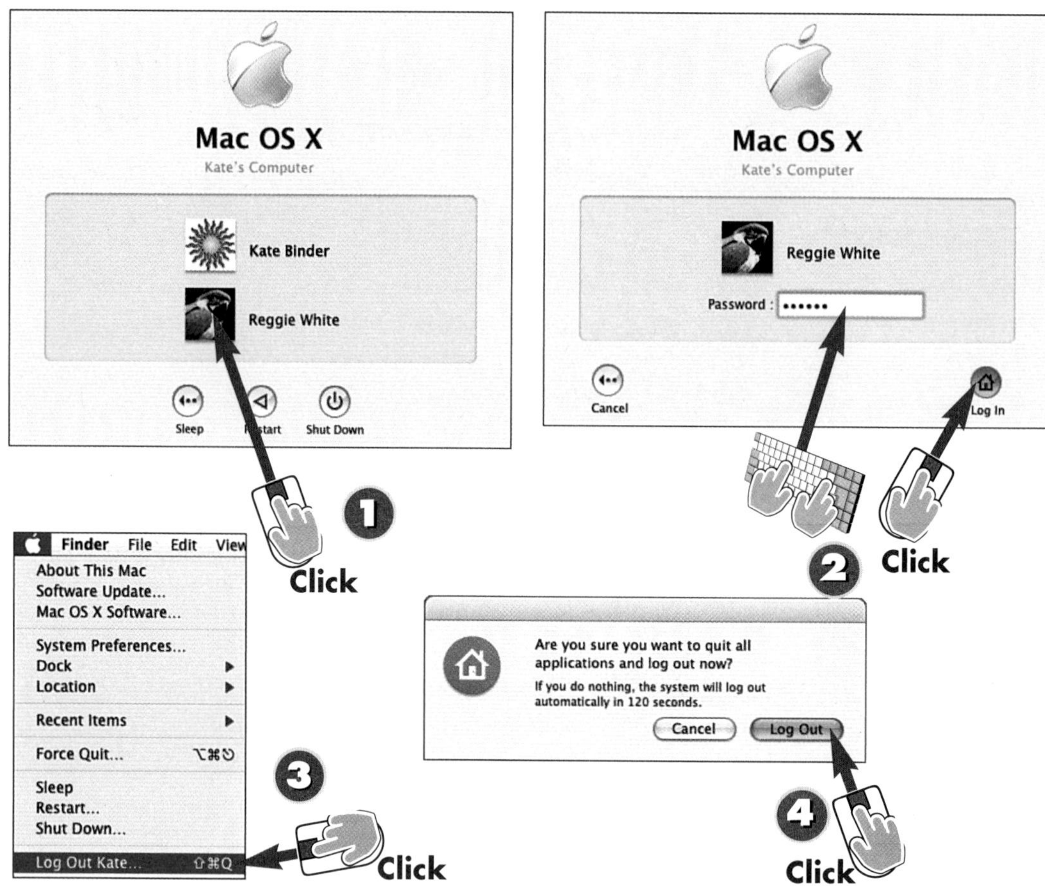

1. In the Login dialog box, click your username in the list of users.

2. Type your password and click **Log In**.

3. To log out, choose **Apple menu**, **Log Out**.

4. Click **Log Out** in the confirmation dialog box. All the applications quit, along with the Finder, and you're returned to the Login dialog box.

INTRODUCTION

Depending on your preferences, you might need to log in to your Mac every day, or you might hardly ever see the login screen. Either way, you do need to remember your login name and password so you can log in when needed—after another user has logged out or after major changes are made to your system.

TIP

Skipping the Login
You can set your Mac so you're automatically logged in at startup. Click **Login Options** at the bottom of the Accounts preferences panel in System Preferences; then click the box labeled **Automatically log in as** and choose a user.

TIP

Faster Switching
Mac OS X's fast user switching feature displays a menu of users in the menu bar; choosing a new user switches instantly to that account. Click **Enable fast user switching** in the Login Options tab of the Accounts System Preferences panel.

Adding Startup Items

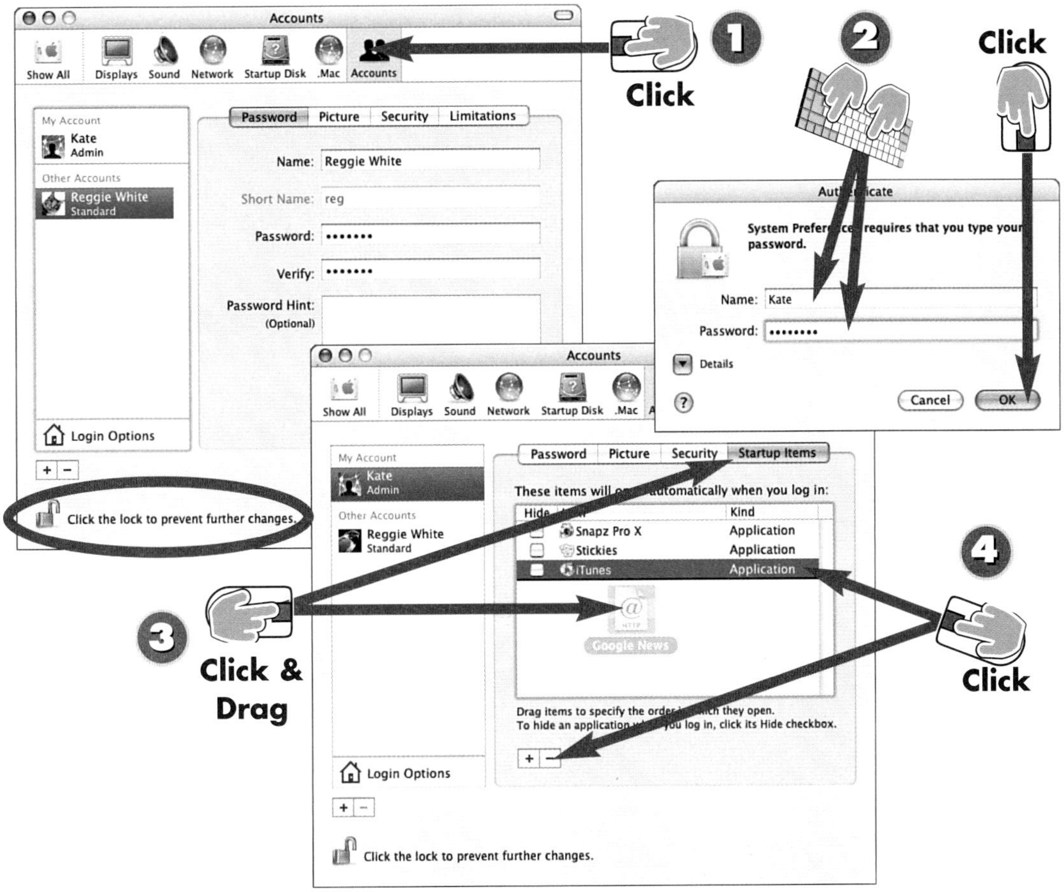

1. In System Preferences, click **Accounts** to see the accounts preferences.

2. If the preferences are locked, click the closed padlock button to unlock them; then enter an admin name and password and click **OK**.

3. Click the **Startup Items** tab and then drag programs, documents, bookmark files, or folders into the window from the Finder.

4. Click an item and click the **Remove** button to remove it from the list.

INTRODUCTION

When you log in, your Mac sets itself up the way you like things. One service it can perform for you when you log in is starting up programs you use all the time, such as your email client, your contact manager, and other constant companions. To make this happen, you add these programs to your startup items.

TIP

What a Drag
Drag items up and down in the startup list to change the order in which they start up when you log in to your Mac.

HINT

Be Creative
Startup items don't have to be programs; you can open any file at login. Examples of files you might want to open every time you use your Mac include a sound file of your favorite song, the novel you're working on, or your recipe database.

Resetting Your Password

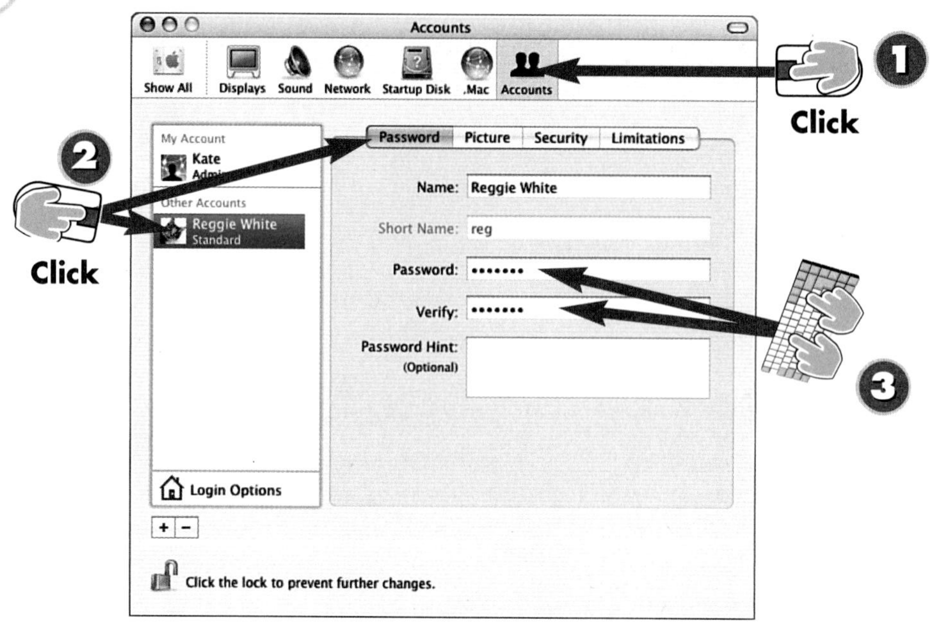

1. If you're logged in, choose **Apple menu**, **System Preferences** and click **Accounts** to see the accounts preferences.
2. Click your username in the list and then click the **Password** tab.
3. Type the new password in the **Password** and **Verify** fields.

INTRODUCTION

Because you need a password to access files on your Mac, be sure to choose a password you can't forget, and take advantage of the Hint feature to provide yourself with a memory-jogging phrase when you need it. If the worst does happen and you just can't figure out your password, here's how to remedy the situation.

TIP

Don't Make It Too Easy
This might seem obvious, but if you enter a hint for your password, don't make the hint too obvious. Even if you're tempted to just use the password itself for the hint, don't!

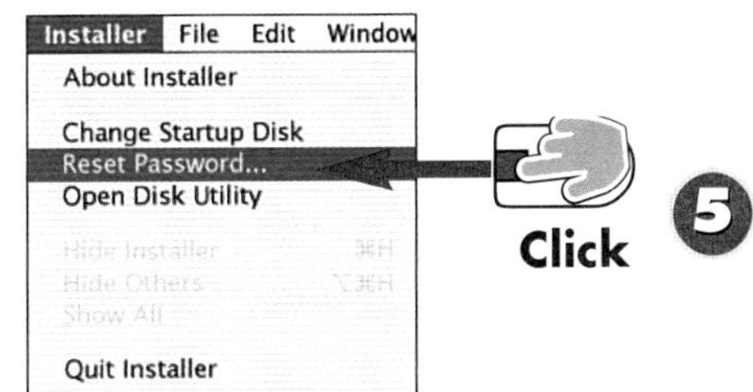

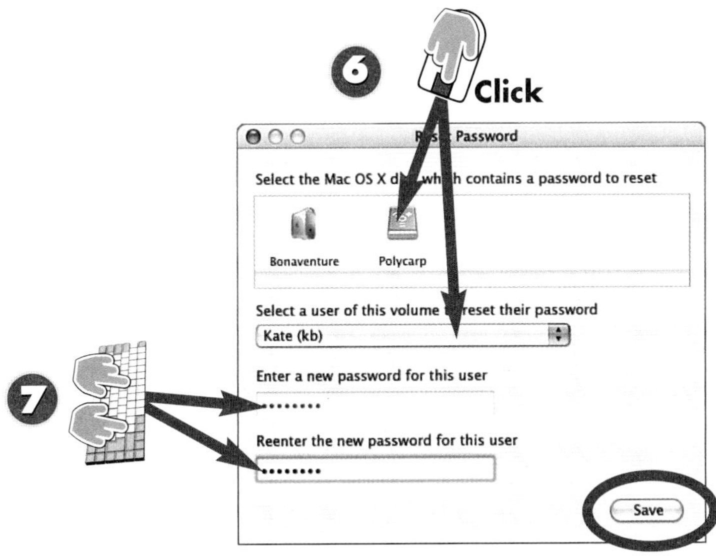

4 If you need to change the Mac's main admin password (the one used by its first admin user), insert the Mac OS X Install Disc 1 CD and restart. Press **C** on your keyboard until you see the spinning gear symbol.

5 When the Installer starts up, choose **Installer**, **Reset Password**.

6 Choose the hard drive where your system software resides and then select your username.

7 Enter the new password twice and click **Save**.

HINT

A Little Help from a Friend

If you forget your password and can't log in or access your home folder (when you're using FileVault), an admin user can change the password for you.

CAUTION

Safe and Secure

Keep your system CD in a safe place so it's not accessible to people who might want to reset the password to gain access to files that aren't theirs.

Sharing Files with Other Users

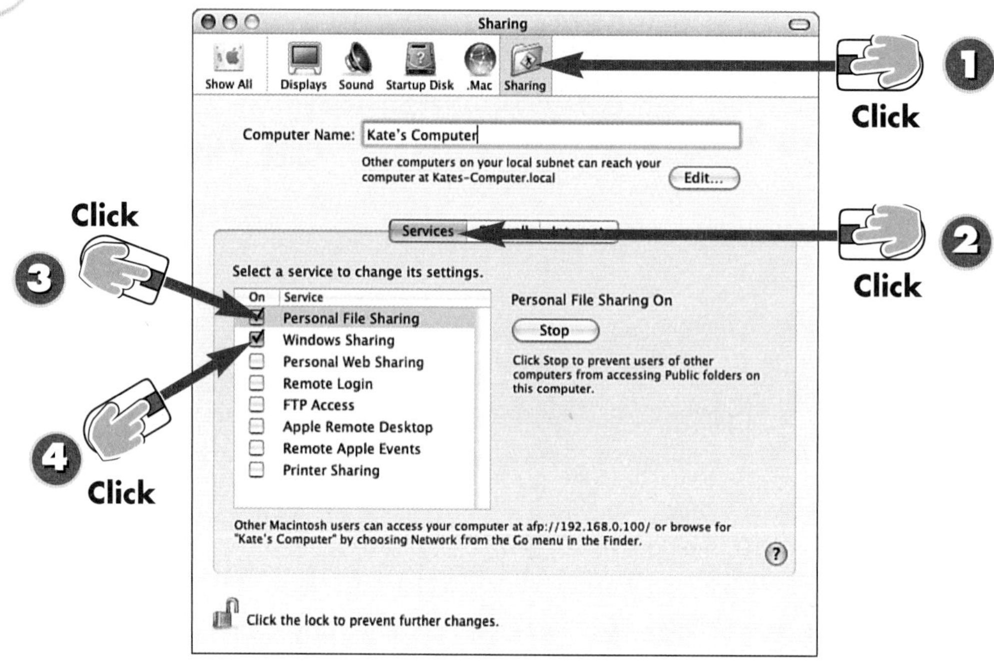

1. To enable network users to access the Public folder in your home folder, open System Preferences and click **Sharing**.
2. In the Sharing pane, click **Services**.
3. Check the box labeled **Personal File Sharing** to share files with other Mac users on your network.
4. Check the box labeled **Windows Sharing** to share files with Windows users on your network.

INTRODUCTION

Some files are meant to be read and even modified by multiple users—a family calendar or a committee report in progress, for example. You can share these files in two designated places, with different results. And you can send copies of your files to other users via their Drop Box folders.

HINT

Skipping It
Why all this rigmarole, you ask? The point is to keep your files as safe as you want them to be. If you want to skip the security routine and share with everyone, you can keep your Mac logged in with a single user account and give all users the password.

HINT

Making the Connection
To learn how to connect to other Macs on a network, turn to "Connecting to Networked Computers" in Part 12, "Creating a Home Network."

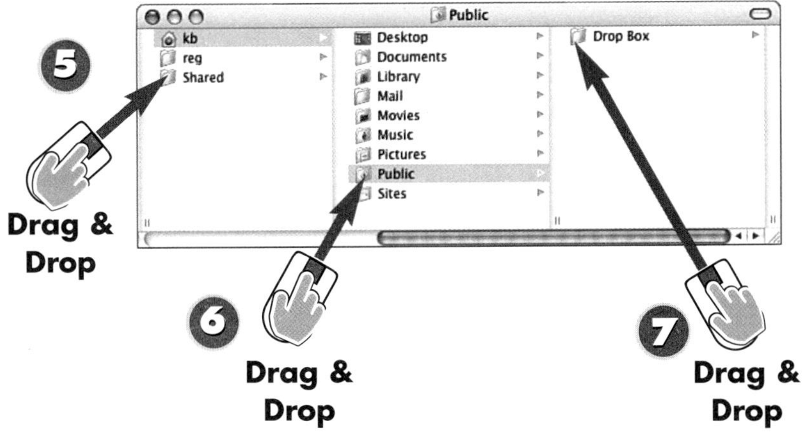

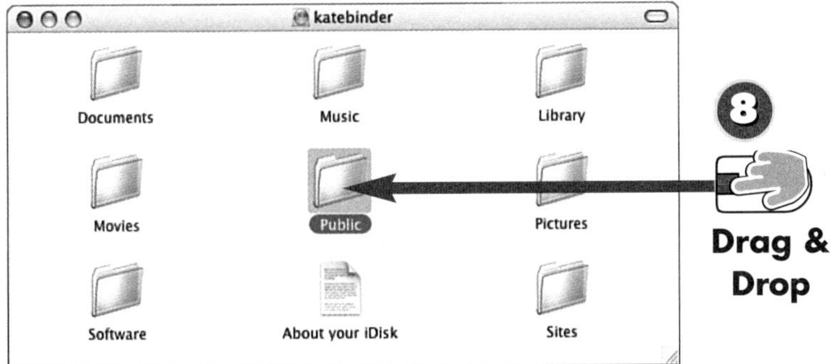

5. Put files you want all your Mac's users to be able to modify in the Shared folder in the Users folder.
6. Put files that you want all your Mac's users to be able to read but not change in the Public folder in your home folder.
7. To give another user of your computer a copy of a file, put the file in that user's Drop Box folder inside her Public folder.
8. To share a file with other Mac users on the Internet, copy it to the Public folder on your iDisk.

HINT

It's Good to Share
Files you might share in a Public folder or in the Shared folder within the Users folder include databases (of recipes, addresses, or clients, for example), templates for letters or memos that everyone uses, and logo graphics.

HINT

Large Attachments
Many email providers limit the size of file attachments. If you want to send someone a larger file than will fit through your provider's email gateway, put it on your iDisk (step 8) and create a File Sharing Web page where she can snag the file.

HINT

Flying Blind
When you drag a file into another user's Drop Box, the Mac warns that you won't be able to see the result of the operation. This is its way of saying that you can't open the Drop Box folder to see what's in it.

Keeping Your Secrets

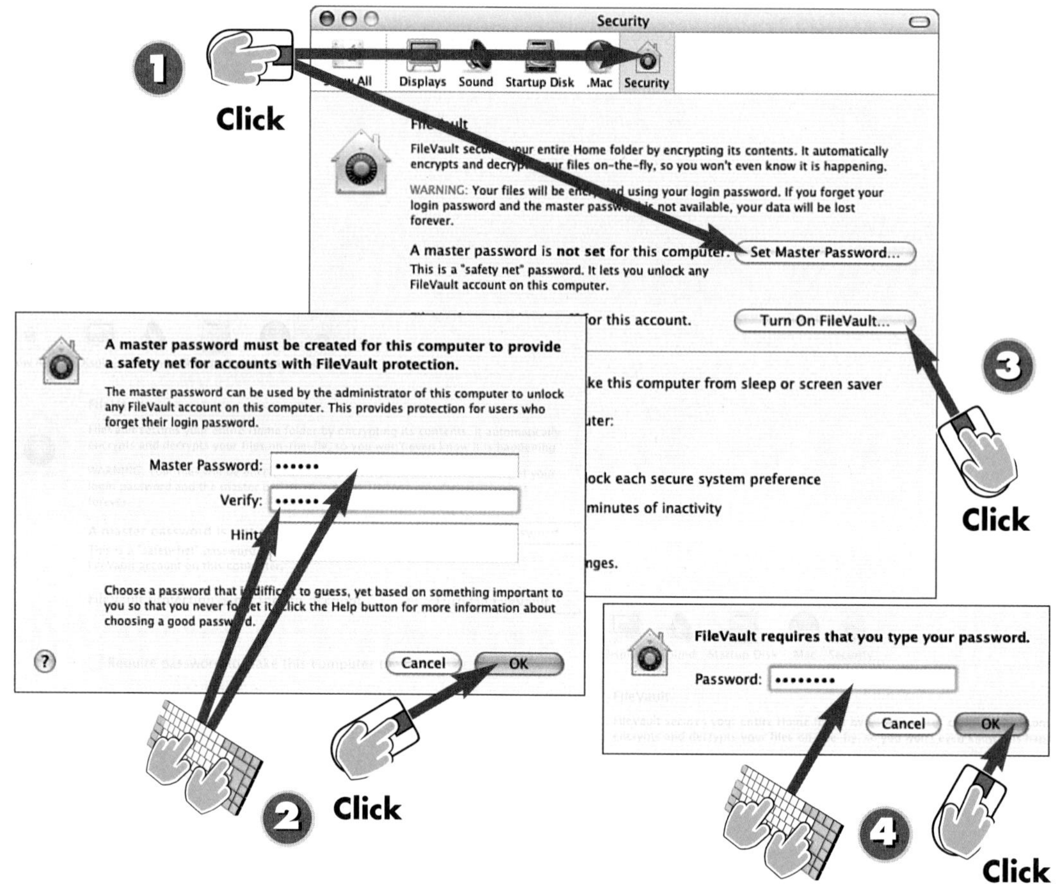

1. In System Preferences, click **Security**; then click **Set Master Password** to create a backup password that opens your home folder in case you forget your login password.
2. Type the master password in the **Master Password** field, type it a second time in the **Verify** field, and click **OK**.
3. Click **Turn On FileVault** to set FileVault preferences.
4. Type your login password and click **OK**.

INTRODUCTION

FileVault is a new feature in Mac OS X 10.3 that encrypts the contents of your home folder so no one can read your files without entering your password. This includes all users, even admin users, under all circumstances—it's the ultimate protection for your files. You must be logged in to your account to turn on FileVault.

HINT

Coffee Break
While FileVault is being turned on or off, you are logged out and can't use your Mac. This could last just a minute or take longer, depending on how much data is in your home folder.

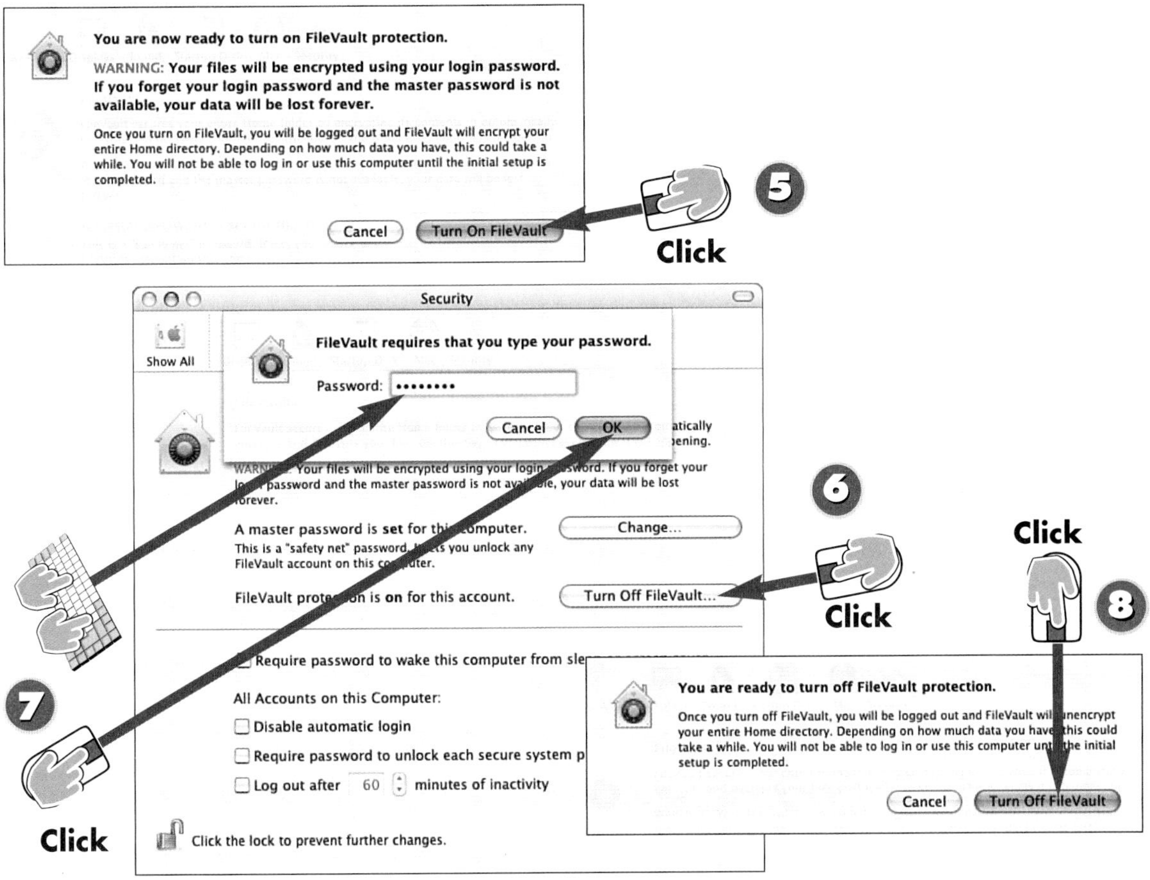

5. Click **Turn On FileVault**. The system logs you out while it encrypts your home folder; it then asks you to log in again.

6. To turn off FileVault, click **Security** in System Preferences and click **Turn Off FileVault**.

7. Type your login password and click **OK**.

8. Click **Turn Off FileVault**. The system logs you out while it decrypts your home folder; it then asks you to log in again.

HINT

How to Tell
When FileVault is turned off, your home folder icon looks like a little house. With FileVault turned on, the folder icon changes to a house-shaped safe with a big combination lock dial on its front.

CAUTION

Deceptive Appearances
FileVault makes your home folder appear to some programs to be a single, constantly changing folder or file, which can interfere with backup software. If you use FileVault, be sure to check that your backups are working correctly.

PART 12

Creating a Home Network

A network, whether it's composed of physical cables or wireless, connects your computer with other computers so you can share files, play network games, and all use the same printers and Internet connection. The Internet, in fact, is simply a huge network comprising many smaller networks. With Mac OS X, setting up your own network in your home or office is easy.

Creating a network has two basic components. First, you need to make the connection by either hooking up your Macs (and Windows PCs, if you like) with Ethernet cables or installing AirPort cards and an AirPort base station so they can talk to each other wirelessly. Then, you need to tell your Mac how your network is set up so the system knows which connector and language to use to communicate with the other computers it's connected to.

In this part, you'll learn how to set up your network and turn on file sharing so both Windows users and other Mac users on your network can exchange files with you. You'll also learn how to share printers connected to your Mac with other users on your network. And you'll find out how to share a single Internet connection among all the computers on a network, as well as how to connect to an AirPort network and get online via a wireless AirPort connection.

Setting Up and Using a Network

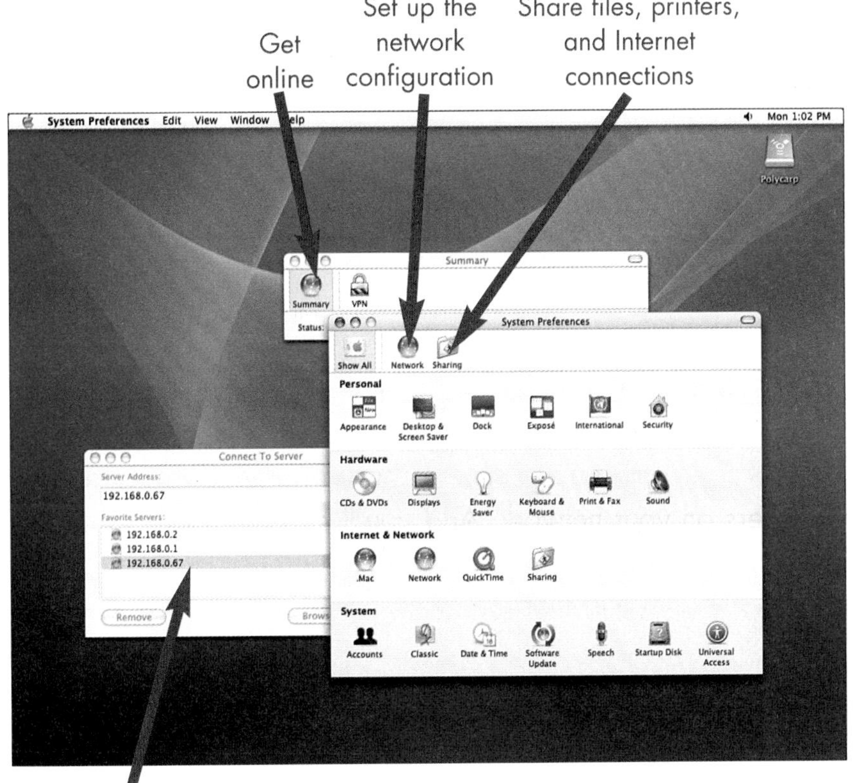

Getting on the Network

Start

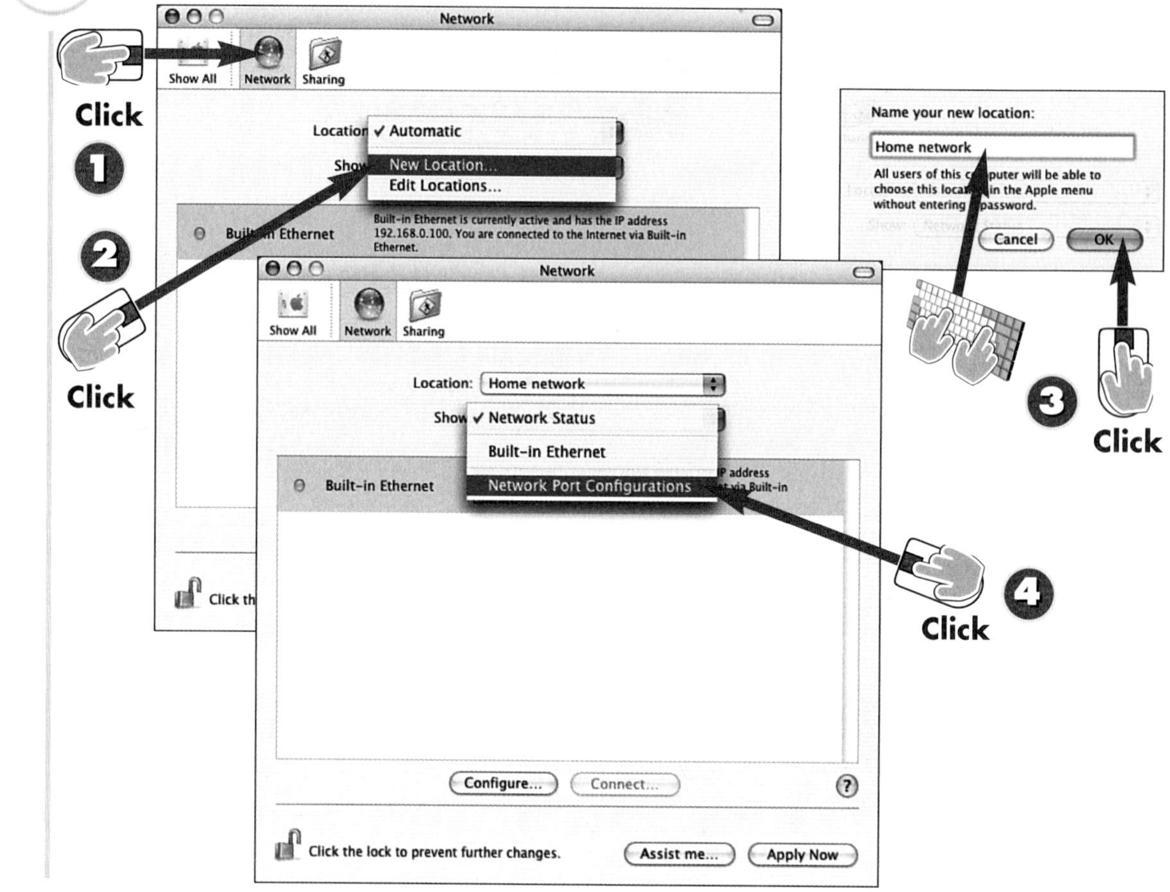

1. Open System Preferences and click the **Network** button.

2. In the Network pane, choose **New Location** from the **Location** pop-up menu.

3. Enter a name for the network configuration you're about to create and click **OK**.

4. Choose **Network Port Configurations** from the **Show** pop-up menu.

INTRODUCTION

The first step to setting up a wired home network is this: Connect your computers with Ethernet cables (a regular one for newer Macs and a crossover cable for older Macs). If you have more than two computers, buy a hub and connect each computer to the hub; otherwise, connect your two Macs directly to each other.

TIP

An Even Easier Way
If network settings completely befuddle you, try using the Network Setup Assistant to get connected. Start up System Preferences and click **Network**; then click **Assist Me** and follow the instructions.

TIP

Looking It Up
Start up System Preferences and click **Network**; then choose **Network Status** from the **Show** pop-up menu. Click the **Built-in Ethernet** or **AirPort** entries in the list to see your IP address.

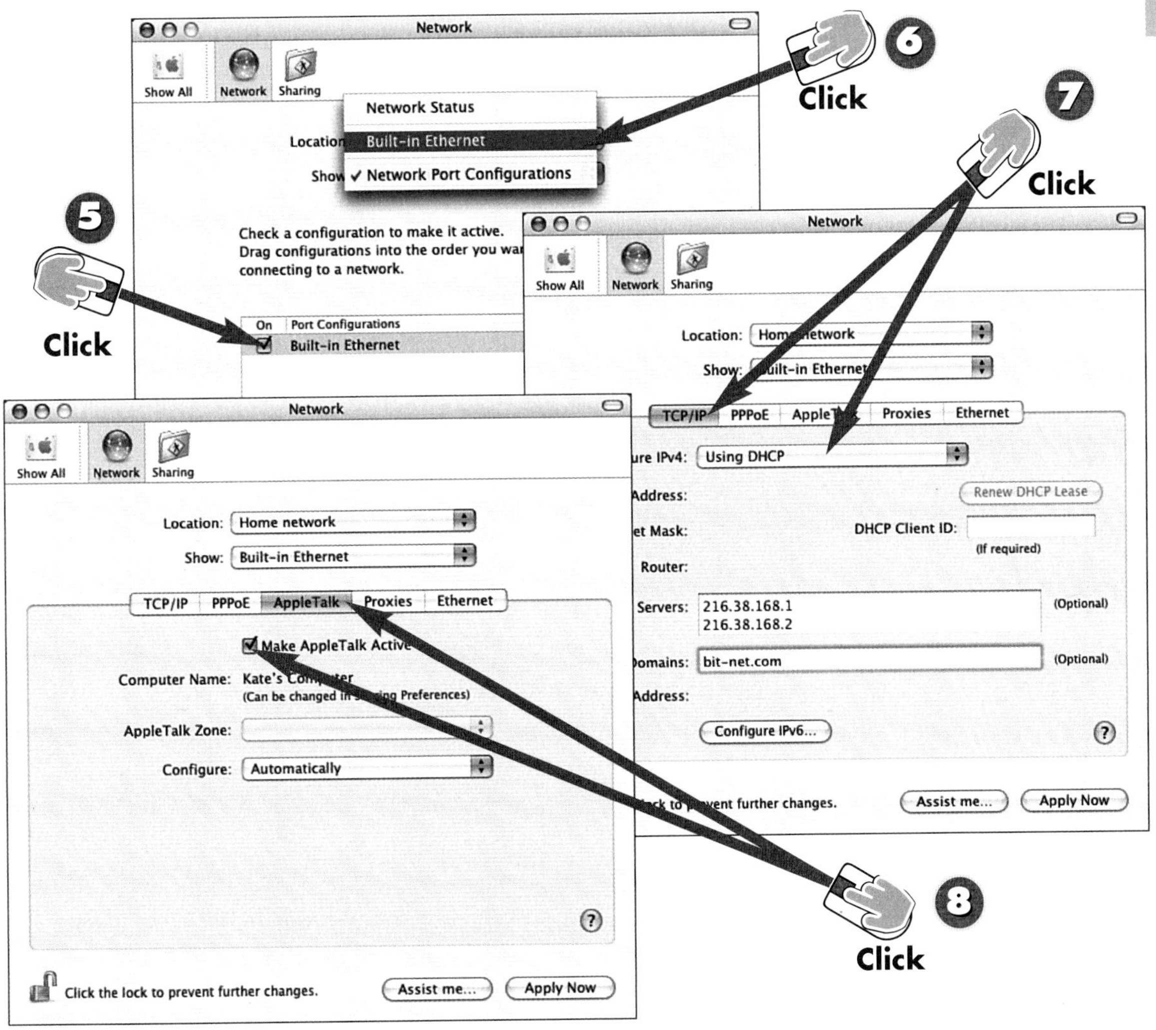

1. **5** Check the box next to the network port you want to use (usually either Built-in Ethernet or AirPort).
2. **6** Choose the active network port from the **Show** pop-up menu.
3. **7** To turn on TCP networking, click the **TCP/IP** tab and make sure that **Configure IPv4** is set to either **Using DHCP** or **Manually** (check with your network admin).
4. **8** To share files with older Macs that can't do TCP networking, click the **AppleTalk** tab and check **Make AppleTalk Active**.

HINT

Going Both Ways
If other users want to connect to your Mac via AppleTalk, both your Mac and their Macs must have AppleTalk turned on as directed in step 8.

HINT

By the Manual
When you choose Manually in the Configure IPv4 pop-up menu, you must enter your Mac's IP address, your router's IP address, and the subnet mask. If all this is gibberish to you, go to Threemacs.com (**www.threemacs.com**) to learn about creating networks.

Connecting to Networked Computers

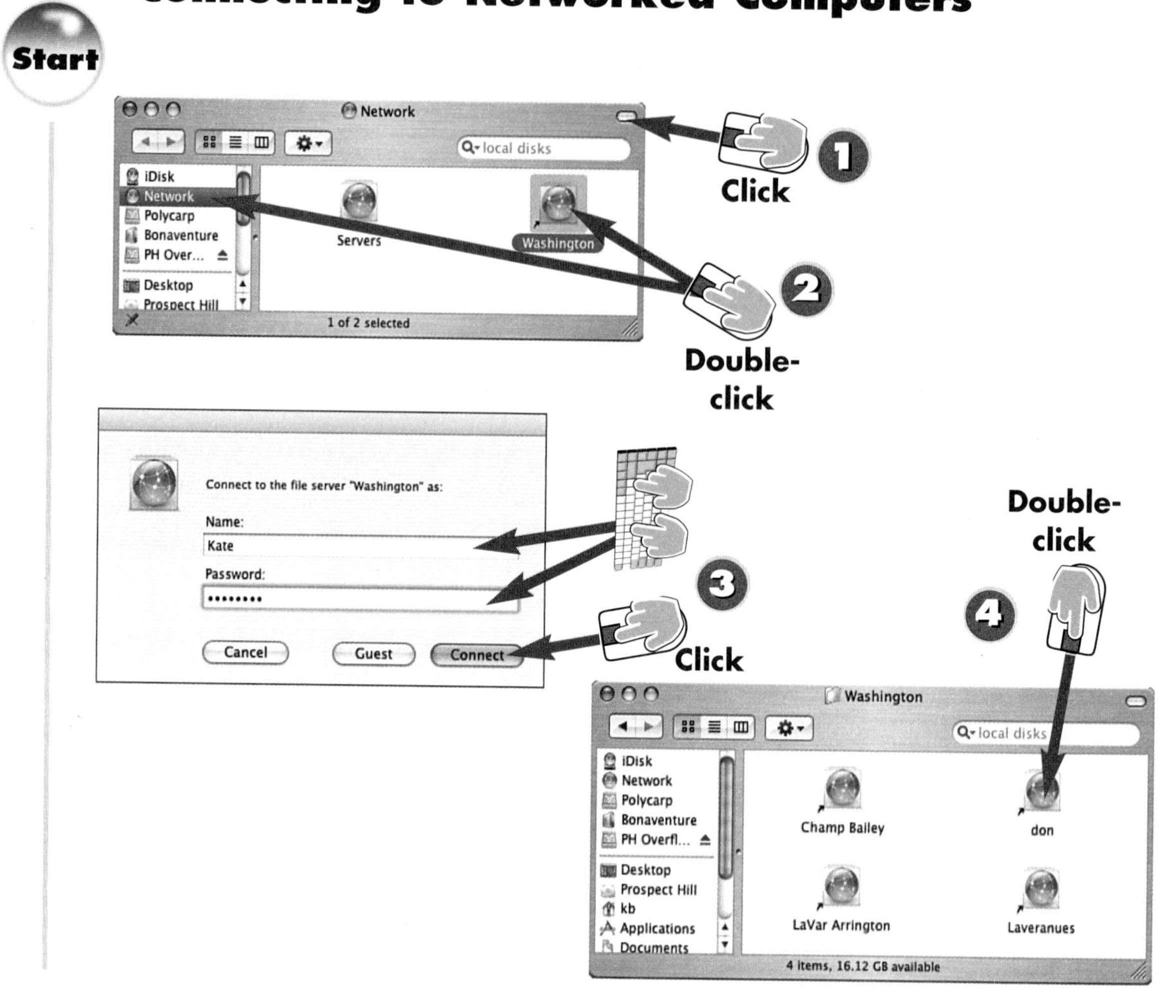

1. In the Finder, click the transparent button to display the Places sidebar if it's not already visible.

2. Click **Network** and double-click the computer to which you want to connect.

3. Enter your username and password and click **Connect**.

4. Double-click a drive or folder to connect to.

INTRODUCTION

Networking has always been easy with Macs, but now the system's networking features are easier to use and more powerful than ever. You can connect to any Mac or Windows computer on your network using either AppleTalk or TCP networking, but all you need to know is the computer's name or IP address.

TIP

Frequent Flying
If you frequently connect to a server that's not listed, drag its hard drive icon into the Favorites sidebar in a Finder window. Then it appears in the sidebar in every Finder window; double-click it to connect.

HINT

Connecting with the Other Side
To connect to a Windows computer, assign it an IP address (refer to Windows documentation). Then enter its address in the Connect to Server dialog box in this form: **smb://192.168.0.102**.

Sharing Files on a Network

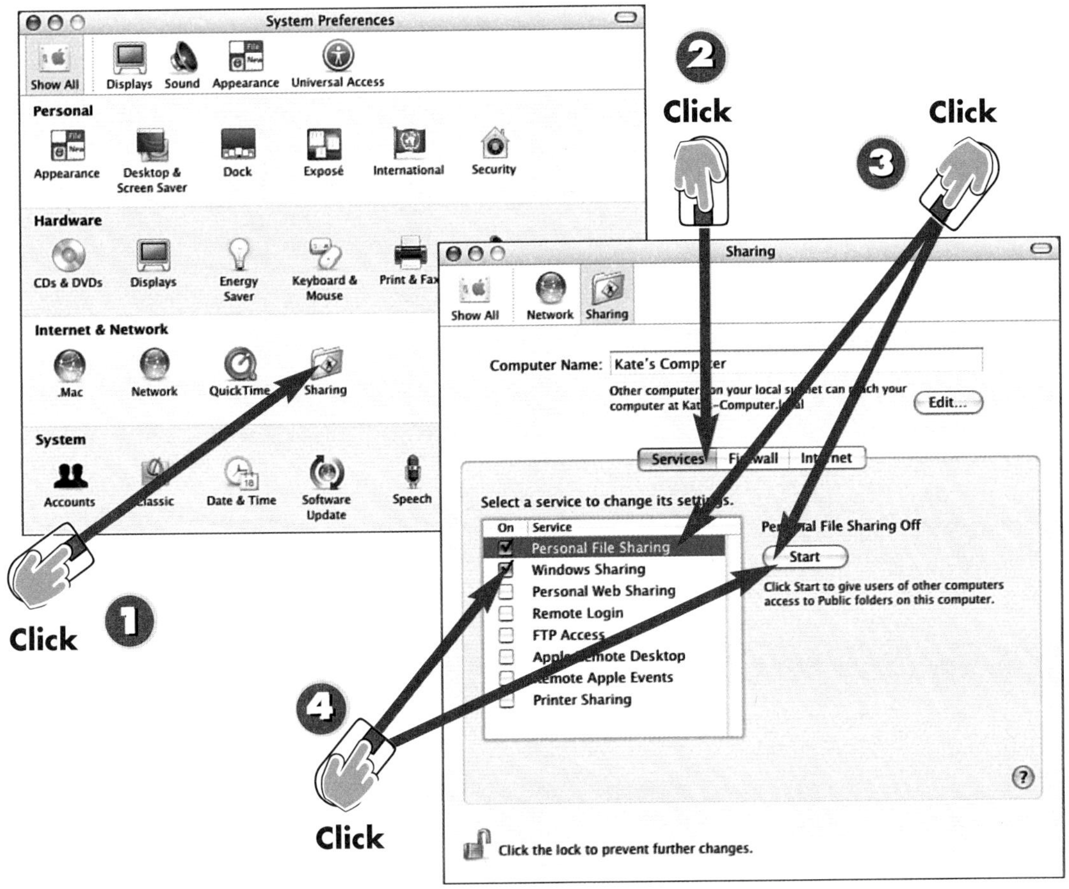

1. Open System Preferences and click **Sharing**.

2. In the Sharing dialog box, click the **Services** tab.

3. Click **Personal File Sharing** and click **Start**.

4. To share files with Windows users as well as Mac users, click **Windows Sharing** and click **Start**.

INTRODUCTION

When computers aren't networked, sharing files requires the use of sneakernet: physically walking a removable disk to another machine. Fortunately, creating a network is easy enough (see "Getting on the Network," earlier in this part) that Mac users rarely have to resort to sneakernet. Here's how to share your files on a real network.

TIP

When You Get There

To connect to another Mac on your network, see the preceding task, "Connecting to Networked Computers." When you connect to another Mac, you'll see the home folders of that Mac's users. If you log in as a registered user of that Mac, you'll be able to access the same folders as if you were sitting in front of the Mac. Otherwise, you must connect as a Guest; in this case, you'll be able to see only the contents of the user's Public folder (see "Sharing Files," in Part 11, "Sharing Your Mac with Multiple Users").

Sharing a Printer on a Network

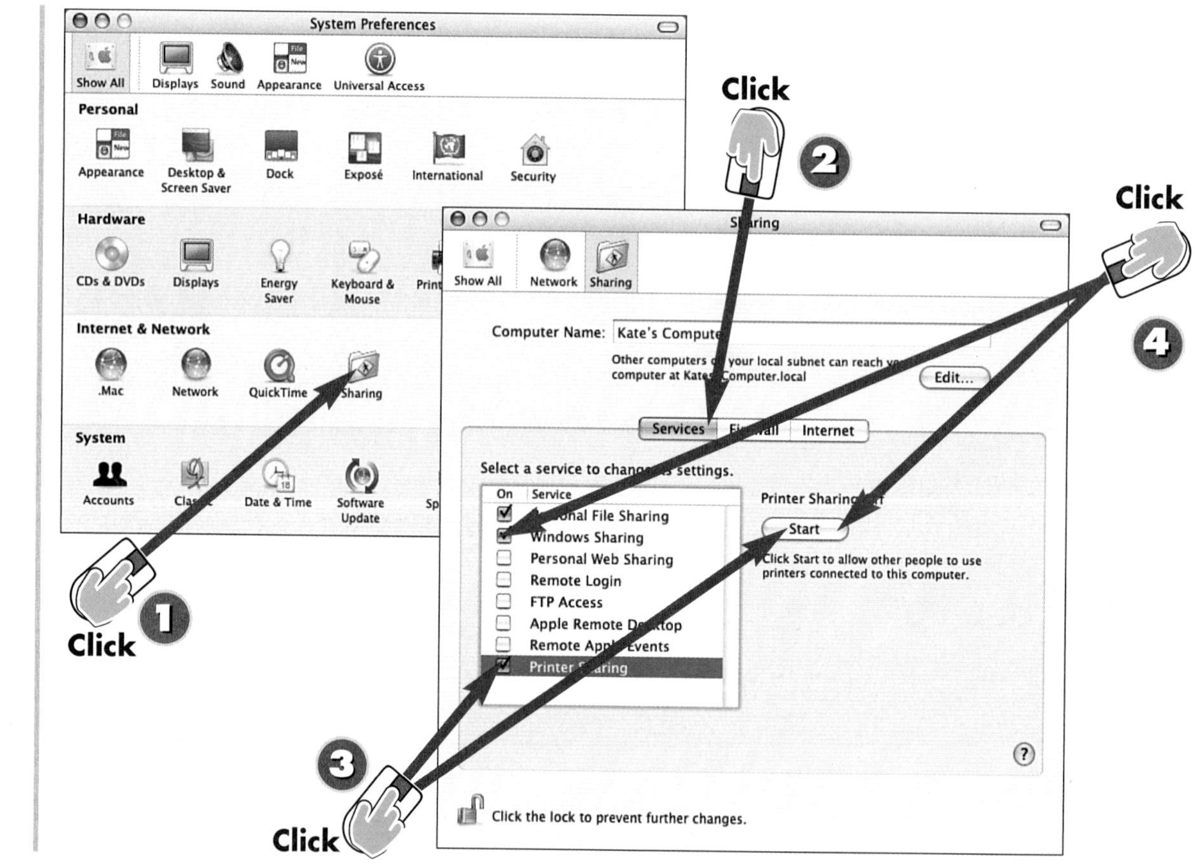

1. Open System Preferences and click **Sharing**.
2. Click the **Services** tab.
3. Click **Printer Sharing** and click **Start**.
4. To share printers with Windows users as well as Mac users, click **Windows Sharing** and click **Start** (if it's not already started).

INTRODUCTION

You can share printers connected to your computer with other computer users on your network. Starting up printer sharing is simple; you can choose to restrict it to Mac users or enable Windows users to use your printers as well. Network users can add shared printers to their Print dialog boxes just like network printers.

TIP

Where in the Office...?
To let other people know where shared printers are physically located, start **Printer Setup Utility** (in the Utilities folder in Applications). Select the printer and click **Show Info**; then add a description (such as "Kate's office") in the **Location** field.

HINT

What It's For
Printers on your network are already shared with other users on the network, even if the printers are located in your office. Printer sharing gives network capabilities to devices such as USB inkjets, which don't usually have network connectors.

Sharing an Internet Connection

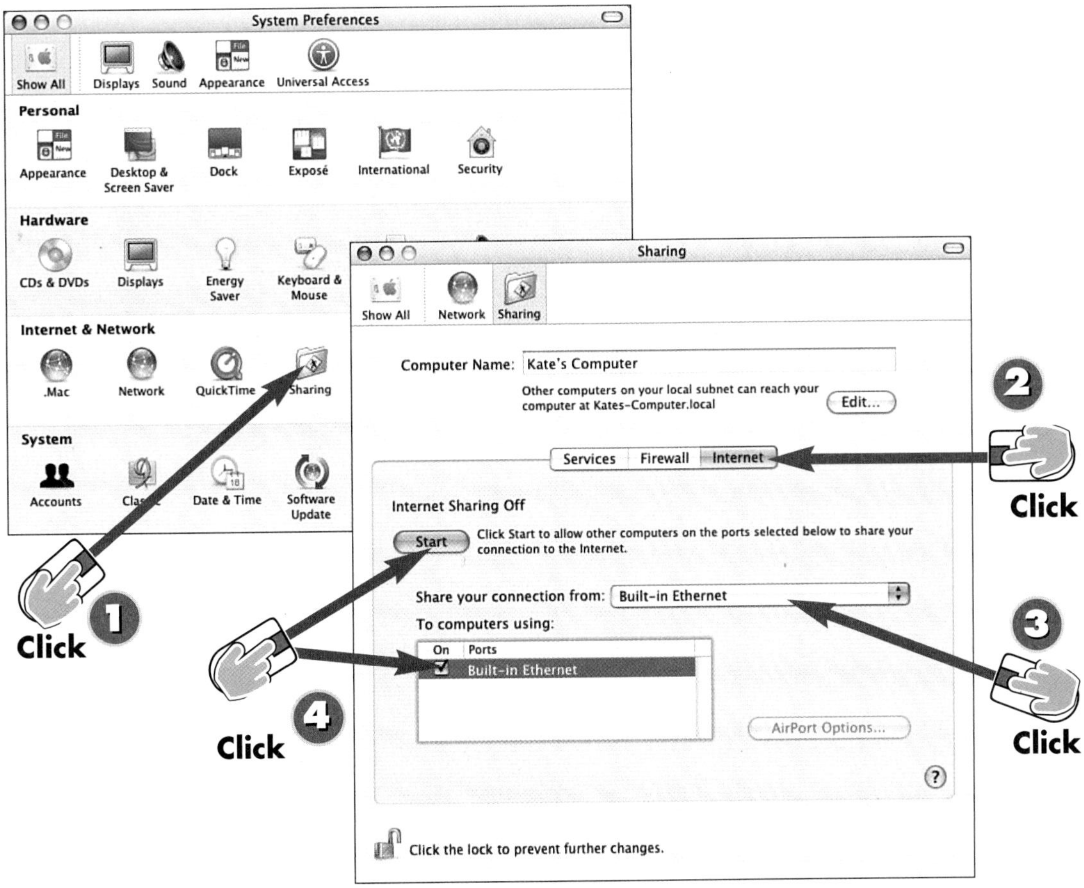

1. Open System Preferences and click **Sharing**.
2. Click the **Internet** tab.
3. Choose a connection to share. For direct cable modem and DSL connections, choose **Built-in Ethernet**; if you have a wireless connection to the Internet, choose **AirPort**.
4. Check the box next to the connection method the other computers on your network use; then click **Start**.

INTRODUCTION

If you've ever suffered through life with two Internet-capable computers and only one phone line, you'll appreciate the ability to share an online connection with all the computers in your house or office. And life gets even better when your connection is broadband, such as a cable modem or a DSL line.

HINT

When Not to Share

If you connect to the Internet and your network via the same port, sharing your Internet connection can disrupt the network by telling other computers to access the Internet through it when they shouldn't (such as when you take your laptop to the office).

HINT

Another Way to Share

If you're sharing an Internet connection through another Mac, you'll be able to get online only when that Mac is up and connected. If that doesn't work for you, consider buying a hardware router that can keep you online all the time.

Joining an AirPort Network

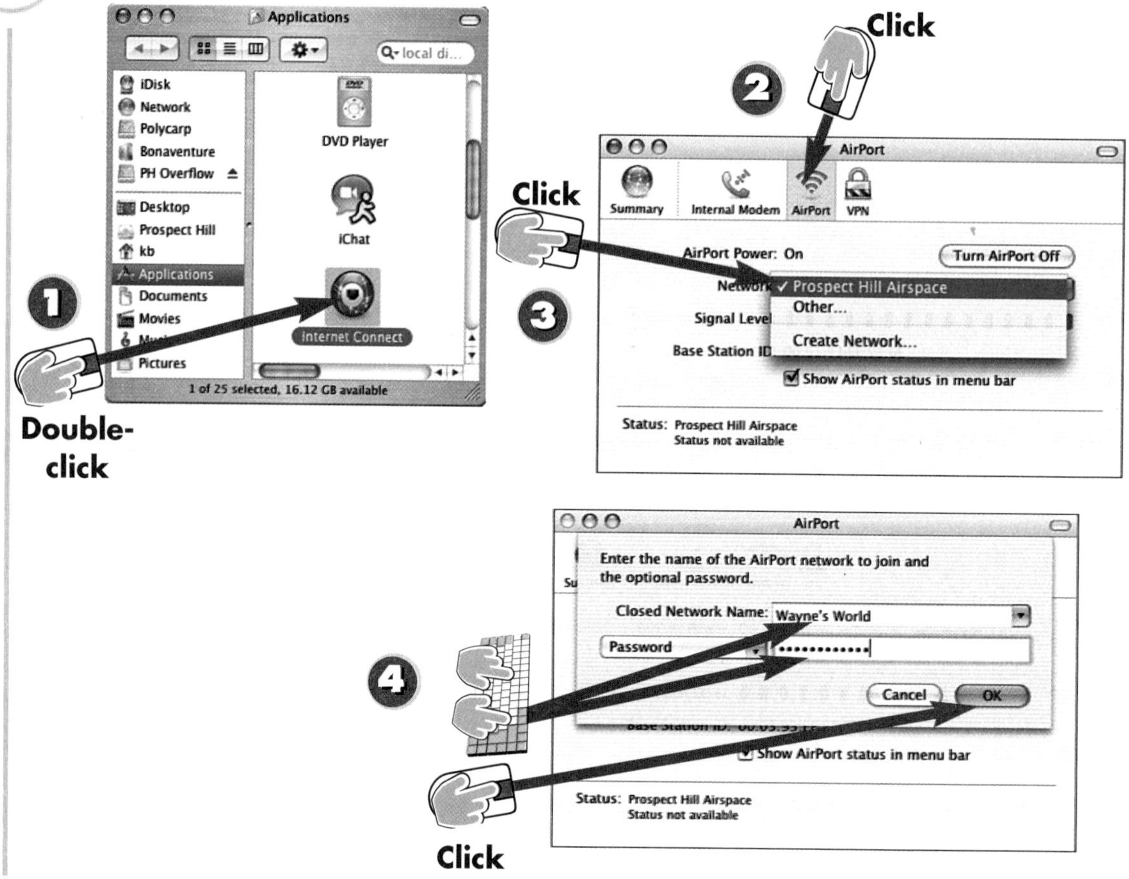

1. Double-click **Internet Connect** (located in the Utilities folder in Applications).

2. Click the **AirPort** icon in the toolbar.

3. Choose a network from the list and enter its password (if required).

4. If the network you want isn't listed, choose **Other** and enter the network's name and password in the login dialog box.

INTRODUCTION

With an AirPort card, you can get rid of those annoying network cables and connect to your network from wherever your computer happens to be, as long as you're close to an AirPort base station. AirPort is great for PowerBooks and iBooks, but you can use it for desktop Macs, too.

TIP

AirPort in Your Menu Bar
With the AirPort status menu, you can switch networks, turn AirPort on or off, open Internet Connect, or connect to AirPort-equipped Macs. Check the **Show AirPort status in menu bar** box in Internet Connect's AirPort settings.

HINT

Close to Home Base
If AirPort is turned on in Internet Connect but you can't get in touch with the network, you might be out of range. AirPort base stations have a range of about 150 feet; you must be within that area to connect to the base station.

Getting Online with AirPort

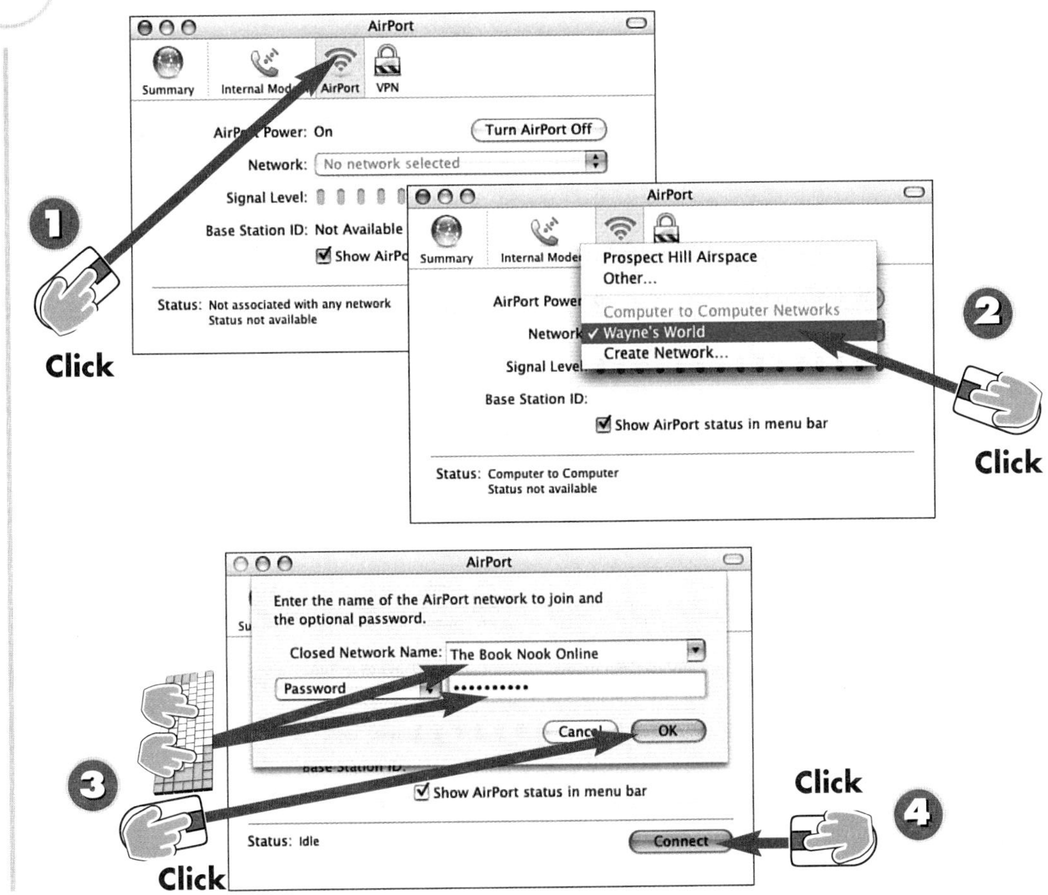

1 Open **Internet Connect** (located in the Utilities folder in Applications) and click the **AirPort** icon in the toolbar.

2 If you're not already connected to an Airport network, choose a network from the list and type its password (if required).

3 If the network you want isn't listed, choose **Other** from the Network pop-up menu and type the network's name and password; then click **OK**.

4 Click **Connect**.

INTRODUCTION

If you're connected to an AirPort network, you can share the Internet connection on that network. It might be configured to connect automatically when you need it (such as when you start up your Web browser), but if it's not, you'll need to know how to tell it you want to get online.

TIP

Closing the Connection
You can disconnect AirPort from the Internet manually, too. Just open Internet Connect again, click the **AirPort** icon in the toolbar, and click **Disconnect**.

HINT

How About My PC?
Yes, Windows PCs can connect to AirPort networks, too. AirPort cards work only in Macs, but there are third-party wireless cards made for PCs; what you're looking for, says Apple, is a "802.11b Wi-Fi certified wireless card."

Maintaining Your System

Most of the time your Mac just hums right along, cheerfully complying with your requests and sitting quietly in the corner when you're not using it. Every once in a while, however, even the best-behaved Mac needs a little maintenance or a minor repair. This part covers the basics of keeping your Mac happy and healthy.

In this part you'll learn how to fix disk errors and reformat disks—both removable disks and hard drives—as well as ways to remedy problems with Classic. Also covered are updating and installing system software, setting the date and time automatically, and calibrating your monitor for accurate color. Some of these techniques are one-time jobs (calibrating your monitor), and others are things you'll do on a regular basis (formatting removable disks).

Along the way, you'll learn a variety of useful tricks, such as displaying system information, rebooting from a different system, and force quitting programs when necessary. Whether you're a power user or a weekends-only Macster, the tasks in this part will teach you things every Mac user should know.

Mac Maintenance and Repair Kit

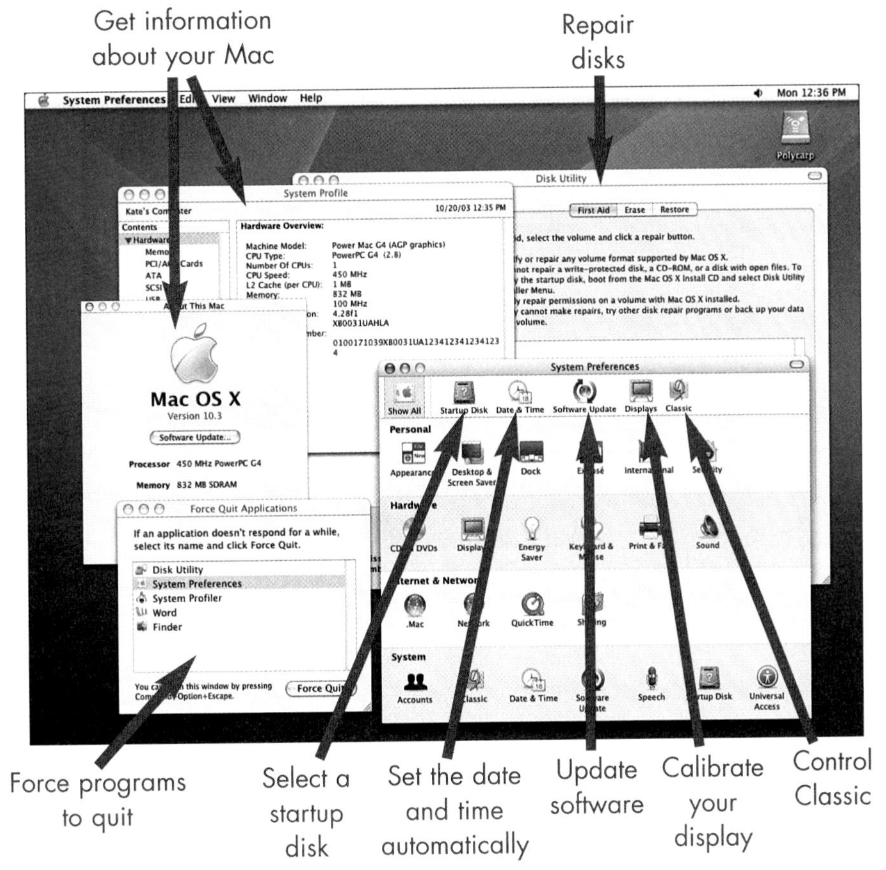

Fixing Errors with Disk Utility

Start

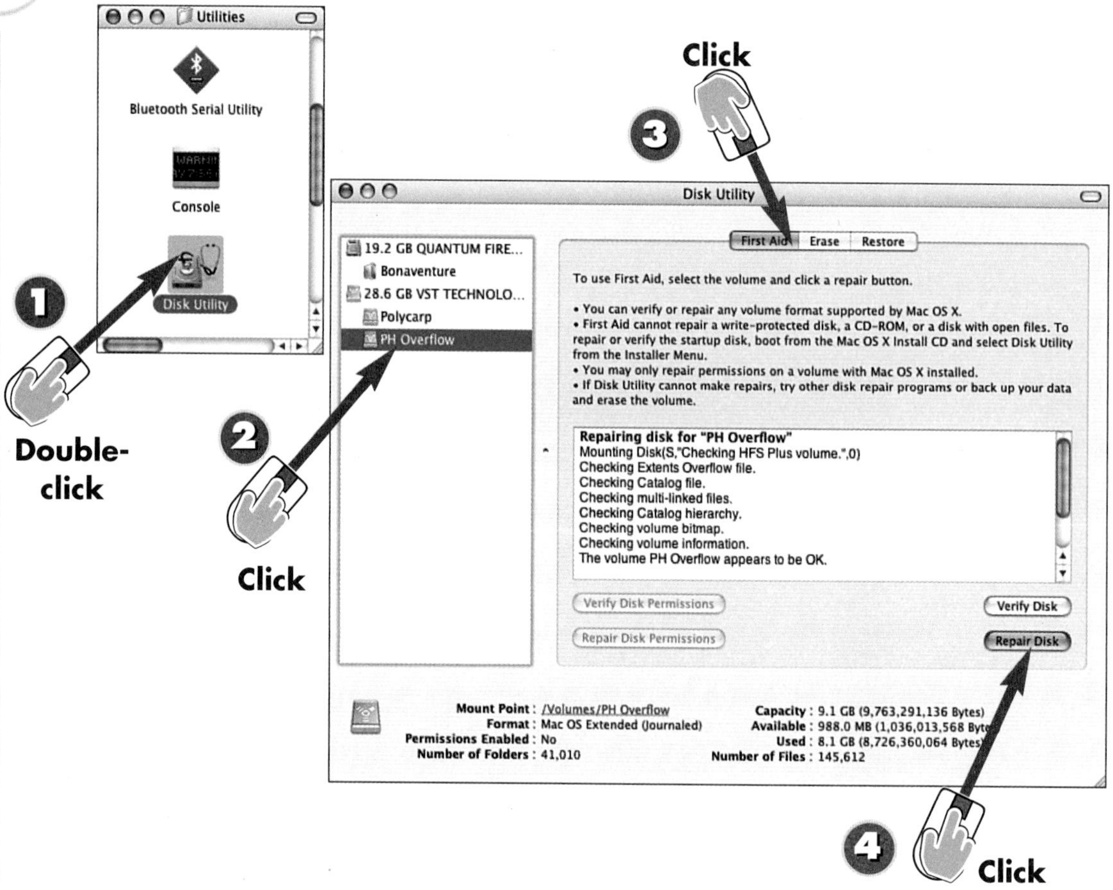

Double-click

Click

Click

Click

1. Double-click **Disk Utility** to start it (it's in the Utilities folder within Applications).

2. Select the disk to be repaired in the list.

3. Click the **First Aid** tab.

4. Click **Repair Disk**.

End

INTRODUCTION

Over time and with use, the formatting structure of a disk can become scrambled, either slightly or seriously. If you have trouble reading files from or saving files to a disk, or if you experience other mysterious problems, it's time to run the repair program Disk Utility. (To use Disk Utility on your startup disk, see the next task.)

TIP

Verify or Repair?

Usually, you should click Repair Disk Permissions or Repair Disk right off the bat. If, however, you're concerned about modifying a disk in any way at all, you can check its status without making any repairs by using the Verify commands.

HINT

What Are Permissions?

Disk Utility can repair permissions. Each program, document, and folder in a Mac OS X system has permissions describing who can open and modify it. Incorrect permissions can prevent programs from running or cause them to malfunction.

Repairing the Startup Disk

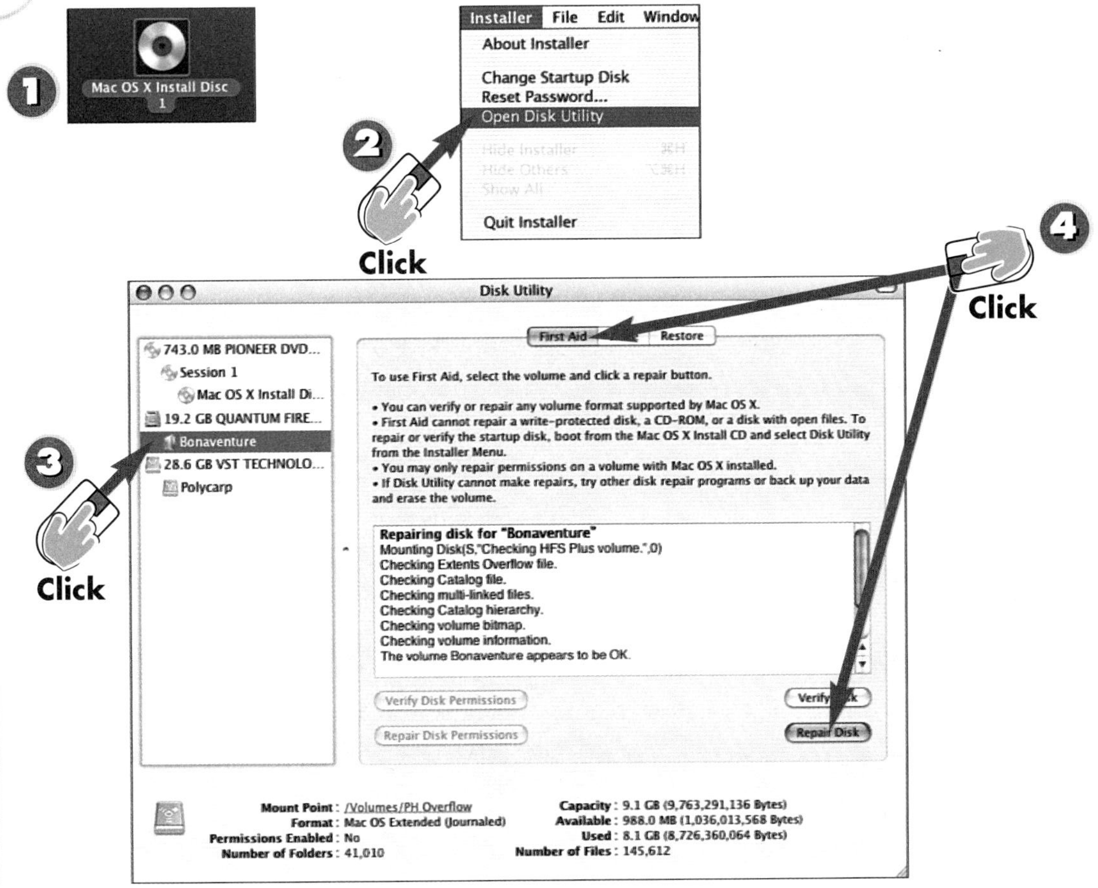

1. Restart from the Mac OS X Install CD (see "Starting Up from a Different System," later in this part).
2. Choose **Installer**, **Open Disk Utility**.
3. Select your hard drive in the list.
4. Click the **First Aid** tab and click **Repair Disk**.

INTRODUCTION

Disk Utility can't repair the startup disk because the program can't modify the section of the disk where it resides. If you have a second hard drive with a Mac OS X system installed, you can start from that drive to run Disk Utility or use your installation CD, as described here.

HINT

What's Going On?

The Open Disk Utility command (located in the Installer menu when you start up from your installation CD) isn't anything special. It simply starts up the Disk Utility program that's installed on the CD, which is the same as the one installed on your hard drive.

Updating Programs with Software Update

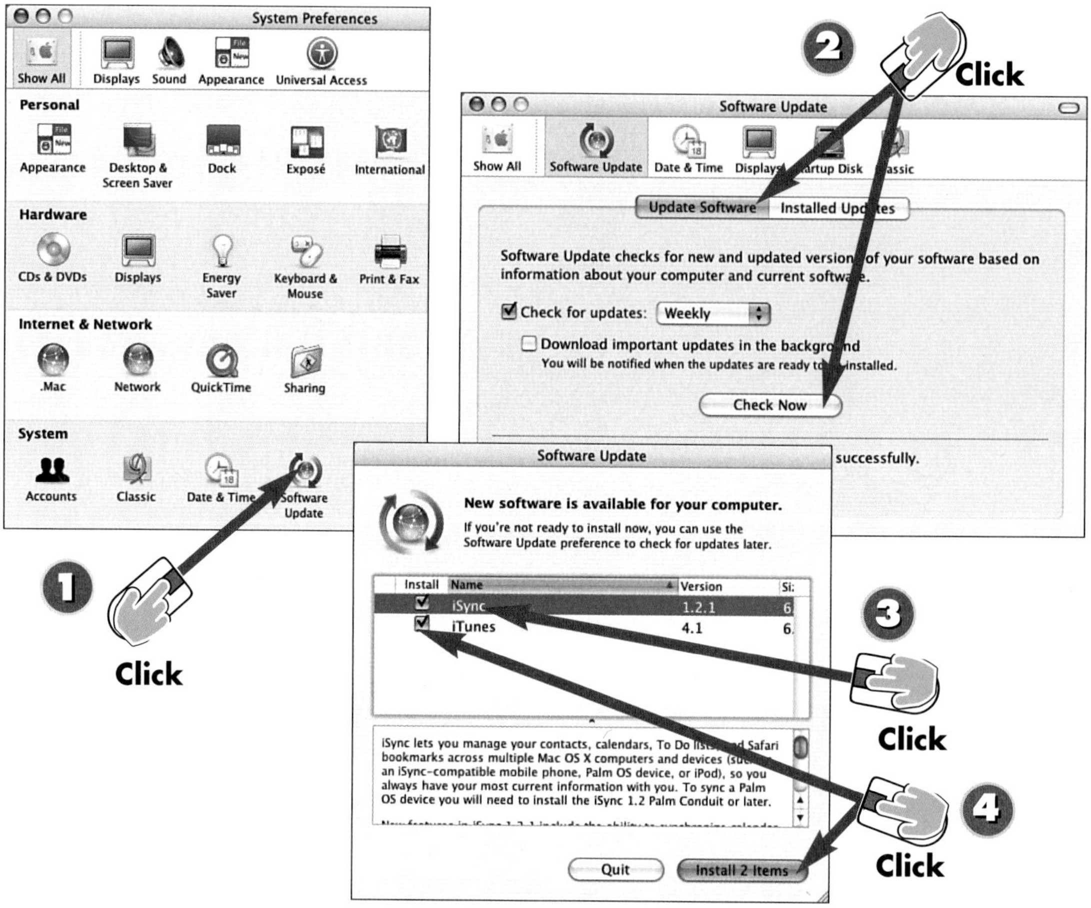

1. Start System Preferences and click the **Software Update** button.

2. Click the **Update Software** tab and click **Check Now**.

3. If updates are located, click the name of each update to see information about it.

4. Check the boxes next to each update you want to install and click **Install**.

INTRODUCTION

Software Update checks the Internet to see whether updated versions of your system software and preinstalled programs are available. Then it can download and install updates for you. You enter an admin name and password when you update your software. Mac OS X assumes only admin users are authorized to change software.

TIP

Behind the Scenes

If you have a broadband Internet connection, check **Check for updates** and choose an interval. Do this at the time of day when you want the check to occur—Software Update starts counting the time interval from the time you make this setting.

TIP

Keeping Track

If you want to know which updates have been installed and when, click the **Installed Updates** tab to see a list. Click the column headers to sort the list by the date, the update's name, or the version number.

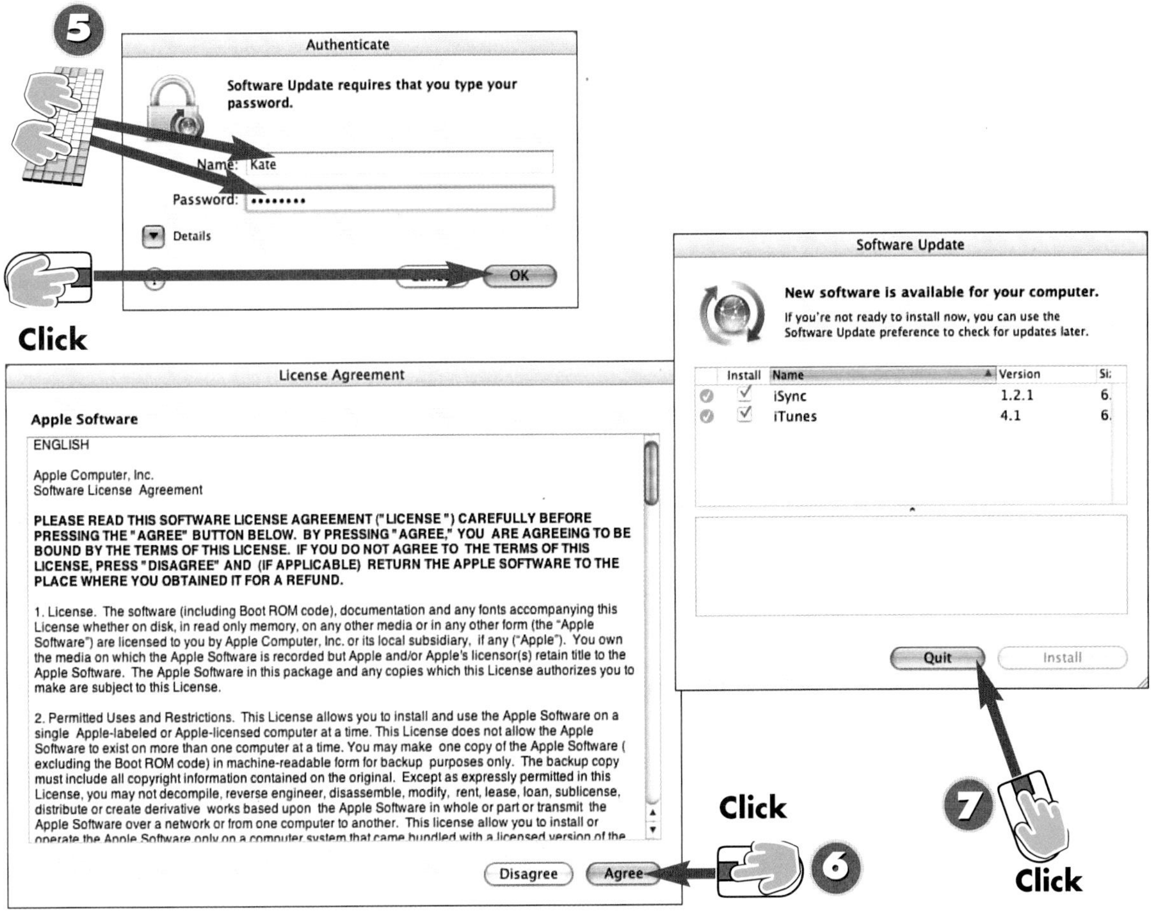

5. Enter an admin name and password and click **OK**.

6. If a license agreement appears, click **Agree**. Software Update downloads and installs the update.

7. Click **Quit**.

HINT

Updating a New System
Some updates don't show up until after other updates are installed. After installing system software from your original CDs (see "Installing the System Software," later in this part), run Software Update repeatedly until it doesn't show any updates.

HINT

Don't Go First
If you're not sure whether to install a system update, take a quick trip to MacFixit (**www.macfixit.com**) to see whether other users who've already updated their Macs have reported any problems with the update.

Using the Date & Time Preferences

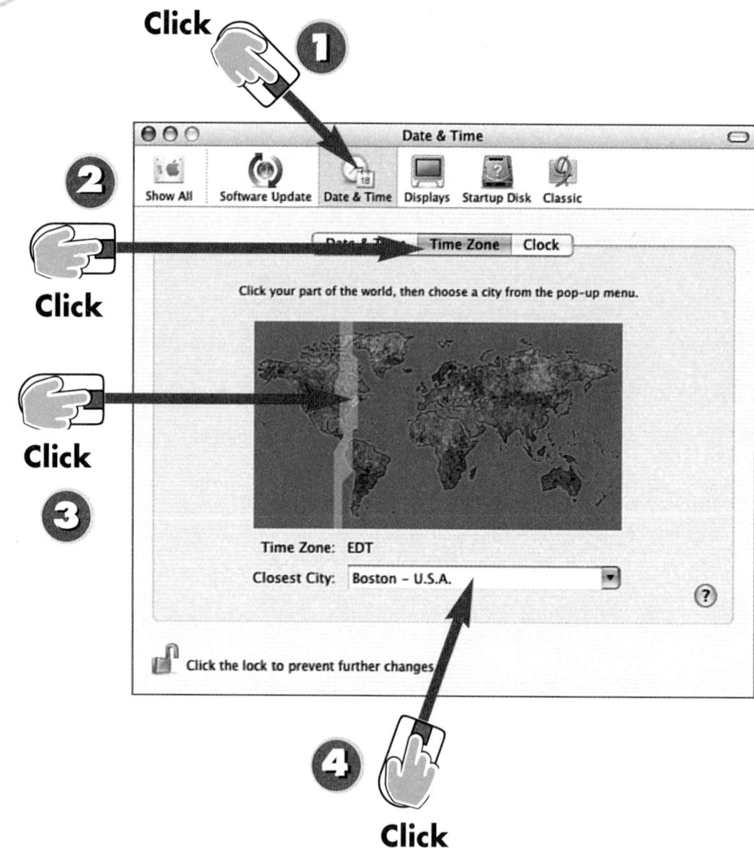

1. Start up System Preferences and click the **Date & Time** icon.
2. Click the **Time Zone** tab.
3. Click the map near where you live.
4. Choose the nearest city from the **Closest City** pop-up menu.

INTRODUCTION

It's important that your Mac knows what time it is. Every file on your hard drive is time-stamped, and the system uses that information to determine which files contain the latest data or the most recent software versions. Using the Date & Time preferences, you can ensure that the date and time stamps on your computer are accurate.

TIP

Blink Blink

Another useful setting in Date & Time preferences is located on the Clock tab. Check the box marked **Flash the time separators**. Then, if the colon stops blinking, you'll know your Mac is frozen and you can restart it.

HINT

Today's Date Is...

To see the full day and date, click the menu bar to reveal its own menu. You can also open the Date & Time preferences from this menu, as well as changing the menu bar clock to an analog icon instead of the standard digital alphanumeric display.

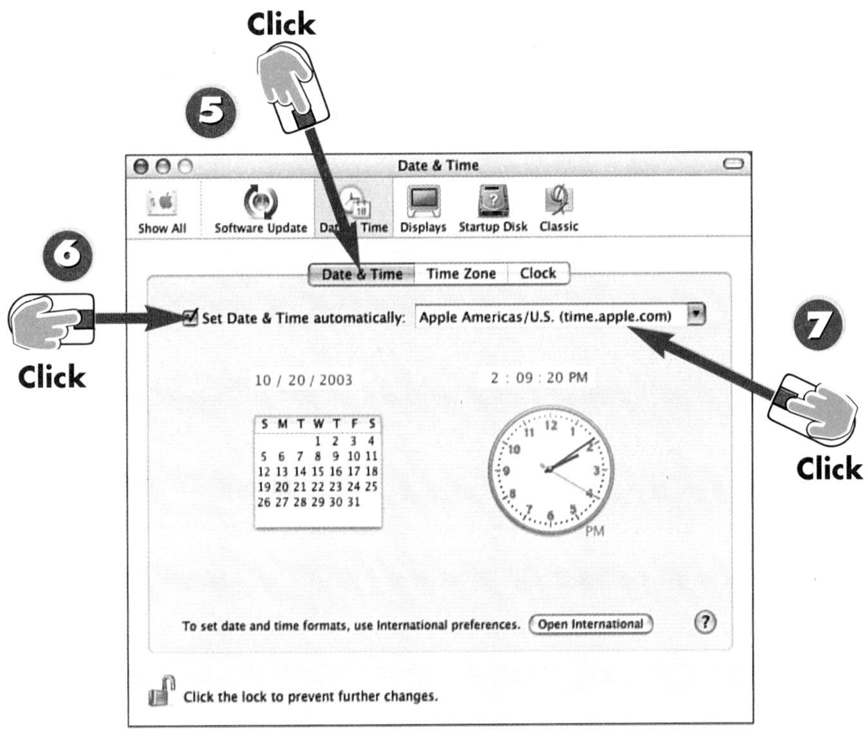

5. Click the **Date & Time** tab.

6. Check the box marked **Set Date & Time automatically**.

7. Choose the nearest timeserver from the pop-up menu.

HINT

More About NTP
To learn more about how network timeservers work, you can visit the Network Time Protocol Web site at **www.ntp.org**. There you'll also find links to lists of alternative timeservers, including servers around the world.

Calibrating Your Monitor

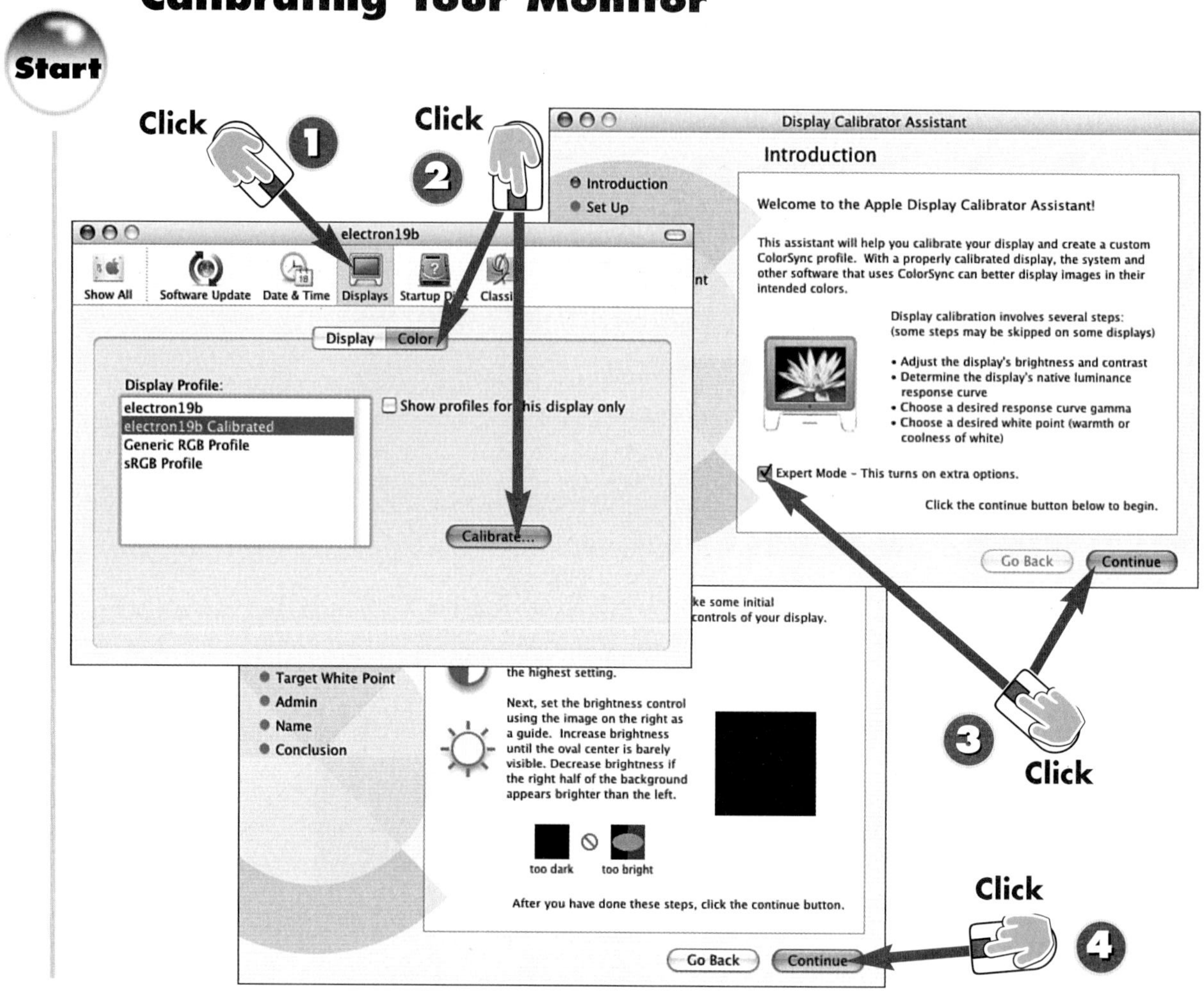

Start

1. Start System Preferences and click the **Displays** icon.
2. Click the **Color** tab and click **Calibrate**. The Display Calibrator Assistant opens.
3. Click the **Expert Mode** box to create a more precise profile; then click **Continue**.
4. Make the monitor settings shown in the window and click **Continue**.

INTRODUCTION

It wasn't all that long ago that computers had grayscale monitors, but now it's all about color. To make sure color looks right on your screen, however, you need to calibrate your system. Here's how to create a color device profile that tells your Mac how your monitor displays color and makes appropriate adjustments.

HINT

Managing Color

The software components that translate color between your Mac and your monitor comprise a color management system (CMS). In its full-fledged form, a CMS ensures consistent color throughout your system, from scanner to monitor to printer.

HINT

Where to Start

The Color tab of the Displays preference pane includes a list of profiles. If one of those matches or is close to the monitor you're using, click to select that profile before you start the calibration process. You'll get a more accurate profile that way.

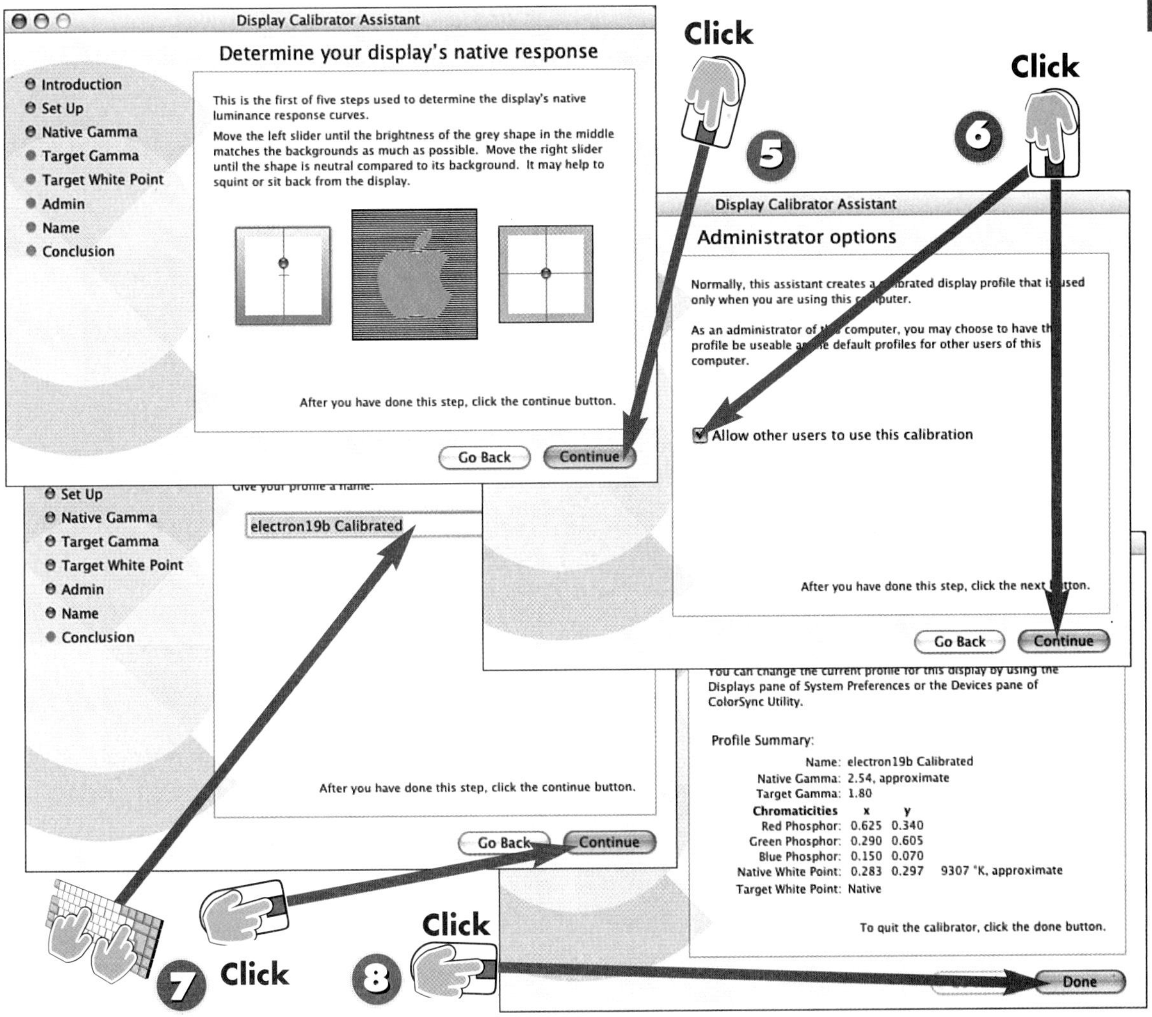

Display Calibrator Assistant

Determine your display's native response

- Introduction
- Set Up
- Native Gamma
- Target Gamma
- Target White Point
- Admin
- Name
- Conclusion

This is the first of five steps used to determine the display's native luminance response curves.

Move the left slider until the brightness of the grey shape in the middle matches the backgrounds as much as possible. Move the right slider until the shape is neutral compared to its background. It may help to squint or sit back from the display.

After you have done this step, click the continue button.

Go Back Continue

Click 5

Click 6

Display Calibrator Assistant

Administrator options

Normally, this assistant creates a calibrated display profile that is used only when you are using this computer.

As an administrator of this computer, you may choose to have the profile be useable as one default profiles for other users of this computer.

Allow other users to use this calibration

After you have done this step, click the next button.

Go Back Continue

- Set Up
- Native Gamma
- Target Gamma
- Target White Point
- Admin
- Name
- Conclusion

Give your profile a name:

electron19b Calibrated

After you have done this step, click the continue button.

Go Back Continue

You can change the current profile for this display by using the Displays pane of System Preferences or the Devices pane of ColorSync Utility.

Profile Summary:

Name:	electron19b Calibrated		
Native Gamma:	2.54, approximate		
Target Gamma:	1.80		
Chromaticities	x	y	
Red Phosphor:	0.625	0.340	
Green Phosphor:	0.290	0.605	
Blue Phosphor:	0.150	0.070	
Native White Point:	0.283	0.297	9307 °K, approximate
Target White Point:	Native		

To quit the calibrator, click the done button.

Done

7 Click

Click 8

5 Follow the instructions on the Native Response, Target Gamma, and Target White Point screens, clicking **Continue** after each screen.

6 If you're an admin user, check the box to make the profile available to all users of this Mac; then click **Continue**.

7 Enter a name for the profile and click **Continue**. The Display Calibrator Assistant saves the profile.

8 Click **Done**.

HINT

Native Gamma, Target Gamma, and Target White Point, used in the Display Calibrator Assistant, might sound very technical, but they simply refer to how your eye perceives the lightness, darkness, and overall color cast of your monitor's display.

HINT

A Step Further

If you're in the market for truly accurate color, you'll have to spend a little to get it. Look into a color profiling application such as MonacoEZColor (**www.monacosys.com**), which can create custom scanner and printer profiles for your system.

Starting Up from a Different System

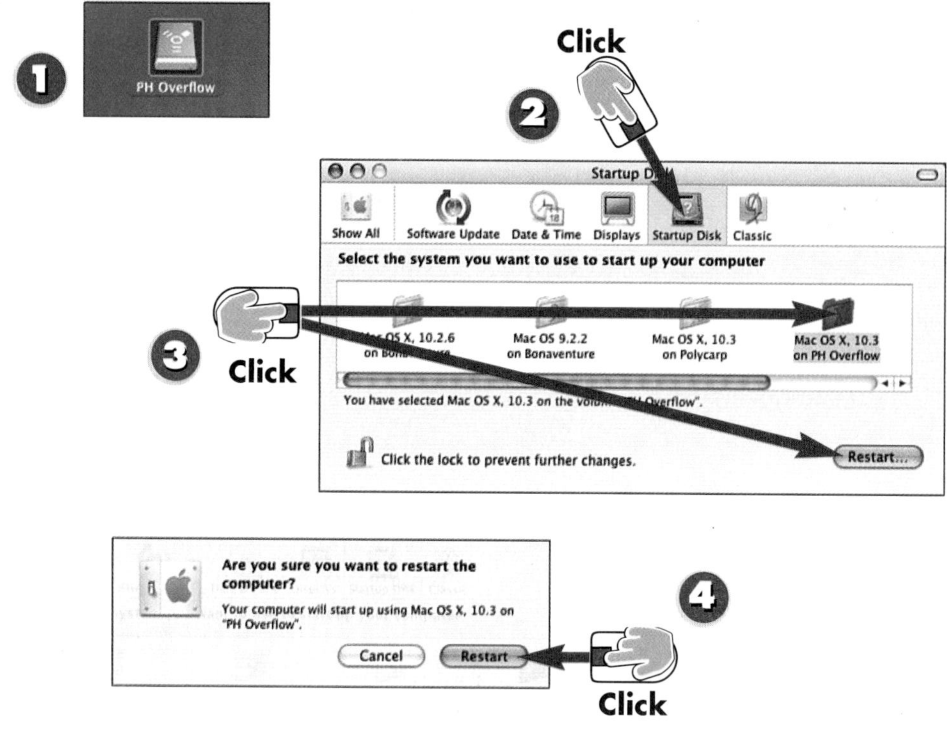

1. If needed, insert or hook up the disk that contains the system from which you want to start up.
2. Start up System Preferences and click **Startup Disk**.
3. Click to select the system installation you want to use; then click **Restart**.
4. Click **Restart** again.

INTRODUCTION

Starting up your Mac is easy using any Mac OS system software it can find. You might use this feature to restart in Mac OS 9 because some older programs won't run in Classic. Or you can play it safe by installing a new Mac OS X system update on an external drive and test it before installing it on your main hard drive.

TIP

Getting Back Where You Belong

If you restart using a Mac OS 9 system, you can get back to Mac OS X by choosing **Apple menu**, **Control Panels**, **Startup Disk in Mac OS 9**. The control panel doesn't look the same as in Mac OS X, but it works the same way.

Forcing an Application to Quit

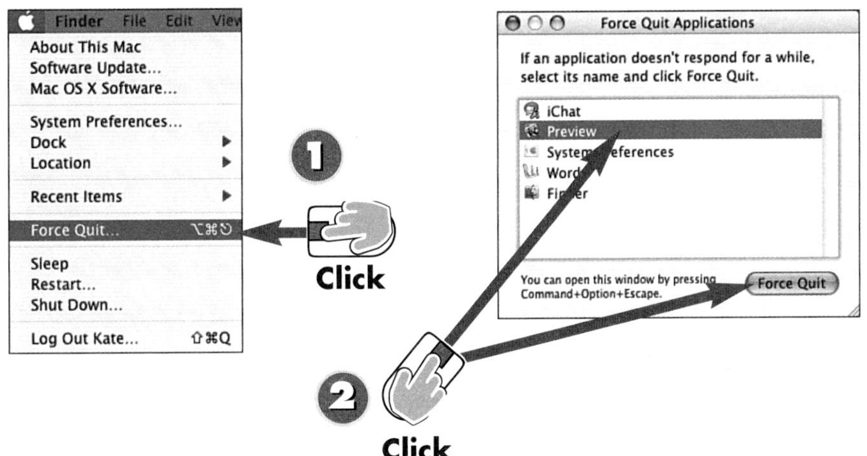

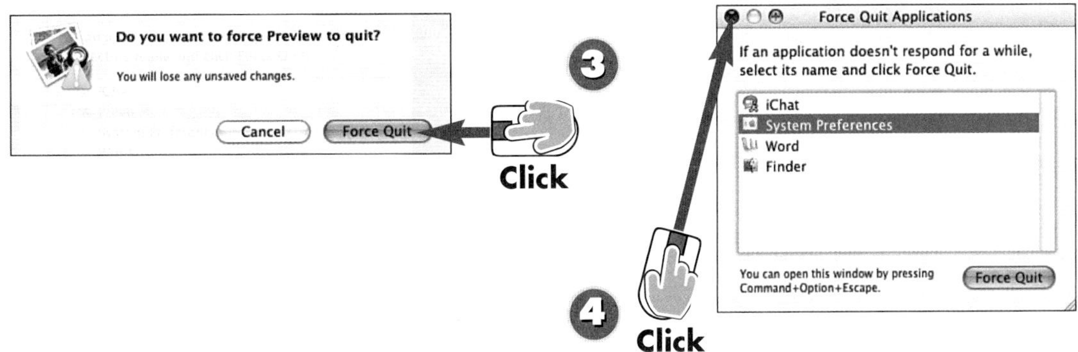

1. Choose **Apple menu**, **Force Quit**.
2. Choose the program you want from the list and click **Force Quit**.
3. Click **Force Quit** again.
4. Click the **Close** button to dismiss the Force Quit dialog box.

INTRODUCTION

When a program isn't working right, your first tactic should be to quit and restart it. But sometimes a program is so off-track that the Quit command doesn't work. Then you can force the program to quit. It doesn't affect the other programs that are running, but unsaved changes in documents within the problem application are lost.

HINT

In the Olden Days

Apple used to recommend that you restart your Mac after force quitting an application. But Mac OS X uses protected memory; each program runs in its own area of memory so that when it malfunctions, no other program is affected. No need to restart!

HINT

Classic Quitting

If you force quit an application running under Classic (see "Starting and Stopping Classic" in Part 3), Classic itself might quit. If this happens, you lose any unsaved changes in all Classic programs.

Displaying System Information

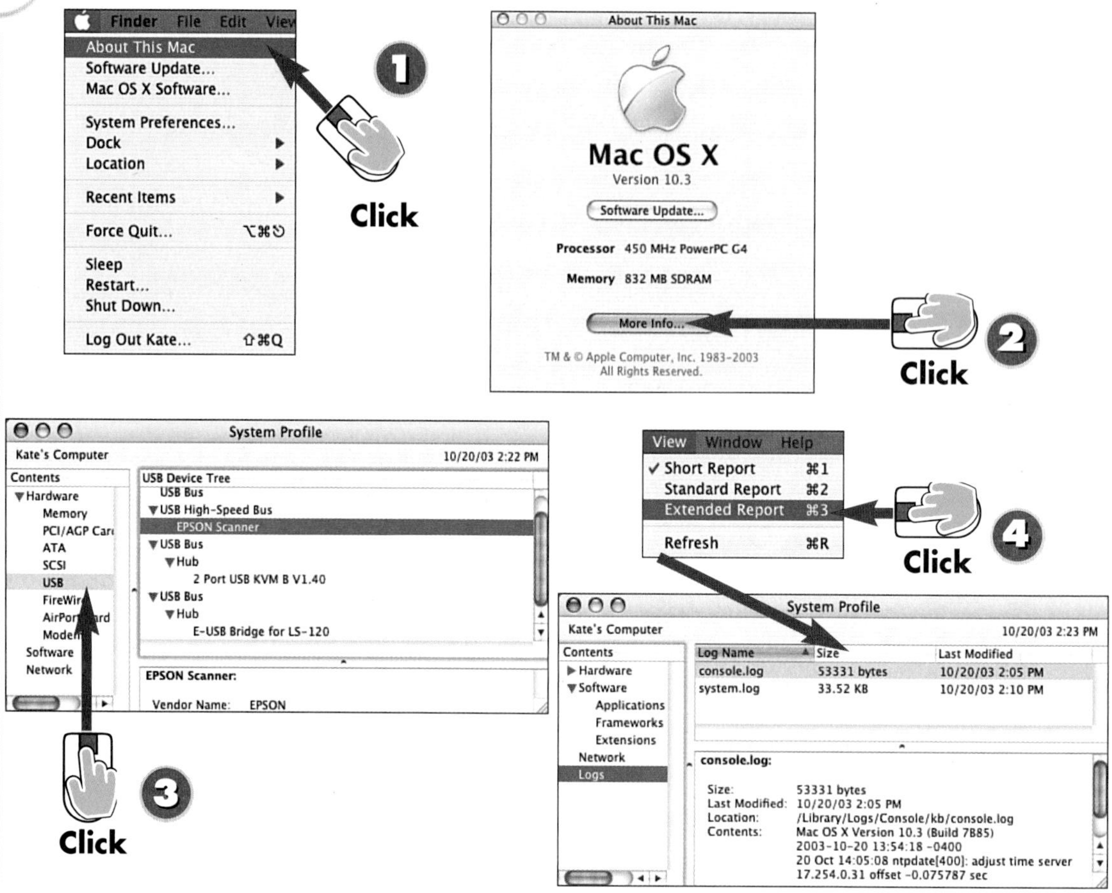

1 Choose **Apple menu**, **About This Mac** to see the system version, your Mac's processor speed and type, and the amount of RAM your Mac has.

2 Click **More Info** to start up System Profiler.

3 Click each entry in the **Contents** column to view that category of information.

4 Choose **View**, **Extended Report** to expand the Software category and see the Logs category.

INTRODUCTION

If you need to know how much memory is installed in your Mac, or how big your hard drive is, or which network card you have—who are you going to call? System Profiler, that's who. This program gives you a complete rundown on how your Mac is configured.

TIP

Sharing Is Good

To share your system information with another person (such as a network administrator or technical support specialist), save a System Profiler report as a text file. Choose **File**, **Export**, **Rich Text**; then enter a name and choose a location.

TIP

Breaking News

If you make changes to your system configuration while System Profiler is open, you can force the program to update its report to include your changes by choosing **View**, **Refresh**.

Formatting a Disk

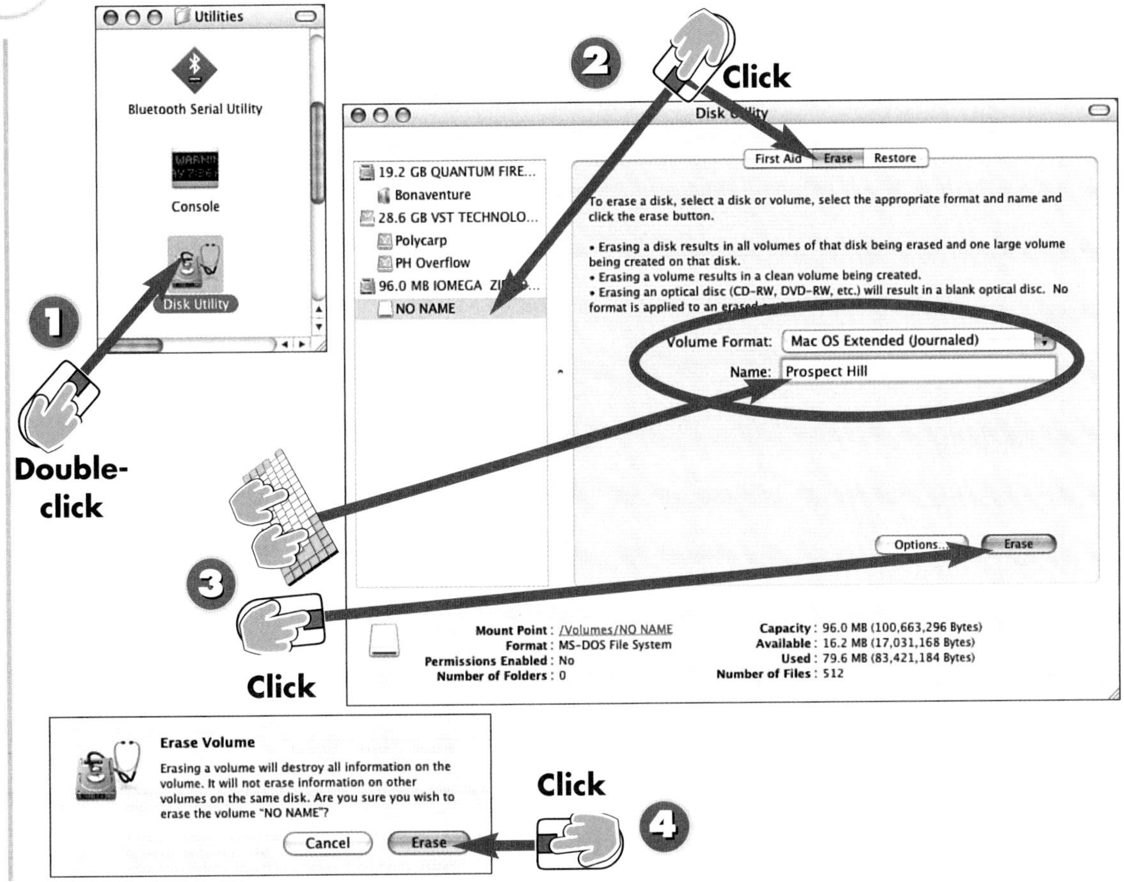

1. Double-click **Disk Utility** to start it (it's in the Utilities folder within Applications).

2. Choose the disk to be formatted in the list on the left and click the **Erase** tab.

3. Choose a **Volume Format** option, type a name for the disk, and click **Erase**.

4. Click **Erase** again.

INTRODUCTION

There are three good reasons to reformat a disk. First, if you want to use the disk on a Windows or Unix computer, it will need a different format. Second, formatting a disk erases all data completely. And finally, reformatting a disk is a last resort if you're having problems opening or saving files on it.

TIP

Lowest Common Denominator
Because Macs can read DOS disks but Windows PCs can't read Mac disks, you usually should choose the MS-DOS File System option when you're formatting removable disks such as Zip disks that might get used on either system.

Maintaining Classic

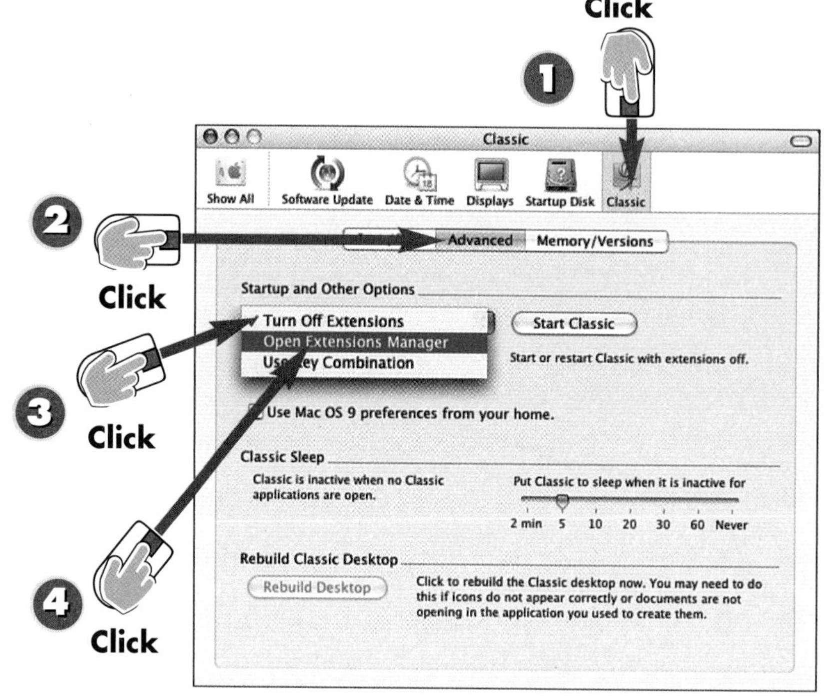

1. Start up System Preferences and click the **Classic** icon.
2. Click the **Advanced** tab to see the Classic maintenance options.
3. Choose **Turn Off Extensions** if you want to start up Classic with a bare-bones Mac OS 9 system.
4. Choose **Open Extensions Manager** if you need to disable or enable specific extensions in your Mac OS 9 system.

INTRODUCTION

You probably know that you can still use your Mac OS 9 programs within Mac OS X. They run in the Classic environment, which uses a regular Mac OS 9 System Folder. So, if you use Classic, you'll occasionally need to do the same system maintenance you would if your Mac were booted from a Mac OS 9 system.

TIP

Fun with Preferences
With the Use Mac OS 9 preferences from your home option, different users can have different Mac OS 9 preferences. They're saved in each user's home folder and used whenever Classic is started while that user is logged in.

HINT

Managing Extensions
Some third-party extensions are incompatible with Classic, and some turn out to be incompatible with each other. If you need to turn off an extension in your Mac OS 9 System Folder—or turn one on—start up Classic with the Extensions Manager.

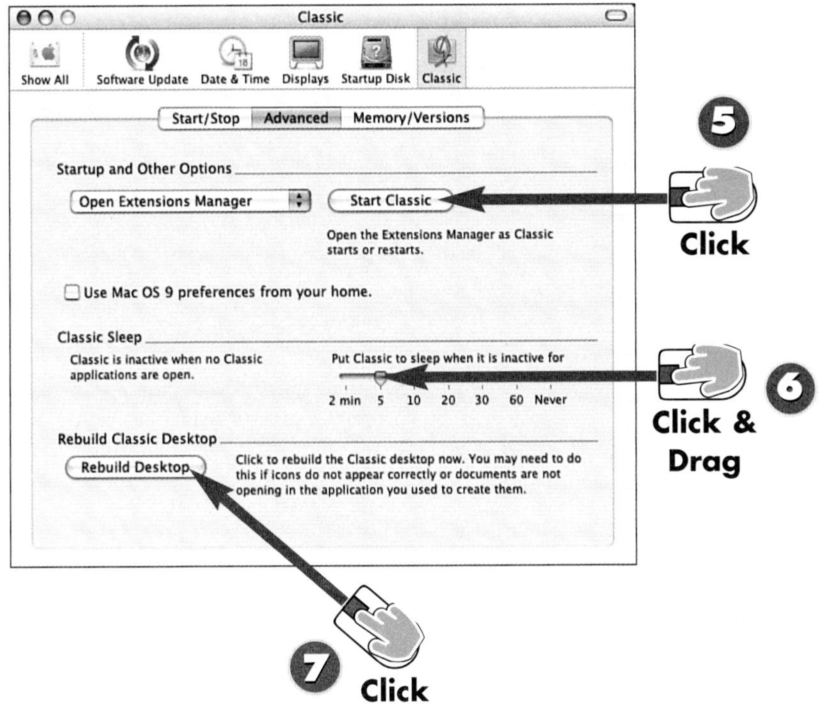

5. Click **Start Classic** to start Classic with extensions off or Extension Manager opened.
6. Drag the slider to determine when the Classic environment will go to sleep.
7. Click **Rebuild Desktop** to rebuild the Mac OS 9 system's catalog of the files on your hard drive.

HINT

Classic Slowdown
Don't keep Classic running if you're not using any Mac OS 9 programs. It slows down your Mac OS X system, even when Classic is sleeping.

TIP

We Can Rebuild
In theory, you rebuild the Classic desktop if you see blank or incorrect icons, meaning that documents aren't linked to their creator applications. It turns out that rebuilding the desktop fixes a host of glitches in both Classic and Mac OS X.

Installing the System Software

Double-click

Click

Click

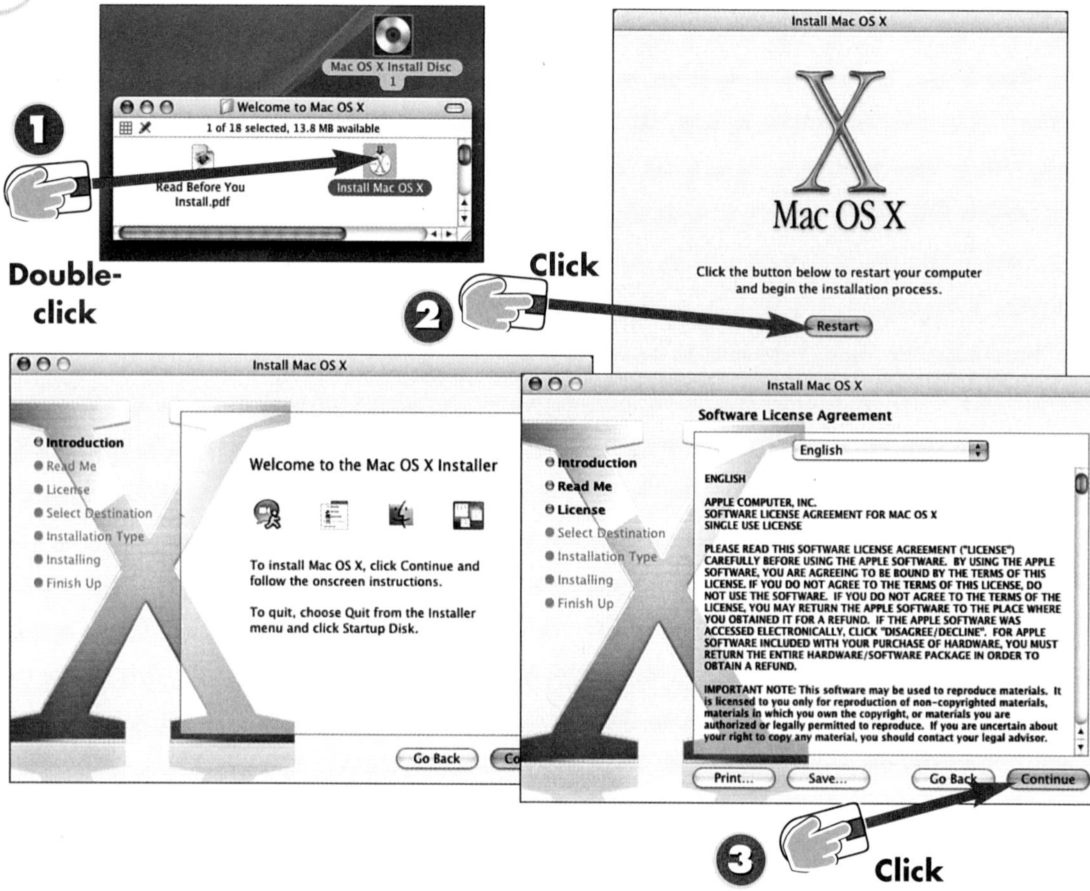

1. Insert the CD labeled Mac OS X Install Disc 1 and double-click **Install Mac OS X**.
2. Click **Restart** and enter an admin name and password. Then click **OK**. Your Mac reboots using the system on the CD.
3. In the Installer's first screen, choose a language and click **Continue** to see the subsequent screens; click **Continue** again on the Introduction, Read Me, and License screens.

INTRODUCTION

When you install a new hard drive (a bigger one, of course!) or want to upgrade an older Mac to Mac OS X, you must install Mac OS X. Using the installer is easy, but it takes a bit of time, and you should be sure your documents are backed up onto another disk before you get started.

TIP

Getting a Fresh Start
Software Update (see "Updating Programs with Software Update," earlier in this part) makes updating your system every time a new version comes out easy. But if you start seeing strange behavior in your system and running Disk Utility doesn't fix it, your best bet is to start fresh with new system software.

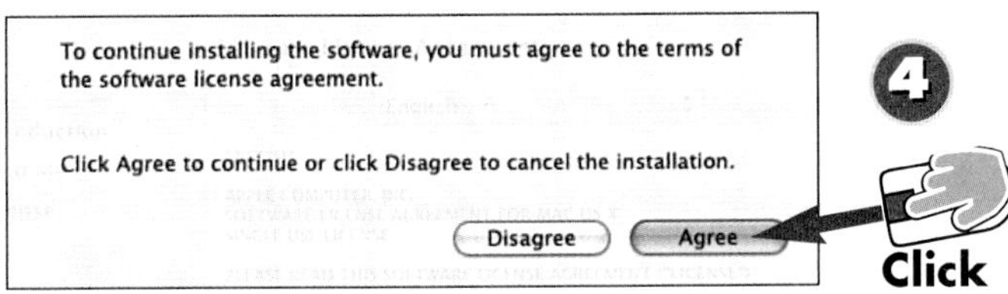

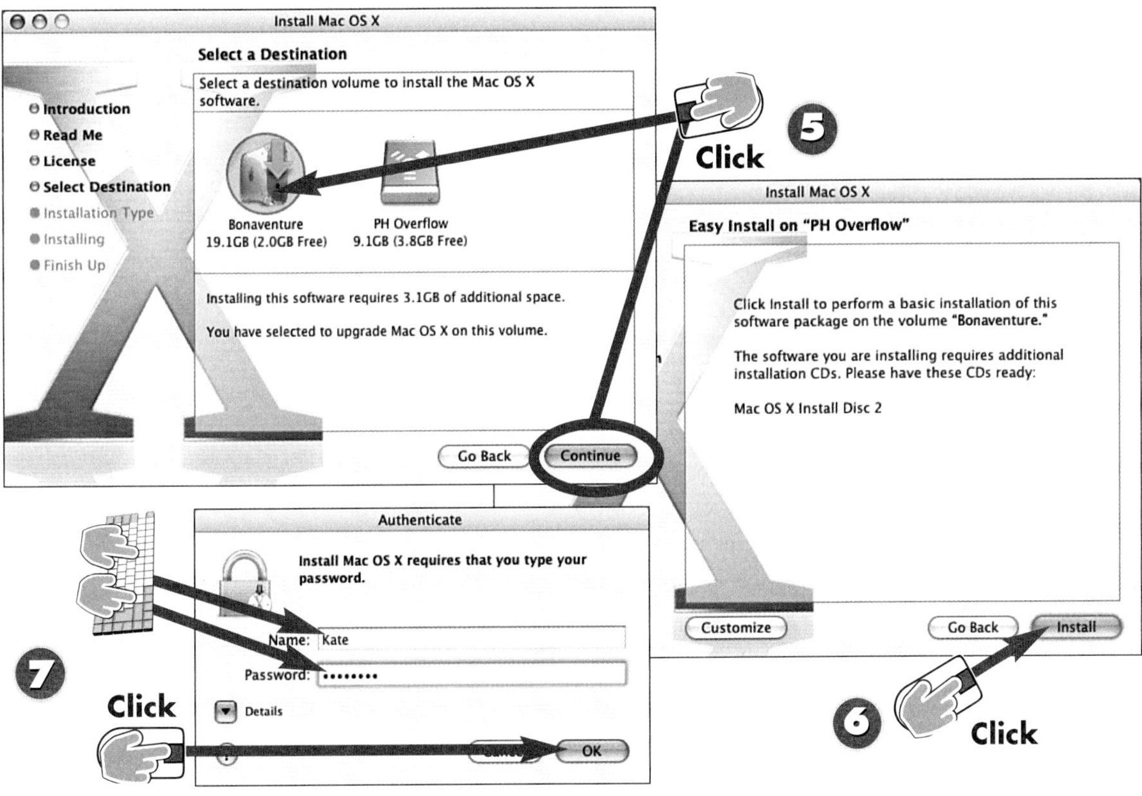

4 Click **Agree** to agree to the terms of the license agreement.

5 Choose a hard drive and click **Continue**.

6 Click **Install**.

7 Type an admin username and password and click **OK**.

TIP

Your Options
In step 6, if the hard drive you choose already has a Mac OS X system installed, you'll see an Options button. Click it to set whether you want the Installer to erase the hard drive before installing, archive the existing system so you can access its files later if you need to and install a fresh system, or just upgrade the existing system (the default choice).

Glossary

A

access permissions Settings that determine who can read, write, or move a file or folder.

accessibility The degree to which a device or program is usable by people with disabilities.

Action menu A pop-up menu that appears in dialog boxes and windows in the form of a gear icon. It provides access to commonly used commands.

admin user An administrative user of Mac OS X; a user who can read, write, and move some files that do not belong to him and who can change locked System Preferences settings and install new software.

AIFF Audio Interchange File Format is a sound file format used by iMovie and other multimedia programs.

AirPort An Apple-branded combination of hardware (AirPort cards and the AirPort base station) and software with which computers can form a network and communicate with each other and the Internet without wires.

alias A small pointer file that, when double-clicked, opens the original file from which it was created.

Apple ID A username for the Apple Web site and the iTunes Music Store.

Apple menu The menu at the left end of the Mac's menu bar; it contains commands such as Shut Down that can be used no matter which application you're using.

AppleTalk A proprietary Apple system for network communication, used primarily by Macs and Mac-compatible devices such as printers.

Application menu The menu that appears to the right of the Apple menu in each program; it's always named with the name of the program.

archive A compressed version of a file that must be dearchived before it can be opened.

B

base station A device that creates a wireless AirPort network in conjunction with Macs equipped with AirPort cards.

Bluetooth A wireless technology that enables computers to communicate with other devices such as PDAs and phones.

bookmark A record of a Web page's location, saved for future reference.

boot To start up a computer.

broadband A high-speed Internet connection such as DSL or a cable modem.

burn To write data to a disc; it usually refers to a CD or DVD.

C

cable modem A high-speed Internet connection that operates over your cable television line.

CD-R Recordable CD, which can be recorded only once.

CD-RW Rewritable CD, which can be erased and recorded again several times.

check box Interface equivalent of the real-world object used to select options in a list or dialog box.

Classic A special program that enables Mac OS 9 to run within Mac OS X so you can use old Mac OS programs that won't run under Mac OS X.

clip A short section of video that can be combined with other clips in iMovie to create a movie.

Clip Shelf The area of iMovie's window where individual video clips are stored before they're used in a movie.

Clip Viewer The area of iMovie's interface where clips are combined with transitions, effects, and each other to form a movie.

collection A group of fonts.

color management The science of translating and adjusting scanned, displayed, and printed colors to produce consistent color from original art to final printout.

Column view A Finder view in which columns of file and folder listings are placed from left to right, with the left columns representing folders closer to the root level of a drive.

compressed A file that's reduced in size by manipulating its underlying data.

contextual menus Menus that pop up wherever you click if you use a modifier key—specifically, the Control key. Their commands vary according to the context in which you're working.

D

database A data file in which each type of information is delimited in a field so the data can be sorted or otherwise manipulated based on categories.

desktop The visual workspace in the Finder.

desktop printer An icon that provides quick access to a printer's features.

device profile A file that describes the color reproduction characteristics of a printer, scanner, or monitor.

DHCP The Dynamic Host Configuration Protocol is a method of automatically configuring a desktop computer's Internet connection.

dialog box A window in which you can click buttons, enter text, choose from pop-up menus, and drag sliders to determine the settings you want to make in a program or your system software.

dial-up An Internet connection over a standard telephone line.

disclosure triangle A button to the left of a folder or category name in a list; clicking it reveals the folder's or category's contents.

DNS server A computer that translates URLs (such as **www.apple.com**) into the numeric addresses where Web browsers can find the files that make up Web sites.

Dock The panel at the bottom of your Mac OS X Desktop that contains an icon for every running program, as well as icons for any other programs, folders, or documents you want to access quickly.

download To copy files from the Internet to a local computer.

dragging and dropping Clicking a file's icon and dragging it into a dialog box, on top of an application's icon, into the Dock, or elsewhere.

Drop Box A folder within your Public folder that other users can use to give files to you; you are the only person who can see the contents of the Drop Box folder.

DSL A high-speed Internet connection that operates over your phone line.

DVD Digital video disc; a CD-like medium that holds several times as much data as CDs and that is generally used to distribute movies.

E

email Electronic mail that travels from your computer to another computer across the Internet or over a local network.

Ethernet A networking technology that enables you to transfer data at high speeds.

export To store data in a new file, separate from the currently open file.

Exposé A set of Mac OS X 10.3 features for moving windows temporarily out of the way.

extension *See **filename extensions**.*

F–G

file sharing A system feature that enables you to transfer files from your Mac to other computers and vice versa; it can also enable other users to access your files if you allow it.

filename extensions Three-letter (usually) codes placed at the end of filenames to signify the type of file.

FileVault A feature that encrypts the contents of a user's home folder so it can't be accessed without a password.

Finder The part of Mac OS X that displays the contents of your hard drives and other drives in windows on your Desktop.

FireWire A type of connector for digital camcorders, hard drives, and other devices.

folder A system-level equivalent of a real-world file folder, in which you can store files and other folders to help you organize them.

font The software that enables your Mac to represent a particular typeface.

format To prepare a removable disk or hard drive to accept data.

function keys The "F" keys at the top of a keyboard are used for performing special functions that vary depending on the program being used.

H

hard drive A device for data storage, usually found inside a computer.

hardware router A device that shares an Internet connection across a local network.

home folder The folder in your Mac OS X system in which you can store all your personal files.

HTML Hypertext Markup Language, which is the coding language used to create Web pages.

hub A device that connects multiple individual computers to form a network.

I–K

icon A picture indicating a file's contents or type.

Icon view A Finder view in which files are represented by graphic icons rather than just lists of names.

iDisk A storage space on Apple's Web site that's available to any Mac user who registers for .Mac.

iLife Apple's bundle of programs, including iMovie, iPhoto, iTunes, and iDVD.

IMAP The Internet Message Access Protocol, which is a less common method of connecting to a mail server.

import To retrieve data from a file using a format other than the program's own format.

instant messaging A method of communicating over the Internet in which users type short messages and instantly send them to other users.

IP address A numerical code that identifies the location of each computer on the Internet, including your Mac.

iPod Small, portable Apple device for playing music in MP3 format.

ISP Internet service provider, which is a company that provides access to the Internet.

JPEG A graphic file format commonly used for photos displayed on the World Wide Web.

L

label A color applied to a file icon in the Finder.

LAN Local area network, which is a small network enclosed entirely within one building.

List view A Finder view in which each window displays the contents of a single folder or drive in the form of a list of files.

local network address An identifier of a computer on a LAN.

log in To identify yourself as a particular user by entering a username and password.

login icon A picture representing an individual user that is displayed when that user logs in or uses iChat.

M

.Mac An online service available to any Mac user that includes an email address and Web storage space, among other features.

mail server A computer that directs email to and from a local computer on the Internet.

memory *See* ***RAM***.

menu bar The wide, narrow strip across the top of the screen that contains drop-down menus in the Finder and in applications.

menu screens Screens on a DVD containing buttons that lead to other screens or open movies.

minimized A folder or document window that has been placed in the Dock, where you can see a thumbnail view of it.

modem A device that enables your computer to connect to the Internet over a standard phone, DSL, or cable line.

modifier keys Special keys (such as Shift, Option, Command, and Control) that enable you to give commands to your Mac by holding them down at the same time as you press letter or number keys or the mouse button.

monitor A computer's display.

motion menus DVD menu screens that incorporate moving video in their backgrounds.

mount To place a disk drive (either one connected to your Mac or one connected to a network computer) on your Mac's desktop so you can access its files.

MP3 A compressed music file that's very small but that retains very high quality.

multiwindow mode Finder mode in which double-clicking a folder displays its contents in the same window rather than in a new window.

N–O

network locations Groups of network settings for specific situations or locations, such as an office LAN.

network port Computer hardware interface used to connect the computer to a network.

NTP server *See* ***timeserver***.

operating system (OS) The software that enables a computer to run.

P

pane A separate page in a dialog box, usually accessible by choosing from a pop-up menu or (as in the case of System Preferences) clicking a button.

pathname The address of a file on a hard drive; it lists the nested folders in which the file resides.

PDF *See* ***Portable Document Format***.

peripheral A device that connects to your Mac, such as a printer, scanner, tape backup drive, or digital camera.

permissions File attributes that determine which user owns each file and which users are authorized to read it and make changes to it.

pixel Picture element; a square on the screen made up of a single color.

Places sidebar A column of disk and folder icons that appears on the left side of each Finder window in multi-window mode.

playlist A collection of songs in iTunes.

PNG The Portable Network Graphic format is a graphic file format used on the World Wide Web.

POP The Post Office Protocol, which is the most common method of connecting to a mail server.

pop-up menu A menu that appears in a dialog box or other interface element rather than dropping down from the menu bar at the top of the screen.

Portable Document Format The file format used by Adobe Reader (formerly Acrobat Reader) and its related software. PDF documents look just like the original documents from which they were created.

PPP The Point-to-Point Protocol, which is a method of connecting to the Internet via a phone modem.

PPPoE PPP over Ethernet, a method of connecting to the Internet via a DSL modem.

printer driver A file that describes the characteristics of a printer and enables programs to use the printer's features.

processor The core of a computer; its brain.

profiles Data files that characterize how a device reproduces color. *See also* ***color management***.

project A collection of files used to produce a movie in iMovie or a DVD in iDVD.

protected memory An operating system feature that places barriers around the areas of a computer's memory (or RAM) being used by each program, so that if one program crashes, the other programs are unaffected.

proxy preview A thumbnail version of a document, usually in a dialog box, that can be manipulated to change the real document in the same way.

queue The list of documents waiting to be printed.

QuickTime Apple's proprietary video format.

RAM Random access memory, which is the part of a computer that stores the currently running programs and the currently open documents so you can work with them.

reboot To restart the Mac.

removable disk Any media that can be ejected from its drive and used in another computer.

resolution The number of pixels per inch contained in a graphic or displayed on a monitor.

rip To convert songs on a CD to MP3 files on a hard drive.

router address The IP address of the computer or device that is providing a shared Internet connection.

RTF Rich Text Format, a format for word processor documents that retains information about bold, italic, and other formatting in a form that almost all word processors can understand.

S

screen name A nickname by which iChat users are identified.

screen saver A moving display that covers the screen to prevent burn-in.

screen shot A picture of the computer's screen.

search field Text entry field at the top of a window where users enter search parameters.

select To choose or designate for action; for example, the user must click a file to select it in the Finder before he can copy the file.

Services A set of ways to access programs' features while those programs are not running.

shelf The space at the top of the System Preferences window where preference icons can be stored for quick access.

Sherlock The Mac OS's built-in utility for searching the Internet to find a variety of types of information.

single-window mode The Finder mode in which double-clicking a folder displays its contents in a new window.

sleep A state in which the Mac is still powered on but consumes less energy because it's not being used.

slider A dialog box control for choosing a value along a continuum.

spam Junk email.

speech recognition A technology by which the Mac can understand spoken commands.

startup items Programs or documents that open automatically when a user logs in.

storage media A type of computer media used for data storage rather than active information exchange.

submenu A menu that extends to the side from a command in a drop-down menu.

SuperDrive An internal drive for writing CDs and DVDs.

sync To synchronize data between a computer and a device such as a PDA or cell phone.

system software *See* ***operating system (OS)***.

T

TCP/IP Transmission Control Protocol over Internet Protocol, the networking method Mac OS X uses; it is an industry standard.

text buttons Buttons in iDVD that don't have video images.

themes Sets of menu and button designs that can be applied to iDVD projects.

thumbnail Miniature image.

TIFF A graphic file format used for images destined to be printed.

timeserver A computer on the Internet that transmits a time signal your Mac can use to set its clock automatically.

title bar The part of a window that displays the folder's or document's title.

toolbar A row of buttons for common functions that appears at the top of a window in Preview or another program.

transition A special effect inserted between scenes in iMovie.

Trash The holding location for files or folders you want to delete.

U–V

URL An alphanumeric address that points to a specific location on the Internet, such as **www.apple.com** for Apple's Web site.

USB Universal serial bus, a type of computer connector.

username An alphanumeric identifier of a single user.

vCard A small file containing contact information that can be attached to an email message.

video buttons Buttons in iDVD that have video images.

virus A program that damages a computer or the computer's files in some way and then reproduces itself and spreads via email or file transfers.

W–Z

Web browser A program used to view Web sites. Safari is the Web browser that comes with OS X.

Webcam A small, digital camera used with iChat or to provide a constantly updated image over the World Wide Web.

WebDAV A type of server that makes iCal calendars available to subscribers over the Internet.

wireless The capability to communicate without cables; for example, AirPort is Apple's technology for creating a wireless network between multiple Macs. *See also* ***AirPort*** and ***Bluetooth***.

word processor A program used for composing, laying out, and printing text.

Zip disk A removable disk larger than a floppy disk that holds at least 100 times as much data as a floppy.

Index

SYMBOLS

A

B

E

F

J - K

Q - R

T

W

X - Y - Z